RELIGION IN VICTORIAN BRITAIN

VOLUME IV

CONTROVERSIES

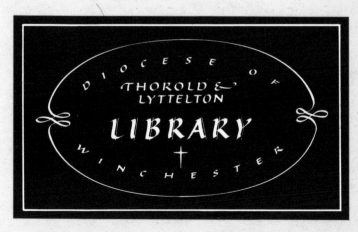

RELIGION IN VICTORIAN BRITAIN

VOLUME II
CONTROVERSIES

EDITED BY
GERALD PARSONS
AT THE
OPEN UNIVERSITY

MANCHESTER UNIVERSITY PRESS
MANCHESTER AND NEW YORK
IN ASSOCIATION WITH THE
OPEN UNIVERSITY
DISTRIBUTED EXCLUSIVELY IN THE USA AND CANADA
BY ST. MARTIN'S PRESS

Copyright © The Open University 1988

Published by Manchester University Press
Oxford Road, Manchester M13 9PL, UK
and Room 400, 175 Fifth Avenue, New York, NY 10010, USA

Distributed exclusively in the USA and Canada by St. Martin's Press, Inc.,
175 Fifth Avenue, New York, NY 10010, USA

British Library cataloguing in publication data
Religion in Victorian Britain.
   Vol. 2: Controversies
   I. Great Britain. Christian church, 1837–1901
   I. Parsons, Gerald   II. Open University 274.1′081

Library of Congress cataloging in publication data
Religion in Victorian Britain.
   Includes bibliographies and index.
   Contents: v. 1. Traditions — v. 2. Controversies —
v. 3. Sources — [etc.)
   1. Great Britain — Church history — 19th century.
2. Great Britain — Religion.   3. Great Britain —
Religious life and customs. I. Parsons, Gerald.
BR759.R43 1988   274.1′081   88–12359
ISBN 0 7190 2512 5 *hardback*
     0 7190 2513 3 *paperback*

This book forms part of an Open University course A331 *Religion in Victorian
Britain*. For information about this course please write to the Student
Enquiries Office, The Open University, PO Box 71, Walton Hall, Milton
Keynes, MK7 6AG, UK

Typesetting information
This book is set in 10 point Baskerville
Printed in Great Britain by
Richard Clay Ltd., Bungay, Suffolk

CONTENTS

PREFACE

This book is one of a four-volume series entitled *Religion in Victorian Britain*, published by Manchester University Press in association with the Open University. The four volumes form the nucleus of an Open University Course. Volumes I and II, *Traditions* and *Controversies* (edited by Gerald Parsons, 1988), consist of sets of specially written essays covering the major religious denominations and groups of the period and the issues and controversies between and within them. Volume III, *Sources* (edited by James R. Moore, 1988), is a collection of primary source material from the period, while Volume IV, *Interpretations* (edited by Gerald Parsons, 1988), is a collection of recent essays and articles in the field by other writers.

References to other volumes in the series are given as follows:

RVB, I, 4 (*Religion in Victorian Britain*, Volume I, *Traditions*, chapter 4), or

RVB, III, 1.2 (*Religion in Victorian Britain*, Volume III, *Sources*, item 1.2)

The authors wish to acknowledge the essential contribution made to the production of these volumes by a number of other members of Open University staff: Gillian Kay, Staff Tutor in History, for her comment and criticism, Barbara Humphreys and Wendy Clarke (secretaries), Jenny Cook (course manager), Tony Coulson (Library), Pam Higgins (Design Studio), and Jonathan Hunt (Publishing).

The authors also wish to thank Professor John Kent of the University of Bristol for his careful and constructive comments on first drafts of their essays. Each of the authors has benefited from Professor Kent's criticism and observations: needless to say, any questionable judgements which remain are the responsibility of the authors alone.

The authors are all members of staff of the Faculty of Arts at the Open University:

Michael Bartholomew, Staff Tutor in the History of Science and Technology

David Englander, Lecturer in European Humanities

Antony Lentin, Reader in History

James R. Moore, Lecturer in the History of Science and Technology

Gerald Parsons, Lecturer in Religious Studies

Rosemary O'Day, Senior Lecturer in History

Terence Thomas, Staff Tutor in Religious Studies

Recommended further reading

Books and articles particularly recommended for further reading are marked with an asterisk in the bibliographies at the end of each chapter.

Illustration sources

The sources for the illustrations reproduced in this book are as follows: front cover, *Punch* Jan-June 1855; Introduction, *Punch* 21.9.89; Ch. 1, *Punch*, Jan-June 1850; Ch. 2, *Punch* 18.5.74; Ch. 3, *Punch* Jan-June 1855; Ch. 4 *The Graphic* 13.8.81; Ch. 5, *Illustrated London News* 3.6.43; Ch. 6, *Punch* 13.2.69; Ch. 7, *Punch* 12.7.73; Ch. 8, *Punch* 4.5.78; Ch. 9, *Punch* 5.6.80; Ch. 10, *Punch* 4.11.71; Ch. 11, *Punch* 1.5.65; Ch. 12, *Punch* 31.8.72; Ch. 13, *Punch* 5.10.61.

Acknowledgement

The authors gratefully acknowledge their thanks to the British Library of Political and Economic Science at the London School of Economics for permission to reproduce material from the Booth Collection in Chapters 1 and 12.

INTRODUCTION

"RAISING THE (TRADE) WIND."

Cardinal Manning. "THERE, THAT'S RIGHT! BOTH BE REASONABLE, AND WORK TOGETHER. BLESS YOU, MY CHILDREN!"

FROM CENTRE TO PERIPHERY VICTORIAN RELIGIOUS CONTROVERSIES IN PERSPECTIVE

THE essays in this book comprise the second of a set of four volumes which together make a self-standing series on *Religion in Victorian Britain*. The present volume focuses, as its sub-title suggests, on major religious *Controversies* in Victorian Britain. The essays are grouped in four sections, each section focusing on a broad area of controversy in the religious life of Victorian Britain, and within each area individual essays then address specific aspects of the particular issue or controversy concerned.

Some of the essays approach the area of Victorian religious controversy with which they are concerned predominantly from the perspective of a *particular* religious tradition or denomination. The essays on Anglicanism, Parliament and the Courts, Church and State in Victorian Scotland, Irish Disestablishment and the 'ethics of belief', for example, adopt such an approach. Even in these essays, however, there are references to, and important elements of comparison with, the attitudes and opinions of other Victorian religious traditions towards the issue in question. Other essays in the volume set out, from the start, to take a deliberately comparative and cross-denominational approach to the areas of Victorian religious controversy with which they are concerned.

All of the essays in this collection are intended as individual studies of their particular topics. In each case, however, a basic degree of familiarity with the histories of, and the developments within, the various particular religious and anti-religious traditions and denominations of Victorian Britain is assumed. The authors of the present collection of essays have themselves supplied such surveys and interpretations of the history and development of a number of particular Victorian religious traditions in the preceding volume of this series. *Religion in Victorian Britain* Volume I *Traditions* provides introductory and interpretative studies of the development of the Anglican, Protestant Nonconformist, Scottish Presbyterian, Roman Catholic, Jewish, and Freethinking and Secularist traditions of Victorian Britain.

The third and fourth volumes in the series, entitled *Sources* and *Interpretations*, provide, respectively, a collection of primary sources for the study of religion in Victorian Britain, and a selection of recent studies of aspects of Victorian religion by historians other than those responsible for the writing and compilation of the present series.

The initial and principal aim of the authors and compilers of these collections of original essays and of primary and secondary sources has been the provision of a coherent and integrated body of material for use by Open University students studying a course on *Religion in Victorian Britain*. The two volumes of original essays are thus designed primarily as textbooks, for the use of Honours level undergraduates. The volumes of primary and secondary sources are, accordingly, designed to support that enterprise by supplying a representative variety of contemporary Victorian documents and evidence, and a number of examples of scholarly articles and essays characteristic of recent developments in the academic study of the role and significance of religion in Victorian Britain.

Although thus originally designed with a quite specific purpose in mind, however, it is also intended that both the overall series of books and the first two volumes of original essays will possess a much wider appeal and relevance. On the one hand, it is hoped that the series as a whole will prove a viable and effective basis — a core of essential material — for the study and teaching of the history of religion in Victorian Britain in institutions other than the Open University. On the other hand, the authors of the two volumes of original essays have also attempted to provide not only a pedagogically structured body of information concerning religion in Victorian Britain, but, in addition, an interpretation and overview of the subject itself.

With this in mind, the various authors have written as individuals, each adopting and presenting his or her own particular standpoint and approach to the subject as a whole and to the specific topic of any given essay. At the same time, however, all the authors have endeavoured to write with certain agreed aims and objectives in mind — although, of course, responsibility for the final form and presentation of any particular essay remains the individual author's.

Each essay is conceived as a case study in which the author has written with the aim of supplying, simultaneously, an introduction to the particular topic in question, a survey and assessment of some of the principal developments within that topic during the Victorian period, and an indication of the significance of the subject of the essay in relation to Victorian religious life in general. In so doing, authors have also attempted both to engage with and reflect the results of recent and current research and scholarship in the field concerned.

Within this book (as in Volume I *Traditions*) the authors have sought to avoid *both* a narrow and conventional concentration on 'church history' or the portrayal of Victorian religion as essentially a matter of ecclesiastical institutions and theological ideas, *and* the alternative of an overreaction and consequent over-concentration on the social history of Victorian religion to the exclusion of the still relevant and essential denominational, institutional, and theological aspects of the subject. The essays in both volumes, therefore, reflect the conviction that an adequate understanding of the history and significance of religion in Victorian Britain requires a combination of the insights and perspectives of 'conventional' denominational, institutional and theological history, and those of the more recent trend towards the study of Victorian religion primarily through its social, cultural, intellectual and political content. In short, there is an underlying assumption that if churches, theologies, and religious beliefs cannot properly be understood apart from their social and cultural context, neither can they or their context properly be understood without taking the churches, theologies, and beliefs seriously in their own right.

In *Traditions* the emphasis falls rather more on the traditional, institutional, approach. *Controversies*, on the other hand, tends somewhat more towards the social and cultural history of Victorian religion. That said, the distinction in question is relative, not absolute, and elements of both approaches will be found in each volume.

Each essay and case study which follows is intended to provide a self-standing statement and interpretation of its subject. At the same time, since similar themes and issues occur in several different essays, inevitably and quite properly, individual essays frequently refer to other essays in each of the two volumes. In the present volume, a number of themes and issues noted in particular denominational contexts in the preceding volume are focused upon and developed in their own right. Among the more notable examples of this process are: the development of critical attitudes to the Bible; the emergence of doubts about the morality of traditional Christian doctrines; the ongoing concern over the perceived irreligion of the working classes; and the changing relationship between the state, the religious establishment(s) and the various expressions of religious and irreligious dissent or nonconformity. Conversely, for the particular denominational contexts of the specific issues and controversies examined here recourse must be had to the preceding volume.

There is no attempt in the essays which follow to supply a neatly uniform interpretation of Victorian religion and its place, role and significance in Victorian society. The essays reflect a number of different interpretative standpoints and methodological perspectives. Nevertheless, it is possible to identify, from the evidence presented, several common themes and notable similarities within and between a number of the groups of issues and particular examples of controversy studied here.

It is also, however, inescapably clear that there are notable exceptions to virtually any given similarity or common theme thus identified. This should hardly cause surprise: not the least of the virtues of historical study in general is its capacity to confound the convenient tidinesses of over-neat interpretation by demonstrating the stubborn intractability of the surviving evidence of the behaviour and significance of equally intractable, stubborn, and unique human beings. It is a not uncommon theme in the essays in the first two volumes of this series that received wisdom — both scholarly and 'popular' — concerning the history of religion in Victorian Britain frequently fails to take account of the intriguing (and sometimes baffling and inconvenient) diversity in Victorian religious life and thought.

II

To what extent, therefore, is it possible to identify the emergence of common themes within and between the four broad areas of controversy identified in this volume and the individual essays within them? The three examples noted below do not constitute an exhaustive list of such common themes but, rather, seek merely to locate the more prominent and significant cases of the emergence of common ground.

First, there is a frequently recurring sense of the gradual but steady emergence in Victorian Britain of an increasingly secular society and an increasingly secular political, social and intellectual *milieu*. Christian social thought and attitudes, for example, became, as a whole, less specifically and self-consciously, and especially less *exclusively*, 'Christian' in inspiration. They became, instead, more open both to the recognition of the importance of environmental factors in the creation of poverty and destitution and to the need for secular and state action in the alleviation of poverty and social problems.

Again (as is clear from the essays on aspects of the interrelationship of church, state and society) there was a clear trend — beginning indeed with the pre-Victorian repeal of the Test and Corporation Acts and the passing of Catholic Emancipation — away from the state support of politically and legally privileged religious establishments, and towards the emergence of religious pluralism and the neutrality of the state in matters of religion. Religious establishment was either abolished when patently incompatible with respect for the religious preferences of the overwhelming majority of the population (as in Victorian Ireland, and as was to be the case in early twentieth century Wales), or was modified and curtailed so as to cease to be an intolerable or unacceptable burden to those in the population of different religious persuasion or none (as in Victorian England and Scotland).

The rights of dissenters and Nonconformists (both Protestant and Catholic) were, meanwhile, steadily extended and their disabilities steadily removed — as also were those of Jews, agnostics, disbelievers and atheists. The pace of change was uneven, and the reforms and concessions were often won only at considerable personal cost to individual dissenters and unbelievers and after long political campaigns — but over the six decades of the Victorian era the overall direction of reform was unmistakable.

Similarly, in the various accounts of aspects of Victorian intellectual life in the essays which follow, there are clear indications of the emergence of a more secular intellectual *milieu*. The reforms of Oxford and Cambridge Universities, whereby clerical dominance was reduced and religious tests were abolished; the emergence of self-styled secular, agnostic and free-thinking 'dissident intellectuals' and would-be intellectual élites, intent upon the construction of alternative 'creeds' and post-Christian intellectual syntheses according to which the future of national life might be shaped; the emergence of an intellectual environment in which earnest and honest doubt in the manner characteristic of Tennyson's poetry might be parodied and mocked in the manner of Swinburne's poetry; the emergence of a new theological and intellectual gulf between the critical and academic methods of 'professional' biblical critics and students of comparative religion and popular conceptions of the Bible and other faiths: all of these developments also point to a variety of broadly secularizing trends in Victorian society.

Second, a number of the essays which follow suggest a tendency, by the end of the century, towards the increasing dissolution or fragmentation of certain aspects of Victorian religious life, and towards a general 'loosening' of religious conformity and a corresponding increase in the clearly optional nature of religious beliefs and practice.

Thus, for example, whilst it is noted that the social attitudes of early Victorian Christians were never as *uniformly* 'conservative' as some accounts would have us believe, nevertheless it is clear that the relative consensus upon social issues among early Victorian Christians steadily gave way to a diversification — or even perhaps fragmentation — of Christian social opinion in the latter part of the century.

Similarly, the Evangelical tradition is shown to have become, in certain respects, less clearly defined and distinctive, more notably diverse, 'fragmented rather than unitary'. Thus by 1900, whilst some evangelicals clung tenaciously to rigidly pre-critical attitudes to the Bible and active opposition to Anglo- or Roman Catholicism, others adopted more liberal theology and accepted degrees of 'ritual' unthinkable to their predecessors of a generation earlier. Or, again, whilst some evangelicals, hard pressed by the realities of urban poverty, adopted a more social approach, others of more suburban provenance retained a traditional evangelical social outlook. Tensions were also apparent between the traditional evangelical role, rationale, and strategy of simply preaching the Gospel, and the steady growth of the various ancillary agencies for social action and educational or recreational provision which most churches and chapels supported by the end of the century.

The essentially ambiguous role of such ancillary agencies is reflected in several of the essays which follow, as is the not unrelated theme of the extent to which the laity — both middle class and working class — showed themselves both willing and able to choose what they wanted and ignore what they did not see the point of in the variety of religious options available to them in later Victorian Britain. No doubt it was always the case that the actual opinions of many church-goers were at some distance from the official theologies of their churches, but it is clear that in the latter decades of our period this gap became more public: clergy, it is noted, tailored their services to the tastes of their local congregations, whilst the laity — and especially the working-class laity — voted with their feet and attended what they wished to attend, and continued to absent themselves from the rest.

Changing attitudes to the Bible also reflected a process of diversification. A clear consensus on the matter no longer existed. By 1900 one could still, of course, find staunch defenders of a traditional view of the biblical text — but an out-and-out defence of a traditional view of the Bible was beginning to look curiously anachronistic. The generation which had worried intensely about 'genesis and geology' had passed away, and the whole of the Bible was no longer characteristically regarded as literally true. A kind of semi-critical attitude to the Bible was becoming widespread: much of the Old Testament might be regarded as not literally true; the New Testament retained more of its conventional status; there was increasing emphasis upon the moral stories and human examplars to be found in the Bible, but such emphasis on the human did not exclude the miraculous, but indeed retained it. Yet in the universities a new generation of biblical critics was steadily casting doubt on the historicity of the New Testament as well. Between these various approaches there were large gulfs in both awareness and willingness to become aware.

The third, and perhaps the most significant, common theme in the essays which follow is the marked and recurrent recognition of the occurrence of a fundamental and broadly-based change in the ethos, nature, and status of religion in Victorian Britain in the period after approximately 1880.

In the 1880s, it emerges clearly, the churches began to become aware of the limits of the success of their immense Victorian investment of resources and energy in the mission to the urban working classes. Responses to this awareness included yet more initiatives in such evangelism — Settlements and Central Halls for example — and also yet more emphasis upon attracting the unchurched through the provision of ancillary agencies, societies and meetings of an educational, cultural or recreational kind. In the latter kinds of organization — be they PSAs or Bands of Hope or Womens Meetings or whatever — the boundaries between religion and recreation became increasingly blurred, the distinctively religious element increasingly reduced.

The 1880s also emerge as the point at which the characteristic social and political configurations of early and mid-Victorian religion began to break down and be replaced by new alignments. In part, of course, this development reflected the realignments within secular political and social life which also began to occur at this time. The split in the Victorian Liberal party over Irish Home Rule and the slow but steady rise of the Labour movement necessarily affected the political alignments of Victorian religious bodies.

But the changes in religious-political alignments of the 1880s and after were also reflections of changed and changing circumstances in the nation's religious life. By the 1880s the reforms already conceded to English Dissenters and Nonconformists and to Irish Catholics and Presbyterians were sufficient to have brought to an end the classic period of political conflict based upon the confrontation of church-versus-chapel, establishment-versus-dissent. There remained particular issues of contention (Welsh disestablishment; church, chapel and education; Presbyterian reunion or disestablishment in Scotland), but they no longer consistently occupied the political centre stage.

In social attitudes, also, the 1880s emerge as a turning point. The 'Christian Socialist Revival'; the rise to prominence of 'the environmental factor' in contemporary Christian comment upon poverty and social issues; the cautious but definite exploration by the churches of a more positive view of, and relationship with, the Labour and Trade Union movements: each of these was symptomatic of the passing of one era in modern British Christian social and political attitudes and the beginning of another.

Finally, in intellectual life, too, the essays which follow suggest a broad process of dissolution and fragmentation, with the 1880s forming a significant turning point. As already noted above, by the 80s it was possible for Swinburne to poke fun at the earnest religious faith-in-dialogue-with-doubt of Tennyson. Between 1869 and 1880 the Metaphysical Society provided a regular forum for the intellectual meeting of clerics and theologians, scientists and philosophers, agnostics and freethinkers: but after 1880 it disbanded and the various intellectual strands of which it had been made up went their several ways. In the 1860s and 1870s the moral question of the ethics of belief and the nature of clerical honesty in assent to creeds was a major source of debate in the quality periodical press: by the 1890s the issue was again being hotly debated, but this time the debate was concentrated within the church, and the participation of 'secular' intellectuals was much more limited.

III

Having thus identified a number of broadly common themes in the essays contained in the present volume, is it possible, in turn, to relate these to similar patterns discerned, and interpretations offered, by other contemporary historians working in the field of Victorian religious history? The rest of this introduction attempts to set the present collection of essays within the context of a thoughtful and suggestive interpretation of the development of Victorian religious life proposed by Hugh McLeod.

At the end of his study of *Class and Religion in the Late Victorian City* (1974) McLeod argues that the period around 1880 was a significant turning point in the history of Victorian religion (and indeed one of the important points of transition in the history of British religion in general). At about this date the 'Victorian facade of religious consensus began to crumble,' and to do so most especially among the hitherto outwardly religiously conventional and church-going middle and upper-class backbone of Victorian Christianity (McLeod, 1974, p. xi).

From the 1880s onwards, the middle and upper class social and religious consensus of church-going, respectability, duty, and the maintenance of at least outwardly orthodox belief, which had been the characteristic mode of the first two thirds of the Victorian era, steadily gave way. McLeod identifies a number of specific changes in attitude, belief, outlook and behaviour, which, when taken together, both account for and characterize the newly emerging situation of the 1880s and beyond.

On the one hand, he suggests, there began to be an increasingly public expression of hitherto 'latent dissatisfaction' with the conventional orthodoxy — both social and theological — of the preceding era. Such latent dissatisfaction included a sense of embarrassment over some of the practices of conventional middle-class piety, such as daily family prayers. But far more importantly, it involved a widespread rejection of the doctrine of hell and eternal punishment. Until the 1870s at least, hell had remained a definite part of the theological furniture of conventional belief. Until that point open rejection of hell had still tended to be the act of a fairly bold religious or anti-religious individualist — be he or she a middle-class intellectual and ethical honest doubter in the manner of George Eliot, J. A. Froude or Francis Newman, a working-class secularist, or a Broad Church clergyman.[1] For most conventionally religious people, hell remained on the theological agenda even if, as one of McLeod's sources observed, in many more benevolently inclined 'orthodox' households people privately hoped no-one would go there (McLeod, p. 225).

By the early 1880s, however, this situation had begun to change. In 1877 F. W. Farrar — by then Archdeacon of Westminster, and already the author of a highly popular *Life of Christ* — had preached and then published a series of sermons entitled *Eternal Hope*, in which he rejected traditional teaching on hell and eternal punishment. The response to the sermons revealed that in preaching and publishing such ideas he was now saying openly what many people had thought privately for some time.[2] Within a few years, McLeod observes, a sermon in favour of hell, outside a

[1] For a discussion of such openly expressed and morally based rejections of hell in the early and mid-Victorian periods, see *RVB*, II, 8.

[2] For an analysis of the debate which Farrar's sermons on *Eternal Hope* prompted among theologians, see, Rowell, 1974, ch.7. For a brief discussion of the significance of Farrar's *Life of Christ*, see *RVB*, II, 11.

church or chapel specifically renowned for its orthodoxy, would seem as surprising as a sermon against hell would have done twenty years earlier (p. 226).

An important theological change had occurred. It was not that large numbers of hitherto faithfully orthodox believers suddenly had 'crises of faith' and gave up Christianity. What happened, rather, was that significant numbers of believers, for whom acceptance of doctrinal orthodoxy had always been tacit and conventional rather than articulate and specific, now found it socially possible to drop particular beliefs which they found objectionable or unsatisfactory. Their Christianity had openly begun to become less credal, less dogmatic, less specific, and more vague.[3]

In place of the inexorable divine justice of evangelicalism and the barrier between a holy God and sinful man of the Tractarian tradition, there had emerged, McLeod nicely remarks, a God who was easy-going and made allowances. 'It was Pascal's wager in reverse: enjoy yourself; if there is no God you have had a good run for your money, and if there is, he would do the same in your place' (McLeod, p. 228). It is notable that T. C. Smout, in seeking to explain the cooling of much of the ardour of Scottish Presbyterian church life from the late nineteenth century onwards, characterizes emerging popular conceptions of God in a very similar way: 'if there was a God, He was good: if He was good, He would send you to heaven or at least give you a second chance if you had made a mistake; if He would give you a second chance it could not matter tremendously if you were a bit of an agnostic here and now, or didn't go regularly to church. God was good. It would all come right in the end'. As Smout observes, as a bit of home-spun logic it had considerable strength and consistency (Smout, 1986, p. 165).

It was not only latent dissatisfaction over hell that 'came out' in the 1880s, however. The breakdown in the hitherto effective Victorian middle and upper-class religious consensus was reflected in other changes too. Other varieties of heterodox religious opinion, apart from the dismissal of hell, began to be discussed without the fuss and furore with which they would have been greeted ten or twenty years earlier. McLeod notes in

---

[3] The emergence of such 'looser,' more diffuse, and less doctrinally and theologically specific versions of Christianity *within* the churches and their predominantly middle-class congregations is an important theme in a number of the essays in both the present volume and Volume I *Traditions*. In the present volume, see, for example, the brief discussion of the relationship between working-class 'diffusive Christianity,' lower-middle class 'non-credal Protestantism', and the development of an internal doctrinal pluralism within many late Victorian denominations (*RVB*, II, 3); and the discussion of changing attitudes to the Bible and the importance of the popularity of 'Lives of Jesus,' (*RVB*, II, 11). In the preceding volume, see, especially, the discussions of the emergence of internal denominational pluralism, the tendency to the decline of doctrinally precise denominational positions, and the increasing popularity of an essentially hymn-centred piety (*RVB*, I, 1, 2, and 3).

particular the effects of *popularized* (and often decidedly garbled) versions of Darwin and the idea of evolution, and the growth in popular (if again also garbled and imprecise) awareness of other religions.[4] Such generalized and popularized knowledge helped to establish a *de facto* relativization of Christian belief in general and orthodoxy in particular (McLeod, pp. 229–31). For those whose orthodoxy had always been tacit rather than articulate anyway, such influences now tended to encourage a more open eclecticism and heterodoxy in their continuing belief.

Heterodox opinion was accompanied by heterodox behaviour: certain norms of mid-century activity (or inactivity) ceased to operate. Most notably, middle and upper-class church attendance began to decline and the strict observance of Sunday began to become the exception rather than the norm. The point must not be exaggerated. The upper and middle classes did not stop going to church in large numbers. But they did (in significant numbers) stop going so regularly and so devotedly. For an increasing number of middle-class families, church-going was one of the things that might be done on Sunday — but one might also (either as well or even instead) go for a walk, go on a family visit, or take part in some form of leisure or recreational activity. McLeod quotes to good effect a sermon of 1906, preached by the minister of the Haverstock Congregational Chapel at the funeral of a stalwart member of the chapel whose own devotional discipline was contrasted with the more lax *mores* of the present generation. For the late Mr Gard, the minister asserted, attendance at the chapel was the most important thing about a Sunday. But now,

> It has become a common thing for Christian people — even members of churches — to make their presence at public worship entirely a matter of inclination. If they think well to be there they will; if from any cause whatever, they choose to be absent, they will be absent ... The extent to which Sunday is used, not only by people who make no religious profession, but by professing Christians as a day of convenience is one of the most depressing features of our times ... It is simply a lax sense of religious obligation.
>
> (Quoted in McLeod, p. 233)

[4] The importance of the combination and coincidence of both the tendency towards *fragmentation* within the intellectual life of late Victorian Britain and the diffusion of *popularized* and *generalized* versions of recent and contemporary scientific and other 'specialist' knowledge has also been noted — although from a different perspective — by Robert M. Young. His final observation at the end of his important study of 'Natural Theology, Victorian Periodicals and the Fragmentation of a Common Context' (1981), is that, by the 1880s, there was a '... break-up of a common intellectual context and its associated literature, leading to the development of specialist careers, societies, and periodicals ... What remained common was popularisation and uncertain generalisation' (p. 96). For a more extended treatment of the theme of intellectual specialization in Victorian culture and society, see Heyck, 1982.

It was, indeed, a change not in overt, articulate opinion, but in under-lying attitudes and *mores*. Perceptions of the range of acceptable leisure activities were extending — and, for many people, religion was now becom-ing less a (and still less *the*) central activity and focus of life, and more one of a number of things which one might do with one's leisure time.[5]

The churches, moreover, were themselves participants in the process. Taken as a whole, the churches of the post-1880 era were more this-worldly than their predecessors of even a generation earlier. They were more con-cerned with the alleviation of this world's problems and more ready, not only to sanction, but themselves to provide facilities and agencies, societies and clubs for straightforwardly recreational as well as devotional and educational activities. Whether the rationale for such church and chapel-sponsored leisure was congregational (the provision of a fulfilling social and cultural life for the church or chapel community itself); or whether it was missionary (the attempt to initially attract the unconverted via such activities and then draw them into the wider life of the church or chapel); either way, the boundary between religion and recreation was apt to become increasingly blurred.

The history and development of the Victorian religious press, it has been noted, reveal the same broad tendency at work (Scott, 1975; Billington, 1986). In the early Victorian period religious periodicals and denomina-tional magazines had tended to focus directly and exclusively upon speci-fically religious issues. Theology, devotional reading, religious instruction, and denominational and general religious news and information were the standard content of such publications. By the 1870s and 1880s, however, a new style of religious journalism was coming to the fore. On the one hand, new large circulation weekly religious newspapers were founded which sought to combine religious news, commentary on secular news and affairs, devotional items and entertainment. On the other hand, many of the older denominational journals began to carry material designed to entertain as well as to religiously improve and instruct. Fiction began to appear, as did accounts of foreign travel and a proliferation of articles and items on a wide variety of cultural and recreational themes. Such developments were in part a product of growing professionalism among publishers and journalists and of the availability of technology suitable for the production of a cheap popular religious press. But they were also a reflection of a subtly changing religious ethos: the new style religious press, it has been observed, blurred

---

[5] For a further discussion of this theme which focuses specifically on the question of changing attitudes to leisure — and especially Sunday leisure — among the middle classes, and the relationship of such changes to the 'traditional' pattern of middle-class church-going and re-ligious allegiance, see Lowerson, 1984.

distinctions between the religious and the secular, and offered 'a reassuring but undemanding faith' (Billington, p. 132).[6]

The collapse of the Victorian middle-class religious consensus; the passing of the era when the denial of hell or the espousal of heterodox theological opinions was almost bound to prove controversial; the coming of the era of secular recreational and leisure activity as a (perhaps the) major challenge to religious practice, and the blurring of the distinction between the two; the passing of the era when the confrontation of church and chapel, establishment and dissent, could fundamentally influence the shape, and even be the centre, of national politics: the 1880s do, indeed, take on the appearance of a significant watershed in the history of religion in modern Britain. Where once they had been central to the life of Victorian Britain, religious issues and controversies were, by the last two decades of the nineteenth century, well on their way towards a new location somewhere nearer to the periphery of national life. It was a new location in which for the most part — odd flurries of atypical twentieth century interest apart — they have continued to reside.

BIBLIOGRAPHY

L. Billington (1986) 'The Religious Periodical and Newspaper Press, 1770–1870' in M. Harris and A. Lee (eds.) *The Press in English Society from the Seventeenth to Nineteenth Centuries*, pp. 113–32, Fairleigh Dickinson University Press.

R. Currie (1968) *Methodism Divided: A Study in the Sociology of Ecumenism*, Epworth.

T. W. Heyck (1982) *The Transformation of Intellectual Life in Victorian England*, Croom Helm.

J. Lowerson (1984) 'Sport and the Victorian Sunday: the beginnings of middle-class apostasy' in *British Journal of Sports History*, Vol. 1, pp. 202–20.

H. McLeod (1974) *Class and Religion in the Late Victorian City*, Croom Helm.

G. Rowell (1974) *Hell and the Victorians*, Oxford, Oxford University Press.

P. Scott (1975) 'Victorian religious periodicals: fragments that remain' in D. Baker (ed.) *The Materials, Sources and Methods of Ecclesiastical History*, pp. 325–39, Oxford, Blackwell.

T. C. Smout (1986) *A Century of the Scottish People 1830–1950*, Collins.

R. M. Young (1980) 'Natural theology, Victorian periodicals and the fragmentation of a common context' in C. Chant and J. Fauvel (eds.) *Darwin to Einstein: Historical Studies on Science and Belief*, pp. 69–107, Longman.

---

[6] For an account of this process at work in a particular denominational context, see the depiction of the secularization of Methodist Magazines in the 1880s and 1890s in Currie, 1968, pp. 135–6.

CHAPTER 1

PURITAN SUNDAY; OR, WHAT WE MUST ALL COME TO.

THE WORD AND THE WORLD: EVANGELICALISM IN THE VICTORIAN CITY

woe is unto me, if I preach not the Gospel
(1 Corinthians 9:16)

A T the close of Victoria's reign Church Evangelicalism appeared to
be a spent force. Within the Anglican communion the soldiers of
Christ, battle-weary and perplexed, seemed set for certain defeat.
'The Evangelical body within the Church of England', wrote Charles
Booth, 'has fallen on hard times. The stream of religious feeling and
tendency (in London at any rate) has flowed on either side and left their
churches stranded' (Booth, 1902, 3rd Series, VII, p. 52). Why, even
Clapham, the very citadel of revived religion, had been overrun by
Romanizing Ritualists (Mudie-Smith, 1904, p. 205). The mission to the
Heathen, long upheld as one of the peculiar glories of Anglican Evangelicalism, was now perceived as a form of spiritual under-consumption. 'The
party everywhere', wrote the Dean of St Paul's, 'has to struggle against
depression and discouragement' (Inge, 1911, p. 181).

Evangelical Nonconformity, by contrast, appeared buoyant. The Nonconformist Conscience, at that point fully aroused, seemed poised to purify
the nation and subdue sin. Appearances, though, were deceptive. 'The
evangelization of the world in this generation' was, as slogans go, comparable with Chamberlain's claim to have secured 'peace in our time'. 'The
Waning of Evangelicalism', the title of a sombre piece in the *Contemporary
Review* for May 1900 signified the doubt and despondence that lay behind
the rush to victory (Heath, 1900). To the more thoughtful elements, 'We
are weak in Him' [2 Corinthians 13:4] seemed a more accurate statement of
their condition and prospects; everywhere irreligion and indifference
appeared triumphant. Redemption seemed remote. 'The fleeing from the
city of Destruction, the crying out against the "burden" of sin, the vision of
the flames of hell flaring close to the Celestial City, represent an apparatus
of experience that is alien to the present', wrote one Christian commentator
(Masterman, 1909, p.267). The despair of the godly reflects the altered
status of organized religion in relation to state and society. It was during
the Queen's reign that Christianity lost its centre-stage position and
became detached from mainstream culture. The process of marginalization,
which is essential to any understanding of religion in Victorian Britain,
supplies the framework within which Evangelical piety needs to be located
and re-assessed (Kent, 1973; Gilbert, 1976).

I

The contrast between the commencement and the close of the Queen's
reign is startling. At the time of the coronation, the forward march of virtue

seemed unstoppable. Much of the machinery of the Evangelical movement was by then in place. Its great voluntary associations — the Church Missionary Society (1799); the Religious Tract Society (1799); the British and Foreign Bible Society (1804); the Society for Promoting Christianity among the Jews (1809); and the Church Pastoral Aid Society (1836) — were fully operational. The Evangelical press, too, prospered. James Stephen, who likened a party without a journal to a bell without a clapper, noted the sonorous tones of the *Christian Observer*, the organ of Anglican Evangelicalism, which month after month relayed its message to the faithful (Stephen, 1849, II, p. 374). The *Record*, a more Calvinist and combative journal, launched in 1828, enjoyed an even wider circulation. Nonconformity, too, had its great 'societies' and was also well served by its press and publications network. Exeter Hall, built in 1831, became the focal point of the 'societies', both denominational and free, and reinforced the cohesion and commitment of the Evangelical community. Its famous 'May Meetings', which brought believers together from all parts of the country for prayer and deliberation, rapidly became a key event in the Christian calendar.

Progress in the reformation of manners and morals, considerable before the Queen ascended the throne, proceeded with unflagging enthusiasm. Vicious, cruel and brutalizing pastimes, so common in the eighteenth century, were increasingly condemned as uncouth, un-Christian and uncivil; vice and depravity, blasphemy and Sabbath desecration were now deemed intolerable. The altered outlook registered the impact of the Evangelical initiatives which began in the late eighteenth century and reached a crescendo with the abolition of slavery in 1833. Evangelicals had by then perfected the apparatus of agitation that was to be used with such signal success later in the century. The leagues, associations, speeches and editorials that so invigorated public life in Victorian Britain were often Evangelical in origin. The mobilization of extra-parliamentary opinion through public meetings, processions and petitions, and all the paraphernalia of pressure group politics, elaborated and applied in the campaign against slavery, supplied a model for subsequent crusades against vice, intemperance and immorality.

Evangelical Protestants at the opening of the Queen's reign made up a fraction of the Established Church; Evangelical Nonconformity, by contrast, was a popular conversionist movement with a broad social constituency. Evangelical pietism was in the main a subcultural phenomenon concentrated in the industrial settlements that were implanted in the century before Victoria came to the throne. It was in the exclusive chapel communities, where religion and culture were spiritually elevating and socially sustaining, that its true strength lay. In addition to the satisfaction of associational, material and recreational requirements, the chapel supplied opportunities for social honour and a sense of belonging. It was here that the basic equipment of evangelicalism, with its emphasis upon lay initiative and missionary methods, was forged. These in due course were appropriated by Anglicans and others so that, by the time of the Queen's accession, evangelical efforts to propagate the Gospel were supported by a dense and sprawling network of charitable educational and philanthropic agencies. Sunday schools, savings banks, church-extension societies, voluntary associations for this, that and the other, all grew with un-diminished vigour. Donations poured in. The annual receipts of the Church Missionary Society doubled during the 1830s; the income of the Church Pastoral Aid Society quadrupled between 1837 and 1849; while the income of the London City Mission increased fivefold during the 1840s (Harrison, 1971, p. 145).

The presence of the latter body underscores the variegated character of Victorian evangelicalism. The efforts of both church and chapel were supplemented by an autonomous lay revivalism that was suspicious of the ministry, urban in orientation and indifferent to denominational boundaries. The London City Mission, with its corps of dedicated profes-sional evangelists, was one of a series of institutions — the others included the Y.M.C.A., the United Kingdom Alliance and the Mildmay Conferences — which gave shape and substance to a distinctive subcultural revivalism that was anti-Catholic in inspiration and Protestant in outlook. The net-work of agents and agencies thus created provided the infrastructure of revivalism that was crucial to Moody and Sankey's subsequent success. It was this environment which also nurtured the Salvation Army and supplied the cutting edge to a popular Protestantism that remained a disturbing and disruptive element in the late Victorian city.

The extraordinary growth of sects and societies and the popularity of revivalism points to a deep sense of dissatisfaction among members of the older ecclesiastical structures. It was their faith and energy that animated the huts, halls and hideaways in which the Gospel was preached, and it was they who furnished the audiences for the numerous American revivalists who visited these shores during the Queen's reign. As John Kent has shown, Palmer, Pearsall Smith, Moody and Sankey, Torrey and others, played a key role in mobilizing these disaffected elements and in giving expression to their unsatisfied yearnings for a truly evangelical faith that lay beyond the reach of doubt (Kent, 1978).

Evangelicalism, then, was a fragmented rather than a unitary move-ment. There were unresolved disputes between Arminian and Calvinist in relation to the doctrines of Election, Atonement and Grace; there was antagonism between clergy and laity, between the polite Protestantism of the Evangelical Establishment and the popular Protestantism of the city missionaries; between the 'natural law' evangelists of the Chalmers school and the pentecostal, pre-millinerian and prophetic elements clustered

around the *Record*; and later there were tensions between the soup'n sand-
wich evangelism of the Salvation Army and the more suburban and socially
less aware sorts across the bridges. Evangelicalism, in short, possessed a
common, though not a unifying, theology. Its doctrines dwelt chiefly on the
fall of man; the atoning death of Christ; grace the sole originating cause of
man's salvation; justification by faith the sole instrumental cause; the need
of a new birth, and of the constant and sustaining action of the Holy Spirit
— and were both a strength and a weakness. By the close of the nineteenth
century, its vision of eternal damnation was said to be alienating and outdated, but at the opening of the Queen's reign it was the Evangelical
emphasis upon the natural equality and moral deficiency of all men before
God that was so attractive.

II

Evangelicalism, which grew up in the shadow of the Industrial and French
Revolutions, appealed to those of uncertain status and precarious position.
It supplied a sense of identity and community, a standard of morality and a
code of conduct, to people experiencing rapid change and social disruption.
First generation Evangelicals, drawn primarily from the Dissenting middle
classes, were reinforced from the fringes of the upper classes. The lesser
gentry and marginal merchants who comprised the core of Evangelical
Churchmen raised a banner to which the more secure elements of the upper
middle classes were subsequently drawn (Balda, 1981). By the beginning of
the nineteenth century Evangelicalism had a broad social base which
embraced slavers and soldiers, manufacturers and merchants, brewers and
bankers, men and women of the professional classes, and those middling
sorts who wished to be goodly and godly. 'The real drama of Evangelicalism', wrote George Eliot, '— and it has abundant drama for any one who
has genius enough to discern and reproduce it — lies among the middle
and lower classes'. By the time the 'Saints' had gone marching in, Evangelicalism had become the very bedrock on which the culture, consciousness and confidence of the middle classes rested. Take away Evangelicalism
and you take away the moral ethos of mid-Victorian Britain: for Evangelicalism was more than a set of doctrines; it was a way of life — and a
very distinctive one at that.

Otherworldliness was its most striking characteristic. The belief that the
present life is merely a preparation for eternity meant the sacrifice of pleasure to duty, indulgence to improvement, and indolence to industry. There
was no time to lose; seconds wasted were sins accumulated. Evangelicals,
knowing that the hour of death was at hand, and that at any time they
could be called to account for their actions, determined to live useful lives
so that on the Day of Judgement they should not be found wanting. Most

were 'workaholics' and expected others to be so. Non-addicts were suspect. J. C. Ryle, a prominent Evangelical Churchman who became the first Bishop of Liverpool, found it difficult to believe that the incumbent of a Hampshire living whom he encountered in slippers and dressing-grown at midday could be numbered among the godly (Toon & Smout, 1976, p. 37). People such as Ryle invariably rose at the crack of dawn and passed the early morning hours in devotional reading, prayer and meditation. By the time the rest of the world was rising, restless Evangelicals had already completed a good morning's work.

Those who lived as though the passing day was their last, monitored their spiritual progress with fear and apprehension. Keeping a diary, a common — but by no means universal — practice among evangelical Christians, assisted the self-assessment process. Their journals, filled with imperfection and infirmity, doubt and deficiency, signify an overwhelming sense of sin and personal unworthiness that found outward expression in comportment and conduct. Some, indeed, received praise as an undergraduate receives an assignment. 'So genuine was his sense of unworthiness that praise became to him a positive pain', wrote W. F. Moulton's biographer. 'He would walk out of the room rather than hear a laudatory passage about himself . . .' (Moulton: 1899, p. 35).[1]

The Puritan conscience affected the psyche and the sentiments. The chase for grace was an endless anguished process of self-scrutiny which left the individual overwhelmed by error, fearful of failure and terrified by the wrath to come. Evangelical diarists filled page after page with confessions, self-abasement, penitence and renewed dedications. The flames of hell charred the mind and tormented the soul long before death beckoned. To its influence may be attributed 'the strange morbid gloominess' from which R. W. Dale suffered, the recurrent fits of depression to which Shaftesbury was prone or the melancholic musing of the reverend gentleman who declared that in the *Congregational Year Book* he 'values the obituaries most of all' (Dale, 1899, p. 45; Peel & Marriott, 1937, p. 30). To its influence must also be traced that sickly sentimentality which critics found so disagreeable.

Evangelicals, like the Devil, were never off duty. Conversazione, for example, subtly but surely turned towards spiritual matters in Evangelical households. 'It was curious to see how, without the least affectation or cant, he was able to make his guests feel that it was an almost natural thing not to separate without a hymn and a word of prayer', wrote Bishop Bicker-

---

[1] I am not, of course, suggesting that Moulton, a Wesleyan, was an Anglican Evangelical. Theologically and socially they were distinct. Wesleyans and Evangelicals were not in the same camp, and this became truer in the last quarter of the nineteenth century. There was always a strong trace of adventism in the Anglican group which was missing from the Wesleyans.

steth's biographer (Aglionby, 1907, p. 183). The call to action was in fact irresistible. One journalist reported having 'heard of two men occupying sittings in a chapel over which one of Mr Spurgeon's most successful students is pastor, paying for two pews that they might accommodate strangers, and prior to every evening service going into the streets and urging the idlers to occupy the seats which they had kept vacant for them'. And such stories were neither apocryphal nor exceptional. (*The Sword and The Trowel*, May, 1870, p. 219).

The Evangelical clergyman was easily identified. Worldly ambition, crushed within him at the time of his conversion, made way for a grave and earnest demeanour. Those who would walk in the paths of righteousness had to appear serious in manner as well as in conduct. Proper projection was important. In 1828 the Rev. H. D. Lowe had his beard cut off by order of the Wesleyan Conference. Thirty-two years later R. W. Dale, the less compliant pastor of Carr's Lane Birmingham, scandalized his congregation by his decision to grow both beard and moustache. The latter was said to invest ministers 'with an air of levity and worldliness' (Dale, 1899, p. 203). Blackcoated pastors, with their silk hats and white ties, were unmistakable, as were their Evangelical compeers in the Church of England. *De rigueur* in the pulpit, where they rebuked Ritualism and proclaimed their Protestanism, the black gown and sombre dark hues of everyday attire expressed their wearer's solemnity, dignity and seriousness of purpose.

Private life was equally austere. For Evangelicals of every denomination the family occupied a pivotal position both in religious practice and in social thought. As with their Puritan forebears the family was perceived as the conduit of Christianity carrying its Revelation from generation to generation. Its importance in role-creation and role-definition and in the placement of men and women in separate spheres of influence was scarcely less profound. Sexual and social subordination were both thereby enforced. Edward Henry Bickersteth, the Evangelical Rector of Watton in Hertfordshire, gathered his children to his study every morning before breakfast to hear them recite selected passages from the Bible which had been committed to memory. Breakfast, attended by the whole household, was followed by family prayers, with a hymn, a reading and exposition of Holy Scripture. This was not unusual. The celebration of family prayers supplied the occasion for the male head of the household to impress his power and authority upon his assembled dependents and the opportunity to reverence property, place and position (Hennell, 1979, pp. 39–40; Davidoff and Hall, 1987).

The roles performed by women were restricted but not unimportant. The organization of the household, instruction of the young, supervision of the servants and management of their morals, were perceived as creating the conditions necessary for the promotion of purity and piety. For dutiful women the path to personal salvation was thereby smoothed. Family duties, when properly discharged, were an atonement for Eve's errors. In short, the godly wife and mother was central to the suppression of sin.

Success here, as elsewhere, was conditional upon conversion. This was the constant aim and endeavour set before parents and teachers, clergy and ministry. Preachers wrestled with God in prayer for conversions and held special services to secure decisions of acceptance. Ministers and office-holders considered something wrong with the preaching or with the spiritual atmosphere when conversions were not forthcoming. Christian parents set their minds on this for their children. They prayed for them and with them, and imparted religious instruction to them with this end in view. They believed in the converting grace of the Holy Spirit and prayed passionately that it might come upon those for whom they prayed.

Serious and spiritual though they undoubtedly were, Evangelical households were not all gloom-ridden dungeons in which children sighed alone and smiles were unknown. Many were dismal, joyless places, but Evangelical childhoods probably contained greater variety than is sometimes suggested. Alas, we really don't know.

What we do know was that between Evangelicals there was considerable variation. Indeed, Evangelicals inhabited two distinct subcultures which touched at several points but in general related to the wider society in rather different ways. The oppositional character and sectarian ethos of extra-establishment evangelicalism reflected the inferior social and political standing of Dissent. By contrast, Anglican Evangelicals identified with the ruling élite and, at the beginning of the Queen's reign, were less estranged from the dominant culture than their Nonconformist counterparts. Anglican Evangelicalism, with its network of local devotional groups, clerical and lay conferences and 'societies' from which the principles of episcopacy and transmitted grace were excluded, possessed a 'particularist spirit', to be sure (Warre Cornish, 1910, I, pp. 50–1). But its manifest sect-structure only emerged in the course of the nineteenth century as the secularization of the dominant forms of culture widened the gap between the World and the Word and reduced Anglican Evangelicalism to a subcultural marginality.[2]

Sabbatarianism, a resource available to all Evangelical pietists, provided both a form of resistance and a means for asserting their separate identities. Whatever their differences, Evangelicals of church and chapel were all agreed that Sunday was special. In Evangelical households Sunday, the Lord's day, was dedicated to public worship and private prayer; all works, other than those of urgent necessity, were set aside and all recreations pro-

[2] On the emergence of sects within the Church of England see *RVB*, I, 1.

hibited. The day was so structured as to prevent contact with the secular sphere. Newspapers and unseemly literature were replaced by devotional works and other suitable texts; private and public transport by shanks' pony. Sunday fare of cold collations and cold sweets enabled servants to attend church. Whether or not Sunday so spent was boring is beside the point. The Sunday Question was about choice as much as belief.

The attempt to impose the Sabbath upon an unwilling public, to legislate against its will and enforce conformity through the courts, was not popular except with that portion of the middle class that was religiously-minded. The Lord's Day Observance Society, the Evangelical body charged with these onerous duties, provoked riots and disturbance and contrived to attract to a single cause just about as much odium as was humanly possible. Sabbatarianism, however, signified something more than the unacceptable face of Evangelicalism; it served, along with teetotalism, the exclusion of worldly pleasure and the company of the wrong sorts, to separate the saved from the damned. Revivalism performed an analogous role. 'Revivalism', writes one scholar, 'worked, not by "conversion" as much as by persuading the converted that their religious experience justified their being alienated from general society, and also necessitated sabbatarianism, teetotalism and other restrictive practices' (Kent, 1978, p. 93).

Revivalism, then, served to sustain subcultural separatism and prepare the faithful for fresh advances. That Anglican Evangelicalism was set to stagnate within a fundamentalist fortress that lay beyond the reach of romish and rationalistic influences was not apparent at the opening of the Victorian age. At that point Keble seemed containable and Strauss an obscure German. From a distance the growth-potential of Evangelicalism appeared considerable. The Evangelical party within the Church of England represented a militant tendency, well organized, well heeled and apparently well placed to secure position and influence. Charles Simeon, the Cambridge don who possessed an acute awareness of place and power, was responsible for a concerted campaign to perpetuate and extend evangelical influence within the Church. Simeon knew that cadres were decisive and sought to acquire rights of representation through the purchase of advowsons. The Simeon Trust, the body responsible for the dispensing of such patronage, worked alongside the Church Pastoral Aid Society, which performed a complementary role in organizing the supply of Scripture Readers and other lay helpers to assist in non-ministerial duties.

More remarkable still was the penetration of the higher clergy. Sumner, elevated to the See of Canterbury in 1848, prepared the way. But for Evangelical Churchmen Palmerston's premiership (1855–65) marked their finest hour. In that time Evangelicals collected mitres like a bankrupt accumulates debts. The prime minister, who in theological issues couldn't tell his left hand from his right, turned for guidance to his devout and informed step-son, the Earl of Shaftesbury, the most Evangelical of Evangelicals, whose reputation as 'the bishop-maker', though somewhat exaggerated, did underscore the Evangelical presence in the highest counsels of the nation.

III

So what went wrong? The simple answer, at least in relation to Anglican Evangelicalism, is that we really do not know. Scholarship, though considerable, tends to present Evangelicalism as a Victorian prelude (Bradley, 1977). There is no satisfactory account of the movement during the Queen's reign. The standard studies of the Evangelical party within the Church of England, all written before the First World War, are now sadly deficient (Moule, 1901; Balleine, 1908; Russell, 1915). The status of Evangelicalism in Victorian Britain, its role, structure, sociology and strategy have not been the object of sustained study. Our ignorance of Victorian Evangelicalism is profound. Of its social origins, age-structure, numerical strength and geographical distribution, we know little. Its relative strength within the Church of England, for example, continues to rely on mid-Victorian guesswork. Much of this — and there was an awful lot of it — was of a polemical or partisan nature and is about as accurate as the official returns of killed and wounded published by combatant nations in times of war. The estimates most often cited, those supplied by Connybeare in 1853, were obtained through an unscientific sample of the *Clergy List* based on the assumption that those whose opinions were ascertainable bore the same proportion to those whose opinions were unknown (Connybeare, 1853, p. 338).

Deficient data are not the only difficulty. Classification and enumeration, too, pose problems which nullify comparison and hamper analysis. The Evangelical party within the Church of England, like its rivals, was not monolithic but contained variety as well as uniformity. Opponents of Ritualism, for example, embraced many shades of opinion ranging from the ultra Protestants at one extremity to those who declined to officiate in a chasuble but unashamedly upheld dignity and beauty in public worship at the other. Opponents of Biblical criticism displayed similar division. Some were uncompromisingly hostile; others decried obscurantism and insisted upon the necessity for engagement; and there were those, the 'Evangelical Higher Critics', who felt that faith was strengthened by such encounters. 'The fact is', said Canon Money in 1884, 'that the division which exists in the Church at large reappears ... in the Evangelical body. There are amongst us the high, and broad, and low' (Bentley, 1971, pp. 168–9; Balda, 1981, pp. 246–8).

Contemporaries, whatever their particular preference, were acutely conscious of the interactive and dynamic character of church parties, and aware that a shift in the position of one affected the relative standing of all. The reciprocal relationship in which they were engaged, moreover, meant that perceptions and identities were not fixed for all time but structured by a continuing process of alignment and re-alignment as the parties responded in their varying ways to changing circumstances. Evangelicalism and Anglo-Catholicism, for example, acted and reacted upon one another in a negative dialectic. Indeed, the Oxford Movement in all its phases — Tractarianism, Ritualism and Liberal Catholicism — was until the unsettlement of faith in the late nineteenth century the dominant influence upon the Evangelical party.

Fear of Rome drove the Evangelical party into an anti-Ritualist alliance with the Low Church party and transformed Evangelical priorities and practices. The absorption of Low Church prejudices led to the denial of its mission and deformation of its message. Evangelicals forgot that the Reformation in England began not in opposition to Rome but with the preaching of the Gospel. Evangelicalism assumed a polemical and punitive character that found outward expression in the Church Association. Pulpits were mobilised and services modified in defence of Protestant principles. Beauty was banished and ceremonial curtailed as panic-stricken Evangelicals, heedless of their own traditions, strove to decontaminate public worship and cleanse the service of any trace of papal pollution. 'Evangelical piety was debased by that association', wrote the High Church historian Charles Smyth, who considered the party's preoccupation with ultra-Protestantism an excrescence upon an otherwise positive movement (Smyth, 1943, p. 17). Aberrant or not, the departure caused confusion when, by the close of the century, fears of Rome had subsided sufficiently to permit the revival of ritual within Evangelical churches.

The Catholic Revival was by no means the sole source of change. Liberal theology, as we shall see, was also important. Its disintegrative effects, though uneven in incidence, operated upon all parties so that Evangelicalism presented a decidedly different appearance at the end of the Queen's reign, compared with its beginning. Then, religion appeared dominant: the conversion of the country, if not at hand, still seemed a realizable ambition. By the time of her passing, Christianity was widely perceived as recessive rather than resurgent. For the Evangelical party the crisis of Christianity deepened a growing crisis of identity. The things which had previously seemed so contentious — elaborately-decorated churches, stained glass, encaustic tiles, costly hangings, ornate metalwork, choir stalls, open seats, choral service, surpliced choir, weekly communion, general offertory and surplice in the pulpit — were increasingly viewed as useful improvements without sacramental significance, or simply irrelevant to the task in hand. The Rev. J. Piper, the Evangelical incumbent of St Paul's, Upper Holloway, who was of the opinion that 'a surplice would look more cheerful' than the black gown in which, out of deference to the wishes of his trustees and congregation, he continued to preach, in confidence declared that he 'does not care a dump what he preaches in' and 'always tells his people that such questions are utterly trivial'. Piper, a former missionary, added: 'as long as a man leads a Christian life I don't care a rap about anything else; a good many R.C.s [sic] are better than their creed and will go to Heaven, and lots of Evangelicals will go to Hell' (B205, pp. 171–3).

Charles Booth's survey of religion in London disclosed a degree of ritual in their services which might have horrified a generation of Evangelical clergy which had been brought up to regard anything other than a simple service as a snare and a delusion.[3] 'Though his church is evangelical', wrote Booth's assistant of the Rev. D. H. Chambers D.D., Vicar of St Anne's, Poole Park, 'Dr C. [sic] has a good musical service and one of the best-known organists in North London, who is probably largely accountable for the congregation being so large as they are, as he is something of a draw in the neighbourhood' (B205, p. 155). Other Evangelicals presented a more guarded approach. The septuagenarian incumbent of St Bartholemew's, Islington, the Rev. L. Stanham, welcomed the sound of music, but resisted its indiscriminate application. The service was reported to be of an old-fashioned Evangelical type: 'it used to be all spoken but now the Psalms are usually sung: the young people now want more music, and Mr S. [sic] would gladly introduce it: but objects to an intoned service, it seems un natural to address God in prayer in a feigned voice' (B196, p. 39). Where, however, the incumbent was half-hearted in his response, as at Holy Trinity, Marylebone, innovation could produce an unpleasing outcome. The ill-paid surpliced choir introduced by the Rev. W. S. Muntz — 'They stick to the prayer book', he told his interviewer — did little for the beauty of holiness. 'They read but on one note', said a colleague, 'it is a mongrel musical service' (B219, p. 201).

The gradual abandonment of the sombre service in favour of brighter and bonnier forms of worship was not, then, a uniform process. By some it was seen as an instrumental response to empty pews. Ernest Aves, Booth's penetrating research associate, had no doubt that, in the market for souls, Evangelical Churchmen were placed at a disadvantage by the sober solemnity of their services. 'The obligation to worship and to keep the Sabbath can never be made as strong as that of taking sacraments that are held to be essential of the Christian life', he wrote. 'The active Ritualist, like the R.C., has a tremendous pull in this respect over his Evangelical brethren.

---

[3] Some evangelical Nonconformists and Scottish Presbyterians similarly developed more liturgical aesthetically self-conscious, musical and 'Catholic' dimensions to their worship in the latter part of the century — q.v. *RVB*, I, 2 and 3.

Their services are more symbolical and they can ask the people to do more definite things' (B203, p. 89). The market for souls, being both localized and subject to various rigidities, however, was insensitive to rapid changes in demand. The form of service in Evangelical churches was the outcome of a process of negotiation in which the laity, as patrons and communicants, were important partners. The rate at which services were brightened, then, depended upon particular conditions in each parish.

The absence of a free and unified market, an important limiting factor, meant that the pace of change was irregular and its direction uncertain. The movement towards brighter services was, however, sufficient to arouse apprehension. Whether market-led or not, an adjustment to altered circumstances that crossed party lines created confusion among the rank and file. Those schooled in the bitter, protracted and still-continuing struggle against Anglo-Catholicism found it difficult to accept the restoration of ritual as a return to an authentic Evangelical tradition of worship. 'Why even some of our so-called Evangelical clergy are now following the obnoxious innovations by encouraging the glorification of the "priest" by the congregation rising upon the approach of the officiating clergy in the House of God . . .', wrote one of the bewildered. 'Fancy a Mohammedan, or a Jew, or even a Catholic, standing up in the sanctuary, which they consider to be the House of God on the entrance of their ecclesiastical leaders!' (*Sussex Daily News*, 23 May 1900).

Communicants were by no means alone in their confusion. Trained observers, when confronted by complex characters like the Rev. Septimus Buss of St Leonard's, Shoreditch, were equally at sea. 'Mr Buss', Booth's research associate explained, 'is the superintendent of two London City Missionaries: as he received me in a cassock, talked about choral celebration etc. this rather surprised me, and I had to ask him plainly what he was in order to explain the mystery. "Well", he said, "I was brought up in the strictest evangelical school, used to preach in a black gown and so on: but gradually I have fallen in line with the more modern school. We don't have any ritual, any incense or genuflections in the church, though I think they are very suitable to the church of a great parish like Shoreditch . . ."' The interviewer concluded that Buss was 'a broad High Churchman', though the respondent thought otherwise. 'I've still got a good deal of the old Evangelical leaven in me', he insisted. 'My great aim is to bring people to Christ' (B232, pp. 43–5).

Ritualism affected Evangelicalism in other ways. The Romanizing tendency and the sacerdotal assumptions and practices of the High Church party largely conditioned Evangelical responses to questions of Church order and Church reform. Until the late nineteenth century issues concerning the institutional adaptation of the Church and the improvement of its methods and procedures in a rapidly changing environment were but little considered by Evangelical Churchmen (Thompson, 1970). And while nothing constructive was forthcoming from their own ranks, proposals for ecclesiastical self-government and administrative reforms emanating from other parties were automatically suspect. Evangelicals, thoroughly alarmed by the secession of Newman and Manning, and the atmosphere created by the Gorham Case and the Papal Aggression, were convinced that the revival of Convocation simply paved the way to priestly despotism. Diocesan organization was likewise dismissed as a form of episcopal entrapment, a cunning attempt to incorporate their 'societies' and undermine their independence, rather than a measure necessary to improve the practical efficiency of Church work. Church autonomy, they felt certain, must culminate in disestablishment and bring with it an increase in popish practices. Evangelicals in consequence held aloof from the three important reform movements of the sixties — the Church Congress in 1861, the Diocesan Conference in 1864 and the Lambeth Conference in 1867. Evangelical traditions of personal piety, if they made for non-involvement, did not, however, require disengagement. The neglect of the corporate life of the Church reflected an adversarial style of politics and a willingness to resort to coercive legislation to resolve spiritual conflicts.

The Church Association, formed in 1865, tried to do for anti-Ritualism what the Lord's Day Observance Society had done for Sunday. Opponents of Ritualism, like the Sabbatarians, sought through litigation to compel compliance with their practices and convictions. The Church Association, known to contemporaries as 'the Persecution Society', provoked disturbances and sent clergymen to prison but failed utterly to halt the forward march of Anglo-Catholicism. Worse, the policy of prosecutions exposed divisions within the Evangelical party, compromised its principles and undermined its practices — the legality of removing the surplice before entering the pulpit was called into question — and held them up to contempt and ridicule. The need for a new departure, underscored by the mass defections from the Church Association, found expression in the set of reform proposals advanced by J. C. Ryle and his circle. These were designed to mobilize the laity against the lawless extension of popish practices into public worship. Parish Church Councils, one of their favourite measures, were, for example, intended to transform the incumbent 'from an arbitrary despot into a constitutional officer and minister of the parish in which he is ordained to serve'. Similarly, their advocacy of greater self-government within the Church was based on the assumption that, the courts having failed, the defence of decorum and decency rested with the priesthood of the laity (Bentley, 1971; Barlow, 1902).

This high-risk policy met with a muted response from the majority of Evangelicals and outright opposition from an irreconcilable element represented by the *Rock*, a noisy and extremist journal, which denounced them as

'Neo Evangelicals', and jeered at their 'ecclesiastical-mindedness'. For Evangelicals, then, the salvation of individual souls remained the dominant preoccupation. The corporate life of the Church, tainted by Anglo-Catholic initiatives for its improvement, provoked hostile rather than creative responses when it provoked any Evangelical response at all. No important measures for its reform and regeneration issued from that quarter. The Gospel and nothing but the Gospel was all that mattered.

The conjoint effects of a tradition of personal piety and an adversarial style of politics also served to accentuate Evangelicalism's increasingly out moded character. But they were not the only factors at work. Darwinism dealt the faithful a fearful blow which evangelical evolutionists, like Henry Drummond, failed to parry. The progress of Biblical criticism was altogether more devastating and left its supporters stranded in an intellectual backwater. The tendency to elevate emotion over reason — embodied in Shaftesbury's dictum, 'Satan reigns in the intellect; God in the heart of man' — debarred Evangelical Churchmen from any effective contribution to the intellectual defence of Christianity. The Bible was regarded as not only containing the Word of God, but as itself being that Word. Criticism — mere 'human science' — was destructive (Hodder, 1886, III, p. 19). 'We will have a whole Bible, or no Bible', declared C. H. Spurgeon; any departure, he added, was to go 'down grade' towards scepticism. Spurgeon's statement summarized the dominant view of most Anglican Evangelicals and some Nonconformists.

'Such was the fame and deserved authority of the great preacher,' wrote the Congregationalist R. F. Horton, 'that to lie under his censure was to forfeit the ear of by far the larger proportion of evangelical Christians' (Horton, 1917, p. 88). Horton wrote from bitter experience. His *Inspiration and the Bible* (1888), an attempt to restate Evangelical theology in the light of modern scholarship, drew 'wild, unreasoning, fanatical denunciation' from the votaries of orthodoxy. Horton's approach, which gave a preeminent place to the Person of Christ, suggested a more convincing engagement with literary and historical criticism. The fact that much textual criticism was methodologically unsound was equally suggestive. The process of adjustment was, however, painfully slow. *The Bible and Modern Criticism* (1902), a volume of essays, edited by Sir Robert Anderson, the former head of Special Branch, was in its unmeasured condemnation of recent scholarship a truly evangelical work.

Between Anderson and his associates and Horton and his more modish sorts lay an unbridgeable chasm. The Rev. William Pierce of West Hampstead Congregational Church, who described his opinions and teaching as 'liberal Evangelical', appeared to Booth's research associate to personify these polarities. '"Evangelical" . . . in the mouth of Mr P. or Horton means something very different from what it used to mean', ran the record of their interview, 'it is consistent with the broadest and most advanced opinions as to the inspiration of the Bible, questions of date, authorship etc., and men of this school look upon the Evangelical party in the Church of England as "hopelessly retrograde": a brother minister of Mr P.'s watched the clergy departing from their great annual meeting at Islington the other day, and described them as "the frowsiest set of frumps", and in this description I am sure Mr P. agreed'. The respondent, though, was aware that ministers of his school were in advance of their congregations, 'that the preaching of "liberal Evangelical" doctrine tends to the slow growth of a church' and that 'Horton's work would have gone much quicker if he'd been less liberal in his views' (B218, pp. 151–3). By the outbreak of the First World War evangelical Protestantism had still to abandon its unreasoning faith in Biblical infallibility. In the Edwardian Church the Evangelical Higher Critics, identified by Dr Hylson-Smith, were a coterie rather than a tendency (Hylson-Smith, 1982, pp. 48–60).

Horton's intervention was prompted by the conviction that 'the infidelity among the people rested on a view of the Bible which the best scholarship of the time did not support' (Horton, 1917, p. 84). R. W. Dale, by contrast, thought that the discrepancy between morality and doctrine was more damaging. 'If Christian men are not actually controlled in their common life by all that they profess to believe; if their worship has no effect upon their common work, they are contributing more powerfully to the temporary triumph of scepticism than the writers who are most hostile to religious truth'. From the 1860s onwards he pressed the case for an ethical revival to complete the unfinished work of the Evangelical Revival of the previous century. The chief defect of the latter, he argued, lay in its failure to provide a proper conception of practical righteousness, and an appropriate moral training. Preoccupied with man's salvation, it had neglected the necessity of man's perfection. The outcome was a reformation in manners rather than a new morality. In Dale's opinion, the true source of unbelief was to be located in these shortcomings. 'The wonderful story of the Incarnation — it is we who are making it incredible, if we are not manifestly trying to live a nobler life than those who deny it. The authority of God, — it is we who are teaching men that there is nothing in it, if we are not afraid to sin against Him' (Dale, 1899, p. 221).

Calls for an ethical revival were, however, beside the point when it was the immorality of the Bible itself which repelled. Everlasting punishment was particularly odious. It was this doctrine of eternal torment which had allegedly contributed more to the spread of atheism and infidelity than any single cause.

Evangelical Nonconformists acknowledged the force of the argument but were often loth to say so. Most had quietly, almost unthinkingly, abandoned belief in endless punishment. 'The doctrine of our forefathers',

R. W. Dale told the Congregational Union in 1874, 'has been silently relegated with or without serious consideration, to that province of the intellect which is the home of beliefs which we have not rejected, but we are willing to forget' (Dale, 1899, p. 312). The substitution of annihilation for eternal damnation, and the shift from the Atonement to an incarnationalist theology and from the Blood of Christ to the Sermon on the Mount, were all part of this process of adjustment by stealth. Nevertheless, there were hardline Calvinists, like C. H. Spurgeon, who held fast to the auld vision of Hell and were none the less popular for so doing. Evangelical Churchmen were equally fearful of the wrath to come. The scripture reader at St Michael's Church, Caledonian Road, an aged and somewhat deaf gentleman who was with difficulty interviewed for the Booth survey, was, for example, 'very much in earnest about the certainty of damnation for those who don't come to church or belong to other denominations' (B203, p. 111). And he was by no means an isolated or untypical figure. The faithful refused to believe that the central truths of evangelical theology — the doctrines of original sin and substitutary redemption — were themselves the cause of the very infidelity they sought to combat.

The finality of its theological doctrine evidenced the growing particularism of Establishment Evangelicalism. It wasn't always so. Until the advent of the Victorian age Evangelicals shared the cultural and intellectual attitudes of their contemporaries and were rather less special than is sometimes imagined (Rosman, 1984). Estrangement and alienation became the distinctive traits of Anglican Evangelicals during the Queen's reign as the conviction hardened that God was no longer in possession and that the world belonged to the Devil (Hennell, 1972). Disengagement and despair accompanied the flight from darkness into a more intensive spirituality. Holiness revivalism, as presented by Phoebe Palmer, the influential American Methodist who preached in Britain in the early sixties, was important — and not only because it supplied William Booth with an off-the-peg doctrine of sanctification — but because it served to rally middle-class evangelicals and strengthen their resolve to resist temptation. Mrs Palmer's teaching, with its repudiation of worldly pleasure, represented a systematic recapitulation and reinforcement of traditional Evangelical pietism. Its most novel feature, apart from its perfectionism, was the insistence upon teetotalism as a condition of sanctification. Acceptance of the latter, particularly among Church Evangelicals, underscores the desperate straits of Anglican Evangelicalism and the importance of holiness revivalism in preserving its cohesion and identity (Kent, 1978, pp. 88–9, 317–20).

'All one in Jesus Christ' became the motto of those who argued for increased spirituality as the solution to disunity, dejection and disintegration. The Evangelical movement was by its nature peculiarly susceptible to the appeal of personal religion. Local meetings for prayer and fellowship, an important source of spiritual renewal, had from the beginning of the

Revival played a prominent part in defining Evangelical piety. The doctrine of sanctification by union with Christ and the indwelling of the Holy Spirit, which later became the essence of the holiness movement, although long present in Evangelical teaching and practice, aroused the gravest apprehension when brought to these islands by the Pearsall Smiths in the late sixties and early seventies, In turning from the higher criticism to the higher life Evangelicals did not find a quiet life.

'Pearsall Smithism', in the opinion of the *Record*, was simply a species of perfectionism, an unsound and unscriptural doctrine that pointed towards antinomianism and worse. In the United States, whence came the Pearsall Smiths, it had given rise to various sects — the Pauline Church, the Perfect Church, the Bible Communists and the Sanctificationists; in Britain its pernicious doctrine was peddled by the Agapemonites, 'a weird and sexually perverted sect' to which certain sorts of Churchmen were apparently drawn. 'Their method was mysticism run mad', wrote an early historian of the Evangelical party. 'They urged their converts to stand up and "profess Sanctification", then and there to yield their bodies to the Holy Ghost, and to believe that from that moment they could never sin again' (Balleine, 1933, p. 303; Bentley, 1971). Sinless perfection was deemed to be a dangerous doctrine from which godly people needed protection.

On this, as on virtually every other issue, however, Evangelicals were divided. Pearsall Smith's uncertain grasp of theology was readily conceded, even by his supporters. He was only a layman after all! said clerical admirers who, while mindful of doctrinal deficiency, were inspired by his fervent feeling for spiritual growth and Christian unity. His perfectionism they repudiated as contrary to the central truths of Christianity; the pursuit of personal holiness, by contrast, directly addressed the requirements of the faithful, and this they warmly commended. But notwithstanding their distinctions and disclaimers, the holiness movement remained suspect and its promoters under a cloud.

The Keswick Convention, first held in July 1875, was its most potent expression. From a semi-private meeting of Evangelical clergy and laity of a kind that was by no means uncommon, it rapidly became the most famous mass gathering of Christians, attracting upwards of 10,000 souls each summer. Its proceedings were carefully monitored lest the supercharged atmosphere in which it operated encourage error as well as excess. Evangelicals were themselves acutely conscious of the dangers into which unrestrained revivalism could lead. The *Record*, for example, fearing the substitution of personal holiness for Christ's atoning sacrifice, warned against the confusion of sanctification with justification. The former, its readers were reminded, was imputed, not imparted; the latter, a cumulative development, was attained by the leading of the Holy Spirit within the soul (Bentley, 1971, pp. 399–400).

The Keswick conveners were aware of their probationary status and pitched their appeal at the faithful rather than the undecided. The emphasis was upon consolidation rather than conversion, upon developing and deepening individual spirituality, and upon a qualitative improvement in the standard of Christian commitment. Holiness, however, was unmistakeably revivalist in procedure and practice. Although the term 'second conversion' was studiously avoided, the holiness movement sought through a comparable experience to secure a reconciliation in Christ in the expectation, not of forgiveness, but of power, through the inspiration of the Holy Spirit. Similarly, the after-meetings at Keswick conventions performed a function analagous to revivalist inquiry meetings.

Sanctification and service went hand-in-glove. The holiness movement supplied a spiritual stimulant which enabled its members to tackle parochial problems with renewed vigour. Such, at any rate, was the theory. The retreats, promoted by Bishop Bickersteth, which at first were greeted with equal scepticism, performed a similar function. Good morale, however, was a necessary but not a sufficient condition of victory. In the struggle against sin strategy and tactics were deemed no less vital.

IV

The propagation of the Gospel was for evangelicals the alpha and omega of their faith. But if their message was unchanging their methods were not. 'My preaching will never fill the place' said one candid cleric. 'If we want the people to come we must go and fetch them.' 'Visitation', he added, 'is to save the church. It is the thing to solve the problem' (B198, p. 6). An army of lay helpers — district visitors, deaconesses, Bible women, missionary women etc. — raised in the course of the nineteenth century, made for efficient house-to house visitation and enlarged the scope of evangelical action in other spheres. Innovations designed to extend the outreach of the Church found form in the provision of bible classes, clubs, schools, societies and guilds. Not all provision was church-centred. Evangelicals, aware of the off-putting effect of the middle classes at prayer, had through the Public Worship Act of 1855 secured authority for additional services in unconsecrated buildings to attract the unchurched masses (Hardman, 1964, pp. 235–90). Special services and missions, often revivalist in character, were held in theatres, music halls, railway stations, factories and tents.

The role of the clergy was transformed. Increasingly the preacher of the Gospel found himself cast as a team leader charged with the co-ordination and control of trained bands of lay helpers. Their efforts were undoubtedly extensive but were they effective? The question of pastoral performance came readily enough to Evangelical Protestants but did not admit of any simple solution. Church attendance and church membership, then as now the most commonly used performance indicators, suggest that in relation to the unskilled urban working class the results of mission-methods and energetic evangelizing were not commensurate with the expenditure of time and effort. There were some slum missions which registered an impact upon the lowest of the low, but these were exceptional.

Away from the slums things were markedly brighter. But even in the suburbs, with still flourishing congregations, there were nagging doubts. Had the social crowded out the spiritual? The object of Evangelical social action was to bring sinners to Christ, but in some parishes and on some circuits the social agencies were reported to be 'far more numerous than the purely religious and appear rather to dwarf that part of the work than lead up to it' (B187, p. 73). Even when, as rarely happened, the rough and respectable presented themselves for communion, it was said to be for the wrong reasons. The poor came to receive the loaves and fishes; the clerk to sustain his social standing. 'Neither one nor the other care the least about points of doctrine,' said the Rev. A. L. Jukes of West Hackney: 'if I should stand on my head in the middle of the church the clerks might be mildly shocked but they would come to church just the same; the poor would not go so far as being shocked . . .' (B196, p. 21).

For clerks, religious observance was a condition of respectability; for others it was a form of entertainment. In the opinion of the Rev. A. R. Clemens, Vicar of St Bartholomew's, Bethnal Green, those who attended the meetings at Charrington's Assembly Hall in the Mile End Road went 'not with any idea of giving service, but rather with that of receiving enjoyment of a pious kind.' His colleague from nearby St Peter's was equally critical. The attraction of Charrington's for young church-goers, he told Ernest Aves, was that 'they can get in the gallery and talk and kiss and do what they like' (B228, pp. 175, 199).

Mission methods were not the only form of Evangelical enterprise in need of elevation. Bible classes, Sunday Schools, Christian Endeavour Societies and the like were thought of as an escalator, carrying people forward to regular worship in church and chapel. Mothers' Meetings, which in theory provided access to the family and household, were supposed to perform a similar role. The spiritual spin-offs, however, were often no less difficult to identify. The Vicar of St Marks, Tollington Park, thought that the fifty-odd women who attended his church would for the most part 'be much better at home cleaning up their place and making it decent and tidy for their husbands to come home to. The majority do no work at the meetings, but sit and gossip and like to be waited on' (B209, p. 9). The incremental additions to church membership, often the sole test by which performance was measured, were equally depressing. 'Not two had joined the church from it,' said the Rev. W. Mincher of King Street Primitive Methodist Chapel, Camden Town, when explaining the decision to wind up his 120-strong Mothers' Meeting. 'When you are in a denomination like

ours that measures everything by statistics you are obliged to watch closely
and direct your energies in the direction that appears best for the church'
(B216, pp. 59–61).

The 'best direction,' though, was often difficult to identify and even more
difficult to follow. By the close of our period there was a feeling that Evangelicals, in Church and Chapel, had failed to do either. Contemporary
explanations varied. Some settled upon a simple supply side analysis.
Improve the quality of personnel and you improve performance. The *Christian Observer*, for example, complained of 'the increased number of young
men with a certain Evangelical electro-plated character about them' and
too little of 'the genuine gold and silver stamp upon them'. 'Too many of
our rising generation', it continued, 'are *negatively* Evangelical only. They
are not Anglo-Catholic; not Ritualistic; not Broad Church; not Latitu-
dinarian. Their preaching contains no elements of an exceptionable kind at
all; it is smooth, commonplace, general, well-rounded, uncontroversial, safe
... And as with their preaching, so with their pastoral work. They lack
interest, eagerness, enthusiasm ... The needs of the day demand men cast
in a more apostolic mould. Respectable, gentlemenlike, educated, ordinary
persons, ornaments to society — these are not the generation of Evangelical
clergy who can now do God's work. They will never rouse a stagnant
Church; guide a restless, enquiring, sceptical generation; convince gain-
sayers; storm Satan's strongholds; hold fast the faith, and hand it down
untarnished to those who shall come after' (Anon, 1873, pp. 89–90). The
formation of the London College of Divinity in 1863 and the foundation of
Wycliffe Hall, Oxford (1877) and Ridley Hall, Cambridge (1881), the institutional outcome of such criticism, did not, however, produce satisfaction.
Wimps, better suited to pleasant curacies in eligible situations, continued to
be presented to tough inner city parishes for which they were quite unfitted.
The Rev. Arthur Woods, Vicar of Christ Church, Somers Town, according
to Ernest Aves, was one of them. Their interview left Aves convinced that
Evangelicals of this sort were best transferred to lighter duties elsewhere.
'The idea of men like Mr Woods effecting anything in a parish like Christ
Church is absurd. He ought to be sent to Bournemouth, or be made
Chaplain of a Workhouse' (B215, p. 79).

Others connected the extreme voluntarism of the Evangelical party to its
weakness within the Church of England. Indifference towards the corporate
life of the church, a function of the Evangelical preoccupation with personal
religion, was sustained by the system or organised antagonisms through
which ecclesiastical policy was — or, more accurately, was not — made. A
war on two fronts, with the ritualists in one party and the rationalists in
another, deprived the evangelical party of any real influence within the
church, while its clumsy insistence upon the quality of its Churchmanship
deprived it of any real influence without (R.E.B, 1878, p. 29). Oppor-

tunities for closer and more brotherly relations between church and chapel undoubtedly existed; for as the Ritualists touched the fringes of Rome, so on its furthest reaches Anglican Evangelicalism touched Nonconformity. The Evangelical Alliance, the institutional expression of this sentiment, nevertheless remained undeveloped. Perhaps it was incapable of further development.

For some Evangelicals, however, it was intellect rather than strategy that was most wanting. The Congregationalist R. F. Horton identified Evangelical doctrine, above all the belief in inspiration and inerrancy, as a major source of weakness. In his opinion it was 'the wrong and indefensible view of the Bible which nullifies the preaching of the Gospel by exciting unbelief in the minds of the people' (Horton, 1917, p. 90). Whether any proposed revision could have arrested the growth of unbelief does, however, seem doubtful.

Indeed, the question arises: what difference would it have made to the prospects of national regeneration if Evangelicals had been more dynamic, more liberal-minded and more astute? The answer, I think, is precious little. Booth concluded that 'there is little real ground for the natural assumption that the churches fail because they preach Evangelical doctrine'. In his view the disintegration of Evangelicalism reflected the removal of the middle classes and their replacement by a non-church-going working class (Booth, 1902: I, 3rd series, pp. 133–4). The importance of demand over doctrine is also suggested by the fact that, at present nearly one in five of the population of the United States — 27 million people — believes in the literal truth of the Bible (Princeton Religion Research Center, 1982, pp. 31–2).

Similarly, the failure to contextualize the problem, above all the neglect of structural changes, leads to an over-emphasis upon church parties and ecclesiastical politics and to the erroneous supposition that church-chapel divisions were a source of retardation. In its formative stages, however, Evangelical Nonconformity drew strength from its sectarian self-sufficiency. 'Far from exercising socially integrative functions on behalf of the dominant culture,' writes A. D. Gilbert, 'its mediation of personal religious satisfactions was through a subcultural orientation which involved withdrawal from the 'world' and which was open only to individuals making a voluntary religious commitment which implicated them in a more or less totalitarian community' (Gilbert, 1976, p. 140). In the course of the Queen's reign the strength of these chapel communities was sapped by the rise in the social and economic status of their members, the removal of disabilities, and by the disappearance from a maturing industrial economy of the distressed and disrupted elements who formerly supplied the principal source of recruits. The decline in the birth rate in the second half of the nineteenth century reduced throughput in the Sunday Schools at the same time as the cultural gap between the churches and the 'world' widened to reduce the prospect of replenishment from external sources. As to Anglican Evangelicalism, all we can say is that, while its social base requires investigation, its marginal status is not in doubt.

Evangelicalism, of church or chapel, had no solution for the crisis of Christianity. 'Mission methods', directed at those who were least responsive to their appeal, failed to address problems of structural change, demographic decline and the peripheral position of religion in mainstream culture. Those who felt that the poor were a distraction — and many evangelical clergy were so minded — could not, however, suggest ways in which middle class support could be retained or regained, not at any rate this side of the Second Coming.

What other options were available? If there were alternatives historians are not at present able to specify them. In the current state of knowledge all we can say is that the decline of Evangelicalism during the Queen's reign was not a function of the 'hidden hand'; of secularization but of a unique conjuncture (Cox, 1982). The evangelical experience in the United States suggests strongly that indifference, irreligion and infidelity are not the inevitable outcomes of modern secular society. American churches are not empty and evangelicalism is not negligible. Its failure in these islands was a peculiarly British failure, just one of the many bequeathed to us by the Victorians and their forbears.

BIBLIOGRAPHY

The following abbreviation has been used in the text:

B — refers to notebooks in the Booth Collection, British Library of Political and Economic Science, London School of Economics.

F. K. Aglionby (1907) *The Life of Edward Henry Bickersteth*, Longman.

Anon. (1873) 'On the present position of the Evangelical Party in the Church of England', *Christian Observer*, Vol. 73, Feb. 1873, pp. 83–96.

W. D. Balda (1981) 'Spheres of Influence: Simeon's Trust and its Implications for Evangelical Patronage', unpublished Ph.D. thesis, University of Cambridge.

G. A. Balleine (1933) *A History of the Evangelical Party in the Church of England* (first published 1908), second edn., Longman.

R. E. B. (1878) 'On the position of the Evangelical Party in the Church of England', *Fraser's Magazine*, Vol. 17, pp. 22–31.

M. Barlow (ed.) (1902) *Church and Reform: Being Essays Relating to Reform in the Government of the Church of England*, Bemrose.

A. Bentley (1971) 'The Transformation of the Evangelical Party in the Church of England in the Later Nineteenth Century', unpublished Ph.D. thesis, University of Durham.

C. Booth (1902) *Life and Labour of the People in London*, 3rd Series, 7 Vols., Macmillan.

I. Bradley (1976) *The Call to Seriousness: The Evangelical Impact on the Victorians*, Jonathan Cape.

W. J. Connybeare (1853) 'Church Parties', *The Edinburgh Review*, Vol. 98, pp. 273–342.

F. W. Cornish (1910) *A History of the English Church in the Nineteenth Century*, 2 Vols., Macmillan.

*J. Cox (1982) *The English Churches in a Secular Society, Lambeth, 1870–1930*, Oxford, Oxford University Press.

A. W. W. Dale (1899) *The Life of R. W. Dale of Birmingham*, Hodder and Stoughton.

L. Davidoff and C. Hall (1987) *Family Fortunes: Men and Women of the English Middle Class 1780–1850*, Hutchinson.

*A. D. Gilbert (1976) *Religion and Society in Industrial England: Church, Chapel and Social Change 1740–1914*, Longman.

B. Hardman (1964) 'The Evangelical Party in the Church of England, 1855–1865', unpublished Ph.D. thesis, University of Cambridge.

B. Harrison (1971) *Drink and the Victorians*, Faber.

R. Heath (1900) 'The waning of Evangelicalism', *The Contemporary Review*, Vol. 123, pp. 649–65.

*M. Hennell (1972) 'Evangelicals and the world, 1770–1870' in G. J. Cumming and D. Baker (eds.) *Studies in Church History*, Vol. 8, pp. 229–36, Oxford, Blackwell.

*M. Hennell (1979) *Sons of the Prophets: Evangelical Leaders of the Victorian Church*, S.P.C.K.

E. Hodder (1886) *The Life and Work of the Seventh Earl of Shaftesbury*, 3 Vols., Cassell.

R. F. Horton (1917) *An Autobiography*, George Allen and Unwin.

K. Hylson-Smith (1982) 'The Evangelicals in the Church of England 1900–1939', unpublished Ph.D. thesis, University of London.

W. R. Inge (1911) 'The Universities' in W. K. L. Clarke (ed.) *Facing the Facts or An Englishman's Religion*, James Nisbet.

J. Kent (1973) 'The role of religion in the cultural structure of the later Victorian city' in *Transactions of the Royal Historical Society*, fifth series, Vol. 23, pp. 53–73.

*J. Kent (1978) *Holding the Fort: Studies in Victorian Revivalism*, Epworth.

C. F. G. Masterman (1909) *The Condition of England*, Methuen.

H. C. G. Moule (1901) *The Evangelical School in the Church of England*, James Nisbet.

W. F. Moulton (1899) *William F. Moulton, A Memoir*, Isbister.

R. Mudie-Smith (ed.) (1904) *The Religious Life of London*, Hodder and Stoughton.

A. Peel and A. R. Marriott (1937) *Robert Forman Horton*, George Allen and Unwin.

Princeton Religion Research Center (1982) *Religion in America 1982*, Princeton (NJ), Princeton Religion Research Center.

D. Rosman (1984) *Evangelicals and Culture*, Croom Helm.

G. W. E. Russell (1915) *A Short History of the Evangelical Movement*, Mowbray.

C. Smyth (1941–3) 'The Evangelical movement in perspective', *Cambridge Historical Journal*, Vol. 7, pp. 160–174.

J. Stephen (1849) *Essays in Ecclesiastical Biography*, 2 Vols., Longman.

K. A. Thompson (1970) *Bureaucracy and Church Reform: The Organisational Response of the Church of England to Social Change 1800–1965*, Oxford, Oxford University Press.

P. Toon and M. Smout (1976) *John Charles Ryle, Evangelical Bishop*, Cambridge, James Clarke.

CHAPTER 2

A NEW ARCH-BISHOP.

Joseph Arch (to Bishop of Manchester). "AH! MY LORD, I NEVER EXPECTED TO FIND YOUR LORDSHIP ON OUR SIDE!"

[See the BISHOP OF MANCHESTER's Letter to the *Times* on the Lock-out of the Labourers — "Are the Farmers mad?" &c., &c.]

SOCIAL CONTROL TO SOCIAL GOSPEL: VICTORIAN CHRISTIAN SOCIAL ATTITUDES

'T HE British Labour movement owes more to Methodism than to Marx.' 'The Church of England is the Tory party at prayer', or, in its more contemporary form, 'the Church of England is no longer the Tory party at prayer' (but was, it is implied, until quite recently). The popular durability of such slogans is considerable. Their accuracy is, at best, a matter of sustained ambiguity. In their popular, boldly stated form, they are largely the product of the deployment of historical apologetic in support of subsequent ideological controversies both within and between denominations, and within the British Labour movement. Christians concerned to advertise the radical social contribution of the churches in modern Britain; socialists concerned to reiterate the diversity of influences in the development of the British Labour movement; Christians — including Anglicans — keen to indicate the contemporary social awareness of the church by confessing past rigidity: such are the characteristic enthusiasts for, and principal exponents of, these historiographical catchphrases.

It is not surprising. Such phrases have a snappy, memorable quality well suited to the construction of 'party' identities. But as historical statements they obscure as much as they reveal. They are caricatures, characteristically supported by other, more extended caricatures, such as that of the prophetic and heroic minority of Victorian Christian Socialist theologians, clergy and bishops valiantly struggling to awaken to its radical obligations a Christian social conscience dulled by long alliance with the political and social *status quo* and the deployment of Christian doctrine as a means of social control.

Like all successful caricatures, they are not wholly without basis in reality. The Methodist contribution to the emergence of both the Labour party and the trade union movement is evidenced in numerous biographies and autobiographies, and in the existence of entire communities, such as those of the Durham and Northumberland coalfield or rural East Anglia, in which membership of, and leadership in, Methodist (especially Primitive Methodist) chapel and local trade union branch were intimately related (Moore, 1974; Scotland, 1981; Howkins, 1985). On the other hand, the Church of England was, certainly until the beginning of the twentieth century, and for some considerable time after that, an institution with predominantly Conservative political inclinations.[1] And the extent to which Victorian Christianity — and in particular the Church of England — was indeed addicted to the presentation of Christian doctrine and morality as a

---

[1] For indications of the way in which some Anglicans sought not only to maintain but in fact to strengthen the relationship between the church and the Conservative party, see Harrison, 1974, and Roberts 1984.

means of supporting and justifying the existing social order and controlling the lower social classes has been demonstrated by, amongst others, Jenifer Hart, in her analysis of the political and social implications of a large number of sermons and pamphlets from the period 1830–80 (Hart, 1977). Or, again, as Edward Norman has recently insisted, many of the leading Christian Socialists, both Anglican and Nonconformist, from Maurice, Kingsley, Ludlow and Thomas Hughes at mid-century, through to Head-lam, Hugh Price Hughes and Westcott at the end of it, are *rightly* to be regarded as prophetic voices, calling the church of their day to a re-appraisal of its stance on contemporary social issues (Norman, 1987, chs. 1 and 10).

Such genuine points of contact between popular catchphrase and his-torical reality must not, however, be allowed to obscure the extent to which conventional caricatures represent a conveniently partial and simplified version of the changes and variations within the social and political attitudes and stances of the Victorian churches. The development of Vic-torian Christian social thought and attitudes was at once uneven, complex, diverse and a good deal richer in variety than a narrow focus upon either 'religion and social control', or upon 'Christian Socialism' and 'the social gospel' tends to allow.

The variations and subtleties in the social attitudes and stances of the Victorian churches (both within particular denominational traditions and between them) and of individual Victorian Christians were considerable. Moreover, the area is also one in which controversy between varying his-torical interpretations has been intense. In particular there is the ongoing debate over the role of Nonconformity in general and Methodism in par-ticular as either a dimension of the control and restraint of the emergent working class of the early nineteenth century, or a means of emergent working-class self-expression and advancement. Was the working-class chapel a source of other-worldly hope and community identity in a world of political powerlessness, uprooted identities and social dislocation? Or was it, rather than being a compensation for dashed worldly hopes, an expres-sion of working-class aspirations, an avenue to self-improvement, and a means of advancement? Historians continue to differ, although, as Hugh McLeod has pointed out, the attempts of Alan Gilbert and T. W. Laqueur to provide, respectively, an overarching interpretation of the rise and decline of Nonconformity between 1740 and 1914, and a thorough assess-ment of the immensely important Sunday School Movement, both favour the view that such religious institutions often appealed to the same broad category of 'respectable' skilled working-class people who also formed the principal membership of popular radical political and secularist groups. Chapel and/or Sunday School offered such people opportunities for leadership, responsibility, personal and family advancement, education, and a potentially socially advantageous community for their children (McLeod, 1984, pp. 23–4; Gilbert, 1976; Laqueur, 1976).[2]

The complex and diverse nature of both the history and the historiography of Victorian Christian social attitudes thus imposes severe limits on what may be attempted in a brief essay. The present essay therefore addresses two specific aims. First, it suggests that — rather than focus in detail upon mid or late Victorian 'Christian Socialism', or upon Primitive Methodist trade unionism as notable exceptions to the general run of Victorian Christian social opinion — it is more instructive to see them as particularly striking examples of a general and steady diversification of Christian social attitudes in Victorian Britain. Second, it suggests a number of themes within that steady process of diversification which it may be profitable to bear in mind in assessing any particular example of Victorian Christian social thought or action.

I THE DEVELOPMENT OF DIVERSITY

Nineteenth-century Christianity, as Eileen Yeo has observed, was not the exclusive possession of any one social group: it was 'contested territory'. To illustrate her point she presents a number of cases of early nineteenth-century social radicals who claimed the support of the Christian tradition — and especially the biblical tradition — for their cause, the majority of her examples being drawn from the Chartist activities of the years 1838–42 (E. Yeo, 1981). Hugh McLeod has similarly noted examples of early nineteenth-century social radicalism among Wesleyan Methodist laymen, despite the official Wesleyan opposition to active political involvement and the essentially Tory stance of the Connexion as a whole (McLeod, 1984, p. 51). More rarely, ministers of traditionally socially conservative and theologically orthodox denominations also expressed support for social radicalism, but not without cost. In 1834 Joseph Rayner Stephens, for example, was obliged to resign from the Wesleyan Methodist ministry because of his active commitment to disestablishment and to factory reform; whilst the Scottish Presbyterian minister Patrick Brewster was suspended for a year by the General Assembly of the Church of Scotland because he not only held socially radical views but had chosen to preach at Chartist meetings (E. Yeo, 1981; Johnson, 1973; Cheyne, 1983, pp. 19–22).

These, however, were exceptions, and marked exceptions at that. Until mid-century genuinely radical Christian criticism of social conditions

---

[2] McLeod (1984, pp. 24–5) also helpfully points out that there is no reason why one or other interpretation of the social significance of such evangelical religion should be definitive. 'In reality', he observes, 'most movements (and most individuals) contain contradictory elements within them'. Quite so: it is an eminently sane, but frequently overlooked, point.

remained substantially the province either of atypical clergy or of theologically unorthodox working-class Christians, outside the denominational mainstream of Victorian Christianity. The predominant Christian social stance was conservative. Its principal ingredients were derived from an amalgam of political economy and evangelicalism, although in the religious context it was not only evangelicals who adhered to them: despite their theological split with evangelicalism, most of the early Tractarians would have shared its characteristic social outlook. That outlook was austere. Poverty was morally tolerable because it was the inevitable product of immutable economic laws which were themselves the product of a divinely ordained and designed world. Hence whilst charity might alleviate poverty, it would be impious, as well as fruitless, to contemplate the transformation of the social structure itself by human reform. Poverty, besides, performed a necessary social function, offering the better off opportunities for the practice of Christian charity and the poor the opportunity for patience, humility and gratitude. Even the practice of charity, moreover, was to be directed towards the deserving poor, whose poverty was identifiably not the result of their own improvidence, intemperance or indolence. Much poverty, it was confidently claimed, was in fact the result of precisely such personal failing, and hence a recompense for sin.

Even evangelicalism, however, was not without its more socially critical elements. As recent studies have demonstrated, by mid-century the evangelical tradition was itself divided in its social stance. On the one hand there were those, such as the mid-century Archbishop of Canterbury, J. B. Sumner, or the pre-eminent Scots Presbyterian of the first half of the century, Thomas Chalmers, who remained fully committed to the principles of political economy, *laissez-faire* social theory, the absolute priority of private charity in the relief of poverty, and the undesirability of state intervention and social reform. On the other hand there were Anglican Evangelicals such as the Tory Radicals and paternalists Bull, Sadler and Oastler and the most famous Evangelical of all, Shaftesbury, who were prepared to advocate a degree of state intervention in social reform — albeit only by extending their underlying concept of paternalism to encompass the state itself.[3]

---

[3] For Sumner and Chalmers, see, respectively, Dell, 1965 and McCaffrey, 1985. For the emergence of alternatives to their stance from within the Evangelical tradition, see Holloday, 1982 and Hilton, 1985. In recognizing the emergence of a strand within early Victorian Anglican Evangelicalism open to the proposition that the state should intervene in matters of social reform, it must also be noted, firstly, that much of the state intervention which such Evangelicals subsequently sought was in fact concerned with matters of morality rather than economics and social conditions (sabbatarianism being the classic case); and secondly, that, after mid-century, Anglican Evangelicals were much less prominent in the emergence of socially critical versions of evangelicalism, the initiative in this area being taken, increasingly, by English Nonconformists and Scottish Presbyterians.

If the early Victorian evangelical tradition was thus more than merely a bastion of the most immutable social conservatism, however, it was also, nevertheless, even its more socially critical form, incapable of providing a fundamentally prophetic critique of the social *status quo*. It was not until the Christian Socialist movement of 1848–54 that such a prophetic social critique emerged from within the mainstream of Victorian Christianity.

In April 1848, the evening after the planned Chartist march from Kennington Common to Parliament had ended in rain-soaked fiasco, J. M. Ludlow, Charles Kingsley and F. D. Maurice met at Maurice's London house. They worked until 4 am to produce a manifesto entitled, 'To the Working Men of England' and signed it, 'A Working Parson'. So began the brief mid-century Christian Socialist movement — although its members did not actually designate themselves 'Christian Socialists' until 1850. In 1851 Maurice observed, in a famous phrase, that their purpose was to influence 'the unsocial Christians and the unChristian socialists'. The movement lasted, formally, only until 1854, by which time it had become clear, on the one hand, that their practical initiatives in founding co-operative enterprises were not succeeding, and on the other hand that the leading spirits of the movement — namely Maurice, Ludlow and Kingsley, together with Thomas Hughes and E. V. Neale — were fundamentally divided among themselves as to the direction the movement should take.

Their activities during their six-year existence as a formal movement were varied and energetic. Less than a month after their manifesto to the working men of England they published the first number of a penny journal, edited by Maurice and Ludlow, and entitled *Politics for the People*. They aimed at a working-class readership but were too moderate and donnish in style (Kingsley's contributions apart), to succeed in attracting and holding such a readership. The journal folded in July 1848 after seventeen numbers.

They next tried the establishment of co-operative ventures, beginning with a working tailors' association in 1849 and subsequently extending their initiative to include further associations for builders, shoemakers, printers, bakers, and a number of other trades. In 1850 they actually adopted the title 'Christian Socialists' and planned a series of 'Tracts on Christian Socialism', the first of which appeared in November 1850. In June 1851, in the course of a series of sermons designed to coincide with the Great Exhibition, Kingsley preached on 'The Message of the Church to the Labouring Man' and was sufficiently outspoken to prompt the incumbent of the church in which he was preaching (St John's, Charlotte Street) to denounce his sermon at the close of the service. Such condemnation, which was reported in the national press, together with the practical efforts in co-operative enterprises and a willingness to actually meet with and listen to working men and their opinions, meant that by 1851 the Christian

Socialists had secured a considerable respect and popularity within the working-class community.

On the other hand, by 1851 the strains within the movement were also beginning to show. The co-operative associations, for example, were already showing signs of being in financial difficulty. Despite this, however, the chief philanthropist and provider of funds, E. V. Neale, wished to press on with such co-operative ventures and make them genuinely national in scope. Maurice, by contrast, was wary of practical initiatives altogether. Kingsley, on the other hand, was inclined to a robust and assertive, even aggressive style, whilst Ludlow wished to proceed slowly but steadily, creating small but well co-ordinated groups which were genuinely both Christian and Socialist. After 1851 the movement began to become less and less co-ordinated and in 1854 it dissolved as a distinct entity — although not without first establishing, in 1854, the Working Men's College with Maurice (by then sacked from his professorship at King's College for not believing in hell) as its principal.

It is something of a commonplace that the Christian Socialists were, in reality, barely socialist in any substantial sense at all. They believed in the mutual co-operation of classes but not in the ending of class distinctions; they retained many of the traits of an enlightened Tory paternalism; they were not politically radical. As Edward Norman has put it, 'the surviving references to traditional social attitudes were thickly distributed within their thought' (Norman, 1987, p. 1). Given such apparently substantial elements of residual conservatism, wherein, then, lay the Christian Socialists' significance? It is possible to identify at least four respects in which, their residual conservatism notwithstanding, they represented an important development in Victorian Christian social thought.

First, they were significant for the very boldness of their association of Christianity and socialism: their understanding of socialism may have been at once conservative and vague, but to suggest at all that the two were in fact compatible, rather than intrinsically in opposition, and to do so without incurring immediate and decisive marginalization within the church, was to break new ground. Second, in their rejection of the necessity of naked economic competition and the essentially individual nature of humanity, and in their advocacy of social and economic co-operation and the essentially communal nature of human life, they struck directly at the traditions of political economy. Similarly, in advocating co-operation between classes for their mutual advancement in the realization of the Kingdom of God as a present reality, they presented a radical alternative to the predominant Christian social teaching that social harmony was to be maintained simply by a patient endurance of present inequality on the part of the poor, the alleviation of the worst of suffering by a benevolent and Christian charity on the part of the better off, and a mutual recognition that in any case the present life was a preparation for eternity rather than an end in itself. Third, the example and writings of the mid-century Christian Socialists exercised an enormous influence on subsequent generations of theologians and clergy. It became a near universal theme of late Victorian Anglican Christian Socialists (but also one echoed by many Nonconformists as well) that it was in Maurice and the mid-century Christian Socialists that they had found inspiration and support for their own Christian Socialist opinions and instincts. Last, but not least, a number of the practical endeavours of Maurice, Ludlow, Neale and company survived the demise of their 'official' movement. The Working Men's College was the most successful of these ongoing ventures, but the continuing contribution of Neale, Ludlow and Hughes to the co-operative and trade union movements were also important and continued to remind the mid-Victorians of the Christian Socialists' essential vision.[4]

It sometimes appears from accounts of the history of Victorian Christian social thought and attitudes as if, with the Christian Socialist 'collapse' of 1854 and the advent of some twenty five years of mid-Victorian prosperity, Christian social thinking and activity simply stood still until, in the mid-1870s, the end of the mid-Victorian 'age of equipoise' gave rise to a 'Christian Socialist revival'. In point of fact, however, the 1850s, 1860s and early 1870s witnessed a number of significant developments and initiatives in Victorian Christian social thinking and attitudes. Anglican, Nonconformist and Scots Presbyterian examples may all be found to illustrate the way in which, after 1850, the former predominance of the values of non-interventionist evangelicalism and political economy continued to be steadily eroded by other alternative Christian social values and perceptions.

One of the most striking examples of such changing Christian perceptions of social issues and responsibilities during the third quarter of the century was the development, especially among Nonconformists, and pre--eminently in mid-Victorian Birmingham, of the ideal of the 'civic gospel'. The combination of concepts and principles involved first developed and then triumphed in Birmingham during the 1850s, 60s and early 1870s, and by the late 1870s and early 1880s had turned Birmingham from a somewhat backward borough into a model of what progressive and efficient local municipal government could be.

In practical terms the civic gospel meant the conviction that local government that was efficient, public-spirited and directed to the well-being of the community as a whole could bring immense benefit to municipal life. Specifically, in the Birmingham of the 1870s and 80s, it meant new provi-

---

[4] For the detailed history of the movement between 1848 and 1854, see Christensen, 1962. For the co-operative aspect, see Backstrom, 1974. Allen, 1968, offers a brief re-assessment of the leadership of the movement. For the most recent assessment, see Norman, 1987.

sion for sewage disposal, new action on public health, municipal ownership of the gas and water companies, a major scheme of town improvement and slum clearance, and the provision of improved educational and cultural facilities, including a municipal museum and art gallery. It was, in short, a variety of civic 'gas and water socialism'.

The civic gospel of mid-Victorian Birmingham was, of course, the product of a number of influences, not least among them the wider ambitions of local radical and liberal politicians of whom Joseph Chamberlain was the most prominent. On the other hand, however, secular political ambition was by no means the only major factor in the evolution of Birmingham's civic gospel. Much of the energy and vitality, zeal and idealism of the civic gospel in mid-Victorian Birmingham came specifically from its powerful and influential middle-class Nonconformist community.

In the formative years of the ideal — the 1850s and 60s — the leading Nonconformist advocate of municipal duty and its potential was George Dawson. Dawson had come to Birmingham in 1844 as minister of Mount Zion Baptist chapel. His liberal theological opinions quickly led to a break with his Baptist congregation, however, and in 1847 he opened his own church, the Church of the Saviour, in the centre of Birmingham. From the pulpit of this church Dawson addressed an influential congregation which included many of the leaders of Birmingham's civic, cultural and political life. Dawson remained minister of the church until his death in 1876, proclaiming a message which was theologically liberal — he became Unitarian in his theological views — and socially and politically centred on a vision of civic brotherhood and of the city as a community in which a common municipal purpose transcended the interests of individual classes and groups. Until his death in 1876, Dawson was the leading Nonconformist exponent and advocate of the civic gospel in Birmingham. He was not, however, alone. Other notable Nonconformist advocates of the ideal included Dawson's Baptist successor at Mount Zion chapel, Charles Vince, the Unitarian H. W. Crosskey, and, most importantly, the Congregationalist R. W. Dale.

Dale had come to Carrs Lane Chapel, Birmingham as assistant pastor in 1853 and remained pastor there until his death in 1895. He listened to much of Dawson's preaching, came to admire both the man and his message, and in the 1860s began to formulate his own version of the civic gospel. The result was an expression of the civic gospel which was more systematic and thorough, and also more deeply rooted in a specifically theological and evangelical morality, than Dawson's version had been. For whereas Dawson had been a remarkable but theologically highly unorthodox minister, Dale was a dedicated liberal in politics and an orthodox — though by no means narrow — evangelical in religion. He was also one of the leading ministers, not only of his own Congregationalist tradition, but of mid and late Victorian English Protestant Nonconformity as a whole.

After Dawson's death it was Dale who assumed the role of leading Non-conformist spokesman for the civic gospel. His finest statement of its principles came in a collection of sermons entitled *The Laws of Christ for the Common Life*. At the centre of the collection was the assertion of the relevance of Christian morality to everyday life and of the sacredness of commercial, municipal and political activities. The first sermon in the collection set out these themes in its title: 'Everyday Business a Divine Calling'.

The civic gospel itself was addressed directly in the sermon on 'Political and Municipal Duty'. Here Dale proclaimed his conviction that municipalities might sometimes do more for people than Parliament. With even their existing powers, he argued, they could do much to improve health and morality, diminish disease and premature death, and 'redress in many ways the inequalities of human conditions'. The churches, he asserted, would never be able to remedy the evils of urban social conditions without the additional action of municipal authorities: medicine and municipal action, and not the gospel alone, were necessary to cure the sick and improve the homes of the poor.

It is true that this collection of sermons dates from 1884 — after, that is to say, the beginning of the 'Christian Socialist revival' and the end of the age of mid-Victorian prosperity. But Dale's sermons of 1884 on this theme were not the product of immediate circumstances. On the contrary, they were the mature statement of a Christian social and civic ideal which had already been undergoing theoretical development and practical application in Birmingham for some twenty five years. The force of Dale's statement of the civic gospel in 1884 derived precisely from the fact that it was the expression of an already changed and carefully developed alternative Christian social vision — and one, moreover, from an impeccably, if critically, evangelical source.[5]

It is not only English Protestant Nonconformity, however, which offers evidence of the increasingly widespread development of a more socially critical evangelicalism in the 1850s and 1860s. In Victorian Scotland in the 1850s and 60s it was the proverbially evangelical Free Church which took the lead in first investigating and subsequently calling for reform in respect of working-class housing conditions. It is clear that a large part of the intensity of the Free Church concern over this issue arose from the link which Free Churchmen clearly perceived between bad housing and sexual immorality, illegitimacy and infanticide. That, however, does not render any less notable the fact that from 1858 to 1867 a Free Church Committee on 'Housing for the Working Classes in Connection with Social Morality'

---

[5] For a fuller discussion of Dawson, Dale, and the civic gospel within the context of Victorian Birmingham and its politics, see Hennock, 1973.

regularly reported to the Free Church General Assembly, and did so in terms which called for state-supported social reform in this area (Boyd, 1980, ch. 3).

Even more notably in the present context, the convener of the Committee, and the most markedly outspoken Free Churchman on the issue at this time, was none other than James Begg — otherwise most renowned for his intensely conservative evangelical opposition to theological liberalism and worship reform in the Free Church and his no less intense anti-Catholicism. On this issue, however, Begg could speak (in 1866–7) of, 'our obligation to promote sanitary and social reform' being based on the direct command of God, and claim that 'the social reformer and the Christian minister must not only combine in seeking to alleviate and remove the destruction of many generations, but they must be combined in the same individuals' (quoted in Brown, 1987, p. 173 and Boyd, 1980, p. 32).

A third brief example, and this time an Anglican one, of the on-going development of more liberal Christian social attitudes in the third quarter of the century is to be found in James Fraser, appointed Bishop of Manchester in 1870. Fraser believed that the church should firmly support attempts to improve social conditions. He supported the Co-operative Movement and was the first bishop to address one of its congresses. He mediated, with varying success, in industrial disputes which occurred in his diocese. Most famously of all, in 1872 he defended the right of Joseph Arch and the agricultural workers to found a union and in 1874, during a lockout of striking agricultural workers, defended the strikers and criticized the farmers (Bowen, 1968, pp. 274–5; Mayor, 1967, pp. 91–2 and 101–3).

In the course of the third quarter of the nineteenth century the social thought of the churches was thus already beginning to exhibit a marked degree of diversity and flexibility when compared with the situation which had existed prior to 1850. In the final quarter of the century, however, the extent of this process of diversification was to become even more marked.

On the one hand there appeared a number of seminal protests, programmes and reports which both indicated the extent of the change which had already occurred in Christian social attitudes and acted as a catalyst for further change. The most celebrated example was the appearance, in 1883, of the short but shocking pamphlet *The Bitter Cry of Outcast London.* Written by Andrew Mearns, the secretary of the London Congregational Union, it noted what the churches were already attempting in the slum districts of London but went on to describe the appalling living conditions, bad housing, overcrowding, insanitary environment, poverty, sexual immorality and sheer human misery which existed there. Such misery and such conditions, Mearns asserted, could not be overcome by the voluntary action of the churches alone. Important though such work was (and Mearns both called for yet more effort and announced new initiatives on the part of the London Congregational Union), the action of the state was also necessary.

Seven years later there appeared William Booth's *In Darkest England and the Way Out*. In many respects it remained a very conservative tract. Its origins lay in matters of evangelistic strategy: Booth (like other commentators on urban religion before him), had come to recognize that many of the urban poor would remain beyond the reach of effective evangelism unless their appalling social conditions were alleviated. His proposals, moreover, placed the traditional evangelical virtues of personal responsibility, hard work and self-improvement high on the agenda. But, significantly, Booth called his proposals a 'scheme of social [sic] salvation', and recognized that self-help and the gospel alone would not, in the worst of environments, redeem urban society: self-help itself required the aid of an enabling environment. He also provided further shocking descriptions of urban poverty and destitution.

In Scotland the tradition of church investigation of social and moral conditions, begun in the 1860s in the Church of Scotland and Free Church committees and commissions on housing and 'Life and Work', was continued in the 1880s and 90s. Notable landmarks included the 1888 petition of the Glasgow Presbytery of the Church of Scotland to the General Assembly requesting an enquiry into 'Non-Church-Going and the Housing of the Poor'; the report of the ensuing enquiry; and the mass of data gathered by the Church of Scotland Commission on the Religious Condition of the People. The fundamental significance of environment was consistently recognized. The original petition of the Glasgow Presbytery included the observations that intemperance was often the consequence, not the cause, of poverty, and that the churches' primary duty was to create a right public opinion (quoted in Withrington, 1977, pp. 163–4).

Such reports and revelations reflect a number of significant common themes: evangelism is not sufficient of itself, either strategically or morally; the effects of environment must be recognized by Christian social thought; the worst of those effects must be removed, not merely accepted and endured; the question of housing and living conditions was a central concern. The latter point is most significant, for it was housing conditions and their social and moral implications which also supplied the mainspring of much of the increasing *secular* social concern and campaigning of the post-1880 era. The churches' concern for housing conditions nevertheless had specifically Christian origins — most notably in the experiences of urban mission and pastoral care — and was not merely a reflection of current secular concerns.[6]

[6] For a discussion of the place of *The Bitter Cry* within the general development of late Victorian social concern, see Wohl, 1968.

Equally indicative of the ongoing diversification of Victorian Christian social attitudes, however, was the re-emergence (or as it is more commonly styled, 'the revival'), of Christian Socialism. Beginning with the foundation (by an Anglo-Catholic curate, Stewart Headlam) of the Guild of St Matthew in 1877, there followed over the next three decades a remarkable proliferation of societies, leagues and unions committed to a more or less precise and overt Christian Socialism. In 1886 came the inter-denominational Christian Socialist Society. This was followed in 1894 by the inter-denominational (and mainly Nonconformist) Christian Socialist League, which was in turn followed in 1898 by the Christian Social Brotherhood. After the 1906 general election and the return of fifty-three Labour MPs, there were founded the (Anglican) Church Socialist League in 1906 and, in 1909, the Free Church Socialist League, both of which were specifically committed to the Labour cause and not merely to a general and undefined 'socialism'.

All of the groups noted above were either small or short-lived (and often both) and represented the opinion of ministers, clergy and laity of uncharacteristically 'advanced' socialist or left-wing liberal views. The largest and most influential of the societies formed during the 'Christian Socialist Revival', however, was the Christian Social Union. Founded in 1889 (by the same younger and more liberal generation of Anglo-Catholics that produced, also in 1889, the collection of theologically critical essays, *Lux Mundi*), by 1895 it already had 27 branches and almost 3000 members, and at its maximum reached a membership of almost 6000, which included a number of bishops.

Such societies were the expression of socially committed minorities within their denominations and certainly not representative of the opinions of their denominations as a whole. This was true even of the CSU with its much larger membership, and it is significant that the large membership of the CSU in turn reflected its own very moderate stance. Although a produce of the 'Christian Socialist Revival' it was itself barely 'socialist' at all. As one historian has observed, for the CSU the word 'socialism' meant the ideal of brotherhood, not a political and economic system (Mayor, 1967, p. 197). On the other hand the various societies and leagues and their individual members (including the more genuinely socialist ones), even if minorities, were not actually disowned by their denominations: their opinions had become an element (even if a debated one) within the overall make-up of the late Victorian churches.

Moreover, the exponents of a revived Christian Socialism or of the need for a 'social gospel' or a 'social Christianity' included many of the most prominent church leaders of the day. Undeniably this also often meant that the Christian Socialism and social Christianity of the clerical, episcopal and ministerial élites of the late Victorian churches were unrepresentative of average clerical and lay opinion. On the other hand, to the extent that the public image of the churches — and also much of their influence in public life — was (and for that matter is) mediated by its leading public, and usually clerical, personalities, the tendency of leading figures to take socially radical positions was more significant in establishing the overall tenor and ethos of late Victorian Christian social thought than their numerical strength alone would imply.

The roll-call of the section of the late Victorian clerical élite which adopted a socially radical stance is an impressive one. The CSU numbered among its leading and most ardent members B. F. Westcott, Henry Scott Holland and Charles Gore. Westcott, as well as being president of the CSU until 1900, presented a famous paper (subsequently published by the CSU) on 'Socialism' to the 1890 Church Congress. Other notable Anglicans who described themselves as Christian Socialists included leading figures in the Settlement Movement, most notably Samuel Barnett and E. S. Talbot.

Among Nonconformists the most outstanding examples of members of the clerical élite who advocated Christian Socialist or social gospel ideas were John Clifford and Hugh Price Hughes. Clifford, one of the giants of late Victorian Nonconformity as a whole, and twice a president of the Baptist Union, was President of both the Christian Socialist League and the Christian Social Brotherhood, desired that the churches should promote social welfare work, and wrote a Fabian Tract, entitled *Socialism and the Teaching of Christ*. Hugh Price Hughes, editor of the *Methodist Times* (which he used to promote his social opinions), minister of the prestigious late Victorian Wesleyan Methodist 'showpiece' West London Mission, and President of Conference in 1898, consistently called upon his denomination to embrace the principles of a 'social Christianity' and to advocate social reform. His manifesto took the form of a collection of sermons published in 1889 and entitled *Social Christianity*. Christ, he argued, came to save society as well as individuals.

Other leading ministers who advocated similarly critical and activist social views included the Wesleyan Methodists Samuel Keeble and John Scott Lidgett (the founder of the Wesleyan Settlement in Bermondsey), both of whom in fact found Hughes' stance too moderate; William Robertson Nicoll, the founder and editor of the widely read Nonconformist paper the *British Weekly* which, like the *Methodist Times*, was used to promote the cause of Christian social reform; and prominent Congregationalist ministers such as J. B. Paton, Andrew Mearns and R. F. Horton. Moreover, behind such individual representatives of the socially conscious clerical élites of late Victorian Christianity, there was also, as K. S. Inglis noted, a discernible tendency towards more socially radical opinion among those sections of the clergy who were most likely to be elected to the various Church and Free

Church Congresses, assemblies and other representative gatherings (Inglis, 1963, p. 254).

In Scotland a similarly socially radical group of ministers emerged in the two decades from about 1890 onwards. They included John Marshall Lang and Donald Macleod (both of whom were contributors to the Glasgow Presbytery petition of 1888 on non church-going and housing), A. S. Matheson, David Watson, and John Glasse. Glasse was minister of the prestigious Old Greyfriars Church, Edinburgh and a member of the Independent Labour Party. Watson was a leading figure in the interdenominational Scottish Christian Social Union, which was founded in 1901.[7]

In the late Victorian Roman Catholic church, Cardinal Manning also became both famous and popular for his sympathies for the social conditions of the poor and the rights of trade unions — most notably in the case of the 1889 London Dock Strike, when he voiced support for the dockers and persisted (eventually with success) in his efforts to mediate in the strike, despite the fact that the Archbishop of Canterbury had quit the role of mediator when the first attempts at mediation proved unsuccessful. Manning had also, along with the Anglican Bishop of Manchester, James Fraser, voiced support for Joseph Arch and the agricultural workers' union in the 1870s.[8]

The cumulative effect of seminal and catalytic texts such as *The Bitter Cry*, *In Darkest England*, and the housing reports of the Church of Scotland, the foundation of a new generation of Christian Socialist groups, and the socially committed preaching, writing and campaigning of leading clergy was considerable. The appropriate Christian response to poverty and other social issues was, by 1900, a matter of ongoing and vigorous debate within the Victorian churches. It was characteristic that official and semi-official gatherings would stop well short of advocating specific policies or precise

[7] The potential complexities of Victorian Christian social thought are neatly illustrated by the fact that both Lang and Watson found part of the inspiration for their turn of the century social gospel stance in the social commitment and concern of none other than Thomas Chalmers (McCaffrey, 1985, p. 55).

[8] The social thought, attitudes and commitment of Victorian Catholicism remain in need of thorough re-assessment. Historiographical orthodoxy has tended towards the portrayal of Manning as the originator of Victorian Catholic social concern. A number of recent essays, however, suggest that a more profitable approach would be to see Manning and his 'social Catholicism' as a late Victorian *continuation* of a longer-standing development in Victorian Catholic social concern, which moved, broadly, away from the predominance of concepts such as 'holy poverty' and the humble acceptance of social deprivation, and towards concepts of Catholic voluntary social action and communally focused philanthropy, co-operation, social reform and social awareness. For indications of the possible potential in such an approach, see for example, Connolly, 1984, p. 103; Aspinwall, 1978a and b, 1980 and 1986. For a description of the 'holy poverty' tradition, see Gilley, 1971.

measures of reform, but it was also characteristic that they would discuss issues of social reform, suggest that reform of some kind was desirable, and, in marked contrast to earlier in the century, would actually debate rather than simply presuppose the fundamental causes of poverty and social destitution.

II   SOME CENTRAL THEMES

Victorian Christian social thought and attitudes were thus a good deal more complex and variegated than conventional and convenient generalizations about, for example, either religion and social control or the emergence of Christian Socialism tend to imply. Although complex, however, it remains possible to identify a number of broad themes within the development of Victorian Christian social thought which, together, provide something of a framework for the assessment of more particular and detailed aspects of the phenomenon as a whole.

In a process analogous to that which occurred in the area of theology and doctrine, most of the major ecclesiastical denominations of Victorian Britain moved in the course of the Queen's reign from a predominantly uniform stance on social issues to one which was essentially pluralist. Just as most of the denominations, either implicitly or explicitly, willingly or reluctantly, accepted the necessity of a *de facto* internal pluralism in matters of doctrine, so also, they came to accept the legitimacy of a range of Christian social attitudes co-existing within their individual communions. The Church of England, the Church of Scotland, the Methodists (Wesleyan and Primitive), the Baptists, the Congregationalists, or any other major denominational example chosen, did not, as a whole, go Christian Socialist, or, as a whole, adopt a social gospel as a priority. Christian Socialists and advocates of a social gospel remained articulate minorities within their various denominations. The great difference between their position in 1900 and that of their radical predecessors of sixty or seventy years earlier, however, was that in 1900 radicals in social matters such as Headlam, Westcott, Clifford, Hugh Price Hughes, J. M. Lang or John Glasse could occupy respected positions, and indeed could even be leading, if also often controversial, figures in their denominations. The turn of the century Christian Socialist might publish Christian Socialist opinions or appear on platforms with secular socialists and yet be in no danger of suffering the kind of denominational fate which had awaited, for example, Patrick Brewster or John Rayner Stephens some half a century earlier.

Again analogously to the position in respect of doctrine and theology, it is much less easy to characterize accurately or succinctly the social stance and attitudes of any given denomination in 1900 than it is for the period prior to 1850. To do so accurately would necessarily require the description of a *range* of opinions, albeit some of them more prominent than others. In terms of the examples of the popular historical wisdom with which this essay began, even by 1900, it was possible to describe the Church of England, without qualification, as the Tory party at prayer, only by ignoring a vocal, prominent and influential minority of Christian Socialist and socially critical bishops, clergy and societies. The same point is equally applicable to other denominations. Moreover, if denominations as a whole did not adopt Christian Socialism or the social gospel as 'official' policy, it was, nevertheless, characteristic of the thinking and attitudes of all the major denominations that, even whilst well short of 'social Christianity', their social attitudes were, by 1900, less passive, less geared to a simple acceptance of the existing social order, less sharply focused upon the individual and his or her responsibility for self-improvement, less likely to attribute poverty and destitution to personal sin, and more aware of the need for state intervention in social matters, more conscious of the effects of environment, and more likely to acknowledge the social and corporate dimensions of both 'sin' and 'salvation'.

The point is one of balance. Late Victorian Christian social thought did not stop emphasizing the importance of individual character and effort, any more than early Victorian Christian social comment had completely failed to recognize the degrading, morally and spiritually destructive effects of poverty, destitution and grotesque social conditions. By the end of the century, however, the recognition of the significance and limitations of 'the environmental factor' was more widespread and more profound, calls for social reform were more frequent and more extensive in range, and political commitment on social issues was more readily perceived as a concomitant of Christian belief. The shift of emphasis was broadly based and not the product of any single or sudden turning point. From the 1880s onwards, however, the intensification and diversification of Christian social awareness and criticism became increasingly pronounced. As Edward Norman has observed, the early influence of Maurice and his circle was negligible, but by the end of the century, 'the Christian Socialists' critique was lodging itself effectively enough in the mind of the church' (1987, p. 185).

If they had thus begun to affect the social thinking of their churches as a whole, however, it is also important to recognize the limits of the 'Christian Socialism' even of many of the leading Christian Socialists of the post 1880 era. Most of them remained aloof from, and wary of, direct political action. The various social gospels and social Christianities put forward tended to be expressed in terms of general principles rather than specific policies or practical programmes. Thus Westcott, in his famous address to the Church Congress of 1890 on 'Socialism', asserted that socialism had 'no necessary affinity with any forms of violence, or confiscation, or class selfishness, or financial arrangement'. It was, rather, a principle. It was the spirit of co-operation as opposed to the spirit of competition. The particular applications of the principle of brotherhood would proceed in different ways. It was not his purpose to discuss questions of detail and the manner of application of that principle. Westcott was here representative of the tone and policy of the CSU as a whole. He tended, in Edward Norman's words, to generalize the content of Christian Socialism 'to the level at which imprecise objectives and commonly held human principles enabled acceptance'. As for the CSU in general, it became, in Desmond Bowen's phrase, 'the conscience of the episcopate' (Norman, 1987, p. 179; Bowen, 1968, p. 284). Perhaps more surprisingly, even Stewart Headlam, founder of the more radical Guild of St Matthew, also asserted in 1901 that it was not his role to suggest any definite action on social and political problems, but rather to propose the principles of such action (quoted in Norman, 1987, p. 119). The 'social Christianity' of Hugh Price Hughes, it is true, did include an element of collectivism, but also combined this (inevitably, given Hughes' prominence in the broader stream of the Nonconformist Conscience) with an even greater emphasis upon the ending of wrong *personal* conduct rather than wrong *social structures* (Norman, p. 159).

In 1900, as K. S. Inglis observed at the close of his survey of the English churches and social reform in the Victorian period, the thorough-going secular socialist could easily assume that a 'lofty neutrality' was the most to be expected from the churches: a generation of renewed social Christianity and Christian Socialism had not shaken the basic conviction of the churches that capitalism and social justice were compatible (Inglis, 1968, pp. 320–1). In Scotland, as Callum Brown has noted, the rise of a late Victorian social theology gave rise to a church-labour group which brought the churches and the socialist movement into direct contact between 1890 and 1914. The number of churchmen involved was relatively small, however, and of them only a minority were actually themselves socialists. Moreover, with the passing of its founding generation and the subsequent leftward move of the Scottish labour movement, the church-labour group dissolved and Scottish Christian Socialism, despite the existence of the Scottish Christian Social Union, was reduced to 'a political and ineffectual minority' within the churches (Brown, 1987, p. 194). The ambiguities of actual *political* alignment in late Victorian Christian social radicalism were also exhibited in the case of Primitive Methodist trade unionism. The classic alliance of Primitive Methodist chapel and trade union branch was characteristically geared to the promotion of political Liberalism and a conciliatory stance in labour relations. With the decline of Liberalism and the emergence of a more militant labour movement, however, leadership of union and chapel became less closely linked. Even when union activists were still Methodists they tended to be less orthodox in theology and less in harmony with their chapel community (McLeod, 1981, pp. 122–3; 1984, pp. 54–6; Moore, 1974; Scotland, 1981; Howkins, 1985).

The Primitive Methodist example of increasing tension between the more conservative, conciliatory line of the chapel leadership and the socialism of individual chapel members was not unique. McLeod has drawn attention to other examples of Nonconformist socialists being forced to choose between their socialism and their chapel and choosing the former, whilst also, in some cases at least, retaining their Christian belief. Moreover, as Nonconformity began to experience a crisis of identity from the 1880s onwards and socialism began to become more widespread, many younger Nonconformists found socialism a more effective outlet for the ethical and moral idealism which they had derived from their Nonconformity. Thus late nineteenth and early twentieth-century British socialism included a significantly religious strand within its membership and even in some respects itself took on the style and ethos of a religious movement, a trait which it displayed both in its organization and in an often intensely ethical and humanitarian idealism which led some socialists to speak of the movement's 'spiritual' objectives and to claim that it now embodied the true spirit of Christianity (McLeod, 1981, p. 123 and 1984; S. Yeo, 1977; Ainsworth, 1977; Lambert, 1976, pp. 111–12).[9]

Such lay (and often working-class) 'Christian Socialism' and 'Christianity becoming Socialism' are often over-looked in an unfortunate, and also distinctly ironic, concentration upon the largely middle-class and clerical leadership of the church centred Victorian and Edwardian 'Christian Socialist revival'. But in any attempt to explain the reasons for the absence in Britain of any clear-cut or fundamental division between the churches, religion, and the modern labour movement, the existence and role of such grass-roots, lay Christian Socialists, combining their religion and their politics as a matter of everyday conviction, must be regarded as at least as important as the existence of prominent, but often in fact decidedly apolitical, clergy proclaiming that the churches were not the enemies of social and political radicalism and reform, whilst simultaneously declining to move beyond such statements of ideals and principles to actual policies and programmes.

At the end of an essay which has argued that whilst Victorian Christian social thought always displayed a capacity for diversity there was a crucial

---

[9] The tension experienced by individual chapel members who held explicitly socialist views is, moreover, indicative of a broader ambiguity in respect of the actual *political* alignment of late Victorian Christian social thought. The fact that the 'Christian Socialist revival' and the emergence of a variety of 'social gospels' and 'social Christianities' coincided with the emergence of the Labour party as a significant factor in British politics did not mean that the majority of the exponents of such socially critical religion became Labour party members or voters. The majority of late Victorian 'Christian Socialists' and exponents of a social gospel would probably have continued to regard the Liberal party as the most appropriate political vehicle for the expression of their views. Certainly this was the case for the majority of Nonconformist social critics and social reformers.

extension of that diversity in the period after 1875, there remains the question, why did the expansion of Christian social options occur then? For those tempted to marginalize theological factors and reduce the churches' changing awareness to mere political pragmatism or the influence of a changed and changing social, political and intellectual context, the wider secular context of the last quarter of the nineteenth century offers plenty of scope for reductionism. By the 1880s the political alignments and concerns of the early and mid-Victorian eras were giving way to new alignments and concerns which were first to influence, and then to dominate, the politics of twentieth-century Britain. The passing of the era of mid-nineteenth century middle-class politics, in which church versus chapel confrontation had been near the centre, if not itself the centre, of national political life, was succeeded by the era of Liberal party division, the rise of the Labour party, and the centrality of class, economics and social issues in national political life. The end of the old church, chapel and political party alliances, and the rise of the labour movement thus invited, even if it did not compel, reflection on the possibilities of political re-alignment by the churches. Moreover, the last two decades of the nineteenth century were a period of increasingly systematic social investigation and, as a result, growing social awareness and social criticism in the purely secular realm: the social surveys of, for example, Booth and Rowntree, were symptomatic of the development.

Was the late Victorian diversification of Christian social thought no more, then, than the pragmatism — political and intellectual — of a Christian tradition adjusting its allegiances to meet changing social and political circumstances, and adopting and adapting contemporary ideas in order to do so? Such a conclusion is possible, but only, as David Thompson has also observed, at the price of positing a radical dichotomy, rather than a subtle relationship, between political, social and theological ideas (Thompson, 1986, p. 200). Certainly the late Victorian Christian Socialist critique was part and parcel of the general growth of social awareness, social surveys and research, social criticism, and rising social concern of the post 1880 era. But it was also a *Christian* Socialist critique. The various strands of Christian Socialist and social gospel thought brought to their analyses of the Christian duty towards society a variety of religious and theological insights and inspirations. It is only possible to discount such theological insights by first diagnosing *them* as also essentially the product of adjustment to changing social and political influences. The latter is, of course, a possible interpretation, but a curiously reductionist one. More profitably, one might reckon with the possibility that late Victorian Christian social critiques genuinely depended upon specifically Christian and theological inspiration *as well as* both the changing intellectual *milieu* of the surrounding late Victorian culture and society and the church's own developing awareness of the intractable nature of urban poverty, living conditions and housing. For some fifty years the churches had regarded the mission to the urban working classes as a priority. By the 1880s the limited achievements of that mission, and the accumulating awareness of social conditions which arose from it, led church leaders to reassess their social stance and to increase the volume and vary the content of their social criticism.

When they did so, the theological legacy of the early and mid-Victorian periods provided a considerable range of resources for the task. By the 1880s the focus of the theology of the Victorian churches had shifted significantly from that of the 1830s. Broadly, it had moved away from the centrality of the doctrine of the Atonement, the wrath of God, the fear of hell, and a drama of redemption conceived in sharply doctrinal terms. It had moved towards the centrality of the doctrine of the Incarnation, the love, mercy and Fatherhood of God (and the corollary of the brotherhood of man), the call to redeem this world as well as prepare for the next, and a drama of redemption conceived less in terms of abstract doctrine and more in terms of the redeeming participation of the divine in the human. The shift of emphasis was neither the product nor the property of any one theological tradition. Anglo-Catholic sacramentalism, Broad Church, Liberal Nonconformist and Presbyterian moral critiques of hell and substitutionary atonement, and the rediscovery (partly through the rise of biblical criticism) of the ethical message of the prophets and Jesus' preaching of the Kingdom of God as a present reality, were all aspects of a theological re-orientation which rendered late Victorian Christianity as a whole more immanentist, more this-worldly, and less doctrinally severe than its early Victorian predecessor. By the 1880s theological trends of this kind provided a variety of theological inputs and resources for the emergence of more socially critical versions of Christianity.

Through such theological convictions, and via a range of societies and personal involvements, a variety of late Victorian Christians — lay and clerical, prominent and obscure — sought to relate their various versions of Christianity, their increasingly radical social awareness, and their chosen brand of politics. Christianity remained contested territory. But by 1900 the contest was less clearly between a large majority of conservative Christians, backed by their denominations, and a small minority of socially radical Christians (often rejected by their denominations) in sympathy with working-class radicals claiming the Christian tradition for themselves. The contest over the social significance of Christianity had now lodged itself firmly *within* the churches.

The churches as institutions would increasingly find themselves not only confronted with the challenge of internal pluralism in theology and doctrine, but also with internal pluralism in matters of politics and social teaching. And, as in doctrine, so in politics: in order to preserve institutional unity, church leaders, when speaking officially, would usually find it expedient to suggest general principles and eschew specific policies and commitments. Active and specific Christian social and political commitment became, increasingly, the private choice of individual Christians. Christian Socialists, Christian Liberals and Christian Conservatives formed their various societies, pressure groups and organizations and urged their varying perceptions of the social significance and implications of Christian belief. That in itself, however, was a measure of the change which had occurred in Christian social thought in the Victorian period. By 1900 Christian Socialism and social Christianity were firmly established as on-going options and the churches as a whole were more conscious of the potentially socially radical implications of Christian belief, and of the case for a social mission, than their early Victorian predecessors had been. There was, by the turn of the century, a genuine range of ecclesiastically acceptable Christian social attitudes, running from continuing conservative attempts to deploy religion as an instrument of social control, to the advocacy of a social gospel or of Christian Socialism; and the churches as institutions had shifted, if not *to* a social gospel, at least *closer* to a social gospel, and consequently further away from a gospel in which social control was a central concern.

BIBLIOGRAPHY

*A. Ainsworth (1977) 'Religion in the working class community and the evolution of socialism in later nineteenth century Lancashire', *Histoire Sociale — Social History*, Vol. 10, pp. 354–80.

P. R. Allen (1968) 'F. D. Maurice and J. M. Ludlow: a re-assessment of the leaders of Christian Socialism', *Victorian Studies*, Vol.11, pp. 461–82.

B. Aspinwall (1978a) 'The Scottish dimension: Robert Monteith and the origins of modern British Catholic social thought', *Downside Review*, Vol. 97, pp. 46–68.

B. Aspinwall (1978b) 'Robert Monteith (1812–1884): a Scottish layman and modern Catholic social thought', *Clergy Review*, Vol. 63, pp. 265–72.

B. Aspinwall (1980) 'Before Manning: some aspects of British social concern before 1865', *New Blackfriars*, Vol. 61, pp. 113–27.

B. Aspinwall (1986) 'The welfare state within the state: the Saint Vincent de Paul Society in Glasgow, 1848–1920' in W. J. Shiels and D. Woods (eds.) *Voluntary Religion*, pp. 445–9, Oxford, Blackwell.

P. N. Backstrom (1974) *Christian Socialism and Co-operation in Victorian England*, Croom Helm.

D. Bowen (1968) *The Idea of the Victorian Church: A Study of the Church of England, 1833–1889*, Montreal, McGill University Press.

K. M. Boyd (1980) *Scottish Church Attitudes to Sex, Marriage and the Family, 1850–1914*, Edinburgh, J. Donald.

C. G. Brown (1987) *The Social History of Religion in Scotland Since 1730*, Methuen.

A. C. Cheyne (1983) *The Transforming of the Kirk: Victorian Scotland's Religious Revolution*, Edinburgh, St Andrew Press.

T. Christensen (1962) *Origins and History of Christian Socialism 1848–54*, Aarhus.

G. P. Connolly (1984) 'The transubstantiation of myth: towards a new popular history of nineteenth-century Catholicism in England', *Journal of Ecclesiastical History*, Vol. 35, pp. 78–104.

R. S. Dell (1965) 'Social and economic theories and pastoral concerns of a Victorian archbishop', *Journal of Ecclesiastical History*, Vol. 16, pp. 196–208.

A. D. Gilbert (1976) *Religion and Society in Industrial England: Church, Chapel and Social Change 1740–1914*, Longman.

S. W. Gilley (1971) 'Heretic London, holy poverty and the Irish poor, 1830–70', *Downside Review*, Vol. 89, pp. 64–89.

B. Harrison (1974) 'For church, Queen and family: the Girls' Friendly Society 1874–1920', *Past and Present*, No. 61, pp. 107–38.

J. Hart (1977) 'Religion and social control in the mid-nineteenth century' in P. Donajgrodzki (ed.) *Social Control in Nineteenth Century Britain*, Croom Helm.

E. P. Hennock (1973) *Fit and Proper Persons*, Arnold.

*B. Hilton (1985) 'The role of providence in evangelical social thought' in D. Beales and G. Best (eds.) *History, Society and the Churches*, pp. 215–33, Cambridge, Cambrige University Press.

J. D. Holloday (1982) 'Nineteenth century Evangelical activism: from private charity to state intervention, 1830–50', *Historical Magazine of the Protestant Episcopal Church*, Vol. 50, pp. 53–79.

A. Howkins (1985) *Poor Labouring Men: Rural Radicalism in Norfolk 1870–1923*, Routledge.

*K. S. Inglis (1963) *Churches and the Working Classes in Victorian England*, Routledge.

D. A. Johnson (1973) 'Between Evangelicalism and a social gospel: the case of Joseph Rayner Stephens', *Church History*, Vol. 42, pp. 229–42.

W. R. Lambert (1976) 'Some working-class attitudes towards organised religion in nineteenth century Wales', *Llafur*, Vol. 2, pp. 4–17.

T. W. Laqueur (1976) *Religion and Respectability: Sunday Schools and English Working-Class Culture, 1780–1850*, Yale University Press.

*S. Mayor (1967) *The Churches and the Labour Movement*, Independent Press.

J. F. McCaffrey (1981) 'Thomas Chalmers and social change', *The Scottish Historical Review*, Vol. 60, pp. 32–60.

J. F. McCaffrey (1985) 'The life of Thomas Chalmers' in A. C. Cheyne (ed.) *The Practical and the Pious*, pp. 31–64, Edinburgh, St Andrew Press.

H. McLeod (1981) *Religion and the People of Western Europe 1789–1970*, Oxford, Oxford University Press, Opus.

*H. McLeod (1984) *Religion and the Working Class in Nineteenth Century Britain*, Studies in Economic and Social History, Macmillan Educational.

R. I. Moore (1974) *Pit-men, Preachers and Politics: The Effects of Methodism in a Durham Mining Community*, Cambridge, Cambridge University Press.

*E. Norman (1987) *The Victorian Christian Socialists*, Cambridge, Cambridge University Press.

M. J. D. Roberts (1984) 'Pressure-group politics and the Church of England: the Church Defence Institution 1859–1896', *Journal of Ecclesiastical History*, Vol. 35, pp. 560–82.

N. G. A. Scotland (1981) *Methodism and the Revolt of the Field*, Gloucester, Alan Sutton.

D. M. Thompson (1986) 'John Clifford's social gospel', *The Baptist Quarterly*, Vol. 31, pp. 199–217.

D. J. Withrington (1977) 'The church in Scotland, c.1870–c.1900: towards a new social conscience?', *Records of the Scottish Church History Society*, Vol. 19, pp. 155–68.

A. S. Wohl (1968) 'The Bitter Cry of Outcast London', *International Review of Social History*, Vol. 13, pp. 189–245.

E. Yeo (1981) 'Christianity in Chartist struggle 1838–1842', *Past and Present*, No.91, pp. 109–39.

S. Yeo (1977) 'A new life: the religion of Socialism in Britain 1883–1896', *History Workshop*, Vol. 4, pp. 5–56.

CHAPTER 3

FROM THE MINING DISTRICTS.

AN ATTEMPT AT CONVERTING THE NATIVES.

Assiduous Young Curate. "WELL THEN, I DO HOPE I SHALL HAVE THE PLEASURE OF SEEING BOTH OF YOU NEXT SUNDAY!"

Miner. "OI! THEE MAY'ST COAM IF 'E WULL. WE FOIGHT ON THE CROFT, AND OLD JOE TANNER BRINGS TH' BEER."

A QUESTION OF MEANING: RELIGION AND WORKING-CLASS LIFE

OF comments on, and assessments of, the relationship between religion and the working classes of Victorian Britain probably none, as Hugh McLeod has observed, were more famous or more influential than those of Horace Mann in his report on the 1851 Census of Religion. It was clear, Mann concluded, that the majority of that 'sadly formidable proportion of the English people' who were 'habitual neglecters of the public ordinances of religion' were members of the working class, and more precisely the 'labouring myriads' of the urban working class. They were, he suggested, 'unconscious secularists — engrossed by the demands, the trials, or the pleasures of the passing hour, and ignorant or careless of the future': as such they were not actively hostile to religion but merely indifferent to it (McLeod, 1984, p. 57). Mann also suggested that, given sufficient effort on the part of the churches in mission to the urban working classes, and given a sufficiently 'aggressive' (sic) approach to evangelism, the 'unconscious secularism' of the working classes was bound to be overcome. For in the end, Mann argued, their religious dis-inclination was merely negative and inert, 'strong enough to hinder their spontaneous seeking of the passive object of their dis-esteem — too feeble to present effectual resistance to the inroads of aggressive Christianity invading their own doors'.

None of this was new. Mann's remarks, far from being original, were substantially typical of a growing body of concern over the perceived irreligion of the urban working classes, a concern which had been steadily gathering momentum since the 1830s. Mann's remarks were, however, a particularly influential statement of the case. They were based upon a national census of religion: the first (and indeed the only) such census to have been taken. The methods and rigour of the census left much to be desired, but on this particular issue the evidence was plain enough: the absence from organized religion and the life and influence of the churches of the working classes was as general and as substantial as the more pessimistic of previous commentators had asserted. The census confirmed as a national phenomenon what accumulating regional experience already knew to be local reality: the urban working classes were significantly 'unchurched'. The Census confirmed and consolidated — but did not create — the Victorian churches' awareness of the scale of working-class absence and alienation from their life, worship and belief.

Mann's report was also typical in its stated criteria for the evaluation and assessment of the degree of religiousness of the nation and in its concluding justification of the importance of the Census. As to criteria, Mann announced in his introduction that the Census had examined the amount of church accommodation available and the levels of church attendance: such matters of *practice* being a better guide to individuals' religious states than 'merely vague professions' (of belief). As to the importance of the Census and its findings, Mann observed in his conclusion that, quite apart from the specifically spiritual benefits of religion, no small part of the secular prosperity and peace of both individuals and states depended upon the profession and practice of 'pure religion'. Orderliness, prosperity, peace, industriousness, temperance and providence, Mann suggested, were the fruits of a 'pure and practical' Christianity. In short, social order and well-being were facilitated by religion and threatened by irreligion, and the measure of religiousness was church attendance. Hence, the absence of so large a part of the urban working classes from the worship of the churches pointed to their irreligion and thus to their being a threat to social order and well-being. The churches, for the most part, shared Mann's assumptions and perspective: they aimed to create a churchgoing working class and understood their mission as one to 'civilize' as well as to convert.

Moreover, both for the self-evaluation by the churches of their mission to the working classes and for the analysis of this subject by several generations of historians, the implications of the criteria for the assessment of religious commitment set out in Mann's introduction were considerable. On the one hand the identification of religion with church attendance narrowed the criteria for judging the degree of success or failure of the mission to the Victorian urban working classes. If church-going was the crucial test, then failure to convert a significant proportion of the working classes to such conventional religious practice would be failure, regardless of any other consequences of the urban mission. On the other hand, the definition of religion as church-going also obscured the possibility of the existence of an alternative religious style within working-class life, culture and community. Once church-going was defined as the key test of religiousness, and in the absence of articulate and sustained secularism on the part of the majority of the working classes, the inevitable conclusion to be drawn from a continued absence of the majority of the working classes from regular church attendance must be that they were, indeed, as Mann had suggested, simply 'unconscious secularists,' and indifferent to religion.

Such definitions and consequent conclusions not only dominated the churches' own, increasingly pessimistic, self-assessment of their mission to the Victorian working classes, but also became something of an historiographical orthodoxy in studies of the relationship between religion, class and society in Victorian Britain. More recent scholarship, however, has increasingly questioned such interpretation, challenging the naïvety and inadequacy of the simple 'religion as church-attendance' criterion, and consequently re-assessing both the meaning of the 'success' or 'failure' of the churches' urban working class mission, and the extent, meaning and significance of religion in the life of the Victorian working classes.

The present essay aims simply to indicate, briefly, the variety and nature of the churches' mission to the Victorian working classes; to consider the principal questions posed and conclusions suggested by recent studies of the relationship of religion, church and the working classes in Victorian Britain; and finally to ask how, in the light of such recent scholarship, one might best characterize the place of religion in Victorian working-class life.

I THE MISSION TO THE URBAN WORKING CLASSES

The 'unchurched masses', the 'spiritual destitution' of the urban poor, and the 'irreligion of the urban working classes' were common currency well before 1851. The issue first began to assume its characteristic prominence among the concerns of Victorian churchmen and women in the 1830s. Prior to that decade there had been a general awareness of the issue and the need to address it. Thus, for example, in England there were parliamentary grants for (Anglican) church building in 1818 and 1824. In Scotland, Thomas Chalmers was already energetically engaged in arguing the case for church extension and the godly commonwealth as the only solution to urban industrial poverty. And among both Anglican and Nonconformist Evangelicals in England and the Evangelical wing of the Church of Scotland experiments were initiated in the organization of systematic district visiting and the use of a variety of lay visitors, evangelists, tract distributors and scripture readers (Lewis, 1986, ch.2; Rack, 1973).

In the 1830s and 1840s, however, both the quantity and the intensity of concern increased markedly. In a variety of denominational and inter-denominational contexts the urban mission to the unchurched masses took on a new urgency. Working-class irreligion became the subject of a considerable and expanding literature. In Scotland the 1830s was the decade in which Chalmers led the church extension campaign in the Church of Scotland. In the Church of England both High Churchmen and Evangelicals demonstrated their concern for urban mission. In Leeds, W. F. Hook became a symbol of High Church concern for church extension and mission to the working classes. Among Evangelicals, Baptist Noel's pamphlet *The State of the Metropolis Considered* (1835) presaged Mann in calling for an aggressive, assertive, urban evangelism, and the foundation of the Church Pastoral Aid Society in 1836 consolidated Anglican Evangelical commitment to the use of lay assistants in evangelism. In London, in 1836, following the example of earlier initiatives in Glasgow and Manchester, Bishop Blomfield founded a metropolitan church building society. Among Nonconformists examples of similar concern were the shifts within both the Baptist and Congregationalist Home Missionary Societies in the 1830s towards a greater concern with urban mission, and the appearance of such notable analyses of the subject of working-class alienation from the churches as those of the Congregationalists Algernon Wells and Edward Miall. Wells' contribution appeared in the *Congregational Year Book* of 1848 under the title 'Thoughts on the Need for Increased Efforts to Promote the Religious Welfare of the Working Classes in England'; Miall's appeared a year later as part of his book on *The British Churches in Relation to the British People*. A further important development was the emergence of inter-denominational evangelical projects, most notably the foundation of city missions such as those in Glasgow (1826) and, pre-eminently, the London City Mission (1835). These, moreover, were indeed but particular examples of a much wider and deeper trend within early Victorian Christianity.

From such a perspective, Mann's report, and the 1851 Census itself, clearly appear as the climax of a steadily increasing concern extending over some two decades. The bleak (from the churches' standpoint) findings of the Census merely confirmed the worst fears of church leaders, clergy and evangelists concerning urban working-class 'irreligion,' whilst Mann's analysis of its causes and prescription for its cure confirmed them in their existing strategies: provide more evangelists, especially lay ones; provide specifically working-class services and churches where class divisions would be less evident than in most churches and chapels; and above all engage in 'aggressive' evangelism. The ensuing half-century therefore witnessed a redoubling of the churches' urban mission both to civilize and convert the unchurched urban working classes.

The more dramatic manifestations of the mid and late Victorian mission to the urban working classes are well-known. Sankey and Moody, Protestant revivalism, and the holding of services in secular settings such as theatres; Anglo-Catholic parish and city missions and the work of slum-ritualist clergy in their semi-monastic clergy communities in notoriously poor parishes; the creation of the Salvation Army, and, in the Church of England, the Church Army. In Wesleyan Methodism the 1880s brought the emergence of Central Halls and City Missions, outside the normal circuit structure of Methodism, with long-term ministerial appointments, popular services with choirs and a setting which sought to borrow from the ethos of the theatre and avoid that of the conventional church, and a thorough commitment to the full range of cultural and social work characteristic of the late Victorian Nonconformist 'institutional church'. And in the 1880s and 90s first Anglicans and then also Wesleyan Methodists, founded 'Settlements' in working-class areas of London in which university graduates and undergraduates would live, some permanently, some in vacations. Under the guidance of a resident clergyman and in co-operation with local clergy, they would be active in local recreational clubs, charitable work and educational provision. The presence of such young gentlemen — intended to be the 'squires of the East End' — supporting local clergy, would, it was hoped, facilitate the urban mission to both convert and civilize the working class and simultaneously foster a renewed co-operation and intimacy between the classes. Such phenomena provided the urban mission with high-profile 'showpiece' initiatives and furnished the various denominational and theological traditions with reassuring symbols of their commitment to urban evangelism.

Of even greater importance, however, were the continuation of church and chapel building and the ongoing contributions to urban mission of innumerable local parishes, churches and chapels. Church and chapel building continued to be a major concern of the mid and late Victorian churches, thus establishing a physical presence in urban working-class environments. No less important was the effort devoted in the last quarter of the century to the establishment of mission halls. Denominations, inter- and non-denominational societies, city missions and individuals built and sustained such missions and did so in such quantity that by the end of the century Charles Booth observed of London that, 'In the poorer districts especially, in almost every street, there is a mission; they are more numerous than schools or churches, and only less numerous than public houses'. The aggregate of their work, Booth observed was enormous (quoted in Lewis, 1986, p. 275).

Local Anglican, Scottish Presbyterian and Nonconformist churches meanwhile, along with such mission halls, gave concrete expression to the urban working-class mission through a staggeringly diverse network of voluntary societies, agencies, clubs and organizations. Sunday Schools, Boys' Brigades, Christian Endeavour Societies, Girls' Guilds, Bands of Hope, Bible Classes, Tract Distribution Societies, Women's Fellowships, Working Men's Clubs, Pleasant Sunday Afternoons, Wesley Guilds, YM and YWCA branches, Temperance Societies, Evening Classes, Libraries, Thrift and Penny Savings Clubs, Co-operative Building Societies, Coal Clubs, Dorcas Societies, Sporting Clubs, agencies for the provision of charitable and philanthropic relief, lodging houses and refuges, or medical care — the list of church, chapel and mission-sponsored agencies could be almost endlessly extended, glossed and made more specific. Some of the activities were straightforwardly devotional (although often located outside the regular pattern of Sunday worship); some were predominantly educational; some were essentially for charity and the relief of distress; some were principally avenues for self-help and self-improvement; some were primarily recreational and leisure-orientated. Many combined elements of each of these aspects. Most importantly, however, all of them brought the churches into some kind of active and semi-regular contact with a large part of the working-class population — and vice versa.

As Callum Brown has observed of such activities in Victorian Scotland, on the one hand the various agencies became progressively more specific in their targeting of particular occupational, age, or gender groups for special attention, whilst on the other hand in their collective impact this 'mammoth panoply of religious voluntary organisations' became the principal means of addressing the social and religious problems and challenges of urban life as a whole (Brown, 1987, pp. 143 and 147). Brown's observation applies equally to the English context as well, where, as specific studies such as Jeffrey Cox's analysis of the role of the churches in Lambeth between 1870 and 1930 amply illustrate, the same richness and diversity of voluntary religious organizations was to be found, similarly addressing particular groups and issues but together amounting to an attempt to provide a comprehensive response to the conditions of late Victorian urban life (Cox, 1982).

The investment of the Victorian churches in the mission to the urban working classes was thus a heavy one, not only in resources, human and economic, but also emotionally and psychologically. The returns on the investment were, as we shall see, far from negligible; but they were not, for the most part, of the kind that the churches had hoped for: hence the emergence, by 1900, of a growing sense within the churches of the failure of the urban working-class mission. It is to that sense of failure that we must shortly turn, but not without a brief consideration of a frequently forgotten aspect of the relationship between religion and the Victorian working classes: namely its rural dimension.

II   RURAL RELIGION: IDEALS AND ILLUSIONS

Confronted with the more horrific aspects of rapid and unplanned industrialization and urbanization, one of the more frequent Victorian responses was the flight into rural romanticism. From such tendencies the churches were not immune.

On the one hand, many of the strategies proposed for the overcoming of urban irreligion and destitution (both physical and spiritual) embodied or included distinctly rural ideals. Thus both the Church of England and the Church of Scotland sought to overcome the challenge of the urban environment by the multiplication of the parochial system. By creating new parishes and sub-dividing old ones, and by providing parish clergy, the estrangement of the urban working classes, it was believed, might be overcome, and the urban community redeemed. It was an ideal at the centre of Thomas Chalmers' vision of what the Church of Scotland should be, and in England both Blomfield and Hook, though pioneers of the urban mission, retained a rural parochial concept and vision of both the end in view and the means to achieve it (Mole, 1979).

The rural ideal was to be found also in some of the apparently most determinedly urban of late Victorian missionary efforts among the working classes. The very notion of 'squires in the East End' betrayed the rural origins of much of the philosophy behind the Settlements. Perhaps more surprisingly, when in 1890 William Booth turned his attention from 'pure' evangelism to the question of social rescue work, the founder of the Salvation Army — the very epitome of urban evangelism — produced a 'scheme of social salvation', which included a notable element of rural idealism. Booth's scheme, which he presented in *In Darkest England and the Way Out*, envisaged the rescue of the urban destitute via first a city 'colony', then a suburban one, and then a rural 'farm colony'. 'As the race from the Country to the City has been the cause of the distress we have to battle with', Booth observed, 'we propose to find a substantial part of our remedy by transferring these same people back to the country'. Booth, moreover, was not alone among late Victorian Nonconformists in advocating rural solutions to urban problems. David Bebbington has noted a more general current of rural romanticism running through much of the late Victorian Nonconformist social gospel (as, for example, in the advocacy of planned suburbs and garden cities), despite its overwhelmingly urban origins and aims (Bebbington, 1979).

If the rural idealism of Booth and the rural (and class) assumptions of the Settlement 'squirearchy' each displayed considerable irony, however, the hopes of the English and Scottish establishments in respect of the urban potential of their essentially rural parochial models revealed an even greater lack of awareness of the realities of the urban environment. Occasionally churchmen recognized this. As James Fraser, Bishop of Manchester, put it in his 1872 visitation charge to his clergy: 'The parochial system, as ordinarily conceived, admirably efficient in rural parishes and among limited populations, where the pastor knows and is known to everyone committed to his charge, breaks down in the face of that huge mass of ignorance, poverty and wretchedness by which it is so often confronted in the thickly peopled areas of our manufacturing towns'. Fraser's remark was accurate enough in respect of the impossibility of applying the traditional parochial ideal to an urban environment in which the ecclesiastical parish was in practice just one more private and voluntary association in an increasingly fragmented urban culture. But was he also right to describe the parochial system as admirably efficient in rural parishes? Was rural religious life in reality as unproblematic as the Victorian churches tended to assume?

Research on the state of Victorian rural religion is less extensive than that on its urban counterpart, historians, like the Victorians of whom they write, generally having preferred to concentrate on the perceived drama of the urban context. There is sufficient evidence, however, to suggest that, however ideal some rural parishes may have been, in many others the state of religious life was far from satisfactory when viewed from the standpoint of the churches.

Richard Jefferies, for example, a journalist writing in 1880 on the changes which had taken place in nineteenth-century rural life, observed in

Hodge and His Masters that, 'there exists at the present day a class that is morally apathetic. In every village, in every hamlet, every detached group of cottages, there are numbers of labouring men who are simply indifferent to church and to chapel alike. They neither deny nor affirm the primary truths taught in all places of worship; they are simply indifferent. Sunday comes and sees them lounging about the cottage door. They do not drink to excess, they are not more given to swearing than others, they are equally honest, and are not of ill-repute. But the moral sense seems extinct — the very idea of anything beyond gross earthly advantages never occurs to them. The days go past, the wages are paid, the food is eaten, and there is all.' Similarly, he spoke elsewhere of rural west country parishioners who 'cleaned their boots on a Sunday morning while the bells were ringing, and walked down to their allotments, and came home and ate their cabbage, and were as oblivious of the vicar as the wind that blew. They had no quarrel with the church ... nor apparently any old memory or grudge, yet there was something, a blank space as it were, between them and the church'.

Jefferies' perception of the religious apathy of rural labourers was not unique. In 1875 the Vicar of Farnborough, Berkshire, observed in a Visitation Return that, '*Indifferentism*, if not *Infidelity*, I fear is the prevailing characteristic of the day in most country parishes'. And in 1872 the vicar of Earls Barton, Northamptonshire had complained of 'Dissent, lukewarmness, and indifference, drinking especially on Sunday. Half the population dissenters. But many profess no religion' (quoted in Horn, 1976, pp. 164 and 171). Moreover, even in many religiously observant parishes, the apparent intensity of much rural piety was owed in part to the socially coercive potential of the local pattern of land ownership and the presence of a resident squire. As David Thompson has pointed out, it was not only Nonconformity which tended to flourish in 'open' villages where a more dispersed pattern of land ownership prevailed: in such villages religious observance as a whole was likely to be lower. Greater scope for being a Nonconformist also implied greater scope for being nothing religious at all (Thompson, 1972, p. 275).

The most thorough of recent case studies of rural religion in Victorian Britain both supports the notion that the reality of rural religious life was much less ideal than religious rural romanticism allowed, and also, importantly, points to the existence of an alternative popular religious tradition among the rural labouring population. James Obelkevich's study of religion and rural society in South Lindsey, Lincolnshire, between 1825 and 1875 focuses upon an area and period in which the established church and Methodism — both Wesleyan and Primitive — confronted each other in aggressive competition. As a result of such competition, and the tensions created by an emerging rural class society, Obelkevich concludes, church attendance probably rose during the period in question and religious belief and knowledge became unprecedentedly widespread. At the same time the strength of popular religion, and especially the range and intensity of both Christian and pagan belief in the magical and supernatural declined, as did the more supernaturalist elements characteristic of the Methodism of the early nineteenth century.

Alongside such developments, however, Obelkevich also notes that formal *membership*, as opposed to occasional attendance, in both church and chapel was as low as ten per cent each of the local population. The majority of a village population, he suggests, would have remained without serious commitment to either church or chapel. Moreover, if general Christian belief became more widespread, there remained both considerable ignorance of fundamental Christian doctrine, and a notable tendency to attach to the rites and sacraments of the established church a range of decidedly unofficial and unorthodox beliefs. By the 1870s, Obelkevich concludes, religion, both popular and official, was becoming less intense and less distinctive: in Methodism, evangelism yielded to entertainment, the 'community of saints' to 'fellowship,' and soul-making to character-building; in the Church of England, the 'invention' of harvest festivals 'baptized' a popular rural religious instinct to celebrate the annual rhythm of the year; in popular religion the magical receded (Obelkevich, 1976, passim, especially pp. 324–30).

What is particularly striking about the tone and the content of the descriptions of, and complaints about, *rural* working-class indifference and alternatives to official religion noted above, is that they are in fact remarkably similar to those of commentators on Victorian *urban* working-class religious — and non-religious — attitudes. As McLeod has remarked, in the light of such evidence, it is not inappropriate to conclude that if the formal religion of many Victorian city-dwellers 'extended little beyond the rites of passage and attendance at Watchnight services, this may have been a continuation of habits well established in the countryside' (McLeod, 1974, p. 280).

III   SUCCESS OR FAILURE: 'INDIFFERENCE' OR JUST 'DIFFERENT': A QUESTION OF CRITERIA

Horace Mann had believed that if the more blatant manifestations of class distinction *within* the churches (such as pew rents and the pressure to dress 'respectably') were removed by the organization of exclusively working-class services, and if sufficient 'aggression' were displayed in the evangelization of the urban working classes, then they would be sure to become converts, their 'inert,' 'negative,' 'unconscious secularism' being sufficient only to deter their actively seeking religion, but not capable of resisting its claims once brought confidently to them. He was wrong.

In 1881 a series of local censuses and enquiries into the state of religion, organized by local newspapers in about eighty English and forty Scottish towns, revealed that little had changed. Those editors who expressed an opinion on the matter tended to agree that, if anything, there had been decline. In particular, the 1881 censuses confirmed that the poor and the working classes in particular remained predominantly absent from the regular worship of the churches (McLeod, 1973, p. 43). Thirty years of increased urban missionary aggression had not begun to turn the urban working classes as a whole, or even in large numbers, into orthodox, church-going Christians.

The point was reiterated in various ways in the next two decades. In the Church of England diocesan reports, such as that on the Condition of the Bristol Poor (1885), reports to Convocation, such as those on the 'Spiritual Needs of the Masses of the People' (Convocation of Canterbury, 1885; Convocation of York, 1892), regular reports and sessions at Church Congresses, and the comments and surveys of individual bishops and clergy, all tended to the same broad conclusion: the church remained a middle and upper-class institution; the working class remained substantially aloof (Inglis, 1963, ch. 1; Kent, 1973, p. 858). In Scotland, the Church of Scotland Commission on the Religious Condition of the People, which examined Scottish religious life in a series of reports to the General Assembly between 1890 and 1896, revealed a similar situation and similar reactions: the Scottish working class was apparently a little less alienated from the regular life of the church than its English counterpart, but not to the extent of being, as a whole, a markedly more church-going community than the English urban working class (Boyd, 1980, pp. 19–23).

English Nonconformity also examined its urban working-class endeavours in the 1880s and 1890s and found them wanting. Here too, in a Nonconformist version of the clear Anglican awareness of the Church of England's overwhelmingly middle-class ethos, there was much said in the Nonconformist press, and in the heart-searching of particular denominations, concerning the middle-class and often suburban nature of Nonconformist life, culture and religion. Recognition of the continuing absence of the working classes from the mainstream of Nonconformist activity inspired further new initiatives: the Central Halls and Missions of Wesleyan Methodism; local Free Church Councils to co-ordinate local Nonconformist evangelism and mission and to help reduce or avoid local denominational competition; an increased and self-conscious shift of emphasis towards the range of recreational clubs and societies sponsored by the churches and chapels — the football clubs, PSAs, Bands of Hope, or Boys' Brigades — and somewhat away from the more overtly religious or 'improving' agencies such as the Bible Classes or Sunday Schools. Aware of their continuing failure to turn the working classes, in large numbers, into chapel members, and aware also of the increasing provision of commercial leisure activities,

Nonconformists in particular set out to 'baptize' and 'consecrate' a variety of essentially secular leisure activities as a means of establishing contact with and then influencing the working classes through a combination of recreation and religion. The Church of England also explored the same strategy, as did the Scottish churches (Inglis, 1963, ch. 2; Brown, 1987, pp. 182–3).[1] Last, but not least, although it arose from other sources also, the emergence of a range of Anglican, Nonconformist and Scottish Presbyterian 'social gospels,' 'social Christianities,' and 'Christian Socialisms' owed not a little to the growth of the conviction that the working classes would remain aloof and indifferent to the churches whilst the churches remained uncommitted to working-class social and political aspirations.[2]

In the second quarter of the nineteenth century the churches had become increasingly aware of the 'spiritual destitution' of the urban poor and working classes and had begun the Victorian urban mission. In the third quarter of the century, their fears and efforts reinforced by the 1851 Census of Religion, they had redoubled their missionary 'aggression' and commitment. In the final quarter, faced with the findings of the local censuses of 1881 and their own awareness of the continued absence of the majority of the working classes from their parishes, chapels and missions, they became less sure that simple evangelical aggression would prevail. They therefore also became yet more evangelistically inventive and innovative, yet more socially conscious, and yet more 'market-conscious' in their bid to convert working-class souls via sanctified working-class leisure.

At the turn of the century, Charles Booth produced his seven volumes on the *Religious Influences upon the Life and Labour of the People in London*. Booth's findings reflected the immense activity of the churches but, like the 1881 Census, indicated little outward and visible change in the place of religion

---

[1] Callum Brown, taking his examples from late Victorian Glasgow, cites such cases as a mission hall, which, in the 1890s, displayed a bold notice outside announcing 'NO: Charge for Admission: NO: Long Sermons; No Collections', or the way in which the YMCA in Glasgow moved from a predominantly educational style in the 1840s, through a revivalist phase in the 1870s after the visit to Scotland of Sankey and Moody, to a sporting orientation in the 1880s; or the way in which local Bands of Hope increasingly adopted novelty evenings, magic lantern shows and the organization of football teams in order to attract the young to the temperance cause (Brown, 1987, p. 183). The policy of 'outreach through leisure' was, however, a potentially ambiguous one: the boundary between religion itself and religiously sponsored leisure could become blurred; the recreational agencies could at once demand the support, energy and talent of the parent church or chapel, and yet develop a rationale, direction, and existence of their own, little integrated with the mainstream religious life of the church or chapel. For examples of both the range and vitality, and also the potential ambiguity, of such voluntary recreational agencies, see the case studies of Bristol between 1870 and 1914 by Meller (1976), and of Reading between 1890 and 1914 by Yeo (1976).

[2] For the emergence of the social gospel and the revival of Christian Socialism in late Victorian Christianity, see also *RVB*, II, 2.

in working-class life. The poor and the working class, Booth found, re-mained 'as a whole, outside of all the religious bodies', although the Roman Catholic poor represented something of an exception to this rule. Even allowing that 'those whose professions are fewest' may yet be inwardly re-ligious, 'the fact must be admitted that the great masses of the people remain apart from all forms of religious communion, apparently untouched by the Gospel that, with various differences of interpretation and applica-tion, is preached from every pulpit'. Although traditional working-class objections to the churches as symbols of class distinction persisted, the degree of active hostility to the churches had decreased. Secularism was not widely influential and pronounced atheism rare. But there was also little sign of the 'increased acceptance of the *particular* teaching of the Churches ... The *humanitarianism* of the clergy and others is approved of, but their *doctrinal* teaching carries no weight'. Working men were now perhaps more tolerant of the clergy, but 'no more religious in anything approaching to the *accepted* meaning of the word'. Moreover, Booth added, liberalized versions of Christianity made no better headway, in fact the chapels and missions which were most succesful in attracting working men were those of strict, even narrow, orthodoxy (Booth, quoted in Helmstadter and Phillips, 1985, pp. 256–60, emphases added). For those churchmen and women for whom the success of the urban mission depended upon the creation of a large body of working-class church members conforming to the norms of belief and practice of official Christianity (namely, regular church attendance and the acceptance of one or other of the available versions of doctrinal ortho-doxy), the censuses, surveys, and introspective reports of the quarter cen-tury after 1880 could only be interpreted as indications of failure.

There remained at the end of the century, as there had been throughout it, many working-class Christians of a conventional, regularly church-going, kind. As McLeod has pointed out, the evidence of a growing number of case studies in church membership records suggests that many individaul congregations included a high proportion of working-class members — even if the leadership of such churches and chapels was more often than not middle class (McLeod, 1984, p. 15). All the major denominations had churches, chapels and missions in working class communities and such churches and chapels were not empty. On the other hand, however, it is likely that within the church-going minority of the working classes the 'respectable' and skilled sections of those classes predominated. It was a commonplace that whilst the working classes as a whole were markedly absent from the life of the churches, the scale of absence and alienation increased as the social scale decreased.

Even the often quoted denominational exceptions to the general pattern of working-class alienation from the churches are far from unambiguous. The successes of 'slum ritualists' often reflected the affection and respect felt locally for individual clergy whose devotion, voluntary poverty and dedication to their working-class parishes inspired personal admiration, rather than a widespread commitment to Anglo-Catholic doctrine and practice. Such parishes also often eclectically drew middle-class Anglo-Catholic worshippers from other nearby areas in which advanced ritualism was unavailable (an eclecticism also noted in the regular congregations of some Wesleyan Missions and Central Halls which, despite all their working-class mission work and rationale, tended to become showpiece 'cathedrals' of Methodism) (Rowell, 1983, p. 140; Rack, 1983, p. 140; Munsen, 1975, pp. 391–5; Yates, 1975, p. 66). Primitive Methodism, justifiably quoted as an example of a predominantly working-class denomination, nevertheless moved steadily in the direction of a more middle-class ethos in the second half of the century. Even the Salvation Army, with its equally justifiable reputation for successfully reaching members of the least 'respectable' sections of the working classes, in fact possessed an overall membership which was more heavily lower middle-class than its traditional image implies.

The one notable exception to the 'norm' of working-class absence and alienation was to be found in Roman Catholicism. But the success of the Roman Catholic Church in consolidating a solid working-class base depended not only on administrative efficiency, the pastoral devotion of the Catholic clergy, and the disciplined determination to build tightly integrated, self-sufficient Catholic communities, but also, crucially, upon the 'accident' of large-scale and ongoing Irish immigration and the resultant desire for the retention of a communal identity in which religion combined with national and ethnic loyalties. Moreover, even within working-class Catholicism there was a discernible division between the 'respectable' working class and the poorest of the Catholic community. Practice was highest among the former. Even among the latter, however, if the customary requirements of regular Catholic piety were neglected, it did not mean that religious identity was a matter of indifference: such 'residual' or 'nominal' Catholics remained fiercely loyal to the Catholic Church and the Catholic community, especially if either were attacked by English or Scottish Protestants (McLeod, 1974, pp. 34–5 and 1984, p. 39; ÓTuathaigh, 1981, pp. 165–9).

Whilst working-class participation in conventional church-going Christianity was thus, in total, far from negligible, and was, indeed, probably somewhat greater than both the more pessimistic contemporary analyses and many historians have allowed, it remained, nevertheless, decidedly atypical. In this it shared common ground with both working-class militant secularism and the brief mid and late Victorian phenomena of the Chartist and Labour Church movements. Militant, aggressive, working-class secularism not only shared with its Christian adversaries a penchant for the religious forms — the missionaries, Sunday Schools, catechisms and hymns

— of the religion it opposed, but also experienced a similar inability to 'convert' the working class as a whole to its standpoint. Although an important movement in its own right, organized secularism failed as comprehensively as Christianity in its attempt to foster a genuinely widespread and articulate anti-religious radicalism within the Victorian working classes. Working-class secularism remained the anti-theological creed of an articulate and atypical minority. The Chartist churches of the late 1830s and early 1840s, and the Labour Church Movement of the 1890s, were similarly the products of politically radical minorities within the Victorian working classes. The Chartist churches vanished along with Chartism. The Labour Church Movement lasted barely twenty years and, because of its theologically diverse constituent elements, paradoxically found it possible to operate effectively only by concentrating on political matters and keeping religious and theological issues in the background. By 1900 the Movement was already past its peak and by 1914 it was effectively over (McLeod, 1984, pp. 48–9; Mayor, 1967, pp. 66–9 and 246–9; Inglis, 1963, ch. 6).

Although unable to convert even large numbers, let alone the majority, of the working classes to their standpoint, the working-class secularist and Labour Church Movements were not simply 'failures' without significant historical legacies: each contributed an important dimension to the emergent Labour movement of the late Victorian and Edwardian eras. Similarly, the much more extensive Christian mission to the Victorian working classes, although unable to turn the working classes into a widely, still less a predominantly, church-going, orthodoxly believing group, was not, therefore, without significant and enduring effects. A Baptist minister in Norwood told one of Charles Booth's researchers that Norwood was 'sodden by the Gospel, and not saved by it', and in 1903 the Bishop of Rochester, E. S. Talbot, warned his clergy not to dismiss the widespread 'diffusive Christianity,' which he considered formed a 'penumbra' to the 'embodied' Christianity of the church (both quoted in Cox, pp. 92–3).

What both comments indicated, although the latter much more favourably than the former, was the existence of a widespread working-class *version* of Christianity, at variance with the official versions on offer from the churches, but in the opinion of those holding it Christian nevertheless. Although the existence of such a 'popular' working class version of Christianity has frequently been noted by historians, it has less often been subjected to analysis, not least because the evidence for it is scattered, elusive and impressionistic. There have, however, been some notable attempts to characterize such urban working-class 'diffusive Christianity'.[3] They reveal

---

[3] Most notably those of McLeod, 1974, pp. 49–60, and 1980, pp. 194–5; Kent, 1973 and 1978, pp. 223–224 and 359–362; Ainsworth, 1977. especially pp. 363–72; and Cox, 1982. The characterisation of a working-class 'diffusive Christianity' which follows is based upon the evidence and argument presented in these studies.

a version of Christianity which, although not systematic or precisely structured, possessed its own broad patterns of both belief and practice. In terms
of belief, diffusive Christianity had little or no time for doctrine or dogma.
It was not that doctrine was generally considered and rejected as incredible or offensive — although hell and eternal punishment were widely
repudiated on moral grounds — but rather that it was dismissed, largely
unconsidered, as irrelevant. Particular doctrines, such as the Trinity, Incarnation or Atonement, or the question of the theological status of the Bible,
and the appropriate mode of its interpretation, simply did not matter to
the diffusive Christian. What did matter was practical Christianity, the
morality of the Bible, the ethical discipline of the Ten Commandments, and
the ethics of the Sermon on the Mount and the parable of the Good
Samaritan. The heart of religion was trying to live a good life, being good
to one's family and neighbours, and not doing wrong. The Bible was a
uniquely worthwhile book and was principally useful for its ethical
teaching, being especially valuable in teaching children a proper moral
code. Kent, for example, has noted the preference of working-class wit-
nesses before the Royal Commission on Elementary Education in 1887 for
Board School religious-moral biblical teaching, without the intrusion of 'unnecessary' dogmas (Kent, 1973, pp. 861–2; 1978, p. 361). In such religion,
God was characteristically distant and remote — but certainly benign and
benevolent; Jesus was essentially a moral exemplar; heaven and the life to
come a place where good people would be taken care of and the toils and
tribulations of this life would be past. It was a profoundly stoical, easy-
going, practical, this-worldly, religious outlook with heaven in prospect but
little worried over.

As for practice, diffusive Christianity eschewed a pattern of regular
weekly church-going — which indeed could be regarded as 'showy' or
seeking to be 'better than one was' — but embraced an alternative pattern
of religious practice in which rites of passage and annual festivals were
central. Birth, marriage and death continued to prompt the desire for
baptism, a church or chapel wedding, and a religious funeral. Of annual
festivals there were at least three kinds: major festivals of the Christian year
— but especially Christmas — would attract some working-class worshippers otherwise usually absent from the churches' worship; annual
services such as a New Year Watchnight Service or a Harvest Festival
would do the same for others; and where such rites of passage or annual
festivals created a link with a particular church or chapel, then the chapel
or Sunday School anniversary or the patronal festival might provide another annual occasion for religious worship. Another 'alternative' form of
religious practice was to be found in attendance at some variety of weeknight meeting or society at which a religious service formed part of the
proceedings. For official Christianity and its clerical professionals, such

rites of passage and annual festivals were intended as the high points — personal and annual — within a regular pattern of piety; and weeknight devotional meetings were additional, supplementary exercises in Christian piety. Working-class diffusive Christians, however, re-made such festivals, rites and occasions into an alternative pattern of piety, sufficient unto itself.[4]

It is not difficult to understand why orthodox Christians should have had difficulty in recognizing such beliefs as authentically Christian, or why some clergy should have found it exasperating to witness a consumer-like acceptance of what was wanted, or could be made sense of, by way of rites of passage, ethics and morals, annual festivals, and the religion-cum-entertainment-cum-companionship of weekly meetings, whilst the discipline and obligations of regular attendance, church membership and orthodox belief were ignored. The existence of such diffusive Christianity, however, strongly suggests the inadequacy of the straightforward characterization of the Victorian working classes as simply indifferent to religion. They were not, in many cases, *in*different to religion. They merely possessed *a* different understanding of what religion constituted to that on offer from the churches. For many members of the Victorian working-classes, Christianity — at least in a residual and diffusive form — mattered greatly. Indifference to the doctrinal and participatory norms of orthodox Christian belief and practice did not necessarily imply indifference to the entire legacy of traditional Christian beliefs, rites and moral imperatives.

Once this is recognized the question of the success or failure of the Victorian mission to the working classes also takes on a different appearance. The absence of the majority of the poor from the regular life of the churches was not a new phenomenon in the nineteenth century. The scale of Victorian shock and horror at working-class non church-going and 'irreligion' owed a great deal to a romantic and inaccurate view of the past in which church attendance was assumed to be the norm. The historical reality was otherwise. Pre-nineteenth century levels of church-going among the poor did not constitute an ideal from which the nineteenth century had fallen. What was new in the nineteenth century was the immense growth in

---

[4] Similarly, among 'nominal' Catholics, resistant to regular practice of confession or attendance at Mass, birth, marriage and death 'were seldom celebrated without the Church's benediction' (Ó Tuathaigh, 1981, p. 166). As Sheridan Gilley has observed, it is difficult to indicate clearly the limits set to secularity 'by the strength and substance of popular religious culture'. If the precise meaning of a residual Catholic piety (embodied in little more than a household picture of the Sacred Heart with a red lamp before it, or an enthusiasm for lighting candles before plaster statues, or a devotion to the singing of favourite Catholic hymns) was elusive and unclear, nevertheless it was a residual piety 'which an environment indifferent or hostile to Christianity could only with great difficulty overcome; so that in time of need or at the hour of death, a priest might re-kindle from the burnt out embers a final flame of faith' (Gilley, 1985, pp. 255–6).

population and the appearance of a numerically large and geographically densely located non church-going urban working class. It has even been suggested that, far from being a failure, the Victorian urban working-class mission may have shifted popular religion as a whole *closer* to recognizably Christian beliefs, albeit in the process creating a popular *version* of Christianity rather than an extension of its 'official', churchly form (Lewis, 1986, p. 274).[5]

Moreover, given that the emergence of late Victorian diffusive Christianity coincided with the relative dissolution *within* the major non-Roman Catholic denominations of their traditional doctrinal and confessional orthodoxies, and their replacement by internal pluralisms marked by calculated doctrinal ambiguity and a deliberately unspecific theological ethos, the gap between the more lukewarm 'conventional' church member and the more articulate 'diffusive Christian' may already have been rather less than either Victorian churchmen would have liked or historians have generally supposed. Thus Jeffrey Cox, having examined the extent and nature of diffusive Christianity in Victorian Lambeth, turned his attention to 'church-going Lambeth'. The religion he found in the records of Lambeth's churches and chapels was also 'this-worldly', the typical sermon containing ethical and moral advice, and detailed speculation on matters of doctrine not being part of the 'common currency of ordinary churchgoers'. Similarly, Hugh McLeod, examining religion in London's late Victorian suburbs, concluded that most middle-class people were 'unconscious Broad Churchmen', brought up to attend church and assent to Christian doctrine, but with a conception of religion which was largely practical (Cox, 1982, p. 105; McLeod, 1974, p. 155).[6]

IV CONCLUSION: AN IMPRECISE DIVERSITY

Writing in 1873, in an essay entitled 'Prospects of the Working Classes,' Thomas Wright, who frequently wrote under the pseudonym 'The Journey-

[5] Lewis refers, in particular, to Keith Thomas' suggestion that whereas between the sixteenth and nineteenth centuries popular religion changed little, in the nineteenth century it changed significantly (Lewis, 1986, p. 274; Thomas, 1978). McLeod (1974, p. 280) similarly emphasizes the extent to which interpretations of nineteenth century urban religious (or non-religious) behaviour are prone to distortion by comparison with idealized and unrealistic images of the religious life of the pre-industrial era.

[6] Compare such estimates of middle-class 'this-worldly' and 'unconscious Broad Church' Christianity with Archbishop Randall Davidson's remark of 1918: 'It is to me amazing to find how many good Christian people emasculate Christianity into a sort of sentimental good nature' (see *RVB*, I, 2). The gap between middle and working-class conceptions of Christianity was also bridged by *lower* middle class religious activity and attitudes which, not surprisingly, characteristically combined elements of the ethos and style of conventional and committed 'official' Christianity with aspects of diffusive Christianity. For analyses of such lower middle-class religion, see McLeod, 1977; and Gray 1977.

man Engineer', published one of the more direct contemporary responses to the assumption (in this case recently restated by the Evangelical Archbishop of York, William Thomson) that working-class non-church-going indicated working-class disbelief in God or a future life. This assumption, Wright argued, merely indicated ignorance of the real nature of working-class attitudes. The common sense of the poor told them, 'that to make church-going the be-all and end-all, as a test of religion, is to confound religion with the observance of its mere mechanical rites'. The hypocrisy of some regular church-goers made the poor think little of church-going altogether. But to say that because they thus disregarded church attendance they therefore lacked belief in God or a better life hereafter was to reveal how little the speaker knew of the subject. 'In the essentials of Christianity — the feelings of brotherly and neighbourly love and kindness, and the virtue of patience — the working classes are not lacking. Their non-attendance at places of worship has not the grave meaning that even many of the more charitably inclined in other classes attach to it' — it was the product, rather, of class distinctions perpetuated in church and formalized, mechanical worship. It was not the first time Wright had addressed the theme. In an earlier essay, published in 1868, on 'The Working Classes and the Church', he had again noted that working-class absence from church was widely construed as irreligious in nature and had pointed out that this was sustainable only by equating the essential spirit of religion with outward religious observance. If judged by 'the essentials of Christianity', however — brotherly love, kindness, self-sacrifice, reflection on the hereafter — then the working classes would not be found irreligious. To speak of widespread infidelity or 'active opposition' to religion among the working classes was nonsense. They did, however, see the church as materialistic, hypocritical and prone to criticize the 'sins' of the poor whilst ignoring those of the rich. The church as an institution did not appeal to the working classes, whilst the habits and ethos of working-class life did not prompt, still less necessitate, church-going for social reasons. Working-class indifference to the *church* (sic) was the result of a contempt for 'the desecration of the spirit of religion under the guise of a ceremonial systematization of it', rather than of irreligious feeling.[7]

Was Wright correct in his estimate of the extent of such working-class non church-going religion? Accurate or precise quantification of the prevalence of such religious views and attitudes among the Victorian working classes is probably impossible: the evidence for it is necessarily simply too fragmentary and anecdotal. The analyses of diffusive Christianity by McLeod, Kent, Ainsworth and Cox, referred to in the preceding section of this essay, would, however, support Wright's basic contention. Elsewhere,

---

[7] Wright's essays appeared in two collections of his writings entitled, respectively, *The Great Unwashed* (1868) and *Our New Masters* (1873).

McLeod has also argued that, despite the increasing competition of a commercially organized leisure industry and the rise of an organized labour movement, formal church-going among the working classes remained higher than some commentators allow and more popular than any other similarly systematic view of life on offer (although he acknowledges that a fluid eclecticism owing total allegiance to no single religion or ideology was more common still). As for the diffusive influence of Christianity, he suggests that it had a pervasive influence, spread widely if also thinly, with the majority of the working classes retaining 'some kind of link with the churches' (1984, pp. 15–16 and 66).

Cox similarly concludes that religion remained more important in late Victorian society than either contemporary observers or historians have been able to see, their vision being doubly obscured by the unrealistic hopes and criteria of the practitioners of the urban mission, and an equally inaccurate concept of a religious past from which the nineteenth century fell away. Quite apart from the plethora of church and chapel-sponsored voluntary, recreational, and philanthropic agencies, hardly anyone, he suggests, in an area such as Lambeth, would have escaped some degree of religious teaching either in Sunday School or, after 1870, in either a denominational school or a Board School in which the non-doctrinal teaching of a biblically based religious education fostered just such a 'demystified, ethically oriented popular religion' as the working classes anyway tended towards (Cox, p. 268). Similarly, again, Ainsworth's conclusions in respect of the role and significance of religion in working-class life in late nineteenth-century Lancashire also reflect the conviction that, even if such 'diffusive Christianity' often existed at some distance from the churches, yet not only was it important in its own terms as a means of giving meaning and a measure of hope to working-class experience, but in addition the church or chapel — and especially the chapel — might play an influential role as an 'all-round social institution'. The overall conception of the role of such religious institutions in working-class life, Ainsworth suggests, requires widening (Ainsworth, 1977, p. 367).

Thomas Wright's contention that working-class rejection of the churches' version of Christianity did not involve the rejection of religion in total, but rather the priority of a different understanding of what 'real religion' constituted, was also to receive support some half a century later in the evidence assembled by churchmen concerning the attitudes to religion of English and Scottish soldiers serving with the British Army in France in 1917. In 1917 the YMCA sponsored an interdenominational survey of the place of religion in the minds of the soldiers. The resulting report (published in 1919 under the title *The Army and Religion* and largely written by the Scottish Free Churchman D. S. Cairns on behalf of a committee of churchmen chaired by the Anglican bishop E. S. Talbot) revealed a situation which Wright would have recognized and understood. The soldiers generally had little time for the churches as institutions (regarding them as lacking in fellowship, sources of class distinction, aloof from questions of social justice, prone to cant, and tainted by materialism). They had, similarly, little knowledge of or interest in traditional Christian doctrine, and saw the ethics and morality of churchly Christianity as essentially negative and moralistic — not swearing, not drinking and so forth. On the other hand, belief in God was widespread (although the deity concerned was largely remote), as was belief in life after death. Prayer before or after battle was common, but so was fatalism about the workings (or non-workings) of providence. Jesus was almost universally respected, but as a purely human figure (notions of incarnation or atoning significance were notable only by their absence), and especially as a fellow-sufferer in a good cause: the cross thus figured as a symbol of self-sacrifice. As for ethics and morality, 'real' Christianity was understood in terms of a life of active good will. Individual clergy could inspire respect, but for their personal qualities, not their clerical status. Communion was often valued before battle, less often at camps away from the front-line. Hymns were popular, not only in their frequently rendered alternative, bawdy versions, but also in their original ones: soldiers, it was observed, would turn easily to *Hymns Ancient and Modern* because it was a 'genuine part of our folk-lore' (quoted in Wilkinson, 1978, p. 158).

The pattern revealed is a familiar one: rejection of official Christianity, but retention of an alternative religious framework in which vague theism, practical ethics and occasional worship were prominent, but from which doctrine, church commitment or churchly morality were absent. The war produced circumstances in which the pattern was revealed particularly clearly, but it did not create it. The religious opinions of the men in the British Army of 1917 were above all the product of several decades of steady working-class contact with, but rarely formal membership of, the churches of late Victorian and Edwardian Britain. Moreover, in assessing the extent of 'diffusive Christianity' suggested by the findings of *The Army and Religion* it is important to remember that this inquiry was specifically concerned with the religious attitudes of *men*: it had long been a commonplace that working-class women were more responsive to both conventional and diffusive Christianity than were men.

How, then, might the place of religion in Victorian working-class life be summed up and characterized? The notion of a simple, predominant indifference to religion simply will not do. It is only possible to continue to maintain that working-class life was generally indifferent to religion by adopting the standards, norms and criteria of official Christianity as the definition of religion, and by ignoring or refusing to take seriously the unorthodox, heterodox, eclectic and unsystematic — but nonetheless deeply

held — religious convictions and practices of working-class people themselves. Providing an adequate alternative description and characterization
of working-class religious life is more difficult. It must necessarily be imprecise and tentative, for, as McLeod has observed, the history of working-
class religion in nineteenth-century Britain is many-sided and comprised of
a range of competing, often contradictory tendencies (1984, p. 16).

The range of attitudes to religion among the Victorian working classes
resembled a spectrum. At one end were a variety of articulate, specific and
precise working-class religious and anti-religious sub-cultures, each of them
atypical precisely because their beliefs were systematically and articulately
held. Working-class evangelicalism, working-class ritualism, working-class
Nonconformity, working-class Catholicism (although this remained an
exception and special case because of its scale, ethnic identity and communal integration), working-class secularism, and the brief experiment of
the Labour Churches, whilst in total far from negligible, were all, in one
sense, closer to each other than to the majority of the working class in
general. Each of these groups espoused a definite set of beliefs and expected
a high degree of active participation.[8] At the other end of the spectrum
there was, indeed, indifference: for many (although determining precisely
how many is probably impossible), matters of religion were simply irrelevant. They, at least, would conform to Mann's 'unconscious secularists'.
And for such people there was little or nothing in working-class culture and
lifestyle to prompt, still less to compel, an interest in religion (or irreligion)
if it were not already desired.

Between these two extremes, however, there stretched a long and complex band of more or less articulate, more or less vague, religious opinion,
best described as 'diffusive Christianity'. At its most articulate and least
vague, it maintained an irregular but in its own way loyal attachment to a
particular denomination, or at least a particular local church or chapel,
expressed through attendance at annual festivals and ancillary agencies.
Such religion was clearly 'Christian', but definitely 'diffusively' so. At its
least articulate and most vague, on the other hand, it had precious little
direct contact with the churches and combined this-worldly fatalism with a
residual belief in God, the world to come, and the ethical precept that one
should try to do good to one's fellow beings. At such a point, diffusiveness
of belief and infrequency of practice were taken to a point at which they

---

[8] There were also other, less orthodox, but specific, not merely diffusive, working-class religious minorities. In the first half of the century, for example, there were a number of popular
millenialist movements (for which see Harrison, 1978); and in the second half of the century
spiritualism established itself as a minority option within plebian radical circles (for which see
Barrow, 1986).

became essentially a variety of folk religion and were barely 'Christian' in any remotely traditional sense at all. It was, as Ainsworth has characterized it, 'quite simply, part of their way of life, not devout or theological religion, but a working ethical code by which life might be lived and ultimately judged' (Ainsworth, 1977, p. 367).

It is a difficult phenomenon to study because it is fundamentally elusive, imprecise and characteristically unsystematic: diffusive Christians did not (and still do not) tend to the leaving of spiritual autobiographies, and evidence of their religion is largely to be found in asides and anecdotes, and in the remarks of clergy and other observers and commentators on religious life. But the elusive and imprecise nature of such belief, and the erratic, irregular pattern of its practice, should not be allowed to obscure either its importance in the lives of those who espoused it, or its residual staying power in the allegedly secular century which has followed its late Victorian emergence. As Cox has pointed out, in the twentieth century, despite the continued decline of the churches as institutions, the continued provision for religious education in state schools in the 1902 and 1944 Education Acts, and the advent of devotional and religious broadcasting by the BBC helped to sustain a version of diffusive Christianity — even more attenuated, diluted and pluralistic, but still not negligible (Cox, p. 276). At the same time, as Gilbert has noted, whilst the role of official religion in middle-class culture has declined, the twentieth century has seen the steady extension of the influence of working-class cultural values in a society increasingly dominated by mass media and popular, commercialized leisure (Gilbert, 1976, p. 138).

The conjunction of the two processes noted by Cox and Gilbert is worth pondering. Rather as Mann's inability to interpret religion as more than church-going misled him to conclude that working-class non-church-going meant working-class indifference to religion, so many observers of the decline of official Christianity in twentieth-century Britain too easily assume that such decline also points simply to indifference. A more profitable line of enquiry might be to examine the extent to which, in the last three-quarters of a century, the middle-class backbone of Victorian Christianity has continued to move religiously, not merely in the direction of the 'unconscious Broad Churchmanship' already identified as existing in the late Victorian suburbs of London, but beyond it and into a version of the diffusive Christianity first clearly observable in the life of the Victorian working classes. If such a process has, indeed, occurred, there is a not unpleasing irony in the fact that the actual religious style of a working class long dismissed as merely 'indifferent' to religion, should in time have become the predominant — if still too little recognized — religious style of the majority of the nation as a whole.

BIBLIOGRAPHY

*A. J. Ainsworth (1977) 'Religion in the working-class community and the evolution of socialism in late nineteenth century Lancashire: a case of working-class consciousness', *Histoire Sociale — Social History*, Vol. 10, pp. 354–80.

L. Barrow (1986) *Independent Spirits: Spiritualism and English Plebeians 1850–1910*, Routledge.

D. W. Bebbington (1979) 'The city, the countryside and the social gospel in late Victorian Nonconformity' in D. Baker (ed.) *The Church in Town and Countryside*, pp. 415–26, Oxford, Blackwell.

K. M. Boyd (1980) *Scottish Church Attitudes to Sex, Marriage and the Family 1850–1914*, Edinburgh, John Donald.

C. G. Brown (1987) *The Social History of Religion in Scotland Since 1730*, Methuen.

*J. Cox (1982) *The English Churches in a Secular Society, Lambeth: 1870–1930*, Oxford, Oxford University Press.

A. D. Gilbert (1976) *Religion and Society in Industrial England: Church, Chapel and Social Change 1740–1914*, Longman.

S. Gilley (1985) 'Vulgar piety and the Brompton Oratory' in R. Swift and S. Gilley (eds.) *The Irish in the Victorian City*, Croom Helm.

R. Q. Gray (1977) 'Religion, culture and social class in late nineteenth and early twentieth century Edinburgh' in G. Crossick (ed.) *The Lower Middle Class in Britain 1870–1914*, Croom Helm.

J. F. C. Harrison (1979) *The Second Coming: Popular Millenarianism 1780–1850*, Routledge.

R. J. Helmstadter and P. T. Phillips (eds.) (1985) *Religion in Victorian Society: A Source-book of Documents*, University Press of America.

P. Horn (1976) *Labouring Life in the Victorian Countryside*, Dublin, Gill and Macmillan.

K. S. Inglis (1963) *Churches and the Working Classes in Victorian England*, Routledge.

*J. Kent (1973) 'Feelings and festivals: an interpretation of some working-class religious attitudes' in H. J. Dyos and M. Woolf (eds.) *The Victorian City*, Vol. 2., pp. 855–71, Routledge.

J. Kent (1978) *Holding the Fort: Studies in Victorian Revivalism*, Epworth.

*D. M. Lewis (1986) *Lighten Their Darkness: The Evangelical Mission to Working-Class London 1828–1860*, Greenwood Press.

S. Mayor (1967) *The Churches and the Labour Movement*, Independent Press.

H. McLeod (1973) 'Class, community and region: the religious geography of 19th century England' in M. Hill (ed.) *A Sociological Yearbook of Religion in Britain*, S. C. M. Press.

H. McLeod (1974) *Class and Region in the Late Victorian City*, Croom Helm.

H. McLeod (1977) 'White collar values and the role of religion' in G. Crossick (ed.) *The Lower Middle Class in Britain, 1870–1914*, Croom Helm.

H. McLeod (1980) 'The de-Christianization of the working classes in Western

Europe (1850–1900), *Social Compass*, Vol. 27, pp. 191–214.

H. McLeod (1981) *Religion and the People of Western Europe 1789–1970*, Oxford, Oxford University Press, Opus.

*H. McLeod (1984) *Religion and the Working Class in Nineteenth Century Britain*, Studies in Economic and Social History, Macmillan Education.

H. E. Meller (1976) *Leisure and the Changing City, 1870–1914*, Routledge.

D. E. H. Mole (1979) 'The Victorian town parish: rural vision and urban mission' in D. Baker (ed.) *The Church in Town and Countryside*, pp. 361–71, Oxford, Blackwell.

J. E. B. Munsen (1975) 'The Oxford Movement by the end of the nineteenth century: the Anglo-Catholic clergy', *Church History*, Vol. 44, pp. 382–95.

M. G. A. Ó Tuathaigh (1981) 'The Irish in nineteenth-century Britain: problems of integration', *Transactions of the Royal Historical Society*, 5th series, Vol. 31, pp. 149–74.

J. Obelkevich (1976) *Religion and Rural Society: South Lindsey 1825–75*, Oxford, Oxford University Press.

H. D. Rack (1973) 'Domestic visitation: a chapter in early nineteenth century evangelism', *Journal of Ecclesiastical History*, Vol. 24, pp. 357–76.

H. D. Rack (1983) 'Wesleyan Methodism 1849–1902' in R. Davies. A. George and G. Rupp (eds.) *A History of the Methodist Church in Great Britain*, Vol. 3, pp. 119–66, Epworth.

G. Robson (1978) 'The failures of success: working class evangelists in early Victorian Birmingham' in D. Baker (ed.) *Religious Motivation: Biographical and Sociological Problems for the Church Historian*, pp. 381–91, Oxford, Blackwell.

G. Rowell (1983) *The Vision Glorious: Themes and Personalities of the Catholic Revival in Anglicanism*, Oxford, Oxford University Press.

K. Thomas (1978) *Religion and the Decline of Magic*, Harmondsworth, Penguin.

D. M. Thompson (1972) 'The churches and society in nineteenth century England: a rural perspective' in G. J. Cumming and D. Baker (ed.) *Popular Belief and Practice*, pp. 267–76, Oxford, Blackwell.

A. Wilkinson (1978) *The Church of England and the First World War*, S.P.C.K.

N. Yates (1975) *Leeds and the Oxford Movement*, Leeds, the Thoresby Society.

S. Yeo (1976) *Religion and Voluntary Organisations in Crisis*, Croom Helm.

CHAPTER 4

The Graphic, Saturday, August 13, 1881. Mr. Bradlaugh and the House of Commons on the occasion of the attempted forcible entry. Scene on the Lobby Stairs: Mr. Bradlaugh is carried out.

ANGLICANISM, PARLIAMENT AND THE COURTS

If he'll only turn out a brave, helpful, truth-telling Englishman, and a gentleman, and a Christian, that's all I want.

(Thomas Hughes, *Tom Brown's Schooldays*, 1857)

The true man will desire to remember at every moment of his life the Scriptural precept "Be courteous".

(Frederick Temple, Bishop of Exeter, *Good Manners*, 1883)

Queen Victoria 'indicating with uplifted fan' that a sermon should stop.

(*Quarterly Review*, April 1901)

I N 1833, when Gladstone first entered Parliament as a Tory, the House of Commons consisted exclusively of Christians, almost all members of the Church of England. Degrees of the Universities of Oxford and Cambridge were barred to non-Anglicans. Civil divorce, a concept considered repugnant to Anglican doctrine, was virtually unobtainable. Publishers declined to put out such serious works as Strauss' *Life of Jesus* for fear of prosecution for blasphemy. Forty years later, by the end of Gladstone's first Liberal administration, Parliament and the Universities were open to men of all faiths (and would soon be open to men of none); and divorce was obtainable from a division of the High Court. It was possible publicly to deny the most basic tenets of Christianity and still remain within the law; and to query the accuracy and even the authority of the Bible, to doubt the reality of miracles and of hell and still remain a beneficed clergyman, and even a bishop. In its influence in state and society, the Church, though still a partner, was no longer an equal, still less a dominant partner; while the Anglican Church in Ireland was actually disestablished. To Tractarians like Pusey or Denison, the Church, through her links with an increasingly secularizing state, was being profaned and defiled; to agnostics, like Huxley or Leslie Stephen, she was being put in her place. The change was rapid, to many revolutionary. The process itself was largely the work of politicians (notably Gladstone himself), Parliament and the courts, responding to pressures and ideas from the wider community, Anglican and non-Anglican. It was an age whose belief in representative government, equality before the law, liberty of conscience and, not least, good manners and good form, ultimately outstripped its religious faith. The Victorian Church remained a national church, not because of its orthodoxy, but because it was made accountable and acceptable to the nation. Squire Brown's ambitions for young Tom mirrored the priorities of the ruling classes generally: first an Englishman, then a gentleman, finally a Christian. Establishment and the royal supremacy were the instrumentality whereby the Church was moulded to these *desiderata*. The Head of the Church could stop a sermon with her fan. Her Prime Minister appointed the bishops. Her Parliament, her Privy Council and her Courts governed, checked and influenced the Church and made it serve the nation.

I NON-CHRISTIANS IN PARLIAMENT

Few denied that England was a Christian country or — though Dissenters grumbled — that the Church of England was the national Church by law established. But what precisely did these propositions mean? At one extreme, the young Gladstone (in *The State in its Relations with the Church* (1838)), conceived, romantically, of a theocratic Britain, a confessional state governed by the moral laws and the spiritual dogmas of the Church. In such a theocracy, it followed logically that those who were not members of the national Church – Dissenters and Roman Catholics, for example – ought not, on principle, to enjoy equal civil rights with the majority who were. But the fact was that Dissenters and Catholics had just been enfranchised in the preceding era of Whig reform. Although they could not yet graduate at Oxford or Cambridge, English Nonconformists and Irish Catholics took their seats in the House of Commons alongside Anglicans, and even, as Gladstone admitted, Unitarians, 'who refuse the whole of the most vital doctrines of the Gospel' (Morley, 1903, I. p. 375). Gladstone's book, as he admitted, was politically irrelevant, out of touch with constitutional realities even when it appeared. It was ridiculed by Macaulay, for the Whigs; and the Tories themselves, traditionally devoted to the alliance of Church and State, frowned upon his chimeras.

The Jews, however, were surely a different matter. Dissenters and Catholics at least professed to be Christian. Jews professed not to be Christian. The liberal spirit of the age suggested that they continue to be tolerated; and it was admitted that City merchants like the Rothschilds or Salomons were influential whether in or out of Parliament. But could more be allowed? Could Jews be accorded equality of rights with Christians in a Christian state? It was true that from 1845 they were allowed to hold office in municipal corporations (a measure which Gladstone opposed). But being, if not anti-Christian, at least non-Christian, how could they be admitted to membership of the sovereign Christian Parliament? So at least the opposing argument went. Much was made in this and other contexts of a *dictum* of the seventeenth-century Chief Justice, Sir Matthew Hale, that Christianity is part of the law of England[1] and by Christianity was meant the law and doctrines of the Church of England. Sir Matthew had long

[1] R. v Taylor (1674) 1 Vent. 293

been the oracle of orthodox lawyers, solemnly invoked whenever questions of denominational reform were broached. Were Jews, it was asked, to be part of the English legislature, legislating for a Christian nation and possibly for the Church of England itself? The answer, said Macaulay, was that a nation of Anglicans and non-Anglicans was entitled to be represented by a Parliament of Anglicans and non-Anglicans.

Clearly, however, Jews could not take the prescribed parliamentary oath 'on the true faith of a Christian'. Did that mean that they could not lawfully sit at all? Lionel de Rothschild tried to force the issue. Elected as Member of Parliament for the City of London in 1850, he purported to take the oath, omitting the words 'on the true faith of a Christian', and was thereupon stopped from taking his seat by the formal resolution of an indignant House. The Commons was certainly within its rights. When Salomons, elected Member for Greenwich, made a similar attempt in 1851, he was removed from the Chamber by the Sergeant-at-Arms. The Old Tory, High Church stand, however, though constitutionally correct and sanctioned by the Archbishop of Canterbury, was, as Gladstone now agreed, increasingly incongruous, especially when Salomons became Lord Mayor of London in 1855. On what principle was a man entitled to sit in the Guildhall, but not at Westminster? Change could only be a matter of time. Three years later Parliament duly passed an act relieving Jewish members of the obligation to pronounce the offending words; and Rothschild, after swearing in the amended form and on the Old Testament, lawfully took his seat as the first Jewish Member of Parliament.

Nonconformists, Roman Catholics and Jews having been admitted to the Commons, what was the position of agnostics or atheists? The question imposed a strain on the feelings of most Members of Parliament, the majority, after all, belonging to the Church of England, and all professing some kind of religious belief. The strain was particularly great when incarnated in the large and provocative person of Charles Bradlaugh.[2] Elected to the Commons as member for Northampton in 1880, Bradlaugh, having made plain his lack of respect for the sanctity of the parliamentary oath, was, like Rothschild before him, forbidden by the House to swear it. If Quakers were permitted to make a simple personal affirmation without religious connotations, he objected, why not atheists? Gladstone, much as he detested Bradlaugh and atheism, could not disagree, and boldly attempted to introduce a bill to relieve unbelievers. In successive battles with the Commons, Bradlaugh, at first forcibly ejected from the Chamber and escorted to the Clock Tower by the Sergeant-at-Arms and on another occasion removed by the Metropolitan police, was in and out of the law courts.

[2] See also *RVB*, I, 8

Finally in 1888, the Commons again bowed to the inevitable, and Parliament passed the Oaths Act, whereby in lieu of an oath invoking the name of the Almighty, a solemn affirmation was permitted for all purposes where an oath is required by law. Proceedings in Parliament continued to begin with morning prayers, but these involved no verifiable test of religious belief. Thus, by the end of the period, not even a token recognition of the Deity remained a prerequisite to membership of the legislature. So far had established religion shifted to the ceremonial margin of state affairs.

II ANGLICANISM AND DIVORCE

The same process of secularization was at work at the heart of the Victorian concept of the family. If there was one thing that at first sight seemed contrary to Anglican teaching, it was divorce. *What God hath joined together, let not man put asunder* (Matthew, 19). Matrimony was an indissoluble sacrament. On the other hand it was clear from Deuteronomy, 24, that a man might put away his wife for adultery. But did putting away mean divorce, as eleven bishops argued in the House of Lords, or (as Gladstone contended) merely ecclesiastical separation *a mensa et thoro* (from bed and board), the traditional remedy of the Church courts, which fell far short of divorce and did not permit remarriage? Whatever the answer to the problems of scriptural exegesis, however, the fact was that civil divorce did take place in England, whether the Church liked it or not. Since the late seventeenth century, disgruntled noblemen had been casting off their erring or unwanted spouses by the lawful though unsanctified means of an act of Parliament. Well-known divorcees included the late King George IV and even a number of cuckolded clergymen. The Bishops, as members of the Upper House, had played their constitutional part in these legislative proceedings.

Proceedings were cumbersome and costly: first a decree from a church court of separation *a mensa et thoro*; next a civil action of 'criminal conversation' against the co-respondent; finally the passage of a bill of divorce through both Houses of Parliament. Divorce was thus available only to a wealthy and exclusive minority. The paradox was pointed in sardonic fashion by Mr Justice Maule at Warwick Assizes in 1845. Sending an impecunious bigamist to prison, he declared that want of a thousand pounds to procure a divorce by act of Parliament was no excuse for breaking the law. So glaring a discrepancy between rich and poor was at obvious odds with the Englishman's sense of fair play. The plea of Samuel Wilberforce, Bishop of Oxford, that for the sake of public morality there should continue to be one law for the rich and another for the rest, struck a note of patronising unction that partly explains his popular nickname — 'Soapy Sam'. Besides, Protestant Prussia had civil divorce. It had existed in Scotland since the Reformation. In 1853 a Royal Commission recommended wider provision for divorce in England and Wales, and Palmerston's Government laid its proposals before Parliament.

The religious outcry was tremendous. Six thousand Anglican clergymen formally protested. A lay petition attracted 90,000 signatures. The first attempt to introduce a bill was abandoned. In 1856, after passing through all stages in the Lords, another bill was disrupted by a general election. At last in 1857 it entered the statute book as the Matrimonial Causes Act. Family matters were entirely removed from the jurisdiction of the Church. Marriages in England and Wales could now be terminated other than by death or act of Parliament — through civil proceedings in the High Court; though the only grounds for divorce was adultery, which in the husband, though not the wife, had to be accompanied by some aggravating circumstance (rape, bestiality, sodomy, incest, cruelty or desertion); a case of double standards, as Gladstone rightly protested, which undermined 'the indestructible basis of the equality of the sexes under Christian Law' (Morley, 1903, I, p. 256). What really thwarted the religious opposition, however, was that the clergy were hopelessly divided on the issue. It was one thing to claim that divorce could not be contemplated in a Christian land and the cite Sir Matthew Hale. It was another to reconcile the conflicting biblical authorities. The Bishop of Oxford, for instance (and, indeed, Gladstone) were more concerned to prevent the remarriage of divorcees with their co-respondents; and the Act contained a conscience clause for clergymen reluctant to officiate at such ceremonies. But as for divorce itself, if Christianity and divorce were compatible — and most bishops and the Archbishop of Canterbury reluctantly conceded that they were — how was the average Anglican to gainsay them? Some thought that the Church had surrendered its claims to catholicity, the Roman Church continuing to impose its ancient ban upon divorce. Others, having swallowed the camel of divorce, continued to strain at the gnat of marriage with a deceased wife's sister. Such a union still fell within the 'prohibited degrees' of kinship laid down by Church and law, and the ban was not lifted until 1907.

III BLASPHEMY AND FREEDOM OF SPEECH

How far were freedom of speech and the press circumscribed by the ideology of the established Church? Until the late Victorian period, quite considerably. To deny the existence of God, the divinity of Christ or the veracity of the Bible, was held by successive judges to constitute the crime of blasphemy, though the law protected only Anglican doctrine. Non-Anglican beliefs could be attacked with impunity, and in the case of Roman Catholicism, frequently were. That the law of blasphemy was not a dead letter in mid-Victorian England is suggested by the successive convictions of Holyoake in 1842 and 1857, the conviction of Pooley in the same year (moving John Stuart Mill to protest in 1859 in *On Liberty*) and the case of *Cowan v Milbourn* in 1867. Pooley, it was true, was a simpleton and a loud-mouth, suppressed as a public nuisance rather than as a victim of Anglican zeal, while Holyoake was a militant secularist out for martyrdom, who rejected the life-lines proffered by a courteous judge. But the ruling in *Cowan v Milbourn* was a different matter.

In 1865 a Mr Cowan, secretary of the Liverpool Secular Society, hired St Anne's Assembly Rooms in that city for the purpose of delivering a course of lectures. Their subject matter, advertized outside on placards, included: 'The character and teachings of Christ; the former defective, the latter mis-leading' and 'The Bible shewn to be no more inspired than any other book.' On learning what was scheduled to take place on his premises, the scandalized proprietor, Milbourn, refused to allow them to be used. Cowan sued Milbourn for breach of contract and lost. It was held that the purpose of the contract of hire being the promotion of blasphemous doctrines, the contract was unenforceable, being void at common law for illegality. Cowan appealed to the Court of Exchequer Chamber (1867) and lost again. The conservative and septuagenarian Chief Baron Kelly, confidently invoking Sir Matthew Hale, declared: 'There is abundant authority for saying that Christianity is part and parcel of the law of the land'. From Hale he con-cluded 'that therefore to support and maintain publicly' the ideas announced on the placards was 'a violation of the first principle of the law, and cannot be done without blasphemy. I therefore do not hesitate to say [he concluded] that the defendant was not only entitled, but was called on and bound by the law, to refuse his sanction to this use of his rooms.' This trenchant and unanimous ruling was a last blast by the Old Guard: deeply unimaginative, a wholly reactionary decision, out of step with the thought even of respectable Broad Churchmen. The title of the second lecture echoed the very language used by Professor Jowett himself in his contribu-tion to *Essays and Reviews* (see below).

Even in Pooley's case (1857), a line of reasoning more in keeping with the liberal spirit of the age had been opened up when a distinction was drawn between words calculated to stir up contempt or hatred for Chris-tianity, which *were* blasphemous, and temperate expressions of personal dis-sent on religious topics, which were not. In 1883 this distinction was emphasized by Lord Chief Justice Coleridge at the trial of Ramsay and Foote, manager and editor respectively of a periodical called *The Freethinker*. The indictment for blasphemous libel alleged that they had published blas-phemous cartoons and articles. The fact of publication was not disputed. The sole point at issue was whether the material was blasphemous in law. It was certainly extremely outspoken. If Hale's well-worn *dictum* was correct, as Chief Baron Kelly had affirmed in *Cowan v Milbourn*, the guilt of the accused could not be in doubt.

But Lord Coleridge doubted whether Hale or Kelly any longer represented a true statement of the law. If the mere denial of the truths of Christianity was blasphemous, he pointed out, then, for example, a religious Jew who denied in good faith that Christ was the Messiah must *ipso facto* be guilty of blasphemy. This in Coleridge's view, was no longer the law:

> To base the prosecution of a bare denial of the truth of Christianity *simpliciter* and *per se* on the ground that Christianity is part of the law of the land ... is in my judgment a mistake. It is to forget that law grows; and that though the principles of law remain unchanged, yet (and it is one of the advantages of the common law) their application is to be changed with changing circumstances of the times. Some persons may call this retrogression, I call it progression of human opinion.

It was no longer the denial of Christianity in itself which the law aimed to suppress, but the threat which in a given order of society such a denial might pose to public order. In late Victorian England, Coleridge decided, it was perfectly safe and therefore lawful to question and even to critcise Christianity, provided that this were done in a gentlemanly way, without causing outrage to respectable members of society: 'If the decencies of controversy are observed, even the fundamentals of religion may be attacked' without the writer becoming criminally liable.

This was a revealing landmark in judicial law-making. Coleridge was ruling that the law was not, after all, concerned to uphold the teachings of the established Church, as had hitherto been supposed. Blasphemy was a question of taste, of decorum; and provided that he chose his words carefully, the most avowed atheist, the bitterest enemy of the Church, a John Stuart Mill, a Darwin, a Bradlaugh even, was free to say what he liked and to expound his un-Christian or anti-Christian heresies with impunity. What had changed, of course, as Coleridge emphasized, was the receptiveness of public opinion to new ideas. The ruling in *Ramsay and Foote* marks both the growing tolerance of educated society and the fact that more and more thinking people, some inside the Church itself, were no longer willing to accept unquestioningly the authority of particular dogmas, even though they might be the dogmas of their own faith. The courts were prepared, on the authority of the Lord Chief Justice, to stand aside, to countenance virtually unfettered freedom of expression in matters of religion and to declare that it was no business of the law to interfere unless, in effect, there was danger of public outrage or disorder. 'It cannot be doubted,' Lord Coleridge affirmed, 'that any man has a right, not merely to judge for himself on such subjects, but also, legally speaking, to publish his opinions for the benefit of others.' In the eyes of the law, then, one man's opinion was as good as another's: or at any rate each had an equal right to speak his mind. Here was a fundamental divide between Victorian society and the traditional attitudes of the Church, certainly of the High Church. 'I think that one of the great dangers of the present day,' as Pusey observed, 'is to conceive of matters of faith as if they were matters of opinion, to think all have an equal chance of being right' (Booth, 1972, p. 269). That was precisely what Lord Coleridge was declaring the attitude of the law to be.

IV   FREEDOM OF CONSCIENCE WITHIN THE CHURCH OF ENGLAND

If the law was prepared to extend freedom of expression to non-Anglicans, how did it treat ministers of the established Church? The Gorham Judgement (1850) provides the answer. Phillpotts, Bishop of Exeter, was a notorious High Churchman in a diocese where Low Church views prevailed among the clergy and where the Crown presented a living to Gorham, an outspoken Low Churchman. After probing his views on baptism, Phillpotts refused to institute Gorham to the living on the grounds that he held heretical Calvinist views. According to Phillpotts, belief in baptism as an effective means of spiritual regeneration was an essential dogma of the Church. Gorham, he alleged, regarded baptism merely as a *symbol* of regeneration. Gorham insisted on his right to the rectorship, and commenced an action in the Court of Arches, the archiepiscopal court at Canterbury. He lost. The Dean of Arches found the charge of heterodoxy proven. Gorham then appealed to the Judicial Committee of the Privy Council and won. Now the Judicial Committee ('The Queen in Council') was a secular court, whose main responsibility was to hear appeals from the colonies. Since 1832, however, it also exercised jurisdiction as court of final appeal in ecclesiastical causes in England. In this capacity, it sat with clerical assessors.

The Privy Council took a cautious view of its duties in the Gorham case. Given the controversial and divisive business before it, it was unusually chary of chancing an *obiter dictum*, of venturing an inch further than the issue demanded. A decision in favour of Phillpotts' contention might provoke defection by the Evangelicals; to come down on the side of the Low Church view would antagonize the Tractarians. Contrary to the hopes and expectations of the clergy and of Anglicans generally, High and Low, the Privy Council expressly declined to pronounce on what the religious considered the only issue that mattered — i.e. what the true doctrine on baptism was. 'This Court', declared Lord Langdale, Master of the Rolls, 'has no jurisdiction or authority to settle matters of faith.' The court made no attempt to define the Church's doctrine on baptism, since after reviewing the relevant authorities, it found their meaning vague, unclear and even inconsistent. It therefore concluded that on the subject of baptism there was legitimate scope for divergence of opinion and for private judgement. The Privy Council, then, avoided offering any opinion on the soundness or unsoundness, 'the theological correctness or error', of Gorham's opinions. The sole question in law was whether Phillpotts had shown sufficient cause for excluding Gorham from the living; and this depended on whether Gorham's beliefs offended against the doctrines laid down in the Church's Articles and Formularies. The Privy Council applied, in the normal manner of a secular court, the regular, commonsense, canons of construction, giving words their natural and ordinary meaning and holding to a robustly liberal approach: 'we consider that it is not the duty of any court to be minute and rigid in cases of this sort'. It quoted with approval a precedent of 1809 that 'if any Article is really a subject of dubious interpretation, it would be highly improper that this Court should fix on one meaning, and prosecute all those who hold a contrary opinion'. It decided by a majority that whatever the theological rights or wrongs of Gorham's beliefs, they were not necessarily incompatible with the Articles; and it ordered Phillpotts to institute him to the living.

The scandal was enormous (especially when Phillpotts refused to institute Gorham and threatened to excommunicate anyone who did, including the Archbishop of Canterbury). However much the Privy Council insisted that it was not attempting to define doctrine, what was clear to the clergy was that Gorham's beliefs had been pronounced heretical by a consecrated bishop and by the Court of Arches, and non-heretical by the Privy Council. A state institution, a secular body of laymen, had quashed the verdict of the highest ecclesiastical court. A civil court, which contained a variety of religious opinion and which could theoretically include non-Anglicans and which did include lawyers unversed in ecclesiastical law, had dictated to the Church of England, as it seemed, on a question of holy doctrine. For some High Churchmen, like Manning, this demonstration of Erastianism at work — 'the fact that such a case is to be decided by such a court' (Nockles, 1983, p. 285) — was the final straw. Bishop Wilberforce seethed against 'this vile judgement' (Wilberforce, 1881, p. 41). Gladstone himself was stunned. The Privy Council, in his view, had denied the efficacy of a sacrament and tainted the catholicity of Anglicanism. It undercut these objections somewhat that the Archbishops of Canterbury and York both attended the proceedings of the Privy Council as non-voting technical advisers (together with the Bishop of London) and the Archbishops (though not the Bishop) approved its findings. For those who felt more Anglican than the Archbishops, the path to Rome seemed the only way out. For Low Churchmen and Broad Churchmen, by contrast, the assent of the Archbishops confirmed that on matters of doctrine there was room for more than one voice; and they approved the ruling of the Judicial Committee as vindicating Protestant freedom of conscience against episcopal authority.

A dozen years later the Judicial Committee again adjudicated in the notorious dispute sparked off by the publication of *Essays and Reviews*. The aim of its clerical contributors was to encourage free discussion of Biblical questions in the light of contemporary scholarship. Professor Jowett, the Greek scholar, stated that the Bible should be read critically — 'like any other book.' Professor Baden Powell, Fellow of the Royal Society, suggested the need to test biblical miracles by the criteria of science. The Reverend Henry Wilson argued against literal belief in eternal damnation. The Reverend Rowland Williams, Professor of Hebrew at Lampeter, urged a view of the Prophets as moralists rather than fortune-tellers. It was the intention of these eminently respectable and well-meaning authors to reconcile Christianity with modern thought rather than to provoke a scandal; but their views plainly clashed with orthodox and fundamentalist belief in the literal truth, historical and scientific, of the Bible. Moreover, *Essays and Reviews* appeared at a peculiarly sensitive moment for the Church — immediately after the publication of Darwin's *Origin of Species*. Churchmen and Bishops, High and Low, agreed that a stand must be taken against what they saw as incitement from within the Church itself to heresy and free thought. Wilberforce, fresh from a public attack on Huxley and Darwinism, leaped to the defence of orthodoxy.[3]

The Archbishop of Canterbury denounced *Essays and Reviews* as irreconcilable with membership of holy orders, and called upon its authors to resign their benefices. When they declined, an action for heresy was commenced in the Court of Arches against two of the six, both practising ministers — Wilson, who had edited the collection, and Rowland Williams. Dr Lushington, Dean of Arches, found for the prosecution, though his judgement was moderate and circumspect and he gave them the benefit of the doubt on all counts but two; but he convicted them on two crucial points of doctrine, holding it unlawful for an Anglican clergyman to deny either the literal truth of Scripture or the doctrine of damnation. Both defendants were sentenced to a year's suspension from office. Both appealed to the Judicial Committee.

As in the Gorham judgement, to which it referred as a precedent, the Privy Council again (1864) took the view that it was not its task to elucidate what the doctrines of the Church ought to be or even what they were; only to decide whether the views complained of were or were not consonant with those doctrines as defined in the Articles. Giving judgement, the Lord Chancellor, Lord Westbury adopted a broad and liberal approach to the Articles, declining to treat their 'language as implying more than is expressed' or 'ascribing to them conclusion ... involving minute and subtle matters of controversy' (Brodrick, 1865, p. 287). Without

[3] See *RVB*, I, 1

venturing any theological opinions, the Judicial Committee held that the appellants' views, fairly construed, were not necessarily incompatible with the Articles. Wilson and Rowland Williams were acquitted on all counts. Their sentences were quashed and they were awarded costs.

For High Church and Low, this was another singularly disillusioning verdict, 'this soul-destroying judgement' (Booth, 1972, p. 267) lamented Pusey, speaking for those who had again hoped from the Privy Council for a clear pronouncement on doctrine analogous to a papal pronouncement *ex cathedra*. The dissent of the Archbishops of York and Canterbury, sitting again on the Judicial Committee as assessors, made no legal difference to the verdict (and even the moral impact of their dissent was lessened by the concurrence in the verdict of Bishop Campbell Tait of London). Nor was the post-trial condemnation of *Essays and Reviews* by both Houses of Convocation at Canterbury, though impressive as an expression of strength of feeling among the clergy, of any legal effect, any more than a letter of protest to the Archbishop of Canterbury, drafted by Denison and Pusey and signed by eleven thousand clergymen. The law compelled the Church to be tolerant. The Privy Council, joked a future lord of appeal, 'dismissed Hell with costs and took away from orthodox members of the Church of England their last hope of everlasting damnation'. Lord Westbury poured scorn on Convocation and Wilberforce. More distressing for the orthodox was the fact that the Court of Arches, the highest repository of learning in Church law, had again been overruled by a secular court, 'a court,' complained Denison, 'which is not only incompetent, but morally and religiously unfit to decide', and that the united protests of both Houses of Convocation counted for nothing.

What made the *Essays and Reviews* controversy especially scandalous was that all the contributors but one were ordained clergymen. The next great issue to involve the Privy Council concerned the beliefs of a bishop, no less. John Colenso, Broad Church Bishop of Natal, agreed in a rather literal-minded way with Professor Jowett that the Bible should be approached critically. A one-time Cambridge mathematician and author of arithmetical textbooks, he went over the figures and dimensions in the Old Testament and found that they did not make sense. He also argued that the Pentateuch could not be entirely the work of Moses. In addition he expressed disbelief in eternal damnation and substitutionary atonement. His writings on these subjects were duly condemned by Convocation. Metropolitan Bishop Gray of Cape Town, a Tractarian, deeply worried by the challenge to orthodoxy posed by *Essays and Reviews*, instituted heresy proceedings against Colenso in his episcopal court at Cape Town, found him guilty and deposed him from his see. Colenso, who refused to attend these proceedings, thereupon appealed to the Privy Council; not, this time, in its ecclesiastical capacity, but as final court of appeal in colonial matters.

Lord Westbury, giving judgement on the purely technical issue of jurisdiction, and without touching on theology, found that Gray had no legal authority over Colenso, whose purported dismissal was therefore null and void (1865). Colenso returned to Natal, and continued to preach and publish his controversial beliefs, notwithstanding the fact that Gray, with the approval of Convocation, had excommunicated him and appointed a replacement. Awkward encounters between the rival bishops ensued in the cathedral precincts.

Once again episcopal authority and the verdict of Convocation had been flouted and set aside by a secular court. The Judicial Committee had side-stepped the only issue which mattered to the orthodox: were Colenso's views heretical or were they not? Convocation had unequivocally condemned them. The decision of the Judicial Committee left Colenso free to resume his diocesan functions in Natal and to defy his metropolitan bishop, from whom he derived his spiritual authority and whom he had sworn to obey. Once again the dilemma for High and Low Church was acute. To whom did their first loyalty lie: to the Judicial Committee of the Privy Council or to the Bishops and the Court of Arches? To the Queen in Council or to the Convocation of Canterbury? If to the Queen, was the Church of England tainted with heresy? If to Convocation, was not the case for disestablishment irrefutable? 'Either the Privy Council would destroy the Church', wrote Gray to Keble, 'or the Church must destroy the Privy Council' (Selbourne, 1898, p. 477).

The Gorham judgement, *Essays and Reviews* and the Colenso case go to emphasize the same point. In none of these cases was the Privy Council concerned with theological truth. For Phillpotts, Wilberforce, Gray and for Convocation, the verdicts were a monstrous evasion of the issue. What they wanted — and what the Privy Council refused to provide — was a clear decision between two antithetical theological opinions, one of which, in the view of the orthodox, must be true and the other false, 'to have it adjudged by Law,' as Pusey said, 'whether one is teaching according to the doctrine which one has professed' (Booth, 1972, p. 266). True to the tradition of the common law, the Privy Council invariably preferred to give the appellant the benefit of the doubt, except where he had demonstrably put himself in the wrong (as in the case of the Reverend Voysey (1871), who denied the divinity of Christ). Save in such extreme instances, the Privy Council was reluctant to penalize intellectual integrity and honest difference of opinion in hearings which were, as Lord Westbury observed, 'in the nature of criminal proceedings' (Brodrick, 1865, p. 281), and where a clergyman's livelihood depended on the outcome. Doctrinally, it seemed to follow that ministers of the Church of England were free to believe as much or as little as they chose. From this lack of spiritual authority in the Church, or, as many Tractarians saw it, this usurpation of spiritual authority by the state, some followed Manning into the Church of Rome. Those High Churchmen who remained, men like Pusey, Keble and Denison, had to live with agonising qualms, and even to contemplate disestablishment as a possible solution for a Church, in the words of the hymn,

> sore opprest
> By schisms rent assunder
> By heresies distresst.[4]

The High Churchmen began from a set of general propositions and attempted to translate them into the language of practical conclusions. Their method was deductive. They believed in the Church of England as part of a universal catholic church possessed of eternal truths — the existence of God as creator, the divine inspiration of the Bible, the efficacy of the sacraments. The problems began when they tried to vindicate these general propositions by insisting on uniformity of belief. Such an attitude began to look bigoted and even absurd to an age that not merely had its doubts, but had a high regard for intellectual honesty. While at the beginning of the period, the sceptics and Bible critics were under a cloud, by the 1860s embarrassment was being caused by the attempts of the High Church party under such zealots as Bishop Wilberforce to suppress intellectual dissent. The 'honest doubters' were now among the respectable. As Lord Coleridge remarked in *Ramsay and Foote*: 'There is a grave, an earnest, a reverent, I am almost tempted to say, a religious tone in the very attacks on Christianity itself, which shows that what it is aimed at is not insult to the opinions of the majority of Christians, but a real, quiet, honest pursuit of truth'. Among the respectable and respected supporters of *Essays and Reviews* and Bishop Colenso were Lyell, Darwin, Huxley, Dickens, Trollope, Matthew Arnold and George Eliot.

V   THE CHURCH OF ENGLAND AS A NATIONAL INSTITUTION

Parliament and the courts strove to keep an acceptable balance between Church and state and within the Church. In 1874 Parliament attempted to curb High Church romanizing ritualism through a Public Worship Regulation Act. Several Tractarian clergymen were prosecuted under the act and removed by a lay judge. Here Parliament went too far; and when it became clear that a succession of trials and prison sentences served only to make martyrs of sincere and respected priests, the Act fell into disfavour and abeyance.[5] It emphasized, however, what was expected of the Church.

[4] S. J. Stone, 'The Church's One Foundation', 1866

[5] See *RVB*, I, 1, section III

What Parliament wanted, what the judges wanted, (and behind them what the great Victorian middle classes wanted) indeed what the Church itself wanted (for the High Church was not the whole Church) — was a *via media* — a sensible, reasonable, respectable, accommodating sort of Church, steering a safe course past the three sirens of Rome, Calvinism and unbelief.

Such a concept was anathema to those who took religion literally: who, like the Tractarians, thought of Anglicanism as Christ's apostolic Church on earth, or who, like the Evangelicals, read the Bible as history or science. Those whose conscience could not be reconciled with the comprehensiveness now required of the Church of England, left or called for disestablishment, complaining that the Church had been reduced to 'practically a subdivision of the Home Office for the promotion of morals' (Parry, 1986, p. 90). The majority stayed on. The Church of England survived, internally a collection of warring parties, none strong enough to oust the others. What kept its lay members together is difficult to pinpoint: for some, it was doctrine, for others, an improving moral ethic, for others beauty of language, liturgy and hymnody. For many, no doubt, 'churchgoing was a social or tribal act' (Parry, 1986, p. 78). Critics complained that the Church was all things to all men: its defenders praised its tolerance and comprehensiveness.

The career and changing attitudes of that long-lived and central Victorian — Gladstone — mirror the displacement of the Church in the nation's life to which he himself contributed. The young Tractarian of the Romantic Revival first conceived of a confessional church, national and theocratic: an Englishman is by definition a member of this church. As a practising politician albeit always a High Churchman, he came to see and to accept the unfairness of Anglican privilege in a society which included Catholics, Dissenters and Jews, whose full civil emancipation he was logically compelled to approve. 'We cannot', he agreed, 'compatibly with entire justice and fairness refuse to admit them' (Morley, 1903, I, p. 375). As a Liberal statesman reliant on Nonconformist support he could not reconcile the artificial domination of the Anglican Church with the fact of denominational pluralism and strove to remove those aspects of establishment which offended most. He co-operated with Nonconformists in the struggle for the abolition of compulsory Church rates, in the removal of religious tests at the universities, and in the Education Act of 1870, which provided for non-denominational religious instruction in schools. The logic of his convictions brought him to the radical and heroic step of disestablishing the Anglican Church of Ireland, 'the discharge', as he put it, 'of a debt of civil justice' (*ibid*, p. 258). The task, however, could not be done except by virtue of Establishment — through Parliament's legislative powers over the Church; and the bill, as he said, could not succeed in Parliament without the votes of non-Anglicans, of 'Scotch presbyterians, English and Welsh nonconformists and Irish Roman Catholics' (Morley, II, p. 259).

After disestablishment in Ireland, Gladstone could not but concede the principle of disestablishment in Wales and Scotland, and even predicted its inevitability in England. Religion, though always of central importance to him personally, ceased early in his career to be a matter of discriminating against non-Anglicans. He came irresistibly to the conclusion that forms of confession were and ought rightly to be matters of individual conscience. The established Church, though still the expression of the word of God, had also to be viewed pragmatically as part of the wider social, institutional and political fabric. Hale's *dictum*, so often and as Lord Coleridge observed, 'so glibly cited', that Christianity is part of the law of England, now required a broad and liberal construction. The nation was still overwhelmingly Christian, in the sense that its ways of thinking were deeply infused with Christian values, permeating society afresh through the public schools at one end and the board schools at the other. 'We are still a Christian people' (Butler, 1982, p. 226) Gladstone declared in 1868. But Christian values were not peculiar or exclusive to the established Church, still less to any one party in the Church. The only logical response for practical statesmen — short of disestablishment — was for the State to hold the ring in a pluralist society and to abandon the pretence to a monopoly of religious truth, 'to deal liberally with religious communities,' as Gladstone said, 'and give them all fair play' (Ramm, 1985, pp. 336–7). Establishment kept the Church out of the hands of extremists, High or Low, while keeping moderates of both persuasions within the fold. It guaranteed a workable measure of freedom of conscience. Through the Public Worship Regulation Act (1874), it attempted to control ritualism without persecuting it, and through the very failure of the Act, the bounds of toleration of High Church practices were in fact extended.[6]

The late Victorian Church thus remained part of the social, cultural and moral life of the nation, but its influence was increasingly peripheral. It no longer commanded authority in science or even necessarily in ethics. Year by year it was forced to yield to the logic of events, to bow to the political demands of the Nonconformists and to concede the liberal arguments of the Macaulays, the John Stuart Mills, the Huxleys and the Matthew Arnolds. Clashes between High Church, Low Church or Broad Church provided the occasion for legal rulings, milestones along the road of secularization. The explanation behind these rulings was an altered perspective in society's sense of truth and more especially in its sense of fair play. In the eyes of more and more thinking people, the Church (still less any one sect within

[6] See *RVB*, I, 1, section III

it) could no longer claim to dictate the beliefs of a whole nation as of right. Gladstone promoted the religious equivalent of Free Trade and *laissez-faire* in calling for 'plenary religious freedom' and inviting the various Churches and denominations to 'stand simply upon their merits before the world' (Ramm, 1985, p. 337).

A necessary guarantee of the national Church under challenge from inside and out was the diplomatic poise of its leaders. Among the qualities sought by Gladstone when shortlisting episcopal candidates (he recommended twelve bishops in his first administration alone) were 'tact and courtesy in dealings with men. Knowledge of the world. Accomplishments and literature. An equitable spirit . . . Some legal habit of mind. Circumspection.' These he wished to see combined with 'liberal sentiments on public affairs'. Above all, 'a representative character with reference to shades of opinion fairly allowable in the Church' (Morley, 1903, II, p. 431). These were certainly social and political virtues of a high order. But were they, wondered Denison and the Puseyites, apostolic? Were the qualities desirable in a candidate for the headship of Rugby or membership of the Athenaeum precisely those that should distinguish the successors of St Peter and St Augustine? The answer, as Disraeli, no less than Gladstone, insisted was that they were indispensable, especially in a primate, if the Church was both to hold together internally and to maintain public acceptability. Warning the Queen against her favourite, Campbell Tait, the Broad Church Bishop of London, Disraeli professed to see in him 'a strange fund of enthusiasm, a quality which ought never to be possessed by an Archbishop of Canterbury' (Marsh, 1969, p. 16). But the Queen's judgement was better, and it prevailed. In 1868 Tait was raised to Canterbury in preference to the abrasive Wilberforce. To Victoria, Tait was 'everything that she liked best in a clergyman — a Scot, a Protestant, earnest about the work of the Church without being fanatical about its rights, liberal in taking account of contemporary laymen's feelings without being controversially theological' (Edwards, 1984, p. 211). Tait was a scholar and a gentleman, Jowett's former tutor at Balliol, and Dr Arnold's successor at Rugby. Tactful, sensible and accommodating, he had proved sympathetic to the Divorce Bill in the Lords and was to prove equally co-operative over Irish disestablishment. A convinced Erastian, he approved the link with the State as the means, the providential means, of saving the Church.

It was on similar criteria that Frederick Temple, Tait's successor at Rugby and a contributor to *Essays and Reviews*, no less, became Phillpotts' successor as Bishop of Exeter on Gladstone's recommendation in 1869. The appointment provoked Denison to demand immediate disestablishment, and was thought by Pusey (described by Gladstone as 'rabid' (Morley, 1903, II, p. 432)) to surpass 'in its frightful enormity anything which has been openly done by any Prime Minister' (Chadwick, 1966–70, II, pp. 86–

7). Temple made an excellent incumbent, however (as was to be expected of the author of an essay on *Good Manners*), and the man once denounced by Convocation as a heretic went on to become Bishop of London and eventually — just in time to attend the Queen's Diamond Jubilee — Primate of All England. Patronage, pragmatism, political tact and fair play, not theological rigour or espiscopal zeal, kept the Church of England safe from harm, or at any rate from the extremes of disestablishment or disintegration. Though its critics, High and Low, questioned its doctrinal soundness, the Church survived, under the watchful eye of its headmasterly prelates, sensible men of what Bishop Ellicott of Gloucester called 'Christian good humour and moderation', its zealots kept in check by Parliament and the courts. Gladstone was surely right in feeling that the Church of England retained a place in the nation's affections. Certainly a private motion in favour of disestablishment was heavily defeated in the Commons in 1871, 1872 and 1873. In a moral, social and aesthetic sense, the Church remained, if not altogether a national church, at least a national institution.

BIBLIOGRAPHY

S. P. Booth (1969) '"Essays and Reviews": the controversy as seen in the correspondence and papers of Dr E. B. Pusey and Archbishop Archibald Tait', *Historical Magazine of the Protestant Episcopal Church*, Vol. 38, pp. 259–79.

G. C. Brodrick and W. H. Fremantle (eds.) (1865) *A Collection of the Judgements of the Judicial Committee of the Privy Council in Ecclesiastical Cases*, John Murray.

P. Butler (1982) *Gladstone, Church, State and Tractarianism: A Study of his Religious Ideas and Attitudes 1809–1859*, Oxford, Oxford University Press.

*O. Chadwick (1966–70) *The Victorian Church*, 2 Vols., A. & C. Black.

*A. O. J. Cockshut (1959) *Anglican Attitudes: A Study of Victorian Religious Controversies*, Collins.

D. L. Edwards (1984) *Christian England, Vol. II: From the Eighteenth Century to the First World War*, Collins.

A. Horstmann (1985) *Victorian Divorce*, New York, St Martin's Press.

P. J. Jagger (ed.) (1985) *Gladstone, Politics and Religion*, Macmillan.

G. I. T. Machin (1987) *Politics and the Churches in Great Britain 1869 to 1921*, Oxford, Oxford University Press.

*P. T. Marsh (1969) *The Victorian Church in Decline: Archbishop Tait and The Church of England 1869–1882*, Routledge.

J. Morley (1903) *The Life of William Ewart Gladstone*, Vols. 1 to 3, Macmillan.

P. Nockles (1983) 'Pusey and the question of church and state,' in P. Butler (ed.) *Pusey Rediscovered*, pp. 255–97, S.P.C.K.

J. P. Parry (1986) *Democracy and Religion: Gladstone and the Liberal Party 1867–1875*, Cambridge, Cambridge University Press.

A. Ramm (1985) 'Gladstone's religion', *The Historical Journal*, Vol. 28, pp. 327–40.

D. Schreuder (1979) 'Gladstone and the conscience of the State' in P. Marsh (ed.) *The Conscience of the Victorian State*, pp. 73–134, Harvester.

Lord Selborne (1898) *Memorials, Family and Personal*, Vol. 2, Macmillan.

T. J. Toohey (1987) 'Blasphemy in nineteenth-century England: the Pooley Case and its background', *Victorian Studies*, Vol. 30, pp. 315–33.

R. C. Wilberforce (1881) *Life of the Right Reverend Samuel Wilberforce*, Vol. 2, John Murray.

CHAPTER 5

DR. CHALMERS

CHURCH AND STATE IN VICTORIAN SCOTLAND: DISRUPTION AND REUNION

O N 18th May 1843 the retiring Moderator of the Church of
Scotland, David Welsh, and the dominating figure in Scottish
religious life in the first half of the nineteenth century, Thomas
Chalmers, led a procession of ministers and elders out of the General
Assembly of the Church of Scotland then meeting in St Andrews Church,
Edinburgh. Joined by other ministers and elders sympathetic to their cause
(but not elected to the General Assembly and therefore waiting outside)
they walked in procession to Tanfield Hall, where they constituted themselves the first General Assembly of the Free Church of Scotland, appointed
Chalmers as their Moderator, and signed an 'Act of Separation and Deed
of Demission' by which they separated from the established Church of
Scotland and renounced all rights and emoluments to which they had
been entitled by their previous association with the Church. In all some
454 ministers out of a total of 1,195 left the Church of Scotland for the
Free Church, along with all 14 overseas missionaries, 194 probationary
ministers, and approximately 40% of the laity (Brown, 1982, pp. 335–6).

This Disruption of the Church of Scotland was the climax of some ten
years of ongoing and increasing division *within* the established church and
of steadily worsening relations *between* the dominant faction within the
Church of Scotland and the state in its attitude to the church. Together
with the Oxford Movement in England a decade earlier, the Disruption was
one of two fundamental crises in church-state relations which occurred in
the second quarter of the nineteenth century in the wake of the 'constitutional revolution' of 1828–9 and the beginning of the movement in Victorian Britain towards a state which was constitutionally pluralist in
matters of religion.

The Scottish Disruption was also an important — although often
neglected — influence upon English Nonconformity, and was undoubtedly
the greatest single upheaval in the *ecclesiastical* life of Victorian Scotland,
perhaps indeed in the *religious* life of Victorian Scotland as a whole.[1] Yet,
within a hundred years, the division created at the Disruption had been
ended; the Free Church was itself no more (save for a small Continuing
Free Church, popularly known as the Wee Frees, and largely confined to
the Highlands and Islands); and Scottish Presbyterianism was substantially
reunified within a reformed religious establishment which enjoyed a more
clearly defined and stable relationship with the state than that of the established Church of England south of the border. The process of Disruption,
Victorian rivalry, and post-Victorian reunion therefore merits examination
as a particularly dramatic example of the potential tensions and realign-

---

[1] Although the latter is a more complex question, another contender for the role being the
immense growth in Scottish Roman Catholicism on which see, briefly, *RVB*, I, 4 and further
references there.

ments which could occur in the interrelationships of church, dissent, state and society in Victorian Britain.

I THE ORIGINS OF DISRUPTION

It would be convenient if the Disruption of the Church of Scotland in 1843 could be adequately explained simply in terms of the emergence within the church of two parties — one Moderate, the other Evangelical — the coming to power of the latter, the development of a controversy over patronage, and the eventual secession of the Evangelicals because the state denied the church a proper spiritual independence. Such conveniently neat historical explanations are seldom to be had, however, and certainly are not available in the case of the Scottish Disruption, although elements of this simple approach — the existence of Evangelical and Moderate conflict, the coming to power of an Evangelical majority in the General Assembly, the clash of church and state — remain integral to more complex (and therefore more adequate) versions of the story.

The appropriate starting point for a discussion of the events which eventually led to the Disruption in 1843 is not the division within the Church of Scotland between Evangelicals and Moderates, but rather the emergence in the 1820s of a concerted attack on the whole principle of church establishment from the various groups which together made up Scottish Dissent. The formation of the United Secession Church in 1820 out of groups of eighteenth-century seceders from the Church of Scotland signalled a new vitality in Scottish Dissent. Both the Dissenting Presbyterian groups out of which the United Secession Church was now formed combined Presbyterian church order and Voluntaryism. Moreover, as well as these Presbyterian opponents of church establishment there were also the other *non*-Presbyterian Scottish Nonconformist churches, all of which took a Voluntary stance.

In 1824 the Rev. John Ballantyne of the United Secession Church presented a forceful statement of the Voluntary principle in his *Comparison of Established and Dissenting Churches*, and in 1829 Andrew Marshall, also a minister of the United Secession Church, preached, and subsequently published, an even more effective critique of establishment in his sermon *Ecclesiastical Establishments Considered*. Establishment, Marshall argued, fostered religious exclusiveness, led to persecution, created resentment among those excluded from it, secularized the church, and discouraged Christian liberality and generosity (Cheyne, 1985, p. 22). Marshall's sermon, coming in the wake of the religious-constitutional reforms of 1828–9, inspired the formation of local Voluntary Societies, a central Voluntary organization, and much political lobbying. The 1832 Reform Act then raised the political hopes of Scottish Voluntaryists, who duly increased

their campaigns against establishment and for relief of dissenting disabilities.[2]

Faced with such challenges, members of the Church of Scotland, both
Evangelical and Moderate, defended religious establishment. In particular,
both parties agreed not only on the *principle* of establishment but on the
desirability of programmes of church extension to secure the building of
new churches and thereby the more effective *functioning* of establishment.
The Evangelicals, however, also advocated two further measures for the
revival and greater efficiency of the church: first, the reform of patronage so
as to give the members of local parishes the right to reject a minister
appointed by a patron but to whom they objected; and second, the extension to ministers of chapels of ease (that is to say, churches built in areas
lacking adequate church accommodation but without an official
territorially-defined parish of their own), of the right, enjoyed by parish
ministers, to be members of Presbyteries, Synods and the General
Assembly. On these latter points the Moderates were opposed to reform.

The position of the reforming Whig government, meanwhile, was
necessarily complicated by the politics of the post-Reform Act era: Dissenting votes mattered and establishment could not be favoured — or at
least not much — if Dissent were not to be alienated. The tendency of
government, therefore, was to resist aid for church extension, reform of
patronage and extension of full ministerial rights to the ministers of chapels
of ease. Evangelicals and Moderates were jointly frustrated on the first
count. On the second and third counts, Evangelical frustration with the
state was heightened, but Moderate opinion was placated. Thus the
mixture of theological party interests, ecclesiastical politics and national
politics was a good deal more complex than a straightforward 'Evangelicals
versus Moderates, church versus state,' interpretation of the Disruption
would allow.

The Church of Scotland General Assembly of 1834 was to prove, in
retrospect, a crucial one. It was the first General Assembly in which the
Evangelicals had a clear majority and they passed three Acts of central
importance to the development of the Church of Scotland in the 1830s and
the eventual occurrence of the Disruption. The Veto Act allowed the
majority of the male heads of families in communion with the church in a
particular parish to reject the minister nominated by the patron of the
parish. The Chapels Act granted chapels of ease the status of parish
churches. They received territorial boundaries, were to hold Kirk Sessions,
and their clergy were to be granted membership of Presbytery, Synod and
General Assembly. By a third Act of the General Assembly, meanwhile, the

---

[2] Their disabilities were less than those of English Nonconformists but sufficient nonetheless to
foster militancy, for details, see Machin, 1977, pp. 114–15.

existing Church Accommodation Committee was enlarged, instructed to organize a new church-building campaign, and supplemented by a new Church Endowments Committee with instructions to seek government aid for the endowment of the new churches which the Assembly wished to see erected. Thomas Chalmers was appointed convenor of the Church Accommodation Committee and at once set about organizing a network of local societies for church extension at city, parish and neighbourhood level. Within a year Chalmers was able to report some £65,626 raised in subscriptions and sixty-four new churches either built or in process of building. At the 1835 General Assembly the Church Accommodation and Church Endowment Committees were combined to form the Church Extension Committee with Chalmers as convener. Chalmers was thereby made the single most powerful voice in the Church of Scotland, the head of a powerful Committee with a national network of sub-committees, and the Church's chief negotiator with the government.

Chalmers was a convinced, enthusiastic, indeed passionate, advocate of religious establishment. His entire religious and social vision — with its deep concern for the poor (and especially the urban poor), its belief in the redeeming potential of the 'principle of locality' and the practice of 'enlightened philanthropy', its conviction that irreligion and poverty were the chief evils of the day and the former the chief cause of the latter, and its certainty that only the successful application of the traditional Presbyterian parochial ideal of the 'godly commonwealth' could salvage human dignity out of the slums of industrialization — depended upon the principle of an established church and its efficient functioning. Only by a successful national application of the parochial ideal, Chalmers believed, could modern post-industrial revolution Scotland be redeemed. He consequently spent much of the 1830s writing, lecturing and campaigning for church extension and the effective application of the establishment principle. Under his leadership the Church Extension Committee had funded the building of 187 new churches by 1838. The aims of the Committee, he said in his first address as convenor, were to make the Church of Scotland 'a sufficiently thick-set Establishment ... [with] ... churches so multiplied and parochial charges so sub-divided, that there will not one poor family be found in our land who might not, if they will, have entry and accommodation in a place of worship and religious instruction, with such a share in the personal attentions of the clergyman as to claim him for an acquaintance and a friend' (quoted in Cheyne, 1985, p. 25). Chalmers led the same committee in lobbying Parliament for state funds for church extension and endowment. He also repeatedly reiterated his commitment to the parochial ideal as an instrument of social improvement, and in 1838 he delivered, in London, at the invitation of a group of Anglican laymen, a series of *Lectures on the Establishment and Extension of National Churches.*

Chalmers' 1838 lectures in London were an outstanding success with his pro-establishment audience and within a year over 8,000 copies had been printed. Opponents of establishment in England, however, were less pleased, published replies and critical reviews, and arranged a reply from a Scottish Congregationalist in 1839. Many High Churchmen found him weak on the doctrine and theology of church-state relations, the young Gladstone, for example, being moved to write his own defence of religious establishment in his *The State in its Relations with the Church*. There was, as Stewart Brown has pointed out, nothing new in Chalmers' 1838 lectures. He merely presented again his ideal of the godly commonwealth and his understanding of establishment as an endowed institution providing 'ducts of conveyance' for the spiritual and moral 'irrigation' of the nation, but did so with an intensity born of the hectic church extension campaign in which he was involved and a conviction that without such moral and spiritual instruction the social order was threatened by the growing disaffection of the working classes. He justified establishment on the grounds that the state had a duty to educate its people and that that duty included adequate religious, and hence moral, provision and oversight. The mission to the poor in particular required an established church, for only by means of a national and territorially based church — supported by the state and not the mere supply and demand of the Voluntary principle — could adequate numbers of churches and ministers be supplied in poor areas (Brown, 1982, pp. 269–71).

There is a certain poignancy about Chalmers' *Lectures* of 1838, for by then it was becoming clear that this ardent defender of the principle of establishment was leading a party within the church whose deeply-held convictions were at odds with the policies and pragmatism of contemporary government. On two fronts the Acts passed by the 1834 General Assembly had already met or were meeting with defeat. The legality of the Veto Act had been challenged by Moderates as early as 1834 in the Auchterarder case, in which a patron's nominee, Robert Young, rejected by a majority of male heads of families then took his case to the Scottish civil courts, which eventually decided in 1838 in his favour and against the Act. The 1838 General Assembly appealed to the House of Lords on the issue and in 1839 the Lords upheld the decision of the Scottish courts, thus confirming a fundamental clash of civil and ecclesiastical jurisdictions.

By 1839, moreover, a further long and complex case concerning the Veto Act was causing Moderate and Evangelical lines to harden within the General Assembly. In 1837 the parish of Marnoch in the Presbytery of Strathbogie vetoed a Moderate patron's nominee, John Edwards. The predominantly Moderate Presbytery proposed to institute Edwards nonetheless, whereupon the General Assembly ordered the Act obeyed and the Presbytery capitulated, only to reverse their decision and ordain Edwards once he secured a ruling in the civil courts against the Veto Act. The Assembly then suspended the ordaining ministers, who in their turn gained a civil court ruling against the Assembly. Edwards was eventually inducted to his parish in January 1841, whereupon, in a dramatic local prefiguring of the Disruption, the majority of his congregation left the church, built their own church and appointed a minister. The Evangelical majority in the General Assembly then proceeded to depose from the ministry the seven Moderate ministers who had ordained Edwards, despite civil rulings that they were not entitled to do so and despite the open sympathy of leading Moderates for the seven ministers. The whole saga resulted in the respective positions of Moderates and Evangelicals becoming more entrenched, to the point, indeed, of Chalmers and other Evangelical leaders beginning to speak in late 1841 and early 1842 of the possibility of Disruption. Indeed, in Stewart Brown's judgement, the deposition of the Strathbogie seven was the point at which the Disruption became inevitable, the question rapidly becoming not whether it would occur but what the scale would be (Brown, 1982, pp. 322–4).

The response of the courts and government to the Veto Act was not, however, the only indication of the coming deadlock between church and state which was already evident by the time Chalmers lectured on establishment in 1838. Church extension was an equal problem. Chalmers and his Church Extension Committee had failed to secure the government support which they requested and which Chalmers believed it essential for the state to provide in order that the church might fulfil its proper role in Scottish life. The initial government response to the Church of Scotland's request in 1834 for funds for church extension was to set up a Royal Commission. It reported in 1838 and was mindful of the opposition of Scottish Dissent to the provision of greater support for the established church. It also produced ambiguous findings: there *was* inadequate church accommodation, but what there was already was insufficiently used. The government offered limited help for church extension in the Highlands, but refused help in the towns, which, for the Church of Scotland, was the real point of the exercise.

II THE DISRUPTION

Between 1839 and 1842 Chalmers was active in continuing negotiations with the government in respect of both the patronage issue and church extension, but it became increasingly clear that progress satisfactory to Evangelical opinion would not be forthcoming. The government it seemed might offer some concessions on patronage in return for the church's submission to its authority. An emerging 'middle-party' in the General Assembly meanwhile sought to avoid the rapidly hardening extremes of

Evangelical and Moderate opinion. Chalmers and other Evangelical leaders (many of them younger and more rigidly Evangelical than Chalmers himself) were now beyond compromise, however. At the 1842 General Assembly they proposed and secured the adoption of a 'Claim of Right' which uncompromisingly asserted the spiritual independence of the church and pledged the church to oppose 'illegal' encroachments of the courts on that independence.

The government was unmoved and indicated that it proposed no action. The middle party was rendered obsolete. The courts reiterated their position in a second judgement on compensation in the Auchterarder case — and thereby indicated the likely outcome of a further thirty-nine similar cases by then pending (Brown, 1982, p. 329). In November 1842 Chalmers and the Evangelical leadership held a six-day 'Convocation' in Edinburgh to which only ministers who supported their notion of spiritual independence were invited. They planned the organization and financing of a Free Church, including a commitment to new churches, manses and stipends of at least £200 for ministers, schools, universities, territorially based ministries in both urban and rural settings, and overseas missions: in short, the establishment ideal of the godly commonwealth, but free of the state. Some 354 ministers pledged themselves to leave the established church if the Claim of Right were not met. The Claim was not met, and, indeed, in January 1843 the civil courts reached a final decision in a long-standing debate concerning the General Assembly's Chapels Act of 1834: the act was declared illegal, the territorial parishes created out of chapels of ease were abolished, and the ministers of the churches created in the church extension campaign deprived of their representation in Presbytery, Synod and General Assembly. Chalmers was already organizing local Free Church associations and raising funds. The Disruption finally came at the General Assembly of 1843 — the ranks of the Free Church being somewhat increased by many ministers who had held parishes under the 1834 Chapels Act and now found themselves deprived of their status, some 69.5% of such ministers, 162 in number, joining the Free Church.

The exodus of over 450 ministers, along with many probationer ministers, missionaries and many teachers who lost their posts because of their allegiance to the Free Church, was a remarkable and impressive testimony to their moral courage and strength of conviction. Granted, Chalmers had been planning ahead for some time; granted, also, that he had a remarkably successful record in fund-raising, yet these ministers, prospective ministers and teachers were leaving secure posts for an unclear and as yet insecure future. In the event Chalmers and the Free Church succeeded in their efforts, not least because of the commitment of the Free Church laity, and indeed produced the required churches, manses, stipends, schools and colleges. Because of the scale of the Disruption, moreover, the Free

Church was also genuinely nationwide, although not uniformly strong in all areas: its greatest strength was in the Highlands and the north, its weakest area was in the south. It was strongly supported by younger Evangelical clergy, and it was disproportionately strong in urban areas — a reflection of the evangelical tendency of the church extension campaign of the 30s.

The scale of the achievements of the Free Church, however, the commitment of its members, the numbers of churches built, and the genuinely national scope of its ministry, cannot in the end disguise the essentially ironic nature of the Disruption. The greatest irony was the insistence of the Free Church upon the fact that it was not a Voluntary church, but the true upholder of the principle of establishment and the godly commonwealth, even as it severed itself from the state and its support: '. . . though we quit the Establishment,' asserted Chalmers in a famous remark, 'we go out on the Establishment principle; we quit a vitiated Establishment, but would rejoice in returning to a pure one. To express it otherwise — we are the advocates for a national recognition and national support of religion — and we are not Voluntaries.' Such, indeed, may have been their principle and their theory, but in their practice they had no choice but to behave as Voluntaries.

There was irony also in the fact than the process of church defence and church extension which ended in Disruption and schism had begun, in the early 1830s, as an exercise in reviving establishment and rebutting the attacks of Dissenters and Voluntaries, and again in the fact that one of the results of the urban church extension campaign was the awakening of churchmen to the full bleakness of contemporary urban poverty and housing: what began as domestic visitation, with a view to the practical realization of the ideal of the godly commonwealth, ended with the dawning of the thought that perhaps the godly commonwealth was *not* a viable solution to an urban industrial poverty which, if soluble at all, would require the resources of the secular state (Brown, 1982, pp. 280–1).

The greatest irony of all, however, was a personal one. For more than twenty years Thomas Chalmers had spent his best efforts and energies in advocating the ideal of the godly commonwealth, expressed and nurtured through the local, parochial structure of the established national church, as the only viable means of recovering a sense of individual and communal responsibility and providing adequate social reform in industrial society. Yet he more than any other single individual also ensured that the scale of the Disruption was such that this ideal of the relationship of church and state could no longer even seriously be contemplated as a practical reality. The Disruption, although it issued in *two* genuinely national churches, also decisively eased the way for the steady increase of purely secular authority in Scottish society, a process symbolized within two years of the Disruption with the reform of the Scottish Poor Law and consequent removal of the church from official participation in poor relief (Brown, 1982, pp. xiii and 349).

III FROM DISRUPTION TO REUNION

As Stewart Brown has observed, the building of the Free Church was one of the great achievements of Victorian Britain. Funded entirely from voluntary contributions, within four years the Free Church had 730 churches throughout Scotland, each with an adequately paid and housed minister, over 500 schools, two teacher-training colleges and a ministerial training college. It also had a full territorial structure of Kirk Sessions, Presbyteries, Synods and General Assembly. Such achievement was, however, bought at a price. The Free Church made high demands on its members for funds. Chalmers laid much stress on the idea of the penny-a-week plan, the principle that even the poorest might give a penny a week and that in total this would be a large sum. In practice, however, the various Free Church funds were a considerable burden upon congregations and the Free Church steadily became an increasingly middle-class institution. The confrontation of the Disruption itself, meanwhile, together with the effort of organization and frequent ongoing hostility between the Free Church and the Church of Scotland (Free Church congregations, for example, often had difficulty obtaining land from Church of Scotland landowners, even when funds were available for church building) rapidly gave rise to a defensive mentality and outlook in the Free Church. As a result, even as it achieved the nationwide presence without which *any* claim to be a national church or an expression of the godly commonwealth was untenable, it began to relinquish that very ideal and replace it with an increasingly sectarian ethos, a sense of being a gathered church and bastion of true believers (Brown, 1982, pp. 344–9).

The Church of Scotland, meanwhile, despite the damage caused by the loss of some forty per cent of its members and thirty-eight per cent of its ministers — including many of its young ministers and many of the leading ministers of the pre-Disruption era — survived the Disruption without, as many predicted in 1843, simply declining into a residual and decadent establishment. By the late 60s and early 70s it had regained a lively sense of vitality and in the last quarter of the century grew more steadily and more extensively than either the Free Church or the United Presbyterian Church which (formed in 1847 by union of the Secession Church and Relief Church) constituted the third major branch of mid and late Victorian Scottish Presbyterianism and was committed to a determinedly Voluntary stance.

In the 1860s the Free Church and the United Presbyterians explored the possibility of union, a majority in the Free Church, led by Robert Rainy, having persuaded themselves that establishment could now be relinquished and Voluntaryism embraced in theory as well as practice. The negotiations lasted from 1863 to 1873 but in the end foundered precisely on the issues of establishment, disestablishment and Voluntaryism: a large enough minority of the Free Church, Highland in background and led by the fiercely conservative James Begg and John Kennedy, opposed union on a Voluntarist basis. Their threat of schism was enough to make the majority draw back.[3] Their threat of schism was enough to make the majority draw back.[3]

In 1874, a year after the eventual failure of the Free Church-United Presbyterian negotiations, Disraeli's Conservative government granted the request of the Church of Scotland that patronage be abolished, an earlier request having been refused by Gladstone's Liberal government for fear of offending their Dissenting supporters. Patrons received compensation and ministers were to be elected by parishes and confirmed by Presbyteries. It was hoped that such reform might open the way for wider Presbyterian reunion, patronage having been a major cause of the Disruption and the Free Chruch having initially declared itself willing to return to a 'purified' establishment. Thus intended as a gesture in the direction of the reunification of Scottish Presbyterianism, the measure in the event irked rather than placated Free Church sensibilities. What they had sacrificed so much to build was not to be so readily relinquished. Moreover, the removal of patronage alone did not in their view end the spiritual subordination of the church to the state, and anyway a majority of Free Churchmen had now become outright Voluntarists and opponents of establishment. There thus ensued a twenty-year confrontation between the opponents and defenders of the established status of the Church of Scotland.

The opponents, led by the United Presbyterians and the majority within the Free Church, but also including other Scottish Dissenters, regarded the abolition of patronage as a wrong-headed attempt to strengthen establishment by reforming it, whereas the proper course was to abolish it. The Church of Scotland, on the other hand, defended its establishment with a vigour born of the fact that, not only had it by 1870 substantially recovered from the trauma of Disruption, but in addition by the 1880s claimed to be growing at a faster rate than either the Free Church or the United Presbyterians, and to have more communicants than the other two Presbyterian churches combined. The familiar manifestations of Victorian disestablishment and church defence controversy — associations, committees, petitions, pamphlets, statistical exchanges and lobbying of local political candidates — were prominent features of Scottish religious and political life from 1874 to 1895. On the disestablishment side the main pressure groups were the Church and State Committee of the Free Church General Assembly (led by Rainy), the United Presbyterian Disestablishment Com-

---

[3] For more detailed accounts of the various stages discussed in this section of the essay see Machin, 1983 and 1987, pp. 87–94, 195–8, Dunlop, 1980; and Kellas, 1964.

mittee (led by G. C. Hutton), the Scottish branch of the Liberation Society, the Scottish Disestablishment Association, and the Religious Equality Association — the latter three of which combined in 1886 as the Disestablishment Council for Scotland. For the establishment the principal groups were the Church Interests Committee of the Church of Scotland General Assembly, the Church Defence Association, and from 1890 the Laymen's League, which included lay opponents of disestablishment from the Free Church and United Presbyterian Church. The campaigning reached a peak in the mid 80s, declined somewhat with the split in the Liberal party after 1886, and reached a second peak during the 1892–5 Liberal government. The controversy began to subside after 1895 and the fall of a Liberal government which, despite declaring in favour of all three, had failed to secure Irish Home Rule or either Welsh or Scottish disestablishment. At its height the campaigning of each side proved mutually reinforcing and, Machin suggests, sufficiently successful in building up support on both sides that only stalemate was likely to follow (1983, p. 225).

Stalemate did indeed occur, and when, between 1894 and 1929, the future relationship of the three major strands of Scottish Presbyterianism was eventually resolved, it was by a quite different route. Even as the late Victorian controversy over Scottish disestablishment was being fought out, a quite different solution to the relationship of the Scottish Presbyterian churches was already beginning to gain support, namely that of reunion on the basis of a reformed establishment. The Church of Scotland had made occasional overtures on the subject from as early as 1859, but it was not until 1894 that a series of private meetings between representatives of the three kirks began to suggest the possibility of progress, even if not at once (Dunlop, pp. 165–6; Machin, 1983, p. 228).

Also in 1894, the Free Church and the United Presbyterians began negotiations for union again. This time the negotiations ended in union in 1900. By the late 1890s the ongoing majority in the Free Church who favoured union with the United Presbyterians were prepared to accept, if necessary, the secession of a Highland minority. They had in any case already accepted one such secession in 1892 when the members of the small and Highland based Free Presbyterian Church separated because of their disapproval of the official Free Church relaxation of traditional Calvinism in the adoption of a Declaratory Statement on subscription to the Westminster Confession. The earlier United Presbyterian adoption of such a statement, in 1879, moreover, was a further incentive for the two churches to unite, the majority in both churches now occupying very similar ground not only in church order but also in both theology and matters of church and state.[4] In

---

[4] For a discussion of the theological context of the adoption of these Declaratory Statements on doctrine, see *RVB*, I, 3.

1900, therefore, the overwhelming majority of the Free Church duly opted for union with the United Presbyterians and the formation of the United Free Church, although a determined Highland minority, stayed out as the Free Church Continuing, becoming known popularly as the 'Wee Frees'.

The secession of the 'Wee Frees' was followed by a legal action on their part claiming the entire property of the former Free Church on the grounds that they alone now held the authentic doctrines of the Free Church, especially on establishment and predestination. In 1904 the House of Lords finally found in favour of the Wee Frees. There was, however, a clear absurdity in a church with only twenty-eight ministers receiving all the property of the former Free Church. The matter was resolved by the Churches (Scotland) Act of 1905, which appointed a commission to divide the resources of the old Free Church. At the same time the government took the opportunity to include in the 1905 Act a clause allowing the Church of Scotland to change its terms of subscription to the Westminster Confession independently of the state, thus removing a further potential barrier to Presbyterian reunion by granting the Church the spiritual freedom it had hitherto lacked. The United Free Church Magazine observed that the clause altered the whole relation of church and state (quoted in Machin, 1983, p. 230). In 1910 the Church of Scotland duly adopted a more relaxed form of subscription.

In 1909 negotiating committees from the Church of Scotland and the United Free Church began to discuss union. Conscious of the diminishing differences between them in theology and the increasing number of Scots who claimed no connection with any church, they explored the possibility of reunion on the basis of a church which was recognized as 'national' rather than 'established', in continuity with the Church of Scotland, but free of state intrusion in its affairs. In 1919 a joint committee of the churches described their proposals for reunion as leading to a church which would be '. . . both national and free. The continuity and identity of the Church of Scotland would be maintained, while at the same time the church would bear the character of a purely spiritual institution, in no sense deriving powers from or controlled by the state, nor enjoying any privilege to the prejudice of other churches' (quoted in Machin, 1983, p. 232). In 1921 Parliament passed, without significant opposition, a Church of Scotland Act based on these principles. In 1925 a further Act resolved the question of endowments, and in 1929 the churches united with only a small group of United Free Church members seceding, without rancour, as the United Free Church Continuing.

After some — perhaps more appropriately 'only' — eighty-six years the breach begun in the Disruption thus ended in reunion. It was reunion on the basis of a reformed establishment — 'an attenuated and nominal type of establishment' which guaranteed spiritual independence and self-government to the church but retained 'national recognition of religion'. It was, as Machin has suggested, a belated expression of Chalmers' ideal (1983, p. 333). But it was also a belated expression of only *half* his ideal, for though it embodied national recognition of a spiritually independent church, it did not include the concept of the godly commonwealth — that had passed away along with the pre-industrial world from which it came, lingering only in the tenaciously traditional Calvinism and fiercely regional identity of the Free Presbyterians and the 'Wee Frees'.

IV THE WIDER CONTEXT

The Disruption and its legacy merit more attention than they customarily receive in accounts of religion in Victorian Britain, not least because they are a powerful reminder that Victorian Britain had two religious establishments, not just one, and an equally powerful antidote to the predominantly Anglocentric, indeed Anglican-centred, bias of much writing on Victorian religion.

Moreover, that historiographical bias itself reflects a further dimension of the complex relationship between church and state in Victorian Scotland with which this essay is concerned. The Disruption, although not a 'nationalist' movement, possessed, as David Bebbington has observed, at least some of the characteristics of nationalism. Opposition to patronage was partly opposition to a relatively (sometimes highly) Anglicized landowning patron class on the part of a more distinctively Scottish evangelical middle class. The conflict between the Evangelical party and the government also revealed both an unwillingness on the part of a predominantly English Parliament to take Scottish concerns fully seriously and also a frequent ignorance of the Scottish ecclesiastical establishment and its workings. For many Evangelicals, the government refusal to reform was an English denial of Scottish aspirations, a perspective which, together with the deep theological convictions at stake, explains the intensity of feeling which the Disruption aroused (Bebbington, 1982, pp. 498–9).

The national(ist) dimension remained an integral element of the later disestablishment and reunion debates. In the former case the 'conversion' of a majority of the Free Church to disestablishment was greatly facilitated by the sense of English Parliamentary insensitivy in first denying reform of patronage in 1843, and then granting it in 1874 in an attempt to strengthen the still established Church of Scotland. In the ensuing disestablishment debates from 1875 to 1895 both sides then played the nationalist card and loudly protested their Scottishness and their essential continuity with historical traditions central to Scottish life and identity (Bebbington, pp. 500–1). Similarly, in the debates and negotiations which led to reunion, the idea of a reunified Presbyterian church as an expression of a distinctive national religious tradition and identity was, as we have already noted, an important influence, the concept of a *national* church indeed becoming rather more prominent than that of an *established* one.

If English insensitivity to Scottish ecclesiastical sensibilities thus affected developments in Scottish religious life, however, the impact of the Disruption on English denominational life and relationships was no less influential. There was, on the one hand, the beginning of the use of the term 'Free Church' (and also other linguistic innovations such as the term 'manse' for a minister's house) within English Nonconformity. John Munsey Turner has recently suggested that the use of such terms was only a minor matter (1985, p. 140), but, as David Thompson has observed, the use of the term needs to be seen in the perspective of a century-long transition from self-understanding primarily in the potentially negative terminology of 'Dissent' and 'Nonconformity', to the more positive idea of 'Free Churchmanship'[5] (Thompson, 1978, p. 32).

Then again there were the responses of particular English Nonconformist denominations. Committed Voluntarists, such as the Congregationalists or Baptists, for example, were gratified by the severity of the Disruption's impact on the Scottish religious establishment and hoped for the development of a similar process in England; but they were disappointed by the continuing commitment of the Free Church to the establishment *principle*. Wesleyan Methodists, meanwhile, were unsympathetic to the Free Church congregational appointment of ministers, but were deeply sympathetic to the Free Church attempt to combine spiritual independence and a state connection, Wesleyan Methodism itself still seeking some such middle ground between establishment and voluntaryism. Perhaps most enthusiastic, however, were the Welsh Calvinistic Methodists, whose combination of Methodist respect for the state and Presbyterian style of church order predisposed them to sympathy with the Scottish Free Churchmen (Machin, 1977, p. 144; Thompson, pp. 32 and 46; Turner, pp. 140–1).

Perhaps the most important influence of the Disruption upon English ecclesiastical and religious life, however, was the fact that it occurred in the middle of the second quarter of the nineteenth century, just at the point at which the establishment issue was moving towards the centre of the relationship between English religious and political life. The constitutional reforms of 1828–35 had raised Nonconformist hopes and aspirations, but the remaining privileges of the establishment and disabilities of Nonconformists thereby became all the more irksome and offensive. The Disruption focused attention on the establishment issue and on the theory and practice of church and state, and it provided one (although only one) of the

[5] For a discussion of this transition, see *RVB*, I, 2.

'triggers' for the formation by Edward Miall of the Anti-State Church Association a year later in 1844 (Thompson, pp. 32–3).

An essay on church and state in Victorian Scotland should, however, end with the distinctiveness of the Scottish experience itself rather than its English implications. In England the emergence of constitutional religious pluralism resulted in an era of fierce conflict between Dissent and establishment, which ended with establishment intact but reduced in influence, and Dissent apparently poised to become an alternative establishment but in fact about to enter a period of serious decline. It also produced a remarkable broadening of the bounds of the established church itself which, however, successfully resisted the threat of schism, albeit at the cost of becoming rather less than a genuinely unified body.[6] In Scotland, by contrast, schism occurred and the established church was abandoned by something approaching forty per cent of its membership and clergy. Yet by the end of the century a revived Church of Scotland was successfully seeking to begin negotiations for union with a church itself formed from a union of the two largest Scottish Dissenting churches. There was, however, at least one unifying element between the Church of Scotland and its two principal Dissenting rivals which did not exist in England. Unlike the English situation, in which an episcopal establishment confronted a variety of non-episcopal Dissenting churches, in Scotland the established church and its two main rivals were all Presbyterian. They shared a common theological tradition and a common system of church government, as well as a common sense of being Scots.

BIBLIOGRAPHY

*D. W. Bebbington (1982) 'Religion and national feeling in nineteenth century Wales and Scotland' in S. Mews (ed.) *Religion and National Identity*, pp. 489–503, Oxford, Blackwell.

*S. J. Brown (1982) *Thomas Chalmers and the Godly Commonwealth in Scotland*, Oxford, Oxford University Press.

A. C. Cheyne (ed.) (1985) 'Introduction — Thomas Chalmers: then and now' in *The Practical and the Pious*, pp. 9–30, Edinburgh, St Andrew Press.

A. I. Dunlop (1980) 'The paths to reunion in 1929', *Records of the Scottish Church History Society*, Vol. 20. pp. 163–78.

J. G. Kellas (1964) 'The Liberal party and the Scottish Church disestablishment crisis', *English Historical Review*, Vol. 79, pp. 31–46.

G. I. T. Machin (1977) *Politics and the Churches in Great Britain 1832–68*, Oxford, Oxford University Press.

[6] For which see also *RVB* I, 1 and *RVB* II, 4 and 7.

*G. I. T. Machin (1983) 'Voluntaryism and Reunion, 1874–1929' in N. Macdougall (ed.) *Church, Politics and Society: Scotland 1408–1929*, pp. 221–38, John Donald, Edinburgh.

G. I. T. Machin (1987) *Politics and the Churches in Great Britain 1869–1921*, Oxford, Oxford University Press.

A. A. Maclaren (1974) *Religion and Social Class: The Disruption Years in Aberdeen*, Routledge.

*D. M. Thompson (1978) 'Scottish influence on the English Churches in the nineteenth century', *Journal of the United Reform Church History Society*, Vol. 2, pp. 30–46.

J. M. Turner (1985) *Conflict and Reconciliation: Studies in Methodism and Ecumenism in England 1740–1982*, Epworth.

CHAPTER 6

OUR SIAMESE TWINS.

Mr. Bull. "YOU DON'T THINK THE OPERATION WILL BE FATAL TO EITHER?"
Dr. Gladstone. "OH, NO!"
Dr. Bright. "NOT A BIT!—DO 'EM' BOTH ALL THE GOOD IN THE WORLD."

IRISH DISESTABLISHMENT

O N 26 July 1869 there passed into law an act of parliament for the disestablishment and disendowment of the Anglican Church in Ireland. By the terms of the Irish Church Act, from 1 May 1871 the Church of Ireland ceased to be the official state church in Ireland, the Irish bishops ceased to have seats in the House of Lords, and the wealth and endowments of the church were appropriated by the government. In compensation, the Church of Ireland received all its churches free, its clergy houses on very favourable terms, cash compensation of £500,000 to the church and life incomes to current benefice holders (with provision for an additional cash bonus of twelve per cent from the government on any such incomes subsequently commuted to the disendowed church in exchange for a salary). Gladstone estimated the total resources of the established Church of Ireland at approximately sixteen million pounds: the final value of the compensation in its various forms amounted to rather more than half of this sum. The remaining surplus was to be used for 'relief of unavoidable calamity and suffering' in Ireland.

The Irish Church Act has been described as the 'greatest single nineteenth century triumph for the forces of religious equality in the United Kingdom' (Machin, 1987). It was also, in the perspective of the ensuing century and more, the high-tide of the cause of disestablishment in Britain as a whole, and the turning point at which the centrality of religious issues (and especially the classic conflict between establishment and Nonconformity) within Victorian political life began to give way to a new configuration of political debate in which issues of class and of social and economic affairs would move steadily towards the centre of the political stage, and issues of religion and religious rights would move correspondingly towards the periphery.

The present essay will briefly explore the significance of Irish disestablishment in four distinct yet inevitably interrelated contexts. First, it will consider the changing status of the notion of established religion and of the Church of England within specifically English political and constitutional life between 1828 and 1870. Second, it will examine the prospect, occurrence and consequences of the disestablishment of the Church of Ireland. Third, it will note the significance of disestablishment within the changing pattern of religion in Victorian Ireland as a whole. Fourth, it will review the history of the campaign for religious disestablishment in Britain in the decades following the attainment of Irish disestablishment.

I   IRISH DISESTABLISHMENT AND THE ENGLISH ESTABLISHMENT 1828–69

It was not merely the fact that the Irish Church Act embodied the first permanent constitutionally sanctioned break in the traditional link between the established churches and the state in Britain which made it significant. It did do this, and would have been significant for that reason alone. In point of fact, however, the contemporary sense of the fundamental significance of Irish disestablishment arose not only from the Act itself but also from the forty-year sequence of constitutional adjustments to the relationship of religion and the state of which Irish disestablishment was but the latest and most dramatic example.

From the repeal of the Test and Corporation Acts in 1828 and Catholic Emancipation in 1829 onwards, the clear tendency of church-state relations in nineteenth-century Britain had been towards the reduction of the privileges of established religion, the increase of the rights of other varieties of believer (and also of non-believers), and the reform of the established church itself (at least in the case of the Church of England and Church of Ireland). The tendency, though clear, was neither unopposed nor uniformly successful. Concessions to Nonconformists over university entrance and church rates, for example, or to secularists over the limits of the law on blasphemy, or to Jews in the matter of the right to sit in Parliament, had to be fought for and won. The reform of the Church of England through the Ecclesiastical Commission, and of the Church of Ireland through the Irish Ecclesiastical Commission, was opposed by many churchmen. And in the Ecclesiastical Titles Act of 1851 Parliament even indulged, in a fit of anti-Catholic pique, in an attempt to return to penal legislation in religion. But the 1851 Act was never applied and in its non-application demonstrated both its own anachronism and the general tendency to greater equality before the law in matters of religion.[1]

Moreover, this overall tendency was not only clear, but appeared, in the late 1860s, to be gathering momentum and entering a politically decisive phase. In England and Wales the Liberation Society, founded in the 1840s, reached its peak, both in terms of influence and achievement, in the 1860s. The St Bartholomew's Day celebrations held in 1862, to mark the bicentenary of the ejection of Puritan clergy from the Church of England in 1662, provided a national focus for the Society's aims, and in 1861–2 the Society initiated a two-fold strategy to influence public opinion and secure the election of sympathetic MPs. A body of travelling lecturers was appointed, material from the monthly journal *Liberator* was reproduced in book and pamphlet form, and direct local pressure was brought to bear on constituency Liberal parties and candidates to adopt the policies advocated by the Society. The strategy yielded significant results in England and impressive ones in Wales. In Scotland negotiations for union had begun in 1863 between the United Presbyterians (committed Voluntaryists and

---

[1] For details of various aspects of this process, see *RVB*, I, 2 and 4 and *RVB*, II, 4.

opponents of establishment) and the Free Church (theoretically in favour of establishment but in practice Voluntary, and within which a majority were becoming willing openly to accept Voluntaryism as the price of union with the UPs). Added to the pressure from other Scottish Nonconformists, the reunion negotiations seemed to foreshadow an increasing attack on the privileges of the Church of Scotland. In Ireland the foundation of the National Association in 1864, with the active support of Paul Cullen and the leadership of the Irish Roman Catholic Church, initiated a new and powerful call for a series of social and political reforms in Ireland, an integral part of which was the disestablishment of the Church of Ireland.[2]

Such accumulating anti-establishment pressure secured a notable victory in 1868 with the passing of an Act of Parliament for the abolition of Church Rates: no longer was it possible to levy a compulsory rate upon the local community for the upkeep of the parish church. Then, in the same year the Liberal leader, Gladstone, also brought forward proposals to disestablish and disendow the Irish Church. In the general election which ensued, Irish disestablishment was a central issue. Irish churchmen and the majority of English churchmen campaigned against Gladstone and his proposals. Gladstone, however, won a majority of 110, in the making of which the votes of Irish Catholics, Welsh and English Nonconformists and Scottish Voluntaryists were a key factor. A bill for disestablishment and disendowment was brought forward in 1869. The English bishops, led by the newly appointed Archbishop of Canterbury, Tait, accepted the result of the general election, ceased to oppose the bill outright, and sought instead to secure concurrent endowment (that is, the reallocation of the total wealth of the Church of Ireland among the three major Irish denominations, Anglican, Catholic and Presbyterian) in place of disestablishment and *dis*-endowment. In this too they failed, many Evangelical Protestants being opposed to the endowment of Roman Catholicism, and the Irish Roman Catholics themselves opting for voluntaryism and rejecting the acceptance of aid from a Protestant state. The efforts of Tait and the English bishops at least secured better terms of disendowment, however, than those originally proposed.

Thirty-six years earlier, the Irish Church Temporalities Act of 1833 and its modest reform of the Irish Church had occasioned widespread anxiety that Irish precedent would issue in English parallel; had caused Keble to preach on National Apostasy and initiate the Oxford Movement; and had given rise to Nonconformist hopes and Establishment fears that the radical reform of the Church of England was imminent. In the event only modest extensions of civil liberty in relation to religious profession, and pragmatic

---

[2] For England see Thompson, 1974; for Wales see Jones, 1981; for Scotland see references in *RVB*, II, 5; and for Ireland see below.

reforms of the church by means of the episcopally dominated Ecclesiastical Commission ensued. The English and Scottish aftermath of Irish disestablishment was also to prove (as we shall see in section IV below) similarly moderate, even anti-climactic. But in 1869 the prospects, to many, seemed quite otherwise. Nonconformists rejoiced and Edward Miall prepared to introduce to the Commons bills for the disestablishment of the Church of England. Staunch High Churchmen such as Denison spoke of the 'revolution' of 1869, argued that Irish disestablishment had destroyed the principle of establishment, and began to wonder if the verdicts of the Privy Council in the Gorham, *Essays and Reviews* and Colenso cases did not in any case argue for the end of establishment in order to preserve the church's doctrinal and spiritual integrity.

More moderate churchmen than Denison were divided as to the consequences for English and Scottish establishment of Irish disestablishment. Supporters of the Act who were also churchmen — which included a majority of the Liberal MPs and pre-eminently, of course, Gladstone himself — believed that Irish disestablishment would remove a blatant offence to religious justice and leave what remained of establishment more secure. Opponents of Irish disestablishment saw, in the concession of principle, a precedent which would henceforth prove irresistible in the rest of Britain. The implications of Irish disestablishment for the history of religion in Victorian Britain as a whole thus remained, in 1869, tantalizingly and controversially unclear. The implications for Irish religious history were, on the contrary, much clearer.

II DISESTABLISHMENT AND THE CHURCH OF IRELAND

The case for disestablishment and disendowment of the Irish Church was based upon the fundamental anomaly of a church which claimed to be the national, state church (with all the social, political and economic privileges and advantages that went with such status) possessing the religious allegiance of only 12% of the population. The mis-match of status, resources and religious allegiance had been manifest for decades (indeed it had been even worse, only 10.7% of the population being Anglican in 1834), as had the cogency of the arguments for reform based upon morality and efficiency. Indeed the latter argument alone had been sufficient to secure the Irish Church Temporalities Act of 1833, by which ten bishoprics and two archbishoprics were abolished and the Irish Ecclesiastical Commission set up to administer the revenues thus released to the church. By 1868–9 the arguments from morality and efficiency had been joined by that from political necessity — or at least expediency: Irish nationalism had become a major and militant force in Victorian politics and disestablishment had become part of Gladstone's programme of Irish reforms designed at once to pacify militant Irish nationalism and retain Irish nationalist support for the Liberal government.

The contemporary political context of Irish disestablishment in the 1860s should not, however, be allowed to obscure the extent to which it came as the latest and most radical stage in an ongoing process of nineteenth-century reform, now transformed into revolution, within the Church of Ireland. The Church of Ireland of 1800 was both weak and ineffective. Its bishops and archbishops were political nominees, many of its clergy were pluralists, non-residence was common (even among bishops), parishes were too large for effective pastoral oversight, churches were in poor repair, and 10% of benefices actually had no church at all (S. J. Connolly, 1985, pp. 7–8). D. H. Akenson has summarized its position in 1800 as 'representing a narrow constituency, surrounded by a hostile majority, controlling great endowments, uncertain of its priorities, inefficient in its administration'. It was, he added, a church ripe for reform or revolution (Akenson, 1971, p. 70).

There was, however, within the Irish Church in the early nineteenth century, both an awareness of the need for reform and a willingness to undertake it. The period from 1800 to 1830 has been described by Akenson as 'the era of graceful reform'. Ecclesiastical discipline was tightened, abuses were curbed, residence was encouraged, administration was improved, finances were reformed, and pastoral standards were raised, not least as a result of the increased sense of zeal and devotion engendered by the spread within the Church of Ireland of the effects of the Irish Evangelical revival (Akenson, ch. 2).

By the 1830s, therefore, the Church of Ireland was engaged in a broad process of internal reform. Also by the 1830s, however, reform could no longer be limited to internal initiatives. The era of constitutional reform in Britain which extended from the late 20s to the late 30s and included, in England, the setting up of the Ecclesiastical Commission to supervise the administrative and financial reform of the Church of England, necessarily affected Ireland and the Church of Ireland as well. In contrast to the earlier period of 'graceful reform', Akenson has styled the period from 1830 to 1867, and especially the decade of the 1830s, as the era of 'reform by critical strangers' (1971, ch. 3).

The most famous of the 'reforms by critical strangers' was the Irish Church Temporalities Act of 1833, with its suppression of ten bishoprics and two archbishoprics, its 'tax' on the revenues of rich benefices, its appointment of an Irish Ecclesiastical Commission to administer the revenues thus released in the interests of the Irish Church, and, finally, its appropriation clause allowing the government to use any surplus in the revenues of the Ecclesiastical Commission for Irish charitable or educational ends. The Act was significant not least for its bluntness: the suppression of bishoprics and archbishoprics and the consignment of their revenues to a newly appointed body, plus the possibility (even if in the event it was never realized) of the appropriation of any surplus funds for secular ends (albeit Irish ones and of a social and educational kind), could hardly be mistaken for anything but the direct intervention of the state in the affairs of the church. The changes in the law concerning tithe, on the other hand, could appear at first sight to be essentially matters of social and economic reform. In point of fact, however, they too embodied a further precedent, in line with that of the Irish Church Temporalities Act, for the reform of the church by the state. The annual tithe which the clergy of the Church of Ireland were entitled to levy on the rural population naturally caused offence to non-Anglicans. In the 1830s there was significant resistance to the payment of tithe and the resulting 'Tithe War' issued in coercion and agrarian unrest. Two reforms ensued. In 1832 the tithe in kind was converted into a money payment; and in 1838 the payment became one for which the chief landlord was liable, though he could pass on the costs to his tenants. The basic cause of offence remained: non-Anglicans were obliged to support the Church of Ireland; but the *direct* link of clergy to tithe payment was broken and *direct* confrontation of Anglican incumbent and Catholic farmer removed. That much was gain for the church: but once more government had reformed the church's property and rights. Also, in 1831, the government had abolished its annual grants to Protestant educational societies in Ireland and replaced them with a national elementary education system which was officially non-denominational and in which children were not obliged to receive religious education in a tradition other than their own.

After the reforms of the 1830s the Church of Ireland experienced some two decades of relative calm. Akenson suggests that the reforms (and especially the effects of the 1833 Act) left the Church of Ireland more professional, more pastorally effective, more centralized and more disciplined. Provision of local pastoral oversight and religious services was improved; there were more churches: and if revenues were somewhat reduced, they were nevertheless better allocated. But, if the reforms of the 1830s thus rendered the Church of Ireland more efficient, they also embodied an important shift of emphasis from the earlier, pre 1830s, era of reform. The earlier reforms had tended to affirm the *principle* of establishment and sought to enhance the effectiveness of its resources. The post-1830 reforms implied scepticism about the value and extent of Irish religious establishment and reduced its funds as well as re-allocating them in the interests of further efficiency (Akenson, 1971, ch. 3). It was a change of emphasis which presaged the possibility of disestablishment, should events outside the church render it desirable.

In the 1860s events both in Ireland itself and also in England, Wales and

Scotland took such a turn. In England and Wales, as we noted earlier, the activities of the Liberation Society reached a peak of intensity and effectiveness in the 1860s (the Liberation Society significantly seeing Irish disestablishment as the first step towards disestablishment in the rest of Britain). In Scotland the negotiations for union between the Free Church and United Presbyterians raised the hopes of Voluntaryists and increased the pressure on the established Church of Scotland. As one would expect, however, it was in Ireland itself that the crucial opposition to Irish establishment emerged.

In Ireland by the 1860s three principal factors combined to inspire pressure for disestablishment. First, the period from the 1820s onwards had witnessed a steady deterioration in the relationship between the major denominations in Ireland and a marked sharpening of denominational identities within both the Protestant and Catholic communities. In the 1820s Evangelical Protestants in Ireland — both Anglican and Dissenting — had embarked on a series of missionary endeavours directed at Roman Catholics in what they ardently hoped would prove to be a 'Second Reformation'. The Irish Roman Catholic church responded by tightening its own discipline, improving its pastoral provision and sharpening its Catholic identity — especially through parish missions and the introduction of the Ultramontane piety of the 'devotional revolution' into Irish Catholic life. Denominational consciousnesses and rivalry, thus sharpened, did not encourage Catholic acquiescence in the existence of an established church, in receipt of tithe from Catholic laity, but with a membership of only a small minority of the population. Second, in 1861 the Census revealed that, despite the efforts of the 'Second Reformation' and the impact of the Great Famine of the late 1840s — via death and emigration — on the Catholic population, the Church of Ireland still numbered only 12% of the Irish population.

Third, and crucially, within the process of Roman Catholic revival and consolidation Paul Cullen had emerged as a dominating and co-ordinating leader, building upon the foundations already laid before his arrival from Rome in 1849 and prepared to lend episcopal support to the political campaigns of Irish Catholicism. In 1864 Cullen led the Catholic hierarchy in support of the foundation of the National Association of Ireland. The Association sought the redress of three Irish grievances, namely, legally-required compensation to occupiers for improvements to land, the disendowment of the Irish Church and the use of its revenues for the nation, and the freedom and equality of education for all denominations and classes.

The National Association rapidly entered into negotiations with the Liberation Society; Irish Catholics and English and Welsh Nonconformists set themselves the task of securing the election of a sufficient number of anti-establishment MPs to secure the disestablishment of the Church of

Ireland, in the Irish Catholic case as an end itself, in the English and Welsh Nonconformist cases as a first step towards the disestablishment of the Church of England. In 1868 the electoral efforts and alliance of the National Association and Liberation Society proved a crucial element in securing the parliamentary majority enjoyed by Gladstone after the general election of that year.

The story of the passing of the Irish Church Act, of the negotiations involved in its passage through Parliament, and of the potential constitutional crisis it provoked, is a fascinating one for connoisseurs of political and parliamentary manoeuvre. It has also been told in detail a number of times (Bell, 1969, ch. 4; Akenson, ch. 4; McDowell, 1975, ch. 2; Machin, 1987, pp. 22–30). In the present context our concern is not with the details of the Act's passing but with its consequences for the Church of Ireland.

The Irish church — led by its bishops — continued to resist the bill to the end: even when the outcome was clear they would not compromise and discuss the precise terms of disendowment. That there was prolonged negotiation over the precise terms of compensation — and a considerable improvement on the original proposals — was due to large part to the work of the English bishops, led by Tait and Wilberforce, who, once the 1868 election made the passage of disestablishment an eventual certainty, reluctantly but pragmatically accepted the inevitable and worked for the best financial settlement they could get for the Irish church.

The Irish Church Act passed into law in July 1869 and set 1 May 1871 as the date from which the Church of Ireland would be disestablished. The church received reasonable compensation for its disendowment, and provision was also made in the Act for the setting up of a governing body for the disestablished church, to be known as the Representative Church Body. As well as disendowing the Church of Ireland, the Irish Church Act also ended the annual grant to Maynooth College and the annual payment, known as the *Regium Donum*, to the Presbyterian Church in Ireland for the supplementation of ministers' stipends. Both the Roman Catholic and Presbyterian churches received lump sums in compensation for the abolition of their respective grants.

Once the Act was passed, the Church of Ireland faced a major task of reconstruction. William Connor Magee, then Bishop of Peterborough, later to be Archbishop of York, formerly Dean of Cork, and an astute commentator on the Church of Ireland, observed to an Irish correspondent in September 1869 that, 'Your three rocks are coming over the surface already. 1. Liturgical revision. 2. Lay tyranny, and 3. Schism between north and south. Still, I think you will weather them; but the second is your greatest danger' (quoted in Akenson, p. 275). He might have added, as a fourth problem, the consolidation of the finances of the disestablished church.

In fact the task of financial reconstruction was successfully and quickly carried out. Three factors greatly helped the Church of Ireland economically: the majority of the clergy proved willing to commute the personal life incomes they received at disestablishment to the church, thus the church gained the twelve per cent bonus allowed in the 1869 Act; the laity proved willing to shoulder the level of giving needed in a now voluntary church; and the laity of the Church of Ireland came in any case disproportionately from the wealthier sections of Irish society. The latter built-in advantage should not, however, obscure the basic financial commitment shown to the church by both clergy and laity after disestablishment.

The threat of lay tyranny, Magee's 'greatest danger', was increased by the new financial burden upon the laity: there might prove to be a price in power for generous giving in money. In 1869 the two Archbishops called their respective provincial synods to meet and then the synods met jointly. A conference of laity also met and passed a resolution that in future synods there should be a 2:1 ratio of laity to clergy. A committee was appointed to draft a constitution and it was debated at a General Convention in 1870. The result was a constitution which avoided both 'lay tyranny' and the continuation of the unmoderated power of the clergy in general and bishops in particular. There was to be a General Synod composed of houses of bishops and 'representatives' (clergy and laity). Voting was by orders (bishops, clergy and laity) and no bill affecting doctrine or liturgy could be passed without a two-thirds majority in each house, after a year's delay and consideration of such proposed legislation by the twelve diocesan synods which comprised the next level of government. The diocesan synods normally had two lay members for each clerical one and included election of the bishop and a role in other clerical appointments within their sphere of influence.

The constitution at once received a thorough test in the 'revision controversy' of 1870–7. Irish disestablishment occurred just as the issue of ritualism and its legality, legitimacy and limits was becoming a dominant concern of the Church of England. The royal commission on the subject issued four reports between 1867 and 1870. The Public Worship Regulation Act was to pass into law in 1874. The Church of Ireland, however, existing within the context of a resurgent and assertive Roman Catholic majority, was a self-consciously Protestant church even when it was not overtly Evangelical. The laity in particular, and a minority of the clergy, desired to take advantage of disestablishment and the constitutional freedom which it offered to revise the Book of Common Prayer in a severely Protestant direction.[3] The archbishops, bishops and majority of the clergy, on the other hand, wished to retain the Book of Common Prayer as it was.

In 1871 the General Synod passed a series of revisions of the Canons of the Church of Ireland which were sharply Protestant in effect: a range of liturgical practices acceptable in the Church of England (or at least not clearly *un*acceptable) were ruled inadmissible in the Church of Ireland. They included the use of vestments, the making of the sign of the cross, the use of bells or candles (other than strictly for light), crosses on or behind the communion table, incense, elevation of the chalice or the host and processions or the carrying of crosses, banners or pictures during services. Between 1871 and 1877 debate continued over revision of the Prayer Book itself, and a revision committee reported to the General Synod. Having set out in 1870 to secure substantial changes, the revisionists eventually had to settle in 1877 with a very few, very small alterations which emphasized the spiritual nature of the Holy Communion; modified the absolution used in the visitation of the sick; removed all saints' names (bar those with specially appointed feast days) from the church calendar; made use of the Athanasian Creed optional; and added explanatory paragraphs to the prefaces of certain services explaining that a number of contentious phrases could be interpreted in a manner acceptable to Low Churchmen. Schism — Magee's third fear for the disestablished church — was averted by revision of the most conservative kind.

The Church of Ireland emerged from its disestablishment and its encounter with the challenges of reorganization, lay bids for power, and Book of Common Prayer revision, with a remarkable degree of discipline, dignity and vitality: they successfully made, as one historian has put it, an ecclesiastical virtue out of a Gladstonian necessity (Daly, 1970, p. 23). If, as Bell has pointed out, it took another forty years and the financial impact of a world war to make the Church of Ireland overcome the tenacity of local diocesan and parochial loyalties and come to terms with the need for radical reorganization of parochial structures, then it must also be said that other churches have displayed (and still display) an equal or greater reluctance to grasp this particular administrative nettle. And when the Church of Ireland did eventually act on the issue (in 1919–20) its decisions

---

[3] The pressure for revision stemmed largely from a fear of ritualism in the Church of Ireland. In reality, however, the fear was quite without foundation. The Church of Ireland was already, because of its context, more definitely Protestant than the Church of England and the only examples of Irish 'ritualism' were tame indeed in comparison with the English situation (see Bell, pp. 187–8; McDowell, pp. 58–60). Although as McDowell points out (pp. 79–81), the restrained use of Gothic architecture and style in new churches and also the many restorations and renovations of old ones, facilitated a range of liturgical practices congenial to high(er) churchmen and not ruled out even by the eventually revised Canons and Prayer Book.

were met with an impressive degree of ecclesiastical discipline and order (Bell, pp. 176–80).

Ecclesiastical discipline in general, however, was another of the strengths of the post-disestablishment Irish Church. If the Church of Ireland emerged from the revision controversy of the mid-1870s with a less broad comprehensiveness than pertained in the Church of England (and it was after all inevitable that it would be so: the extremes of incense-using, vestment-wearing, sacrament-reserving Ritualism were never going to prove acceptable in a country whose predominant religious style was post-devotional revolution Roman Catholicism), then at least it was a comprehensiveness overwhelmingly respected by its members and not, as in the contemporary Church of England, secured at its limits only by conscientious clerical disobedience verging on liturgical anarchy (Bell, 1969, pp. 194–6).[4]

The Church of Ireland emerged from disestablishment and the ensuing decade of debate with a clear identity, a sense of order, unity preserved, and a viable relationship between clergy and laity. It also entered the twentieth century with a presence throughout Ireland (albeit one numerically much stronger in the north than in the south) which enabled it to survive partition as a genuinely cross-border institution (Bell, 1969, p. 211). Most of all, however, as Sean Connolly has observed, it emerged with its role within Irish life completely redefined, it was no longer 'the religious embodiment of civil society' but 'the church of a socially advantaged but numerically weak minority' (S. J. Connolly, 1985, p. 32).

III DISESTABLISHMENT AND THE CHANGING PATTERN OF RELIGION IN VICTORIAN IRELAND

In one respect at least the pattern of Irish religion remained remarkably consistent between the 1830s and 1900. Statistically the balance of denominational allegiances did not alter dramatically. In 1834 the division of population between Catholic, Anglican and Presbyterian was, respectively, 80.9%, 10.7% and 8.1%. In 1861 the figures had become 77.7%, 12% and 9%; and by 1901 they stood at 74.2%, 13% and 9.9% (S. J. Connolly, 1985, p. 3). Nor did the geographical distribution shift markedly. The Catholic population was substantial throughout the country, although only a substantial minority in parts of Ulster. The Anglican population was also dispersed across the country but with a much heavier concentration in Ulster. Presbyterianism was overwhelmingly Ulster centred.

---

[4] For the nature of such 'conscientious clerical disobedience', see briefly, *RVB* I, 1 and *RVB*, II, 4.

The areas of dramatic change, on the other hand, were *within* the denominations, in the way in which they related to one another, and in the way in which government was involved (or not involved) in that relationship.

We have noted already the poor condition of the Church of Ireland in the opening decades of the century: administratively, pastorally and spiritually lax and in need of reform. We have noted also a process of internal reform already under way by 1830 and a consolidation of such reform under pressure from without during the 1830s and the decades following. By the time disestablishment took place, the Church of Ireland was a pastorally and administratively efficient institution, served by a dedicated clergy, with a committed laity and a keen sense of its distinctively Protestant identity.

In some respects the condition of the Irish Roman Catholic church bore a remarkable resemblance to that of the Church of Ireland during the first three decades of the century. It too lacked adequate efficiency and discipline, had insufficient numbers of clergy and churches, and faced a significant challenge from the still lively traditions of Irish 'folk religion' — especially in the poorer and more rural areas. Again like the Church of Ireland, the Irish Roman Catholic church had already begun to address its weaknesses within the first three decades of the century, impressively sustained its revival in the 1830s and 40s, and under Cullen's leadership between 1849 and 1878 achieved a consolidation and extension of the earlier achievements which amounted to a fundamental reshaping of Irish Catholicism relative to its early nineteenth-century condition.[5] The reshaping not only involved tighter discipline and greater efficiency, increases in clergy and in buildings, but also, essentially, included the transformation of Irish Catholic devotional life: residual elements of folk religion were pressed decisively to the periphery of Catholic life and Ultramontane piety and devotionalism firmly established at its centre.

Irish Presbyterianism, meanwhile, was internally divided in the early nineteenth century between the Synod of Ulster and the Secession Synod, and within the former there was also a division between an evangelical wing and a group whose theology was much influenced by eighteenth-century rationalism and radicalism and tended towards Unitarianism. In the 1820s the evangelical wing in the Synod of Ulster succeeded in expelling the Unitarians, and in 1840 the two Synods united on the basis of an evangelical majority in both churches committed to both 'Calvinist orthodoxy' and 'vital religion'. As subsequent events were to demonstrate, however,

[5] For details of this process of revival and the relationship of folk religion and official Catholicism, see *RVB*, I, 4. Patrick Corish in particular emphasizes the *early*, pre-famine, pre-Cullen basis and extent of reform and revival (1985, chs. 6 and 7).

such a combination of 'Calvinist orthodoxy' and 'vital religion' lacked internal cohesion: the logic of strict Calvinism and the dynamics of a vital evangelicalism pulled in opposite directions, to the long-term advantage of the latter and the disadvantage of the former.

The extent to which a commitment to an evangelical Protestantism, centred on conversion, vital religious experience, and a fiercely conservative understanding of scripture and doctrine was in practice replacing *traditional* Presbyterianism — with *its* essential ideal of the 'godly community' — was well illustrated by the Presbyterian enthusiasm for the 1859 revival in Ulster. As Peter Brooke has observed, the revival illustrated the extent to which the central organizing principle of traditional Irish Presbyterianism had been undermined: 'In the eighteenth century to be a Presbyterian was to be a member of a self-organizing community. By the 1850s to be a Presbyterian was to be a person with particular religious views' (Brooke, 1987, p. 191). And the particular religious views in question were, moreover, increasingly characterized by a revivalist theology which implicitly undermined the logic of traditional Calvinist doctrine.

The Irish Presbyterian community had always been concentrated predominantly in Ulster. In the Victorian era it became even more so, steadily emphasized its greater size in Ulster than the Church of Ireland, and, especially after disestablishment, took up a political stance which was broadly 'Protestant' (alongside the other Protestant bodies), rather than distinctively 'Presbyterian'. In this its politics mirrored its theological development, for the chief legacy of the 1859 revival in Ulster was to break 'the Presbyterian monopoly of Protestantism outside the Established Church' and provide an opening for other Protestant Nonconformist churches and for the widespread growth of non-denominational Gospel Halls and Missions, whilst at the same time transforming Ulster Presbyterianism from within by replacing strict and traditional Presbyterian polity and theology by a generalized conservative evangelical Protestantism and a markedly revivalist theology (Brooke, p. 193; S. J. Connolly, 1985, pp. 46–7).

Changes *within* the major denominations of Victorian Ireland necessarily effected relationships *between* them. In early nineteenth-century Ireland there was notably little overt sectarian hostility between the denominations, a general willingness to co-exist as separate communities, and even, indeed, a willingness to engage in a limited range of co-operative enterprises. By the end of the century such co-operation had been replaced by, at best, cool co-existence at a distance, at worst, mutually reinforcing militancy and sectarian hostility.

Prior to the 1820s the major religious communities in Ireland, although markedly separate, remained on broadly good terms. Between Anglicans and Catholics such good terms extended even to a degree of practical co-operation: clergy of each church attending the other's public occasions, and laity working together in charitable ventures (Connolly, 1985, p. 25). As Bowen has put it, prior to the twenties, '. . . to a remarkable degree, the Catholic majority people and the minority Protestant ascendancy seemed able to tolerate each other' (1978, p. x). It was a period of moderate 'accommodation' in religious matters.

In the 1820s, however, both religious and political factors combined to undermine such peaceful co-existence. The development of an Irish Evangelical revival had already given rise to a number of Evangelical Protestant missionary societies (such as the Hibernian Bible Society or the Irish Society for Promoting the Education of the Native Irish through the Medium of their own Language), whose specific aim was the conversion of Irish Roman Catholics. In 1822 the newly appointed Anglican Archbishop of Dublin, William Magee, opened his archiepiscopate with a charge to his arch-diocese which sharply attacked Roman Catholicism. The initiative by Magee, not suprisingly, sparked a bitter pamphlet war and encouraged the evangelicals to launch more systematic missionary efforts to Irish Catholics: the proposed 'Second Reformation' was begun. Irish Roman Catholicism responded by a reassertion of its own identity, a new militancy, and a determination to tighten its discipline and efficiency. Whereas sectarianism had previously found it surprisingly difficult to take root, the Second Reformation, with its itinerant preachers (often Irish speaking), bible and tract distribution, free schools (at the cost of Protestant religious teaching), and even 'colonies' for converts, succeeded, in Patrick Corish's phrase, in driving the sectarian wedge further home (1985, p. 155).[6]

The numerical returns for such Protestant efforts were small and short term. The damage done to Catholic-Protestant relations on the other hand was enormous. Politically, meanwhile, the campaign for Catholic Emancipation (which much of the Protestant community had chosen to oppose) mobilized and politicized the Catholic middle class. The feelings aroused by the 'Protestant Crusade' to the Irish Catholic poor thus combined with the religious-political mobilization of the wealthier elements of the Irish Catholic community. In the 1830s this 'alliance' was consolidated in the campaigns over tithes, as was the growing sense of sharper separation between the Protestant and Catholic communities (Bowen, 1978, pp. 156–77).

The crisis and trauma of the famine, especially between 1845 and 1849,

[6] A similar transition from eighteenth and early nineteenth-century co-existence and moderate co-operation to Victorian confrontation occurred in English Roman Catholic-Protestant relations. In England, too, the trigger of change was the initiation of aggressive missionary activity on the part of evangelical Protestants among Roman Catholics. English Roman Catholics naturally responded with an assertion of their own distinctive claims. For a brief discussion of this development and its context within the history of English Catholicism in the Victorian era, see *RVB*, I, 4. For a detailed case study of the transition from co-existence and co-operation to conflict and confessionalism, see G. P. Connolly, 1984.

further accentuated the division. On the one hand the growing mutual distrust of Catholic and Protestant frustrated relief work, the frustration itself then adding to the distrust and ill-feeling. Moreover, in the aftermath of the famine, as Bowen has emphasized, the already polarizing groups within Irish religion were powerfully reinforced by external influences. In the Protestant case, elements within the English Evangelical tradition perceived the aftermath of the famine as an opportune moment to launch a renewed and militant missionary campaign to the Irish Catholic poor. In particular, the work of Alexander Dallas and his Irish Catholic Mission (founded in 1849) displayed a proselytizing and missionary zeal, aggression and assertiveness of a kind and intensity which offended even Irish Protestants. From the Catholic side, the arrival in Ireland of Paul Cullen, in 1849, signalled the beginning of the assertive consolidation of the pre-famine Roman Catholic revival by means of the full range of 'Roman' and 'Ultramontane' discipline, devotionalism and authority (Bowen, 1978, chs. 5 and 6). The work of missionary religious orders and the widespread use of the parish mission proved a more than adequate Catholic response to evangelical Protestant missionary endeavours among the Catholic population. Whilst postfamine Irish religion did not become *exclusively* extreme, to the exclusion of *any* more moderate opinion, it did become fundamentally divided between a militant Evangelical Protestantism, characterized, if not dominated, by the evangelical fervour of the 1859 revival, and an equally militant Ultramontane Catholicism, characterized by the 'devotional revolution' and symbolized by, for example, the Marian devotion which became focused on Knock, Co. Mayo, after claims, in 1879, of the occurrence of visions of the Virgin Mary.

In both basic communities and all three major Irish denominations, therefore, the Victorian period saw a process of increasing self-definition. Placing the Church of Ireland and Presbyterians together and alongside the range of other Protestant Non-conformist denominations and non-denominational Protestant Gospel Halls and Missions which expanded so rapidly after the 1859 revival, it also saw an increasing militancy in the matter of Catholic-Protestant relations. The Evangelical Protestant endeavour to realize a 'Second Reformation'; the successful Catholic resistance and response via the devotional revolution and the institution of the parish mission; the crisis of the famine and the impact of Dallas and the 'Protestant Crusade'; and the heightening of evangelical Protestant consciousness in the 1859 revival and its legacy: out of all these things there emerged after disestablishment in late Victorian Ireland what Patrick Corish has described as 'two church establishments, one Catholic and the other Protestant, despite the fact there was no longer a legally established church' (Corish, 1985, pp. 226–7). In the 1880s, Corish suggests, the existence of the two unofficial church establishments began to foreshadow the existence of two distinct political communities. Catholicism reached an accommodation with the nationalist movement, whilst avoiding the explicit commitment of the church to the nationalist cause. And a *majority* of the Protestant population — Anglican, Presbyterian and Nonconformist — became opponents of Home Rule, whilst avoiding the *complete* identification of Protestantism with Ulster Unionism.[7]

The twentieth-century legacy of this Victorian religious polarization remains (all too tragically) familiar. There is, moreover, in the light of the still passionately interrelated nature of religion and politics in Ireland, a further irony in the Victorian history with which we are concerned here. A case can be made for the view that, from as early as 1831, British governments recognized the moral and political need for governmental withdrawal from denominational preference or privilege in Ireland. In 1831 the setting up of the National Schools, although still recognizing the role of the churches in education, sought to avoid direct denominational preference or favouritism: government aid was available to any denomination and children were not to be taught the doctrines of churches other than their own. Also in the 1830s the reforms of tithe and of the revenues of the Irish church pointed away from the era of government support for the Church of Ireland and towards the era of government disengagement from direct involvement in Irish religious life. In 1845 the British government increased the annual grant to the Roman Catholic seminary at Maynooth, and throughout the period until 1869 the government continued to pay the annual grant of the *Regium Donum* to the Presbyterian church: two financially small but symbolically significant indications of government recognition that if it were to be involved in actively supporting religion in Ireland it must support more than the established church. In 1869, with disestablishment, there ended also both the Maynooth grant and the *Regium Donum*. By 1871 the government had thus *constitutionally* withdrawn from involvement in religion in Ireland more thoroughly than it had in Wales, Scotland or England (indeed more thoroughly than it ever has in the latter two): yet in the twentieth century religion and politics have remained interconnected in Ireland in a manner which had already ceased in the rest of Britain by the 1920s.

IV IRISH DISESTABLISHMENT: THE BRITISH DIMENSION

As G. I. T. Machin indicates at the end of his study of the relationship between politics and the churches in Great Britain from 1832 to 1868, it was unclear in 1868–9 whether Irish disestablishment would prove an end

[7] For more detailed, and contrasting, interpretations of aspects of the relationship between religion, politics and nationalism in Victorian Ireland, see the following: *Catholicism* Larkin, 1975, Steele, 1975, Bowen, 1978 and 1983, and Corish, 1985, chs. 7 and 8; *Presbyterianism* Barkley, 1975, Holmes, 1982, and Brooke, 1987, ch. 9; *Church of Ireland* McDowell, 1975, ch. 5.

or a beginning, whether it would be the climax of mid-Victorian Dissenting pressure or the prelude to general religious disestablishment in Britain (1977, pp. 382–3). Was the future to lie, as Miall, Nonconformists and Radicals hoped and believed, and many churchmen feared, with the steady dismantling of establishment, or was it to lie, as Gladstone hoped, with continuing establishment rendered safe and acceptable by the removal of its manifestly unacceptable aspects?

In the event it was Gladstone's hopes that were fulfilled and Miall's that were never realized. Irish disestablishment proved, in retrospect, the high-water mark of the campaigns for disestablishment in Victorian and post-Victorian Britain. Miall introduced to the Commons motions for the disestablishment of the Church of England in 1871, 1872 and 1873: he lost comprehensively on each occasion. By the mid-1880s, further concessions to English Nonconformity had been granted and the most blatant causes of practical offence to English Dissent removed; Miall was dead; the Liberal Party was in process of splitting over Gladstone's conversion to the necessity of Irish Home Rule; and the mid-century political configuration of religious dissent and political liberalism which had triumphed in 1868–69 was passing away. The Liberal Government of 1892–5 declared in favour of both Welsh and Scottish — but not English — disestablishment, and in any case left office without having secured even these aims. By the time the next Liberal government was elected in 1906, English disestablishment had passed even more decisively off the agenda of practical politics.

In Scotland the early 1870s saw the failure of the negotiations for Union between the Free Church and United Presbyterians — significantly on the refusal of a minority in the Free Church to relinquish their commitment to the principle of establishment and become Voluntaries in theory as well as practice. Moreover, by the 1880s the established Church of Scotland was enjoying an impressive revival and growth in numbers of communicants, and it was no longer possible clearly to demonstrate that the Church of Scotland was smaller than the combined numbers of the Free Church and United Presbyterians. There was, nonetheless, a fierce propaganda war in the 1870s and 80s between Voluntaries and Establishmentarians in Scotland, which reached its height in 1885–6. For all its intensity, however, it did not result in Scottish disestablishment and, indeed, the very intensity of the campaign was due in part precisely to the strength of the defence of establishment. Moreover, even in the midst of the ongoing controversy, another strand within Victorian Scottish Presbyterian life was emerging in the form of a movement for reunion on the basis of a modified, reformed establishment.[8]

[8] For a discussion of Victorian Scotland and the issue of disestablishment, see *RVB*, II, 5 and Machin, 1983 and 1987, pp. 87–94 and 255–60.

Only in Wales did further disestablishment occur. Even there, despite the manifestly minority status of the established church, it took twenty-three years from the date of Irish disestablishment, and a bitterly fought tithe war in 1888–90, before Welsh disestablishment became a viable political proposition (with the election of a Liberal government after an election campaign in which the Liberal programme had placed Welsh disestablishment high on its agenda of objectives); and a further twenty-two years and four bills before Parliament (in 1894, 1895, 1909 and 1912) before Welsh disestablishment finally reached the statute book in 1914 — only to then be delayed for a further five years of world war and its immediate aftermath. Politically, its passage depended upon the election of Liberal governments, dependent in their turn upon a large number of Welsh Liberal MPs, in their turn dependent on Welsh voters, for a majority of whom the Anglican Church in Wales had become (justly or not) the symbol of English, land-owning interests, widely perceived to be fundamentally at odds with the interests of the Welsh people, language and culture. Welsh disestablishment, when it came, was thus the product of the politics of class and nationality as much as of the politics of religion (Bell, 1969, pp. 228–9).[9]

The final question remains why it was only in Ireland and Wales that disestablishment was eventually secured. A crude argument from numbers — that in Ireland and Wales the established churches were the churches of minorities in the population — will not of itself suffice. The 1851 Census in England revealed that the Church of England was the church of rather less than fifty per cent of those who chose to attend worship on Census Sunday, and in Scotland after the Disruption the established church certainly could not claim the allegiance of more than fifty per cent of the people. On the other hand, a modified version of the argument from numbers remains relevant: the Church of England remained the church of almost fifty per cent of English churchgoers, and the Church of Scotland, by the 1880s, had revived to a point at which it could claim more communicants and faster growth than the other main Presbyterian churches put together. In Ireland, on the other hand, the church, while established, had not gone above twelve per cent of the population, and according to the 1851 religious census the Anglican Church in Wales attracted only nine per cent of those

[9] Thus both Bebbington and W. B. George, for example, emphasize the extent to which the Liberation Society, which had exerted so powerful a political influence in Wales during the 1850s and 1860s, was effectively marginalized and then excluded from the disestablishment campaigns of the mid-1880s onwards. In contrast to the perspective of the Liberation Society, the leadership of the late Victorian and Edwardian movement for Welsh disestablishment saw the issue less as matter of religious principle and more as a matter of Welsh national sentiment and the desirability of protesting against all or any 'Anglicizing' influences in Welsh life, society and culture (Bebbington, 1982b, pp. 33–6; George, 1970).

who attended church on Census Sunday.[10] By 1891 the vigorous effort of the Victorian Anglican Church in Wales to revitalize itself had produced some improvement in the situation, but combined Nonconformist membership still numbered almost four times the figure for regular Anglican communicants (Bebbington, 1982a, p. 491). To the argument from numbers, therefore, must be added something further.

The answer that it was only in these two cases that the results of electoral politics produced the necessary pressure to make politicians act, while true enough in itself, is merely to press the question one stage further back and express it in a different way. Arguably the root of the matter lies, rather, in elusive but significant notions of religion and national identity and in the ability of the established churches of England and Scotland to adjust and reduce their definitions and practice of 'establishment'. On the one hand, they remained for a *sufficient* number of the English and Scottish people, at least, *an* acceptable element of their national and religious cultural identity. On the other hand, and equally importantly, by their adjustments to the meaning of 'establishment', they ceased to be a positive, active, grievance to all but a minority of those who remained outside them.

In Ireland and Wales such adjustments were never possible. Not only were the Anglican churches small minorities in the overall demographic structure of Irish and Welsh religion, they were also widely *perceived to be* alien, foreign, English, and, moreover, the churches of a social and economic élite. We have noted already Sean Connolly's observation that the Church of Ireland prior to disestablishment had functioned as the religious embodiment of civil society, ministering to such an élite. By no stretch of the imagination was the established Church of Ireland an expression of the predominant national religious culture and identity of Ireland. In Wales, similarly, a complex combination of social and economic class, language and denominational allegiance rendered Anglicanism at best the expression of a minority Welsh culture and identity (heavily, but not exclusively, English speaking and upper middle class), whilst Nonconformity could claim to represent a majority Welsh culture which was predominantly (but also not exclusively) Welsh speaking and lower middle and working class.[11] It is in *this* sense (though not in the further sense of a direct correlation between

---

[10] Although the *overall* contrast of nine per cent Anglican attenders in 1851 and eighty-seven per cent Nonconformist attenders disguised very large regional variations. The Anglican Church faced a particular difficulty in rural Welsh speaking areas (see Jones, 1981, p. 227).

[11] In fact the Anglican Church in Wales made considerable efforts after 1850 to respond to the demands of Welsh language and culture. As Bell has pointed out, the church in Wales had a sound claim to express a version of 'Welshness' different from that of Welsh Nonconformity — but the political point was a matter of numbers and long-nurtured perceptions and their force, not varying interpretations calmly considered (Bell, 1969, pp. 269–73 and 241–2).

specific churches and equally specific 'nationalist' political parties), that Machin is correct to speak of 'Catholic nationalist force' gaining Irish disestablishment, and 'Welsh Nonconformist national force' securing Welsh disestablishment (1987, pp. 324–5).[12]

In England and Scotland the religious establishments had greater room for adjustment and took advantage of it. Less rigidly the churches of specific, élite minorities, they accepted reform and adjustment of the rights and structures of establishment, relinquished many of their privileges, and moderated many of their claims. In the case of England, as we have seen in other essays in this volume and its companion, the Church of England so adjusted itself that it remained if not a national church, at least a national institution — *an* expression, if not *the* expression, of a distinctively English religious ethos and style.

Similarly in Scotland (where in any case the position of the established church was made easier by the fact that it shared a common Presbyterian identity with the two major Scottish dissenting bodies), in the last quarter of the nineteenth century and the first quarter of the twentieth century the debates over disestablishment were finally diverted into discussion of the possibility of Presbyterian reunion. As the previous essay noted, a succession of developments and changes led from the Free Church-United Presbyterian Union of 1900, through the granting of freedom to the Church of Scotland to change its Confession of Faith in 1905, the adoption of a relaxed formula of subscription in 1910, and negotiations for Union from 1909 onwards, to the Church of Scotland Act of 1921, granting the Church of Scotland spiritual independence of the state. The result, as Machin has put it, was the eventual re-absorption into the Church of Scotland, in 1929, of most of the groups which had left it in the preceding two hundred years, the reabsorption being based not on disestablishment but on 'an attenuated and nominal type of establishment' in which spiritual independence and self-government were combined with a 'national recognition of religion' (Machin, 1983, p. 233).

The Church of Scotland Act passed through Parliament with little opposition, for by the 1920s the world had already moved on. Although the

---

[12] For careful analyses of the very complex and subtle relationships between religion, culture and national identity in modern Britain, and especially Victorian Wales and Scotland, see Robbins, 1982, Bebbington, 1982a, and Brown, 1987, ch. 1. Whilst differing in many specific points, each of these authors clearly demonstrates that the relationship between religion and national identities in modern Britain is anything but simple or straightforward. On the one hand, religion has at times clearly contributed markedly to the development or maintenance of *distinct* Welsh, Scottish, Irish and English senses and notions of national identity and ethos. On the other hand, it is also possible to identify trends and influences in the religious life of modern Britain which have contributed to the consolidation of a more uniform British sense of identity.

relationship between religion and Parliament could still cause an occasional flurry of controversy — as in 1927–8 when the Commons refused to accept a Revised Book of Common Prayer prepared by the Church of England and passed by its Church Assembly — such moments began to look increasingly quaint and anachronistic in an era whose politics were now centred on issues of class, not religion. The age when the disestablishment of the Irish Church could be the centre and focus of national politics and the deciding factor in a general election was past indeed.

BIBLIOGRAPHY

D. H. Akenson (1971) *The Church of Ireland: Ecclesiastical Reform and Revolution 1800–1885*, Yale University Press.

J. M. Barkley (1975) 'The Presbyterian Church in Ireland and the Government of Ireland Act (1920)' in D. Baker (ed.) *Church, Society and Politics*, pp. 393–403, Oxford, Blackwell.

D. W. Bebbington (1982a) 'Religion and national feeling in nineteenth-century Wales and Scotland' in S. Mews (ed.) *Religion and National Identity*, pp. 489–503, Oxford, Blackwell.

D. W. Bebbington (1982b) *The Nonconformist Conscience*, George Allen and Unwin.

*P. M. H. Bell (1969) *Disestablishment in Ireland and Wales*, S.P.C.K.

*D. Bowen (1978) *The Protestant Crusade in Ireland 1800–70*, Dublin, Gill and Macmillan.

D. Bowen (1983) *Paul Cardinal Cullen and the Shaping of Modern Irish Catholicism*, Dublin, Gill and Macmillan.

*P. Brooke (1987) *Ulster Presbyterianism*, Dublin, Gill and Macmillan.

C. G. Brown (1987) *The Social History of Religion in Scotland Since 1730*, Methuen.

G. P. Connolly (1984) 'The transubstantiation of myth: towards a new popular history of nineteenth-century Catholicism in England', *Journal of Ecclesiastical History*, Vol. 35, pp. 78–104.

*S. J. Connolly (1985) *Religion and Society in Nineteenth Century Ireland*, Dundalk, Dundalgan Press.

*P. Corish (1985) *The Irish Catholic Experience: A Historical Survey*, Dublin, Gill and Macmillan.

G. C. Daly (1970) 'Church renewal: 1869–1877' in M. Hurley (ed.) *Irish Anglicanism 1869–1969*, pp. 23–38. Dublin, Alan Figgs.

W. B. George (1970) 'Welsh disestablishment and Welsh nationalism', *Journal of the Historical Society of the Church in Wales*, Vol. 20, pp. 77–91.

R. F. G. Holmes (1982) 'Ulster Presbyterians and Irish nationalism' in S. Mews (ed.) *Religion and National Identity*, pp. 535–48, Oxford, Blackwell.

I. G. Jones (1981) 'Religion and society in the first half of the nineteenth century' and 'The Liberation Society and Welsh politics 1844 to 1868' in *Explorations and*

Explanations: Essays in the Social History of Victorian Wales, pp. 217–35 and 236–68, Llandysul, Gower Press.

E. Larkin (1975) 'Church, state and nation in modern Ireland', *American Historical Review*, Vol. 80, pp. 1244–76.

G. I. T. Machin (1977) *Politics and the Churches in Great Britain 1832–68*, Oxford, Oxford University Press.

G. I. T. Machin (1987) *Politics and the Churches in Great Britain 1869–1921*, Oxford, Oxford University Press.

R. B. McDowell (1975) *The Church of Ireland, 1869–1969*, Routledge.

K. Robbins (1982) 'Religion and Identity in Modern British history' in S. Mews (ed.) *Religion and National Identity*, pp. 465–87, Oxford, Blackwell.

E. D. Steele (1975) 'Cardinal Cullen and Irish nationality' in *Irish Historical Studies*, Vol. 19, pp. 239–60.

CHAPTER 7

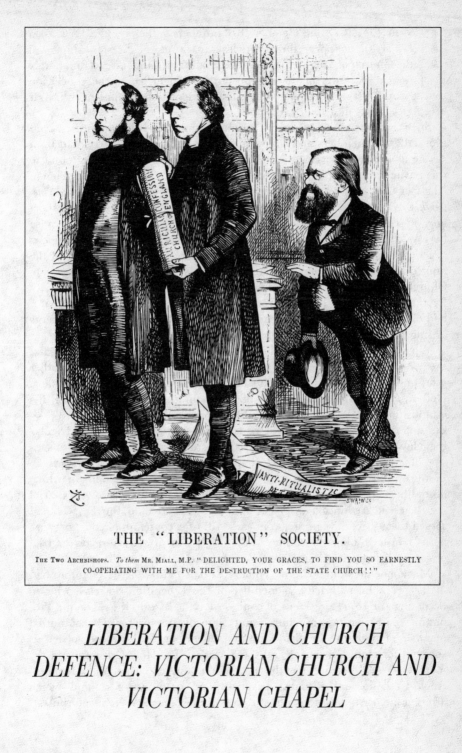

THE "LIBERATION" SOCIETY.

THE TWO ARCHBISHOPS. *To them* MR. MIALL, M.P. "DELIGHTED, YOUR GRACES, TO FIND YOU SO EARNESTLY
CO-OPERATING WITH ME FOR THE DESTRUCTION OF THE STATE CHURCH!!"

LIBERATION AND CHURCH DEFENCE: VICTORIAN CHURCH AND VICTORIAN CHAPEL

I N the June 1877 and October 1878 numbers of the periodical *Nineteenth Century* there appeared two articles advocating the disestablishment of the Church of England. The author maintained that an examination of the practical workings of the existing establishment led to the conclusion that it would be preferable for that establishment to be abolished in favour of a free church in a free state.

Such arguments were hardly original: militant Nonconformists, and especially the members and supporters of the Liberation Society, had been saying as much for several decades. Nor was the immediate background to this particular author's observations on the subject of the state and religion (the fact that, only four months prior to the first of his articles in the *Nineteenth Century*, the state had imposed a prison sentence, albeit only a short one, on a clergyman, of views similar to those of the author himself, because he would not accept the state's authority over certain matters of religious practice) by any means unique. Some forty-three years earlier, one of the immediate causes of the foundation, in 1844, of the British Anti-State Church Association, (which changed its name to the more familiar Society for the Liberation of Religion from State Patronage and Control in 1853), had been the Nonconformist sense of outrage over a series of imprisonments arising from refusal to pay church rates.

What was different about the two 1877–8 articles, however, was that their author, far from being an evangelical Nonconformist, was none other than the Reverend A. H. Mackonochie, Anglo-Catholic Vicar of St Albans, Holborn. The immediate context of his commitment to the cause of disestablishment in 1877–8 was the Public Worship Regulation Act of 1874 — the notorious 'bill to put down ritualism' — but behind that particular issue lay the wider one of the perceived Erastianism of the state in a succession of issues ranging from the Gorham Judgement and *Essays and Reviews* to the disestablishment of the Irish church. The recent imprisonment which no doubt helped to focus Mackonochie's opinions on the issue was that of the Reverend Arthur Tooth, Vicar of St James', Hatcham, Surrey, who had served twenty six days in prison in early 1877 for contempt of court because of his refusal to obey the rulings of the newly constituted court for the trial of cases arising out of the Public Worship Regulation Act.

Mackonochie, along with his equally Ritualist curate A. H. Stanton, had in fact even been, briefly, a member of the Liberation Society, prior to becoming (in 1877) president of a newly founded Church League for Promoting the Separation of Church and State. But he was also a committed member of both the English Church Union (one of the most vociferous societies for church defence) and the Society of the Holy Cross (one of the most vigorous societies for the promotion and extension of 'advanced' Anglo-Catholic and Ritualist practices and opinions of a kind which aroused intense opposition and objection from evangelical Nonconformists).

The example of Mackonochie, his stance on disestablishment, his brief experiment as a Ritualist member of the Liberation Society, and his presidency of an Anglo-Catholic disestablishment society which passed resolutions very similar to those of the Liberation Society itself, is, it must be said, decidedly atypical. Although the Public Worship Regulation Act did stimulate a flurry of Anglo-Catholic calls for disestablishment, the number of Ritualists and High Churchmen who held such views remained a decided minority. Nonconformists, meanwhile, necessarily experienced mixed feelings over such allies: that church and state had got into such a tangle that members of the establishment called for disestablishment must be gratifying; but Mackonochie's reason for desiring disestablishment — that it would aid the spread of Ritualism — could only horrify evangelical Protestant Nonconformists for whom Ritualism was popery in Anglican form.[1]

For all its oddity, however, the case of Mackonochie serves in the present context to suggest something of the complexity of the Victorian encounter between establishment and dissent. That encounter is conveniently reducible to a *straightforward* confrontation of church versus chapel 'church defence' versus 'liberation'. Conveniently reducible, but not accurately so, for although the clash of chapel and church was an integral and prominent part of Victorian religious and political life, and although the *predominant* pattern of that clash was the commitment of Nonconformity to 'liberation' and the counter commitment of the establishment to 'church defence', neither the clash of church and chapel nor the concepts of 'liberation' and 'church defence' are in the end susceptible to simple polarization.

The present essay seeks, briefly, to achieve three aims. First, to indicate the extent to which Victorian chapel versus church confrontation was indeed a clash *between* 'liberation' and 'church defence'. Second, to note some of the ways in which the concepts of 'liberation' and 'church defence' nevertheless provoked or reflected divisions *within* the communities of 'church' and 'chapel'. Third, to suggest that the complex interaction between church, chapel, church defence and liberation in Victorian England and Wales is most appropriately understood within the context of the growth of an increasingly *denominational* outlook and identity in both Non-

---

[1] Mackonochie's Ritualist curate, A. H. Stanton, on the other hand, had no such reservations about adopting and adapting the methods and ethos of Protestant Nonconformity. When C. M. Davies, a Broad Church clergyman turned religious journalist, visited St Alban's, Holborn, to report on a New Year's Eve service there, he found Stanton conducting a Watch-night service of a kind more usually associated with Methodism, complete with revivalist hymnody and decidedly evangelical preaching. Overt ritual was not in evidence. Davies' account of his visit to St Alban's appeared in his collection of reports on the varieties of Anglican religious life to be found in London in the early 1870s. The collection was published in 1876, with the title *Orthodox London: Or Phases of Religious Life in the Church of England*.

conformity and Anglicanism in response to the clear option of the state for growing constitutional pluralism and neutrality in matters of religion.

I CHURCH AND CHAPEL c.1830–c.1870

The constitutional reforms of the years 1828–35 — most notably in the present context the Repeal of the Test and Corporation Acts in 1828, the passing of the Reform Act in 1832, and the Municipal Corporations Act of 1835 — created among Nonconformists the hope that the era of Anglican privilege and Dissenting disabilities might be about to end. In fact, because of the residual strength of the establishment, and the limits of parliamentary reform, it required several more decades of Nonconformist pressure to achieve that end. As a result, throughout the Victorian period the conflict between 'church' and 'chapel' was always present in, and not infrequently central to, the political life of Victorian England and Wales, although by the end of the Queen's reign, despite one last bitter church-chapel confrontation, it was already becoming clear that in English and Welsh political life the domination of the politics of religion was being replaced by the domination of the politics of class.

In order to exploit the political opportunities offered by the reforms of the early 1830s, Nonconformists required an effective political organization, but, as David Thompson has pointed out, in the late 1830s Dissenting politics were in fact in relative disarray. The long-standing Nonconformist political coalition known as the Protestant Dissenting Deputies had been fundamentally weakened in 1836 by conflict between the Unitarians (who had provided much of the political leadership) and the still Trinitarian members of the coalition. Legal cases ensued over the ownership of property now held by Unitarians but originally built or purchased by orthodox believers. Such legal disputes did nothing for political cohesion. Moreover, the political style of the Dissenting Deputies was essentially that of the pre-Reform Act era: it lacked the cohesion of the pressure-group politics which were to be the hall-mark of successful early and mid-Victorian reform movements. On the other hand, the various new and politically radical Dissenting pressure groups, such as the Church Rate Abolition Society, the Society for Promoting Ecclesiastical Knowledge, and the various local Voluntary Church Societies inspired by Scottish precedents, as yet lacked unity and cohesion (Thompson, 1974, pp. 211–3; Jones, 1981, pp. 237–45).

In the early 1840s, however, three factors conspired to produce an effective focus for Nonconformist political activity. From 1839 onwards the persistent conflicts over church rates were given added passion by a series of imprisonments arising from local church rate controversies: John Thorogood in Chelmsford, David Jones in Llanon, John James in Llanelly and William Baines in Leicester provided Dissenters with examples of establishment 'persecution'. Second, in 1841 Edward Miall (Baines' minister in Leicester) gave up his Congregational pastorate to devote himself full time to the cause of Voluntaryism. He founded *The Nonconformist*, a paper which came to symbolize the militant and radical wing of Victorian Dissent, and edited it for some forty years. He also began to seek the means of organizing a new, effective focus of militant Dissenting opinion. Third, in 1843 two events provided Miall with the opportunity he sought. In Scotland the Disruption and creation of the Free Church provided both example and inspiration for English Voluntarists. In England the attempt of a Tory government to pass a Factory Act which included a favoured position for the established church in the proposed factory schools caused Dissenting uproar: Nonconformists (including even the normally apolitical Wesleyan Conference) united in protest, and the offending clause of the proposed legislation was withdrawn.

Miall and other radical Dissenters seized the moment and organized an Anti-State Church Conference in April 1844 which resulted in the foundation of the British Anti-State Church Association. The new society was committed not merely to the relief of Dissenting grievances but to the actual disestablishment of the Church of England. Moreover, although it did not embody the thoroughgoing political radicalism which Miall hoped for (indeed it came to occupy a carefully chosen middle ground within the spectrum of Victorian radical reform), the Society in due course became, for a generation, or perhaps two, an effective focus for Nonconformist political aspirations, one of the best organized of Victorian political pressure groups, a formative influence in the emergence of the Gladstonian Liberal party and even, it has been claimed, 'the epitome of rational agitation' (Vincent, 1966, p. 66; Gilbert, 1976, p. 164; Thompson, 1974, p. 210).

The early years of the Society, until about 1853 when it officially changed its name to 'The Society for the Liberation of Religion from State Patronage and Control', were necessarily occupied with organization. The constitution of the Society vested authority in an elected Council of 500, executive authority between triennial conferences of this Council being delegated to a committee of fifty, chosen from the Council. Initially the three national secretaries (of whom Miall was one) and also the local 'registrars' were honorary and unpaid. The main activities of the Society at this stage were the publication of tracts and organization of lecture tours. In 1847 a major organizational step was taken with the appointment of a permanent salaried secretary, an office staff, and the reorganization of the localities whereby local committees, responsible to the executive committee, were set up. Such local committees in due course became the basis of Liberation Society influence in parliamentary constituencies. The Society also now employed full-time touring lecturers and both full and part-time fund collectors. The first full-time national secretary was John Carvell Williams, who became, in the 1860s, the Society's key strategist and, no less than Edward Miall, devoted a lifetime's work to the Society and its cause.

By 1853 the society was sufficiently confident to embark on a new phase of national policy. As well as starting its own monthly magazine, *The Liberator*, in 1855, and establishing a press and publishing committee in 1854 (which from 1860 had a full-time researcher H. S. Skeats, a historian of the English Free Churches, at its disposal), the Society embarked on a concerted parliamentary campaign, encouraged by its success in securing the election of a small but growing body of pro-Dissent MPs from the 1847 election onwards. To co-ordinate the parliamentary activities of the Society a parliamentary subcommittee was set up in 1854 and an electoral sub-committee in 1855. The former co-ordinated parliamentary action and functioned virtually as a Whips' office for MPs sympathetic to the Society; the latter co-ordinated the Society's attempts to influence local constituencies and elections. As well as supporting such parliamentary measures as the Oxford and Cambridge University reforms of 1854 and 1856, the Society's parliamentary sympathisers introduced bills of their own, most notably a series for the abolition of church rates which in the 1850s met with success in the Commons but defeat in the Lords. By the early 1860s, however, such bills lost even their Commons majority.

In 1861–2 the Society again adjusted its strategy (partly to avoid the disheartening effect of repeated parliamentary failure) and increased its scale of operations. As a result of the conjunction of this increase in activities and a peculiarly favourable political context in the mid-60s, the Society achieved its most striking successes in the ensuing decade. In 1862 the bicentenary celebrations of the ejection of Puritan ministers from the Church of England in 1662 provided an extraordinary focus for the publicity and propaganda efforts of the Society. The Liberation Society both contributed to and exploited the widespread Nonconformist (and especially Baptist and Congregationalist) celebration of their heritage, and also renewed its commitment to the publication of both tracts and major studies such as Miall's book of 1862 on the *Title Deeds of the Church of England to Her Parochial Endowments*.

As well as such ongoing propaganda, however, it was resolved to switch the focus of political efforts from Parliament to the constituencies: supporters were urged to withhold their support from parliamentary candidates who were not prepared to commit themselves to the Society's policies. It was also resolved to make a special effort in Wales, where the strength of Nonconformity and the relative weakness of the established church, together with an emerging alliance of interest between Welsh nationalism and Welsh Nonconformity based on an amalgam of class, language, chapel and culture, promised to yield high support. Finally, but importantly, a political alliance was agreed in Ireland between the Liberation Society and the Catholic National Association. It is open to debate precisely how many seats the Liberation Society decisively influenced in the 1865 and 1868 elections. What is clear, however (and was clear at the time also), is that the Society's influence was indeed decisive in Wales, was also influential in a number of English seats, and, together with the National Association votes in Ireland, helped to create the parliamentary arithmetic which issued first in the abolition of Church Rates in 1868 and then in the disestablishment of the Irish church in 1869. The hopes of Liberation Society members were raised that the disestablishment of the Church of England itself might now be within reach.[2]

Faced with such well-orchestrated Nonconformist organization and the growing realisation that the relationship of church and state was indeed changing radically, members of the established church responded by organizing means of 'church defence'. In the 1840s there began, on the one hand, agitation for the revival of Convocation, and on the other hand the foundation of local church unions and church defence associations. The unions were generally High Church or Ritualist in orientation and arose out of concern over the state's 'interference' in such matters as the church's traditional role in education, the regulation of matters of liturgical ritual and adjudication in questions of doctrine. After 1848 the Gorham Judgement provided a vital catalyst for the emergence of such groups. One of the most notable local church unions was that at Bristol, whose secretary was the militant churchman G. A. Denison. The local church defence associations, meanwhile, developed mainly in areas where the Liberation Society was particularly active.

It was not until the late 1850s that such local initiatives issued in national organizations. In 1859, however, were founded both the English Church Union (which became increasingly prominent in the defence of High Church and Ritualist causes and opinions) and the Church Institution, which sought to mobilize church support and oppose the Liberation Society by the adoption and use of its own pressure group political methods. One of the leading figures in the foundation of the Church Institution was the layman, Henry Hoare, who had also been prominent in the campaign for the revival of Convocation. In both cases the need to mobilize the laity loomed large. The old political dependence of the church upon the landed interest and its political power was increasingly vulnerable

[2] For detailed analyses of the Liberation Society until 1868 see Thompson, 1974; and Jones 1981. For a general account of 'liberation and disestablishment' see Mackintosh, 1972; and for the location of this theme within the broader context of religion and politics in Victorian Britain, see Machin, 1977 and 1987. For the local manifestation of Liberation Society activities, see Jones 1981 for Wales, and Newton, 1980, for an English case study.

in the era of post-Reform Act policies: the church now needed its lay voters as well as its traditional clerical and gentry-aristocratic influence. In 1861 the first Church Congress met in Cambridge, prompted by the local Church Defence Association. Here, too, the defence of the church and the encouragement of lay involvement went hand in hand, as they were also to do in the development of diocesan conferences and synods later in the century.[3]

II   CHURCH AND CHAPEL c.1870–c.1902

After 1870 the English Church Union became increasingly identified with the defence of specifically Ritualist and Anglo-Catholic interests, whilst the Church Institution (renamed in 1871 the Church Defence Institution), formed a *de facto* alliance with the emerging local organizations of the late Victorian Conservative party — just as the Liberation Society had featured in the emergence of the local Liberal party organizations in the 1860s. The Church Defence Institution, however, reached the height of its efficiency and scope as an organization (by 1886 it had branches in every diocese and hoped to reach each large town and rural deanery) just as its definitive rival, the Liberation Society, passed the peak of its influence. After 1870 the form taken by church-chapel confrontation changed somewhat from that of the 1850s and 1860s, and the Church Defence Institution found its own role curiously undermined as its rival diminished as a practical threat to the Church of England. By the 1890s, moreover, the Conservative party was well on the way to establishing its own autonomous local party organiza-tions and was hence less dependent on the role of groups like the CDI, whilst the bishops, led by Benson, Archbishop of Canterbury since 1883, were intent on developing greater self-government and self-regulation within the church and thus securing greater independence from any one political party. Benson duly established a diocese and parish based organization of lay church members — the Central Church Committee — and in 1896 secured, not without CDI resentment, the merging of the CDI with the new organization.

Benson and his fellow bishops were well aware that the late Victorian Conservative party remained the natural ally of the church (just as the late Victorian Liberal party remained the natural ally of Nonconformity); but they were also astute enough to sense that an overt and aggressive Church-Tory party alliance might not be a sound policy in a clearly changing political context. The openly party allegiance of the CDI was, therefore,

---

[3] For the place of such institutional expressions of 'church defence' within the broader history of the Church of England in the Victorian period, see *RVB*, I, 1.

duly absorbed and then muted within a broader organization. 'The age of militant churchmanship', as the most recent historian of the CDI has observed, 'was coming to an end' (Roberts, 1984, p. 580).[4]

A significant change also occurred in Nonconformist politics in the 1880s and 1890s. In retrospect the years 1868–71 were the high point of the career of the Liberation Society and a point of transition in the Victorian confrontation of church and chapel. The abolition of church rates in 1868 and the disestablishment of the Irish church in 1869 were followed in 1871 by Edward Miall's first Commons motion for the disestablishment of the Church of England. The motion failed by 374 votes to 89; but simply to have reached the point at which disestablishment of the Church of England was debated was itself an achievement.

The achievement soon began to look more like an end than a beginning, however. Further motions in 1872 and 1873 also failed: that of 1872 secured 94 votes, with 295 against: that of 1873 only 61 votes in favour with 356 against. The advent of a Conservative government in 1874 rendered further disestablishment motions pointless for the time being: Miall retired from Parliament in 1874. Even when the Liberals returned to office in 1880 there was little progress on the part of the Liberation Society. The Liberals reformed the law concerning burials in parish churchyards, enabling Nonconformist ministers to officiate at such services and removing the more offensive (although not all) Anglican rights and Nonconformist disabilities in an area which caused continuing controversy and offence.[5] But an attempt by the Society to re-activate the disestablishment campaign petered out in 1883: the issue, as David Bebbington has observed, was running out of steam (Bebbington, 1982, p. 19).

So was the Liberation Society. The explanation most favoured at the time and urged by Carvell Williams was that the political context had become unfavourable: popular moral indignation was focused upon wars in South Africa and Afghanistan and atrocities in the Balkans, not on the remaining inequalities of Nonconformists; Irish Home Rule was becoming the central political-moral issue in domestic politics; after 1886 the Liberal party was split. Bebbington's analysis suggests, however, that a number of more serious underlying weaknesses and changes in context lay at the heart of the Liberation Society's movement into decline. Its level of activity dropped from an average of over 850 meetings a year in the mid and late 1870s, to only around 300 a year in the 1880s. The structure and methods of the Society, moreover, remained those of the 1860s, and Carvell Williams

[4] There is also a useful chapter on church defence and its ambiguities in Crowther, 1970.

[5] For details of the burials issue, see Mackintosh, 1972, pp. 274–82; and Bebbington, 1982, pp. 30–2.

led it tenaciously rather than dynamically. Many of the worst and most actively pressing problems of religious inequality had now been removed: education remained a decidedly active issue, but was not the main focus of the Society's efforts.

Perhaps most crucially, however, the Society opted for the priority of party politics rather than the 'purity' of the moral crusade. It chose to ally itself completely with the Liberal party and thereby seek to permeate that party. But in so doing, in exchange for a hoped for adoption of its aims as party policy, the Society sacrificed the ability actually to pressure, threaten and cajole the Liberals. The Liberal party, for its part, was ready to accept the Society's support and profess commitment to its ideals, but also prepared to decline to make the Society's aims official policy. At the same time, the Society, in becoming effectively an adjunct of the Liberal party, lost the crusading moral appeal which it had possessed in the days of imprisonment over church rates and the campaign for Irish disestablishment. Its early appeal had been overtly moral and religious: an appeal to the evangelical conscience in support of religious freedom and against religious disabilities. Its later stance looked increasingly political, and pragmatically party political at that (Bebbington, 1982, ch. 2).

The moral energies of late Victorian Nonconformity turned increasingly elsewhere. Social questions such as temperance and alcohol abuse, prostitution and sexual immorality, gambling, and the poverty and degradation which were perceived as both cause and consequence of such vices, became central to the late Victorian and Edwardian 'Nonconformist Conscience'. The Nonconformist political campaigns thus inspired could easily appear narrow-minded or repressive, as for example when they caused the downfall of the Irish nationalist politician Parnell because of his adultery, or sought to impose the Sunday closing of public houses. There was, moreover, a considerable irony in the action of a Nonconformist community which had but lately campaigned for the removal of restrictive legislation based upon religious principles now seeking to secure restrictive legislation on matters which were as much — or arguably more — religious than moral in nature. But it was also true that such campaigns, whether prompted by pamphlets such as Mearns' *Bitter Cry of Outcast London* or newspaper articles such as Stead's *The Maiden Tribute of Modern Babylon*, or by opposition to alcohol and gambling, possessed a moral and religious passion and a crusading zeal — whereas the stance of the late Victorian Liberation Society appeared increasingly drily and calculatingly political.[6]

---

[6] Mearns' pamphlet appeared in 1883 and addressed the poverty, degradation and consequent sexual immorality of the worst of London's inner city slums. Stead's articles appeared in the Pall Mall Gazette in 1885 and concerned juvenile prostitution. The Nonconformist Conscience was, characteristically, a moral crusade against specific 'wrongs'. Bebbington identifies three

The organizational expression of the late Victorian 'Nonconformist Conscience' was also significantly different from that of the mid-Victorian Nonconformist call for 'liberation'. The Liberation Society was an organization composed of individual members. The principal institutional expression of the 'Nonconformist Conscience' was the National Free Church Council (a body of delegates from local councils, representing local denominations) which was founded in the 1890s and became one of the most effective pressure groups of Edwardian England. The FCC was itself, in due course, as Bebbington has shown, destined to encounter the same problem as the Liberation Society in respect of active political involvement: the Liberal party was its natural ally in its chosen causes, but closer alliance with the party eroded the specifically religious orientation of the organization and its campaigns and consequently caused disquiet within the Free Church community. (Bebbington, 1982, pp. 82–3). The transition, however, from a society of individual Nonconformists to a Council of Free Churches as the principal political organ of Nonconformity was, as we shall note shortly, symptomatic of a broader and deeper transition within the Victorian Nonconformist tradition.

If the classic phase of both 'liberationism' and 'militant churchmanship' was thus over by the 1880s and 1890s, there yet remained one area of marked church-chapel confrontation, namely education. By 1870 the majority of Nonconformists had abandoned their previous commitment to the Voluntary principle in education and come to accept that only with the resources of the state could an adequate system of elementary education be provided for all children. Nonconformists, therefore, welcomed the overall principle of the 1870 Education Act, but fought, successfully, for the exclusion of any specifically Anglican teaching from the new schools which were to be set up under the Act. Under the famous Cowper-Temple clause any 'catechism or religious formulary' distinctive of a particular denomination was to be excluded from the syllabus of the new 'Board Schools'. Nonconformists failed, however, in their attempt to prevent the possibility of poor

---

distinctive features of the 'Conscience', each of which gathered momentum during the 1870s and 80s, namely: a conviction that there is no strict boundary between religion and politics; an insistence that politicians should be men of the highest personal moral character (hence the outcry over Parnell's adultery); and a belief that the state both could and should promote the social welfare of its people by means of legislation, including legislation in moral matters such as the regulation of the liquor trade, gambling and prostitution. The Nonconformist Conscience thus proceeded to moralize any given issue and to campaign in a manner that combined moral and religious zeal with political pressure. The campaigns were also, in consequence, largely negative in aim (seeking the removal of some specific 'wrong' or condemning an existing state of affairs); always urgent in their demands (because a moral wrong required immediate reform); and generally uncompromising, because of the ultimately moral basis of the cause in question (Bebbington, 1982, pp. 11–17). For further assessments which note both the limitations and the strengths of the 'Nonconformist Conscience', see Kent, 1966, and Helmstadter, 1979.

children being sent, at the expense of the ratepayers, to church schools. Numerically it was a very small matter, few school boards making use of the provision, but as a matter of principle Nonconformists objected to Anglican schools receiving funds from the rates.

Until the early 1890s the education issue between church and chapel became muted at the national level, although it was frequently bitterly fought at the local level as church and chapel vied for control of local school boards and, thereby, for control of the precise extent and nature of the local Board School religious education syllabus: all such provision was to exclude specifically denominational teaching, but there nevertheless remained scope for diversity. Such local rivalry not only exacerbated local church-chapel relationships, but also made for discontinuity and widespread local variation in the religious education of the Board School system (Richards, 1970). The Church of England, meanwhile, attempted to erect new schools, especially in rural areas, where it stood a chance of providing sufficient places for school boards to be made unnecessary. Local Nonconformists would then have no choice but to have their children educated in an Anglican setting: there remained a conscience clause exempting such children from denominational lessons, but the school remained Anglican in ethos and recourse to the conscience clause risked social stigma and local notoriety.

In the 1890s church-chapel conflict over education returned to the national level. In 1894 an attempt by High Churchmen on the London School Board to introduce both openly doctrinal elements into the syllabus of the schools and specifically Trinitarian tests for teachers caused a predictable furore. The High Churchmen lost, but the incident not suprisingly raised the temperature of the ongoing debate (Munson, 1975). Militant churchmen, conscious of the relative confidence of contemporary Anglicanism, sought to extend the Church of England's educational role in national life. Nonconformists became more sensitive to their disadvantages under the existing system.

Matters came to a head in 1902. The Education Act of that year sought to bring order to the nation's elementary education. School Boards were abolished and local authorities were given control of local education. Denominational schools were brought within the system and, for the price of one third of the managers of their schools being publicly appointed, were to receive rate aid. Anglicans had long sought such rate aid. Nonconformity reacted furiously to its concession. The Free Church Council organized a campaign which, characteristically, amounted to a moral crusade. As well as public meetings and parliamentary protests, many Nonconformists urged a passive resistance campaign in the form of withholding that part of the rates which was for the maintenance of church schools, and a National Passive Resistance Committee, chaired by the Baptist, John Clifford, was formed. By 1906 some 70,880 summonses had been issued for non-payment of rates, goods had been distrained and auctioned, and in 176 cases non-payment *and* refusal to allow distraint of goods ended in periods of imprisonment (Bebbington, 1982, ch. 7).

After 1906 the controversy subsided. A new Liberal government undertook to moderate the terms of the 1902 Act. There followed eight years of confusion as the more adamant Nonconformist opponents of the 1902 Act refused to accept the various compromises offered by Liberal politicians sympathetic to their cause but aware of the political limits within which they must work. It was only the outbreak of war in 1914 which finally put an end to the debates — and by the end of the war the whole issue was as thoroughly anachronistic as the wider church versus chapel conflict of which it was the final post-Victorian fling.

III 'LIBERATION' AND 'CHURCH DEFENCE': SOME AMBIGUITIES

Opposition to the 1902 Education Act was not the exclusive preserve of Nonconformists. Although most Anglicans were, predictably, supporters of the Act, there were Anglican opponents of it too. At the evangelical extreme of the Church of England there were militant Protestants, including the members of the Protestant Church Union and the Church Association (the latter being the chief prosecutors of Ritualists under the provisions of the Public Worship Regulation Act, and indeed before the passing of the Act also), who opposed the Act on the grounds that it would afford too many opportunities to Ritualist and Anglo-Catholic clergy. Other Low Churchmen opposed the Act for the damage it would do to emerging inter-denominational co-operation with the Free Churches. At the other extreme, a vocal minority of High Churchmen opposed the Act as conceding too much to the state in terms of public representation on management boards in return for financial assistance from the rates (Pugh, 1972). Such reactions, although minority views, effectively demonstrate the extent to which, by 1900, the Church of England had become, in practice, a single 'umbrella' ecclesiastical institution encompassing a range of internal 'sects', often at loggerheads with each other. They also illustrate the potential complexities of the Victorian church-chapel confrontation. Like the example of Mackonochie, the Ritualist supporter of disestablishment, some twenty-five years earlier, the Anglican opponents of the 1902 Act indicate that notions of 'liberation' and 'church defence' were not the exclusive prerogatives of, respectively, Nonconformists and Anglicans.

The Liberation Society was another, Nonconformist, case in point. The Society may have been the principle, even symbolic, focus of Nonconformist political aspirations in the middle decades of the nineteenth century, but it never commanded the unified support of the whole Nonconformist community. The Wesleyan Methodists remained (predictably, given their ambiguous stance in respect of establishment) generally lukewarm to the Society. Other Nonconformists also found the Society too exclusively political and insufficiently religious, however. In 1843 and 1844, when the original Anti-State Church Association was in process of foundation, the influential Congregationalist J. A. James opposed its 'half religious, half political' nature, and John Blackburn condemned it in the *Congregational Magazine* for using the church to promote political ends. R. W. Dale was later to complain that some Liberationists, by virtue of their commitment to particular political aims, were prone to preventing the discussion of religious questions on properly religious principles (Thompson, 1974, pp. 232–3). Both Dale and Guinness Rogers — two of the most influential Congregationalist ministers of their day — found the tone and ethos of the Liberation Society in the 1870s too secular (Bebbington, 1982, p. 27).

'Church Defence' was an even more ambiguous phenomenon. The 'church defence' of the English Church Union rapidly became chiefly a matter of defending the Ritualist and Anglo-Catholic cause against the legal attacks of the ultra-Protestant Church Association — a group whose stated aim was 'to uphold the Principles and Order of the United Church of England and Ireland, and to counteract the efforts now being made to assimilate her services to those of the Church of Rome', and whose prosecutions of Ritualists, following the Society's foundation in 1865, prompted the more moderately Evangelical William Connor Magee to dub them the 'Persecution Company Limited'. (Crowther, 1970, p. 194; Reynolds, 1965, p. 124). Church defence, in the last third of the nineteenth century, might equally well, depending on the context, mean *either* defence of the established church against Nonconformist calls for disestablishment, *or* defence of the Anglo-Catholic understanding of the Anglican Church's identity against the attempts of their Evangelical co-denominationalists to rule them illegal.

'Liberation' and 'church defence' were thus standpoints capable of dividing Nonconformists and churchmen among themselves, and therefore part of the complexity of Victorian denominational interrelationships, not a simple reflection of their polarity. A further example of that complexity is to be found in the cross-denominational alliances which could also be formed. The conflict of church and chapel did not prevent Evangelical Anglicans and Protestant Nonconformists from co-operating on a range of issues. The fact that both groups shared a common debt to the Evangelical Revival of the preceding century enabled them to work together in various fields, even as their own denominational groups became more closely defined and on occasion engaged in bitter institutional conflict. At the national level such co-operation was manifested in organizations such as the Evangelical Alliance, the YMCA, the Bible Society and the Religious Tract Society, as well as a host of less well-known but still national evangelical organizations and societies. At the local level, Evangelical Anglican and Protestant Non-conformist co-operation might lead to the establishment of pan-Evangelical Town Missions — the most famous example being the London City Mission — and to joint local campaigns on issues of common evangelical concern, although (as J. D. Walters has shown in a study of Anglican and Dissenting relationships in Wolverhampton between 1830 and 1870) the co-operation was also subject to the repeated stresses and strains produced by the continuing attachment of Anglican Evangelicals to the establishment principle and the growing Nonconformist opposition to it (Walters, 1981). The basis of such pan-Evangelical co-operation was a combination of a common piety and theology, a common commitment to the evangelization of the working classes, a common concern for moral issues such as a temperance and sabbatarianism, and, frequently, a common anti-Catholicism.[7] .

IV OVERVIEW: CHURCH, CHAPEL AND DENOMINATION

The particular denominational structure and ethos characteristic of English and Welsh Christianity during the twentieth century was itself a product of the changes in religious and ecclesiastical life of the preceding century. The Victorian conflicts of church and chapel, 'liberation' and 'church defence', were at once fought out against the background of that process of change, yet themselves a part of it. In the case of Nonconformity, the development of marked and distinctive denominational identities and structures was the context rather than the product of the search for religious equality. In the case of Anglicanism, on the other hand, the *de facto* reduction of the established church to the status of one denomination among others — albeit a still officially established and residually more powerful and influential one than the rest — was a consequence of the decision of the state to bow to the moral and electoral pressures of increasing democracy and to opt for constitutional religious pluralism and, in consequence, the drastic curtailment of the privileges of establishment.

The precise origins of, and appropriate explanation for, the development of increasingly distinct denominational structures and self-consciousness within early nineteenth century Dissent are matters of lively debate.[8] What cannot be doubted, however, is the marked contrast between the degree of formal denominational structure and cohesion which existed within the major branches of the Dissenting tradition in about 1830 and that which

[7] For a wide-ranging but highly detailed case study of the pan-Evangelical mission to the poor which also examines the nature and bases of Victorian pan-Evangelical co-operation as a whole, see the highly informative study of the London City Mission by Lewis, 1986.

[8] For a discussion of these debates see Thompson, 1985.

existed by 1900. In 1830 there were a variety of Baptist and Congregational societies and general funds, area associations, ongoing attempts to organize national 'Unions', and various magazines and periodicals which reflected 'denominational' identities. In Methodism there was already a definitely 'connexional' structure, but the relationship between centre and locality was still very much in process of definition and still an ongoing cause of friction, controversy and secession. By 1900, however, the Baptist and Congregational Unions and the Wesleyan and Primitive Methodist Connexions were all functioning as fully-fledged denominations and formed the core of the Free Church Council Movement.

By the end of the century, the era in which campaigning for the relief and repeal of Dissenting and Nonconformist grievances and disabilities was a central concern of Victorian Nonconformity — the era in which the Liberation Society was *an* (although never *the*), effective symbol of Nonconformist identity — was over. It had been succeeded by an era in which the ethos and status of Nonconformity was more properly symbolized, not by a society dedicated to the search for religious equality and the relief of dissenting disabilities, but by a Federal Council articulating the opinions and policies, and voicing the continuing concerns and protests of a group of 'Free Churches'. The irony of the transition from the era and ethos of Dissenting Meeting House, via that of Nonconformist Chapel, to that of Free Church lay, however, in the unexpected loss of rationale which occurred somewhere along the way: in the long run it proved harder to articulate and sustain a distinctive and widely compelling rationale for 'Free Churchmanship' than it had been for still 'unliberated' Nonconformity and Dissent.

Whereas the emergence of fully-fledged Free Church denominationalism reflected the increased status and growing influence of the Nonconformist tradition, the development of *de facto* Anglican denominationalism reflected a relative decline in status and loss of influence. If the controversy over the 1902 Education Act revealed the residual strength of the Church of England and the still unequal status of the Free Churches, it was nevertheless now *only* a residual strength. In the long Victorian confrontation between church and chapel, it was the chapel which steadily gained ground and the church which steadily lost it.[9]

---

[9] Although in due course it was to become clear that the religious tradition which advanced its position most securely and significantly during the Victorian period was not Protestant Nonconformity but Roman Catholicism. By 1900, Protestant Nonconformity in some respects appeared poised to assume the role of what amounted to virtually 'an alternative establishment'. In retrospect, however, it is clear that by 1900 English and Welsh Nonconformity had already reached the peak of their influence. In the first three decades of the twentieth century there began to emerge first a crisis of identity and role, then the beginning of serious decline — a process from which English and Welsh Nonconformity have yet to emerge. Roman Catholicism, by contrast, continued to consolidate its position and to expand until the 1950s. For more detailed discussions of both the Nonconformist and Roman Catholic cases, see *RVB*, I, 2 and 4.

The continuing strength of the historiographical tradition which interprets the history of Victorian Anglicanism as *essentially* a history of internal revival after near shipwreck in the preceding century tends to obscure the degree of Anglican decline in the Victorian period. It is, of course, quite true that the Victorian Church of England achieved a remarkable revival in terms of organizational efficiency, pastoral provision, enriched devotional life and general vitality.[10] As Alan Gilbert has observed, the fact that in 1914 a higher proportion of the English population practised Anglicanism than had done so in 1830 indicates that in the Victorian period the Church of England had indeed succeeded in reversing at least one process of decline which was by then already over a century long. But as Gilbert goes on to point out, such revival itself requires to be set within another broader framework of decline: the Victorian Church of England, he insists, was not merely made more efficient but was also 'metamorphosed', in a process amounting to 'gradual disestablishment'. The late Victorian Church of England retained the trappings and residual ethos of its days of official religious monopoly, but in practice accepted the realities of denominational co-existence in an officially pluralist society (Gilbert, 1976, pp. 138–43).[11]

The process of acceptance gave rise to the various manifestations of 'church defence'. Societies such as the English Church Union and the Church Defence Institution provided Victorian Anglicanism with an aggressive front line against the challenges of both militant Nonconformity and an increasingly liberal-pluralist state. The CDI provided the principal organizational response to the Liberation Society and the call for disestablishment. The ECU defended High Church and Anglo-Catholic practices and convictions against the state's perceived 'interference' in liturgical and doctrinal matters, and against the attempt of extreme Evangelical Anglicans to exploit that 'interference' to restrict the spread of Ritualism and Anglo-Catholicism. Behind that front line, however, the bishops as a body displayed a sound grasp of the pragmatism for which Anglicanism is renowned, and frequently compromised in order to preserve the form of establishment whilst relinquishing much of its substance. Other aspects of church defence — such as the revival of Convocation, the development of diocesan synods, the holding of Church Congresses, and the increase in the involvement of the laity in the government of the church — reflected the growth of an Anglican denominational structure and bureaucracy similar to those which arose in the various Nonconformist traditions as they also became self-consciously denominational Free Churches.

[10] For the broader context of the developments in both Anglicanism and Nonconformity discussed here, see *RVB*, I, 1 and 2.

[11] For another important discussion of the extent and nature of the *decline* of the Victorian Church of England, see Marsh, 1969.

The 1902 Education Act, with its blatantly preferential treatment of Anglicanism, ensured that the twentieth century began with a last furious burst of church-chapel controversy. It was, however, a final postscript — though a vitally important one for Nonconformist consciences and sensibilities — to a process of religious confrontation and constitutional adjustment which had begun in the 1830s, peaked in the 1860s, and already passed into decline by the 1880s. The pattern of Anglican-Free Church relationship in the twentieth century was to be quite different. Having spent most of the nineteenth century becoming self-conscious denominations in response to the organizational pressures and demands of an expanding urban industrial society, the various churches began to wonder whether the challenges posed by such a society did not in fact require the application of the combined resources of their several denominations: the ecclesiastical watchword of the twentieth century was to be 'ecumenism'.

BIBLIOGRAPHY

*D. W. Bebbington (1982) *The Nonconformist Conscience: Chapel and Politics 1870–1914*, George Allen and Unwin.

M. A. Crowther (1970) *Church Embattled: Religious Controversy in Mid-Victorian England*, Newton Abbot, David and Charles.

*A. D. Gilbert (1976) *Religion and Society in Industrial England: Church, Chapel and Social Change 1740–1914*, Longman.

R. J. Helmstadter (1979) 'The Nonconformist Conscience' in P. Marsh (ed.) *The Conscience of the Victorian State*, pp. 135–72, Brighton, Harvester.

*I. G. Jones (1981) 'The Liberation Society and Welsh politics 1844 to 1868' in *Explorations and Explanations: Essays in the Social History of Victorian Wales*, pp. 236–68, Llandysul, Gower Press.

J. Kent (1966) 'Hugh Price Jones and the Nonconformist Conscience' in G. V. Bennett and J. D. Walsh (eds.) *Essays in Modern English Church History*, pp. 181–205.

D. M. Lewis (1986) *Lighten Their Darkness: The Evangelical Mission to Working-Class London, 1828–1860*, Greenwood Press.

G. I. T. Machin (1977) *Politics and the Churches in Great Britain 1832–68*, Oxford, Oxford University Press.

G. I. T. Machin (1987) *Politics and the Churches in Great Britain 1869–1921*, Oxford, Oxford University Press.

W. H. Mackintosh (1972) *Disestablishment and Liberation: The Movement for the Separation of the Anglican Church from State Control*, Epworth.

P. T. Marsh (1969) *The Victorian Church in Decline*, Routledge.

J. E. B. Munson (1975) 'The London School Board election of 1894: a study in Victorian religious controversy', *British Journal of Educational Studies*, Vol. 23, pp. 7–23.

J. S. Newton (1980) 'Edward Miall and the diocese of Durham: the disestablishment question in the north-east in the nineteenth century', *Ecclesiastical Durham University Journal*, Vol. 72, pp. 157–68.

D. R. Pugh (1972) 'The church and education: Anglican attitudes 1902', *Journal of Ecclesiastical History*, Vol. 23, No. 3, pp. 219–32.

M. Reynolds (1965) *Martyr of Ritualism: Father Mackonochie of St Alban's, Holborn*, Faber.

N. J. Richards (1970) 'Religious controversy and the School Boards 1870–1902', *British Journal of Educational Studies*, Vol. 18, pp. 180–96.

*M. J. D. Roberts (1984) 'Pressure-group politics and the Church of England: the Church Defence Institution 1859–1896', *Journal of Ecclesiastical History*, Vol. 35, No. 4, pp. 560–82.

*D. Thompson (1974) 'The Liberation Society 1844–1868' in P. Hollis (ed.) *Pressure from Without in Early Victorian England*, pp. 210–37, Arnold.

D. Thompson (1985) *Denominationalism and Dissent 1795–1835: A Question of Identity*, Dr Williams' Trust.

J. R. Vincent (1972) *The Formation of the British Liberal Party 1857–68*, Harmondsworth, Penguin.

J. D. Walters (1981) 'The evangelical embrace: relations between Anglicans and Dissenters in the period 1830–1870', *West Midland Studies*, Vol. 14, pp. 32–8.

CHAPTER 8

MISAPPREHENSION.

Mary Jane (indignant). "COME ALONG, 'LIZA. DON'T STAND LOOKING AT THAT——WHICH I CALL IT SHAMEFUL O' THEM PREFANE DARWINITES! I DON'T BELIEVE IT'S A BIT LIKE HER!"

[Dedicated to Hanging Committees

THE MORAL CRITIQUE OF CHRISTIAN ORTHODOXY

ADAPTING a phrase from Tennyson's *In Memoriam*, the historian Basil Willey identified a group of Victorians as 'honest doubters'. In 1949 he wrote: 'the distinctive nineteenth-century phenomenon is the devout sceptic, the sage who rejects traditional religion not because he is shallow or immoral, but because he is too earnest to accept it' (Willey, 1969, p. 231). The honest doubters rejected traditional religion for a number of reasons, the best-known of which are doubts about the authenticity of scripture, and doubts deriving from the discoveries of science. The subject of this essay, however, is another, but equally potent source of doubt, namely, *morality*. This essay is about a group of honest doubters who felt, as a chief objection to Christianity, that it failed to measure up to the highest moral standards — that it seemed to encourage belief in a vengeful and unjust god, who inflicts eternal torments on people.

Honest doubters were, typically, people who had been reared in evangelical households, who took their own religious beliefs very seriously, who were sure that one had a duty always plainly to speak the truth, and who had had implanted in them a powerful sense of right and wrong. A strange crisis for these people arose when the personal moral obligations engendered by their background, conspired to make it impossible for them to assent to some of the central doctrines of Christian theology. The doctrines themselves, it seemed, failed to measure up to the highest standards of Christian morality, and so had to be rejected as immoral, or even downright wicked. There is a paradox here: the rejection, or at least, the radical criticism of Christianity seems to have been a direct product of Christian values. And religion was far too serious a business for the doubters to keep their doubts private: the ethos of the period demanded that they spoke out.

Before we go on, it is worth noting something of what was demanded of orthodox believers, lest the agonizings of the doubters seem trivial. If the orthodox believers were Anglicans, they would be members of congregations that were obliged, at least once a year, to recite the Athanasian creed, a creed which includes the following terrifying proposition:

> Whoever will be saved: before all things it is necessary that he hold the Catholic faith. Which Faith except every one do keep whole and undefiled: without doubt he shall perish everlastingly ... And they that have done good shall go into life everlasting: and they that have done evil into everlasting fire.

Dissenters of course, were not bound to creeds. In the emphatic words of J. A. James, writing in *The Principles of Dissent*, published in 1841, '*The Holy Scriptures are the sole authority and sufficient rule in matters of religion, whether relating to doctrine, duty, or church government*' (James, 1841, p. 6) But a sole reliance on the Bible seemed, to numbers of morally earnest believers, to require the worship of a God who, in his Old Testament manifestations, seemed often to be a vengeful and capricious tyrant. And the dissenting tradition, just as much as the Athanasian Creed, emphasized the torments of hell that awaited, or which were already being suffered, and would eternally be suffered, by the majority of humankind.

The philosopher Herbert Spencer recorded his own moral revulsion at the Christianity (in his case dissenting Christianity) in which he had been reared. Spencer wrote his autobiography in 1894 and thus was recollecting an experience that had happened over half a century earlier. The mature agnosticism into which he had settled no doubt coloured his account of his early religious struggles, but the account makes clear that his alienation from Christianity had been influenced by what he saw as the injustice and cruelty of its central doctrines:

> I had not at that time [i.e. around 1840] repudiated the notion of a deity who is pleased with the singing of his praises, and angry with the beings he has made when they fail to tell him perpetually of his greatness. It had not become manifest to me how absolutely and immeasurably unjust it would be that for Adam's disobedience (which might have caused a harsh man to discharge his servant), all Adam's guiltless descendants should be damned, with the exception of a relatively few who accepted the "plan of salvation," which the immense majority never heard of. Nor had I in those days perceived the astounding nature of the creed which offers for profoundest worship, a being who calmly looks on while myriads of his creatures are suffering eternal torments. But, though no definite propositions of this kind had arisen in me, it is probable that the dim consciousness out of which they eventually emerged, produced alienation from the established beliefs and observances.
>
> (Spencer, 1904, I, p. 152)

Not all those who felt moral objections left the church. This essay is concerned chiefly with those who did leave, but there were plenty who stayed, attempting to reformulate Christian doctrine in the light of powerful moral objections. Benjamin Jowett and F. D. Maurice, for example, remained Anglican priests and devised ingenious and less desolate (and also a good deal less clear) interpretations of the doctrine of eternal damnation. And overall, perhaps the church's move, during the Victorian period, from a concern with the Atonement (the doctrine that Christ's death atoned for human sin), to a new stress on the Incarnation (the Divine becomes human), was a reflection of widely-felt reservations about the morality of God's dealings with humankind.

Doubt, then, was felt by some Victorians to be a moral obligation, forced on them by what they took to be the ethical offensiveness of certain key aspects of Christian doctrine.

I THE MORAL OBJECTORS

This aspect of Victorian faith and doubt was first opened up in detail by Howard Murphy. In his article, published in 1955, 'The Ethical Revolt against Christian Orthodoxy', Murphy showed that the doubts of numbers of Victorian intellectuals were powerfully present as early as the 1840s — that is to say, well before the impact either of historical biblical studies, or of Darwin's theory of evolution by natural selection could have been felt. He traced the fortunes of a group of early Victorian believers who were caught between two conflicting pressures. On the one hand, they were members of an earnest generation who passionately believed that society and social conditions could be reformed or ameliorated — a belief sustained by the passing of the 1832 Reform Act and by the decade of reforming legislation that the Act signalled, while on the other, they were expected to assent to religious doctrines which, if taken seriously (and they took everything seriously), seemed to turn Progress into a hopeless illusion. Additionally, Murphy's sample were shaken by their knowledge of people whose lives were lived according to rules which seemed to be ethically superior to those of the church. Francis Newman — John Henry's brother — recollected:

> I shuddered at the notions which I had once imbibed as part of religion; and then got comfort from the inference, how much better the men of this century are than their creed. Their creed was the product of ages of cruelty and credulity; and it sufficiently bears that stamp.

(Quoted in Murphy, 1955, p. 804)

Another of Murphy's sample, George Eliot (Mary Ann Evans), took a rather similar view. 'I was considerably shaken', she wrote in 1840, 'by the impression that religion was not a requisite to moral excellence' (quoted in Murphy, 1955, p. 813). We can usefully pursue George Eliot beyond the limits of Murphy's article, in order further to illustrate the argument he was elaborating. Fifteen years later, when George Eliot could express her doubts more confidently, she wrote a stinging review of books by a popular Evangelical preacher, the Rev. John Cumming (Eliot, 1855). What comes through powerfully in her review is the indignation she feels on behalf of all honest doubters. She resents Cumming's imputation that unbelievers are sinful and stupid. The boot, she makes plain, should be on the other foot: it is Cumming who should be adjudged morally odious and intellectually imbecile. She considers that his grasp of the intellectual issues facing the church — biblical criticism and geological theory, for instance — is weak, but, more important, she is offended by his dwelling on divine retribution to the exclusion of divine love and mercy. The precise details of Cumming's theology need not concern us here. His importance for us is that he serves George Eliot as a vehicle for working out an honest doubters' manifesto, a manifesto that has three important elements. The first concerns truth. The 'highest moral habit', she says, is 'the constant preference of truth both theoretically and practically', and, she goes on, 'the stamp of a truth-loving mind' may well be *doubt*. The second two elements are vaguer. One is a definition of the Christianity practised by 'the best minds'. According to this definition, Christianity is 'the perpetual enhancing of the desire that the will of God — a will synonymous with goodness and truth — may be done on earth'. That is to say, God's will must be consonant with the very highest standards of morality. The last element is a statement of the sort of optimistic humanism sketched in the quotation from Francis Newman. In the words of George Eliot, 'human nature is stronger and wider than religious systems' (Eliot, 1855, pp. 442, 448, 455, 460). Her full ethical programmes is not systematically worked out, but it is clear that George Eliot, under the influence of Comte, was trying to establish an ethical system that took elements from New Testament Christianity and from science, grafted them onto a rather imprecise notion of 'humanity', and held them all together with the bonds of a tremendous earnestness. The result is well illustrated by the anecdote of the philosopher F. W. Myers, who walked round the Fellows' Garden of Trinity College Cambridge with her one evening in May 1873:

> she, stirred somewhat beyond her wont, and taking as her text the three words which have been used so often as the inspiring trumpet-calls of men, — the words *God, Immortality, Duty*, — pronounced, with terrible earnestness, how inconceivable was the *first*, how unbelievable the *second*, and yet how peremptory and absolute the *third*.

(Quoted in Willey, 1969, p. 214)

Murphy's general conclusions have been endorsed by other writers, although there is a debate about the precise source of the ethical revolt. Was it the evangelical tradition itself which bred a generation which would turn on its teachers? Or was it rather that all Victorian humanitarians lived on the legacy of enlightened late eighteenth-century views of justice and punishment, and found, to their dismay, that their religion failed to measure up to them? It is a matter of emphasis. John Kent and Don Cupitt, for example, stress the background of penal reform. Writing about critical responses to the hell-fire preaching of the revivalist, Moody, Kent says that 'what made eternal punishment incredible to so many in the long run was the change in the civilized attitude to prisons and punishment, the decay in the serious belief in the value of retributive punishment' (Kent, 1978, p. 195). Josef Altholz, on the other hand, argues for the importance of the specifically evangelical roots of the ethical revolt. He comes to the neatly expressed conclusion that 'perhaps the Victorian religious revival had made men too moral to be orthodox, too humanitarian to be Christian' (Altholz, 1976, p. 66). Like Murphy, Altholz develops his argument chiefly by means of a sequence of biographical case-studies, — in this case, of Tennyson, Jowett, Colenso and Maurice — but he also considers issues like the professionalization of the clergy. Additionally, he very tellingly reproduces a passage from a sermon by Samuel Wilberforce, Bishop of Oxford. The repetitious calls for Truth from the honest doubters may sound somewhat sanctimonious and histrionic (although Victorian discourse is characteristically histrionic), but they seem less so when it becomes clear that for some orthodox clergy, unquestioning acceptance of doctrine was a positive virtue. Wilberforce, for example, was encouraging his flock to abase their understanding:

> Whilst irreverence and doubt are the object of your greatest fear; whilst you would gladly retain a childlike and unquestioning reverence by abasing, if need were, your understanding, rather than gain any knowledge at the hazard of your reverence ...
>
> (Quoted in Altholz, 1976, p. 63)

Against such advice, the famous lines from Tennyson's *In Memoriam*,

> There lives more faith in honest doubt
>   Believe me, than in half the creeds

sound less affected than they otherwise might.

·II WORKING-CLASS MORAL OBJECTORS

Murphy and Altholz built their arguments by steadily accumulating anecdotal biographical evidence, a method that is tailor-made for establishing the views of the highly articulate, hugely productive, educated classes of Victorian Britain. There can be few social groups who have left behind such mountains of correspondence, biographies by devoted contemporary admirers, reviews and articles, as well as the solid books of their scholarship. With such profusion, it is not surprising that Murphy and Altholz do not turn their attention to the ethical doubts, if such there were, of the great, scarcely visible mass of Victorians who left few records.

We can get a bit closer to the Victorian population at large if we follow the work of historians like Susan Budd and Edward Royle. In a much quoted and intriguing article published in 1967, Budd analysed 150 obituaries in the secularist press in order to find out what had caused the deceased to lose their religious belief. Her conclusion closely parallels Murphy's and Altholz's: the reasons for doubt among her sample of chiefly working-class men are the reasons given by middle-class intellectuals like Francis Newman and George Eliot. Budd's conclusion is that 'the revolution in scientific and theological thinking seems largely irrelevant. The loss of faith for Freethinkers was not an intellectual but a moral matter' (Budd, 1967, p. 125). What was crucial in the loss of faith, she argues, was the conviction that the Bible was morally wrong, and that doctrines like eternal punishment, hell, the atonement, and damnation for unbelievers were wicked (Budd, 1967, p. 118). Royle, in his book *Victorian Infidels*, provides a fuller account of the secularist movement, but endorses Budd's conclusions. Like her, he stresses the eighteenth-century ancestry of the secular movement, showing how Tom Paine's *The Age of Reason* (1794) provided nineteenth-century secularists with a vocabulary, and an armoury of anti-clerical arguments. Royle then goes on to reconstruct something of the feeling of the hundreds of secularist public meetings that went on up and down the country. Such meetings might contain rather theatrical jibes of the sort he quotes from a book by C. Southwell called *The Difficulties of Christianity* (1843). Southwell wrote that the God of Moses must be a local god 'who comes down from heaven to take part in the miserable battles of his miserable creatures and teaches those creatures to hate, spoil, or destroy each other' (quoted in Royle, 1974, p. 109). But the force of the moral objection is clear, and Royle's conclusion about the causes of the infidelity of secularist orators, and frequently their audiences, is this: 'infidelity seems to have frequently been inspired by disgust with the church and moral revulsion against Christian doctrines, and then sustained by a growing intellectual conviction of the rightness of such a rejection' (Royle, 1974, p. 108). Royle's sketch of secularist public meetings is borne out by a reviewer in the generally freethinking, but middle class, *Westminster Review*. The reviewer, William Binns, in a survey of 'The religious heresies of the working classes', writes of open air Sunday meetings in Yorkshire at which crowds 'upwards of 5,000 persons' listened to metropolitan secularist speakers. He writes also of smaller, indigenous meetings. His tone is rather patronizing: the women who attended the meetings are pictured as trailing along behind the men, and the standard of argumentation at the meetings is faintly mocked, but Binns is unlikely to have been mistaken about the occurrence of such meetings, although, for his own, Unitarian, purposes he may have exaggerated their importance. Of these meetings in the dales above the West Yorkshire woollen and worsted towns, he writes:

> Hither troop keen-witted men from Bradford, Bingley, Keighley, and the surrounding towns, all toilers and all heretics, and many with

their wives, sweethearts, or children following in their train. In rude dialect, with the ready, common-sense logic of workshop, and often also with the intemperance unfailingly begotten by shallow draughts at the "Pierian spring", [where the Muses drank] homely orators criticize the Bible, are indignant at the immoralities of Calvinism, overturn the Church's house of cards, popularize the metaphysical disquisitions of Hume, and pick flaws in the reasoning of Paley.

(Binns, 1862, p. 70)

For our purposes, it is the critique of 'the immoralities of Calvinism' that is significant.

A slightly less lofty account of working-class doubt came from Thomas Wright, the 'Journeyman Engineer' who published *The Great Unwashed* in 1868. In his chapter on the working classes and the church, he claims that

here and there among working men there will be found some half-educated shallow minded man who, having read a few such books as *The Ruins of Empires* and *The Age of Reason* [i.e. secularist books], has come to the conclusion that to profess infidel beliefs marks him out as a bold and original thinker. But such men are exceptional, and are only laughed at by those among whom they live; and after all their infidelity is of the most harmless character, simply consisting in asking if you really believe that the whale swallowed Jonah, or pointing to the verbal discrepancies shown in the gospels with regard to the inscription placed on the cross at the crucifixion. Among the more thoughtful portion of the working classes there is certainly a considerable amount of that honest doubt in which they believe with the Laureate [i.e. Tennyson, author of *In Memoriam*] there lives more faith than in half the creeds.

(Wright, 1868, pp. 84–5)

The work of historians like Budd and Royle and contemporary accounts of working-class doubt of the sort given by Binns and Wright take us beyond the amply-documented world of the middle-class intellectuals, but we are still a very long way from an answer to the question 'Why did Victorians lose their faith — if they had one to lose?'. Indeed, simply to pose the question is to recognize how partial and incomplete our answers are bound to be. In the face of this task, it is prudent to retreat to well-mapped territory, and for the remainder of this essay I shall be doing no more than supplying two further biographical case studies, drawn from the familiar and inexhaustible store of Victorian middle-class intellectuals.

The two are Charles Darwin, and the poet Algernon Charles Swinburne. Darwin is significant because although he is customarily presented as the man whose scientific theories threatened religious belief, it can be shown that the personal objections which led to his loss of faith were as much ethical and moral, as they were scientific. Swinburne too had moral objections, though of a rather different sort. His importance, for the purposes of this essay, is in demonstrating the change in tone between the discourse of the mid and late Victorian periods. Swinburne is the embodiment of the rejection of the high seriousness and unremitting earnestness of the mid-Victorians.

III CHARLES DARWIN

Darwin is really an unlikely candidate for the role he has been obliged to play in accounts of Victorian religion. Unquestionably, the difficulties that his theory of evolution by natural selection raised for Christian belief were formidable, and Darwin knew exactly how formidable they were. But his personal handling of the religious implications of his theory, and indeed of all matters of religious belief, especially when they touched on his relations with his wife and family, was curiously reticent. This reticence was not due to moral cowardice or to evasiveness, and certainly not to ignorance, but to a sense of propriety. He hated giving offence. In this respect, he is quite different from the general run of self-dramatizing, soul-baring honest doubters. Darwin produced the biggest bombshell to hit Victorian theology, but he rolled it gently into the arena with the utmost courtesy and the least possible self-assertion. His *Origin of Species* (1859) did not dodge the religious issues, but neither did it elaborate them. A few carefully-chosen sentences were all that he proffered. As a rather private (and often unwell) man, he felt that his religious beliefs were his own business; but he knew that certain aspects of his published work had inescapable religious implications, and he recognized a duty to indicate, briefly and judiciously, what they were.

At first sight, when his scattered public and private thoughts on religion are assembled, the collection looks self-contradictory and off-hand. It seems to confirm his own autobiographical comment: 'I do not think that the religious sentiment was ever strongly developed in me' (Darwin, *Autobiography*, p. 53). However, this first impression is not borne out by closer study, for it is possible to reconstruct a reasonably coherent account of his religious life. What emerges from it is a man who seems personally to have experienced few dark nights of the soul, but who steadily developed, albeit informally and unsystematically, a powerful critique of Christianity. And for our purposes, it is significant that moral objections were entwined with scientific objections in his seemingly casual, but in reality very searching critique.

Darwin differed from other honest doubters in not having had an intensely religious upbringing. The family tradition, best exemplified in his grandfather, Erasmus Darwin, was one of freethinking, or of Unitarian dissent. Darwin's father, a successful doctor in Shrewsbury, was not a religious man, but seems to have felt no fierce antagonism to religious institutions: he cheerfully sent the young Charles to conventional middle-class schools. In his autobiography, written when he was in his seventies, Darwin recalled no fervent childhood religious feelings, save for the earnest prayers that he addressed to God when he was late for school. He recalled that he attributed his success in not being late 'to the prayers and not to my quick running, and marvelled how generally I was aided'. His gratitude, however, did not inhibit him using morning chapel as a time and place to do his Latin homework (Darwin, *Autobiography*, pp. 10, 12). He left school, then, a rather placid young man with no strong views on religion — or on anything else, for that matter. At his father's direction, he went to Edinburgh University to study medicine. He did not take to it, and eventually dropped out. His father, now somewhat exasperated, sent him to Cambridge University with a view to his becoming an Anglican clergyman. Charles, hoping that his father's eventual death would bring him into a fortune large enough for him not to have to work at all, was happy enough to go along with the idea of becoming a clergyman, despite a qualm:

> I had scruples about declaring my belief in all the dogmas of the Church of England: though otherwise I liked the thought of being a country clergyman. Accordingly I read with care Pearson on the creeds [i.e. an orthodox book of Anglican apologetics] and a few other books on divinity; and as I did not then in the least doubt the strict and literal truth of every word in the Bible, I soon persuaded myself that our Creed must be fully accepted.
>
> (Darwin, *Autobiography*, p. 31)

This recollection is from the autobiographical fragment that the aged Darwin wrote for his children, so it needs to be treated critically, but it rarely conflicts with evidence drawn from earlier periods of his life. In this particular recollection he did not record which of the dogmas bothered him, but his doubts evidently caused him very little anguish.

At this point, before we push on to the time in Darwin's life when religious issues became important, we need to make an elementary distinction between, on the one hand, convictions and doubts about the truth of particular Christian doctrines — about the immortality of the soul, the everlastingness of damnation, Christ's atonement for human sin, for example — and, on the other hand, convictions and doubts about the very existence of God and about the character of His creation — does nature, for instance, exhibit marks of intelligent and loving design? Now, Darwin's theory of evolution by natural selection bears most pressingly on this second area of enquiry — on whether nature is the handiwork of a good and wise god. And most of Darwin's utterances on the question of religion, as he developed and reflected on his theory, are to do with the matter of Design. But there is another, thinner strand of reflections running through his writings which concern the first area of enquiry — that is to say, Christian doctrine.

Darwin came to feel, much more urgently than he had done as a youth, doubts about the morality of Christianity. Such doubts may have struck him before he devised his theory of evolution, and logically, they could have persisted, quite independently of his biological work, even when this work was well under way. The distinction between on the one hand, the dogmas of theology, and, on the other, the question of whether Nature exhibits evidence of heavenly design, is needed in order to clear the ground for a fuller explanation. The incantation of the word 'evolution' will not do to explain everything in Darwin's religious life.

At Cambridge University, which he attended between 1827 and 1831, Darwin was required to read the standard work by Archdeacon William Paley: *Evidences of Christianity* (1794). Paley's aim was to show that marks of intelligent design are so obviously and abundantly visible in the natural world that we are driven happily to the conclusion that only a good and wise god can have been responsible for its creation. Alternative explanations, Paley argued, and especially those which postulate chance as a sufficient explanation, collapse when one seriously considers the wonderful intricacy, and the fitness for purpose, of an organ like the eye. Darwin recalled that the logic of Paley's book gave him much delight and that he knew it inside out (Darwin, *Autobiography*, p. 32).

The teacher at Cambridge who impressed him most and who became a lifelong personal friend, was the Professor of Botany, The Rev. John Henslow. Darwin Recalled:

> His judgment was excellent, and his whole mind well-balanced ...
> He was deeply religious, and so orthodox that he told me one day, he should be grieved if a single word of the 39 Article were altered. His moral qualities were in every way admirable.
>
> (Darwin, *Autobiography*, p. 39)

Darwin left Cambridge in 1831, it seems, pretty comfortable, if undemonstrative, in his religious beliefs. Little changed during the next five years, which he spent voyaging around the world as a naturalist on the admiralty surveying ship, *The Beagle*.

> Whilst on board the Beagle I was quite orthodox, and I remember being heartily laughed at by several of the officers (though themselves

orthodox) for quoting the Bible as an unanswerable authority on some point of morality.

(Darwin, *Autobiography*, p. 49)

The crucial years for the scrutiny and radical overhaul of his religious beliefs were the three or four years following his return to England with *The Beagle* in 1836. These were the years during which he formulated his theory of natural selection, which he wrote up in 1842 as a private rough sketch from a series of notebooks he had been keeping since 1837. Just as important, from the point of view of this essay, he married, and was obliged, by the gentle promptings of his wife, to reflect on his beliefs. The result was twofold. First, he came formally to make up his mind and reject some central Christian doctrines, and secondly, he began to doubt that nature is the product of, and is constantly in the hands of, a good and wise creator. His recollection of his state of mind at this experience is very carefully analysed in his autobiography and conflicts with nothing we can find in his letters and notebooks of the period.

Let us take his rejection of Christian doctrine first. Here, we are on familiar ground: his reasons are the standard reasons given by ethical objectors and by students of the history of scripture. Darwin recalled that he came to see that miracles are incredible, that the scriptures are historically unreliable, and that the Old Testament attributes to God 'the feelings of a revengeful tyrant'. Accordingly, he concluded, 'I gradually came to disbelieve in Christianity as a divine revelation'. He develops his reason for his disbelief and introduces again the crucial *moral* element:

... disbelief crept over me at a very slow rate, but was at last complete. The rate was so slow that I felt no distress, and have never since doubted even for a single second that my conclusion was correct. I can indeed hardly see how anyone ought to wish Christianity to be true; for if so, the plain language of the text seems to show that the men who do not believe, and this would include my Father, Brother and almost all my best friends, will be everlastingly punished. And this is a damnable doctrine.

(Darwin, *Autobiography*, p. 50)

Darwin had his moments of wit, but I think that he was unconscious of the irony of that last adjective.

Like his father before him, Darwin kept this rejection of Christian revelation private, perhaps even from his wife, and outwardly maintained good relations with his local vicar. He sent his own sons to conventional Christian schools. But his disbelief, as he said, was never shaken, and was almost certainly fortified by the desolation he experienced at the death of his ten-year-old daughter in 1851. The suffering and death of children was a constant source of moral objection to Christianity in the nineteenth, as in any other century, but it is worth generalizing beyond Darwin here to point out that death hovered never far away from Victorian families. Most people would have had fairly close personal experience of a child's death. The Darwins themselves lost three.

By around 1840, Darwin had done with the Christian revelation. Thereafter, his interest in it was the interest of the social anthropologist: Christianity was just one among the many systems of belief and behaviour for which social evolutionists, not theologians, had to account. At a personal level though, he seems to have been content to jog along, in the Kentish village where he lived, within the structures of the Anglican parish, cheerfully taking on the light social duties laid upon the local well-to-do. Darwin personally was no ardent secularist, whatever the long-term social ramifications of his theories may have been.

But he was never able to lay to rest the problem of Design. The problem, as it insistently presented itself to Darwin, can be simply stated. The theory of evolution by natural selection offers a sufficient account of why the living world looks the way it does. Species of plants and animals, including humans, are as they are because accidental minor variations in the structure of their ancestors conferred on them a fitness in the contest for food, for mates, for survival in hostile environments. Species are temporary survivors in an incessant and relentless struggle for existence. The theory depicts nature as a site of general death and extinction, with accidental variations determining the victory of the handful of survivors. Presented like this, the theory is the very antithesis of the providential, benign account of the living world that Darwin had found in Paley's *Evidences* at Cambridge.

Earlier, I made a distinction between moral objections to certain Church dogmas and objections to the argument from Design, as a preliminary to clarifying Darwin's own position. But the distinction is only temporary: it starts to collapse when the particular force of Darwin's critique of designfulness is grasped. His is not essentially a *logical* objection, of the classical sort advanced in the eighteenth century by David Hume. Rather, it is a *moral* objection, deriving from an ethical evaluation of the laws and processes that govern the living world. It is *possible* that a god designed variation and natural selection as a system for producing his creation, but if so, he is a bungling and cruel god — and not altogether different from the god who would condemn people to everlasting damnation or allow innocent children to die painfully. Darwin's critique of religion might well be a unified critique. It is likely that the theological issues of why the innocent suffer (raised by the death of his children), or of the immortality of the soul, were in continuous exchange with problems raised in his scientific work — problems like why a good god should have planned that cats should play with mice before killing them, or how and why early human tribes came to believe in spirits. In Darwin's thought, there is a continuous feedback between theological and biological issues.

The moral objection to the doctrine of a good and wise god, which Darwin derived from his biological studies, was not in essence a novel objection. Rather, it was a particularly stark formulation of the theologian's standard problem, namely, why did a good God create a bad world? The novelty of Darwin's challenge consists in its scientific source. Biology, ever since the seventeenth century, and up until Paley, had been an unfailing supplier of arguments and illustrations that seemed to *demonstrate* divine wisdom and goodness. In Darwin's hands, it started to do the opposite.

I have made it sound as if Darwin's rejection of Design was as final as his rejection of revelation, but it certainly was not. The balance of his statements on the question is pretty clearly towards rejection, but throughout his life he kept indicating that he was not entirely at ease with the idea that living nature is the result of blind chance. A few examples, drawn both from his public and private writings, will make this plain.

The first comes from the closing lines of the *Origin of Species* (1859). Having given a concluding summary of his theory, Darwin rounded off his book with this:

> There is grandeur in this view of life, with its several powers, having been originally breathed into a few forms or into one; and that, whilst this planet has gone cycling on according to the fixed law of gravity, from so simple a beginning endless forms most beautiful and most wonderful have been, and are being, evolved.
>
> (Darwin, *Origin*, p. 460)

This is entirely typical of the tone of many passages in both his published work and in his notebooks. He had no hesitation in using words like 'grandeur', 'beautiful', 'exquisite', or 'wonderful', words which signify approbation of, and delight in, all sorts of aspects of the living world. Nor did he balk, especially in his early notebooks, at the language of 'creation'. He tended to use the notion when he wished to signify the institution of the general laws which govern nature, as opposed to the working out of these laws in particular instances. The following example comes from an unpublished 'Essay' of 1844:

> It is in every case more conformable with what we know of the government of this earth, that the Creator should have imposed only general laws.
>
> (Darwin, 'Essay', p. 154)

Some scholars (Ospovat, Moore, Brooke) have argued for the possibility that Darwin's theorizing, perhaps until the 1850s, was actually driven partly by a desire to dignify God, so to speak, by releasing Him from the obligation to keep fiddling with nature every time a new species is to be created, and to assign Him to the nobler role of framer of grand laws of evolution. Passages like those I have quoted, and a close reading of the early notebooks support this view.

It is generally agreed, though, that the possibility of this motive fades when one considers the sections of his later writings which dwell on the cruelty and waste implicit in natural selection. Darwin was initially attracted by an argument that sought to detect the providential hand of God guiding *successful*, adaptive variations. This line of argument would have preserved the notion of an ultimately benign heavenly control over evolution. But he could not, in the end, accept this line of argument, and his reason was classically simple: if God designs and sustains the adaptive, helpful variations, where do the maladaptive, doomed variations, come from? He expressed his awareness of the darker side of the processes of variation and natural selection most vividly in an outburst in a letter to a colleague in 1856:

> What a book a devil's chaplain might write on the clumsy, wasteful, blundering, low and horribly cruel works of nature!
> (F. Darwin, 1903, Vol. I, p. 94)

The public debate which was generated by *The Origin of Species*, which was published three years after this statement, is not the subject of this essay, and in any case, Darwin did not publicly enter into debate about the issues that his books raised. Privately, though, he debated with his intimate correspondents the issue of an omniscient god who seems to have left large and decisive areas of nature to work themselves out by chance. His own contributions to these debates, which stretch over years in his correspondence, were forceful and concrete. Typically, he would try to put his correspondent (invariably a close friend or colleague) on the spot with an uncomfortable question: the raw material of evolution is the range of tiny variations that any group of plants or animals exhibits; does God personally design those variations which natural selection will unerringly pick out? Years earlier, Darwin had nearly failed to be selected for his post on *The Beagle*, because the captain didn't like the shape of his nose. Since *The Beagle* voyage had been crucial in opening up new worlds to him, Darwin often used the nose incident, in his arguments about design, as an example of the importance of quite accidental variation. He would be greatly obliged, he would write, if his correspondent would honestly tell him if he thought that God had personally designed his nose. The unsophisticated, seemingly deliberately unphilosophical, tone of Darwin's argument should not be taken as evidence of flippancy. He was going to the heart of the matter: either God stands remote from the processes that shape the living world, or he is continuously present in them. If the former, his existence is of no great consequence: if the latter, He is involved in some pretty shady dealing.

Commonly, Darwin's letters on the subject end on a self-deprecating, head-scratching note, as if he had become aware of having inadvertently stumbled into a debate about fundamental issues for which he lacked credentials. So he would, as it were, back out, confessing that he was 'bewildered' or 'muddled':

> The conclusion which I always come to after thinking of such questions is that they are beyond the human intellect: and the less one thinks on them the better. You may say, Then why trouble me? But I should very much like to know clearly what you think.
>
> (F. Darwin, 1903, Vol. I, p. 194)

Whatever he says here, in this letter of 1861 to the geologist Sir Charles Lyell, Darwin continued to think on such questions and devoted a lengthy passage of his autobiography to his eventual conclusions — although he was again entirely typical in calling them only 'vague conclusions' and in returning to them from time to time to make marginal corrections. It's worth giving a passage at some length:

> The old argument from design in nature, as given by Paley, which formerly seemed to me so conclusive, fails, now that the law of natural selection has been discovered ... There seems to be no more design in the variability of organic beings and in the action of natural selection, than in the course which the wind blows ... That there is much suffering in the world no one disputes. Some have attempted to explain this in reference to man; by imagining that it serves for his moral improvement. But the number of men in the world is as nothing compared with that of all other sentient beings, and these often suffer greatly without any moral improvement. A being so powerful and so full of knowledge as a God who could create the universe, is to our finite minds omnipotent and omniscient, and it revolts our understanding to suppose that his benevolence is not unbounded, for what advantage can there be in the sufferings of millions of the lower animals throughout almost endless time? This very old argument from the existence of suffering against the existence of an intelligent first cause seems to me a strong one.
>
> (Darwin, *Autobiography*, pp. 50–2)

Darwin joins hands here with other moral objectors: his understanding revolts at the prospect of a God who is not benevolent.[1]

IV ALGERNON CHARLES SWINBURNE

The case of Algernon Charles Swinburne (1837–1909) is altogether different. With honest doubters like Darwin, the moral gravity of the critique of Christianity is fairly plain. With Swinburne, it is not. His most famous lines on Christianity, from the poem 'Hymn to Proserpine', published in 1866, are those he puts into the mouth of a fourth-century Roman who is reflecting on the establishment of Christianity as the official religion of the Roman Empire. The Roman laments the waning of the old gods and addresses this line to Christ:

> Thou hast conquered, O pale Galilean; the world has grown grey
>   from thy breath.

It is an extraordinary line. It expresses a criticism of Christianity which is utterly different from those we have been looking at so far. Whereas former critics had objected chiefly to the tyrannical god of the Old Testament, Swinburne is here expressing a dislike of the world that was ushered in by Christ himself. To Swinburne, the new Christian world is pallid, grey, and full of prohibitions. The old, colourful, libertarian, pagan world is preferable. The difficulty with Swinburne, though, is in deciding the real force of the objection. Was he, in lines like this, dramatizing his own, deeply-held convictions, or was he just trying to send a frisson of outrage through polite society? Was he a true moral objector — on the grounds that Christian morality was dehumanizing and constricting — or was he merely an adolescent blasphemer?

One preliminary point, however, is pretty clear. With Swinburne, we have moved from the earnest world of the mid-Victorians into an altogether different sensibility. It will be recalled that when George Eliot's religious beliefs collapsed around her, the notion of personal moral duty survived the wreck. Indeed, her novels can be seen as a species of sophisticated moral instruction. The vocation of the artist, she believed, was to turn literature into a repository of the moral values which survived the disintegration of formal religion. The artist, above all, should be a moralist. Swinburne would have none of this. His rejection of the role of moralist comes out most clearly in an essay he wrote in 1868 on William Blake, the unorthodox and then unfashionable poet, whom he championed. The essay turns into a sort of manifesto of Swinburne's own programme for what he calls 'art for art's

---

[1] For a different view of Darwin, see *RVB*, I, 8.

sake first of all'. He rails against those who would turn art into the hand-maiden of morality, and especially of 'the puritan principle of doing good'. Here is a sample of his manifesto:

> Art is not like fire or water, a good servant and bad master; rather the reverse. She will help in nothing, of her own freewill: upon terms of service you will get worse than nothing out of her. Handmaid of religion, exponent of duty, servant of fact, pioneer of morality, she cannot in any way become; she would be none of these things though you were to bray her [i.e. pound her] in a mortar ... Once let art humble herself, plead excuses, try at any compromise with the Puritan principle of doing good, and she is worse than dead ... Let us hear no more of the moral mission of earnest art.
>
> (Swinburne, 1970, pp. 322–3)

His rejection of moralizing could not be plainer, and his rejection increases the difficulty of establishing whether there is, despite his protestation, a consistent moral view present in his own verse. The difficulty is further increased when we observe the elementary literary critical rule of never assuming that any line from a poem straightforwardly expresses the carefully formulated personal views of the poet. There are exceptions of course. When Tennyson writes, in *In Memoriam* (1850),

> I falter where I firmly trod,
>   And falling with my weight of cares
>   Upon the great world's altar-stairs
> That slope thro' darkness up to God.

We can fairly readily interpret it as autobiography — as a statement of his own, faltering religious belief. But when Swinburne puts lines into the mouth of a fourth century Roman, or, in the poem 'Anactoria', gives the following lines to Sappho, a seventh century BC Greek poetess who celebrated female homosexual love, we cannot be so sure:

> Him would I reach, him smite, him desecrate,
> Pierce the cold lips of God with human breath,
> And mix his immortality with death.

Nearly all Swinburne's poems are *dramatic*. That is to say, they are narrated by a character who is not manifestly identical with the poet himself. Swinburne himself made this point in a published reply to his critics (who, as we shall see, were not slow to respond unsympathetically to his verse). He asked them to bear in mind that 'no utterance of enjoyment or despair, belief or unbelief, can properly be assumed as the assertion of its author's personal feeling or faith' (quoted in Hyder, 1970, p. 49). Nonetheless, it is possible to make some progress in tracking Swinburne's own views. A rapid sketch of his life is the first step.

His parents were Admiral Charles Swinburne and Lady Jane Ashburnham. As a child of this impeccably upper class couple, he naturally was sent to Eton, where he was introduced not only to the classics, but also to regular flogging, a punishment which seems permanently to have perverted his sexuality. Thereafter, personal pain became for him a necessary feature of sexual pleasure. The Victorian cult of manliness had its darker side. He progressed from Eton to Balliol College, Oxford, an accomplished classical scholar. There he was tutored by Benjamin Jowett. This is important, for no matter how debauched Swinburne later became, no matter how much public opprobrium his scandalous verses were stirring up, he was always welcome at Jowett's. Birth and education within the charmed circle of the Victorian upper classes seems to have given Swinburne a license that would not have been granted to working-class blasphemers. It seems also to have ensured that he would not be barred from the society of the liberal intelligentsia. He is, for instance, recorded as having read his rather salacious and blasphemous poem 'Les noyades' (The Drownings) to a company that included the Archbishop of York and Thackeray and his two daughters (Henderson, 1974, p. 69).

Swinburne went to Oxford in 1856. The Oxford Movement, which gripped the university during the late 1830s and 1840s, had died away, and Swinburne gives no impression of having been at a place where religion was a burning issue. Since he had, as a child, been subjected neither to fierce Nonconformism, nor Anglican evangelicalism, there seems to have been no corresponding violent reaction. He felt sufficiently strongly on religious matters, however, to join the Old Mortality Society, a free-thinking student group. He also refused to attend college chapel. But he left no account of his beliefs and doubts. They have to be pieced together from odd fragments, and largely, from his verse.

His studies at Oxford were erratic and he acquired a reputation for debauchery. On Jowett's advice, he left without sitting his final examinations. He was not formally expelled, but he left under a cloud. Thereafter, financed by his parents' wealth, he lived a strange, long and often solitary life of travel, devotion to the cause of Italian patriotism, drunkenness, sexual perversion and sea bathing. But in the most important aspect of his life — his writing — he was at one with the most earnest of High Victorians: he was amazingly productive. His collected works run to twenty volumes. His first collection of verses, *Poems and Ballads* (1866) caused such a scandal — there were calls for prosecution for obscenity (Henderson, p. 118) — that the publisher lost his nerve and withdrew the volume, obliging Swinburne to take the book to another, rather dubious publisher.

Succeeding volumes caused less of a stir, and his first scandalous volume went through edition after edition, making a tremendous impression on young readers: Thomas Hardy, for example, was so enraptured that he walked through the streets reading it (Millgate, 1982, p. 88). Swinburne was never prosecuted, either for obscenity or blasphemy, probably for reasons suggested by Morley, an early reviewer of *Poems and Ballads*. Morley wrote: 'the only comfort about the present volume is that such a piece as 'Anactoria' will be unintelligible to a great many people, and so will the fevered folly of 'Hermaphroditus', as well as much else that is nameless and abominable' (Hyder, 1970, p. 24). That is to say, a book of obscure poems, nominally about the classical world, was likely to do little public damage, and the writer, as the son of a notable family, need not be prosecuted.

Swinburne died in 1909, aged seventy-two, in the house of a highly respectable admirer, Theodore Watts-Dunton, who had taken him into his household thirty years earlier when his bouts of drinking threatened to put an end to him. Swinburne made no deathbed repentance. Indeed, he gave strict instructions to Watts-Dunton to make sure that the Church of England burial service was not read over his coffin. Watts-Dunton wrote: 'If he had made a slight matter of his antagonism against Christianity, as so many free-thinkers do, it would have been different but with him it increased with his years and at the last ... it was bitterer than ever' (Henderson, p. 282).

It is generally reckoned that Swinburne's earliest published poetry is his best and it is principally to the early collections that I propose to turn, in order to sample and analyse his religious views.

Many of the poems are violent and erotic. Often, characters are simultaneously suffering and enjoying pain. Love is presented as a virtual impossibility. The imagery is of blood, biting, bruising, stinging. Here is a lurid example, from 'Ilicet':

From boy's pierced throat and girl's pierced bosom
Drips, reddening round the blood-red blossom,
    The slow delicious bright soft blood ...

And another, from 'Hesperia', which makes an extravagant and surely deliberately impious comparison:

As the cross that a wild nun clasps till the edge of it
        bruises her bosom,
So love wounds as we grasp it, and blackens and burns
        as a flame.

This is the sort of thing that made critics see Swinburne as a crude and heartless blasphemer. The reviewer in *The Athenaeum* in 1866, for example, wrote: 'It is quite obvious that Mr Swinburne has never thought at all on religious questions, but imagines that rank blasphemy will be esteemed very clever' (Hyder, 1970, p. 33). In one sense, the reviewer was correct: Swinburne certainly did not systematically work out a theological stance and then embody it in verse. His method was to assume a sequence of dramatic personae and, by means of them, to reflect on the character of God, the relationship between God and humans, and the nature of love. Doubtless, much of his verse was intended to give offence, but his central concerns can properly be called religious, as long as we are not looking for systematic theology. Within all the ranting and posturing is a real despair and rage at the cruelty of God.

The rage comes through most powerfully in 'Anactoria', the narrator of which is Sappho. She is brooding on the simultaneous love and hatred she feels for her lover:

> O that I
> Durst crush thee out of life with love, and die,
> Die of thy pain and my delight.

It is tempting to read such lines merely as an expression of a pathological sexual deviance. But this would be to miss the impact of his characterization of God and nature. Sappho goes on to answer the charge of cruelty that might be laid against her, by saying that if she is truly made in the image of God, then her cruelty is divinely legitimated:

> were I made as he
> Who made all things to break them one by one,
> If my feet trod upon the stars and sun
> And souls of men as his have always trod,
> God knows I might be crueller than God.

And she goes on to give a terrible catalogue of 'the mute melancholy lust of heaven'.

Maybe Swinburne was here merely dramatising feelings he did not personally share, but it seems unlikely, for this frame of mind, in one guise or another, informs all his verse. What is consistently present is the rage or despair at being a victim of a god, or gods, who create people only to torture them. Sometimes the rage is unfocused and incoherent, firing off at a vaguely specified company of pre-Christian gods. In this mode, Swinburne is very much the world-weary, classical scholar, recreating a pagan world in which, like a character in a Greek drama, he could rail against the capriciousness of the gods. Sometimes, a particular god or goddess is singled out, and not always for scorn. Venus, the goddess of love, crops up frequently. She was a particularly rich source of meanings for Swinburne:

he draws extensively on the myth of her birth (she was the result of a union between the sea and Uranus, whose genitals had been torn off and flung in the ocean by his son, Cronos). Sometimes, the Christian deity is addressed: Christ, Swinburne's 'pale Galilean' is the subject of 'Hymn to Proserpine'. And sometimes, as in this poem, and in the lines that enraged his critics, he had the effrontery to compare the pagan and Christian gods. The Roman narrator of the poem compares the Virgin Mary with Venus and gives his allegiance to Venus, 'the blossom of flowering seas', and not to Mary, 'a slave among slaves'. The same comparison is made in 'Laus Veneris' (Praise of Venus), in which the narrator, a sixteenth-century knight, rejects Christ and embraces Venus:

... thou didst heal us with thy piteous kiss
But see now, Lord; her mouth is lovelier.

But his choice of Venus brings the knight no lasting satisfaction. He has rejected the chivalric, ascetic code of the Christian knight, in favour of an obsessive, sensual liaison with a pagan goddess. But the knight does not triumph. The love that he is drawn towards is presented as predatory, violent, doom-laden. It is likened, in one place, to a panther, down whose 'hot sweet throat' the bleeding carcase of the lover/victim is gulped. The knight's own grim conclusion is that there is no better life than to have known love, to have known how bitter love is, 'and afterwards be cast out of God's sight'. The knight may not be speaking exactly for Swinburne himself, but the world view which 'Laus Veneris' dramatizes is recognizable in much of Swinburne's poetry. It is a world view in which love is, paradoxically, both realized and denied in the experience of the pain and the cruelty that always attend it. And in pursuing love, Swinburne's characters see themselves as defying the moral laws framed by God and refined by His son, the 'pale Galilean'.

There is finally no neat proposition which will sum up Swinburne's religious broodings. Reading him is an odd experience. Posturing, debunking and showing off are all prominent in his verse: but so are vivid passages in which characters express agonized feelings about their blighted place in the scheme of things. Swinburne's starting place was not George Eliot's or Tennyson's. By comparison, the subject of their doubts is relatively straightforward. Swinburne, though, took as read all their conclusions about the veracity of scripture or the moral character of the biblical God. Starting in the bare intellectual world that they had cleared, operating from within a personal sexuality that offered small chance of lasting fulfillment, and determined never to let his art subserve morality, Swinburne tended to rave somewhat indiscriminately, but his concerns were real enough.

He had odd moments of comedy, though, and one of them is worth quoting in conclusion, for it shows the distance between him and Tennyson. The solemnities of the Poet Laureate became a subject for a joke. In 1869 Tennyson had published a poem called 'The higher pantheism'. Here are the first two and the final two verses:

> The sun, the moon, the stars, the seas, the hills and the plains —
> Are these not, O soul, the vision of Him who reigns?
>
> Is not the vision He? though He be not that which He seems?
> Dreams are true while they last, and do we not live in dreams?
>
> Law is God, say some: no God at all, says the fool;
> For all we have power to see is a straight staff bent in a pool;
>
> And the ear of man cannot hear, and the eye of man cannot see;
> But if we could see and hear, this vision — were it not He?

Such a poem was a sitting duck for Swinburne. In 1880, and still relishing his reputation as an *enfant terrible*, and displaying wicked skill as a parodist, he replied with 'The higher pantheism in a nutshell':

> One, who is not, we see: but one, whom we see not, is:
> Surely this is not that: but that is assuredly this ...
>
> Doubt is faith in the main: but faith, on the whole, is doubt:
> We cannot believe by proof: but could we believe without? ...
>
> God whom we see not, is: and God, who is not, we see:
> Fiddle, we know, is diddle: and diddle, we take it, is dee.

Thus Swinburne despatches the honest doubters: they command his respect and allegiance no more than do the believers. Here, he could make a joke of it, but as we have seen, he was sometimes graver. The issues that shook Tennyson and George Eliot were lifeless as far as he was concerned. Or rather, the sharply doctrinal formulations of the issues were dead. But they left a residue of questions about the moral character of the universe, and that residue was still given theological form in Swinburne's verse.

The final point can be drawn from Altholz. His suggestion is that honest doubters of George Eliot's generation were 'living on the ethical capital of the Christianity which they had abandoned' (Altholz, 1976, p. 77). When the capital was all used up — when the religious culture which had formed their characters withered — the weakness of the alternative, secular bases of their ethics was exposed. Swinburne, from a later generation, and for whom religion certainly had withered, felt no cultural pressure to behave in one way rather than another. No terribly earnest avowals of the inescapability of Duty came from him. Even the codes of respectability, decency and gentlemanliness meant nothing to him (although he would shamelessly deploy them when it suited him). He went his own way, practising a personal libertarianism and developing a new aesthetic of 'art for art's sake'. The difference between his savage dramas of blasphemy and perverted eroticism, and the dignified, pious doubting of *In Memoriam*, mark, albeit melodramatically, a cultural shift between mid and late Victorian Britain.

BIBLIOGRAPHY

*J. Altholz (1976) 'The warfare of conscience with theology' in *The Mind and Art of Victorian England*, University of Minnesota Press.

W. Binns (1862) 'The religious heresies of the working classes', *Westminster Review*, Vol. 77, pp. 60–97.

*J. H. Brooke (1985) 'The relations between Darwin's science and his religion', in J. Durant (ed.) *Darwinism and Divinity*, pp. 40–75, Oxford, Blackwell.

S. Budd (1967) 'The loss of faith', *Past and Present*, No. 36, pp. 106–25.

D. Cupitt (1972) *Crisis of Moral Authority*, Lutterworth.

C. Darwin (1974) *Autobiography*, G. de Beer (ed.), Oxford, Oxford University Press.

C. Darwin (1958) 'Essay of 1844' in G. de Beer (ed.) *Evolution by Natural Selection*, Cambridge, Cambridge University Press.

C. Darwin (1968) *On the Origin of Species* (first published Murray, 1859), Harmondsworth, Penguin.

F. Darwin (ed.) (1903) *More Letters of Charles Darwin*, 2 Vols., Murray.

G. Eliot (Mary Ann Evans) (1855) 'Evangelical teaching', *Westminster Review*, pp. 436–62.

*P. Henderson (1974) *Swinburne: the Portrait of a Poet*, Routledge.

C. K. Hyder (1970) *Swinburne: the Critical Heritage*, Routledge.

J. A. James (1841) *The Principles of Dissent*, Hamish Hamilton.

J. Kent (1978) *Holding the Fort: Studies in Victorian Revivalism*, Epworth.

M. Millgate (1982) *Thomas Hardy*, Oxford, Oxford University Press.

J. R. Moore (1979) *The Post Darwinian Controversies*, Cambridge, Cambridge University Press.

*H. Murphy (1955) 'The ethical revolt against Christian orthodoxy', *American History Review*, Vol. 9, pp. 800–17.

D. Ospovat (1981) *The Development of Darwin's Theory*, Cambridge, Cambridge University Press.

E. Royle (1974) *Victorian Infidels*, Manchester, Manchester University Press.

H. Spencer (1904) *An Autobiography*, 2 Vols., Williams and Norgate.

*A. C. Swinburne (1970) *Poems and Ballads: Atalanta in Calydon*, M. Peckham (ed.) Indianapolis and New York, Bobbs-Merrill.

B. Willey (1969) *Nineteenth Century Studies* (first published Chatto, 1949), Harmondsworth, Penguin.

T. Wright (1970) *The Great Unwashed*, Frank Cass (first published pseudonymously — by 'the Journeyman Engineer' — in 1868).

CHAPTER 9

DANGERS OF DOGMATISM.

Brown (a mild Agnostic, in reply to Smith, a rabid Evolutionist, who has been asserting the doctrines of his school with unnecessary violence). "ALMOST THOU PERSUADEST ME TO BE A CHRISTIAN!"

ON SPEAKING PLAINLY: 'HONEST DOUBT' AND THE ETHICS OF BELIEF

ENNYSON's *In Memoriam* has been described as the representative
poem of its age, its representative status deriving from the fact that
it was a poem neither of belief nor of unbelief but, rather, one of
doubt — that is of 'doubtful belief' (Houghton, 1957, p. 22). As befitted the
representative poem of its age, it was also astoundingly popular, selling
60,000 copies within a few months of its publication in 1850, and then
averaging a new edition per year for two decades.

As Owen Chadwick has observed, a large part of the poem's significance, (and also a large part of the explanation of its immense popularity),
lay in the way in which it presented the dilemmas of faith and doubt, and
in particular the perceived clash between science and religion, in a non-
technical form which reached the 'popular non-philosophical mind'
(Chadwick, 1971, p. 567). It was, moreover, a form which combined both
honest confrontation of the intellectual challenges to traditional belief posed
by geology and natural history, and a sense of the depth and intensity of the
emotional implications of that confrontation. In *In Memoriam*, the implications of Lyell's *Principles of Geology* or Chambers' *Vestiges of Creation* were not
merely *faced*, but were *felt*: intellectual challenge and religious instinct were
evoked simultaneously and with equal effect.

This was important, for, by 1850, however much conservative and orthodox preachers and theologians might enjoin the suppression of intellectual
doubt by the flight to 'known truths', and however much militantly
aggressive secularists and atheists might insist that contemporary science
showed Christianity to be simply incredible as well as clearly immoral,
there was a growing number of people for whom neither set of certainties
was adequate, and for whom the whole business of what one wished to
believe or what one could believe was a matter of disconcerting perplexity,
not self-confident assertion.

It was to such people that *In Memoriam* spoke. The poem's evocation of
an individual's struggle between faith and doubt corresponded to the actual
experience of many perplexed mid-nineteenth century minds. It expressed
the simultaneous persistence both of the fundamental questions which so
many of the orthodox said should simply be suppressed and the religious
intuitions that the militantly secularist asserted were illusory. Moreover,
although the poem ends with belief, it is a belief based on hope and trust,
not on certainty. And this belief is but loosely defined and by no means
orthodox.[1] It was belief which 'faltered', 'stretched lame hands of faith',

---

[1] As R. H. Hutton put it, in an article in *The Spectator* in 1892, 'The lines of his [Tennyson's]
theology were in harmony with the great central lines of Christian thought; but in coming
down to detail it soon passed into a region where all was wistful, and dogma disappeared in a
haze of radiant twilight.' Although Hutton also observed that because of the way Tennyson
combined a 'generally faltering voice' with 'the ardour of his own hope', he touched the heart
of 'this doubting and questioning age, as no more confident expression of belief could have
touched it' (quoted in Willey, 1956, p. 104).

'called to what it *felt* was Lord of all', 'faintly trusted the larger hope', and 'believed where it could not prove.' Perhaps most memorably of all, it was belief which allowed that:

There lives more faith in honest doubt,
Believe me, than in half the creeds.

But what was '*honest* doubt'? Were the demands of honesty fulfilled if the doubter simply declared, openly, his or her perplexity? Did such perplexity concerning specific aspects of traditional Christian orthodoxy constitute grounds for ceasing to call oneself a Christian, and ceasing, therefore, to attend public worship with the apparent endorsement of orthodox belief which such attendance would seem to imply? Most pressingly of all, could a clergyman be an *honest* doubter? Could a clergyman both experience and express doubts about specific aspects and traditional interpretations of orthodox doctrine and belief and yet remain both a practising clergyman and an honest man? Such questions exercised the Victorians greatly, (especially in the third quarter of the century and in the aftermath of the *Essays and Reviews* and Colenso cases), and gave rise to an ongoing and deeply felt debate about 'the ethics of belief'.

To begin to appreciate the character and intensity of the moral earnestness of the mid-Victorian era it is necessary first to understand the nature and significance of this debate over 'honest doubt', 'plain-speaking' and 'the ethics of belief'. The present essay seeks to suggest something of that nature and significance. It does so by examining, briefly, a number of particular reactions to the question of whether a clergyman — whilst continuing to practice as a clergyman — might be simultaneously a doubter (or indeed a disbeliever) in the *traditional* meaning of particular Christian doctrines and yet also an honest man.

I THE BROAD CHURCH AND TRUTHFULNESS

The persistence of popular perceptions of the 'Victorian crisis of faith' as essentially a matter of science versus religion, Darwin and geology versus the Bible, notwithstanding, it is abundantly clear that the essence of the crisis was, in fact, moral in nature. The fundamental conflict was not one between science (or for that matter biblical criticism) and theology, but, in Josef Altholz's apt phrase, one between 'conscience and theology' (Altholz, 1976). It was considerations of morality which gave rise to the soul-searching and conscience examining which constituted the heart of the 'Victorian crisis of faith'. There were, however, at least two quite distinct types of moral 'crisis of faith'.

On the one hand there was a widely felt crisis over the morality of certain aspects of traditional Christian doctrine. Were the notions of hell and everlasting torment, or of substitutionary Atonement, indicative or suggestive of a genuinely moral deity? Similarly, were some of the incidents recounted in the Old Testament and attributed to the action or direction of God, (the killing of the Egyptian first-born or the slaying of whole populations, for example), the acts of a moral being? Or again, was the history of waste and suffering in nature which was revealed by the fossil records which so fascinated Victorian minds suggestive of a benign, benevolent creator? For a significant number of Victorians the answer to such questions was 'no', and they duly renounced their Christian belief out of loyalty to a concept and understanding of morality which seemed to them higher than that of Christianity itself.[2]

On the other hand there was also a crisis over the morality of no longer believing in the traditional version of Christian doctrine, (either because it indeed appeared immoral in certain aspects, or because developments in science and historical consciousness seemed to render particular traditional beliefs incredible), but nevertheless still believing oneself a Christian because one believed the essence of Christianity itself to be capable of expression in terms other than those of traditional doctrine and theology. The issue was especially acute when the believer concerned was a clergyman. In mid-century the classic example of this version of the moral crisis of faith was to be found in the case of the Anglican Broad Churchmen.

The classic Broad Churchmanship of the generation of A. P. Stanley, the authors of *Essays and Reviews* and Bishop Colenso was characteristically composed of a combination of three things. Firstly, the moral rejection of traditional teaching on hell and the Atonement. Secondly, the conviction that the essence of Christianity was in any case to be found in experience, morality and relationship, not in intellectual assent to doctrine. Thirdly, a firm commitment to the proposition that Christianity was not only falsely placed if it resisted the insights of science and historical criticism, but that, in fact, it had much to gain from accepting such insights and incorporating them within its worldview. Moreover, the Broad Churchmen also frequently justified their theological and doctrinal stance in terms of the need for the church and for Christianity to be strictly honest and truthful. Thus, for example, Stanley had asserted as early as 1841 that he believed the besetting sin of the clerical profession to be 'indifference to strict truth', and complained of the clerical 'habit of using words without meaning, or with only a half-belief' (quoted in Altholz, 1976, p. 63).

Similarly, Jowett, in a letter to Stanley in 1858 in which he sought

---

[2] For discussion of some examples of such moral rejections of Christianity, see Altholz, 1976; Murphey, 1955; and *RVB*, II, 8.

(unsuccessfully as it turned out) to persuade Stanley to write for the projected volume of essays which eventually emerged as *Essays and Reviews*, laid great emphasis upon questions of clarity and plainness of speech:

> The object is to say what we think freely within the limits of the Church of England. A notice will be prefixed [in the projected volume of essays] that no-one is responsible for any notions but his own. It is, however, an essential part of the plan that names shall be given ... we are determined not to submit to this abominable system of terrorism, which prevents the statement of the plainest facts ... I do not deny that in the present state of the world the expression of them [Stanley's theological opinions] is a matter of great nicety and care, but is it possible to do any good by a system of reticence?
>
> (Quoted in Faber, 1957, pp. 230–1)

Jowett also addressed the theme of truth in his own contribution to *Essays and Reviews*, where he observed that, 'It would be a strange and incredible thing that the Gospel, which at first made war only on the vices of mankind, should now be opposed to one of the highest and rarest of human virtues — the love of truth.' Yet that, Jowett insisted, was precisely the case whenever Christianity rejected criticism simply because it conflicted with traditional understandings of doctrine or traditional theological views. As things stood, he asserted, 'No-one can form any notion, from what we see around us, of the power which Christianity might have if it were at one with the conscience of man, and not at variance with his intellectual convictions.'

Or again there was the example of Bishop Colenso who, in 1862, in the preface to the infamous first volume of *The Pentateuch and Book of Joshua Critically Examined*, (for the writing of which he was to face accusations of heresy), explained that, whilst translating the Bible into Zulu, his Zulu helper asked him of the story of the Flood, 'is all this true? Do you really believe that all this happened thus?' 'My heart answered,' said Colenso, 'in the words of the Prophet, "Shall a man speak lies in the name of the Lord". I dared not do so.'

Such observations, protestations and explanations would seem to suggest, at first sight, that it would be the Broad Churchmen who would possess the moral high ground in a debate over the ethics of belief. In point of fact, however, quite the opposite occurred. It was the Broad Churchmen who found themselves charged with dishonesty — and not only by orthodox believers. That this was so both requires some explanation and reveals much about the nature of the Victorian debate concerning intellectual honesty and the ethics of belief.

The Victorian debate over the ethics of belief and the morality of certain kinds of intellectual attitude towards the interpretation of religious doctrine did not begin with the Broad Churchmen. It began, in fact, some twenty years earlier with the Oxford Movement and the attempt — especially in Newman's crucial Tract 90 — to justify the interpretation of the Church of England's doctrinal formularies (and especially the Thirty Nine Articles) in a thoroughly Catholic manner. To many observers, the Tractarians in general, and Newman in particular, seemed to propose to interpret the Articles in a manner that moved beyond mere subtlety and into deliberate sophistry and casuistry of a kind which smacked of dishonesty and intellectual sleight-of-hand (Livingston, 1974a, pp. 2–3).

The passion and bitterness of the debate also owed much, of course, to the sheer dislike of apparently 'Romanising' theology. But when in Tract 90 Newman argued, for example, that Article 22, (which condemned the 'Romish' doctrine of purgatory), did not condemn the present Roman Catholic doctrine on the subject because that had not been defined until after Article 22 was written, a distinct impression of evasiveness was created. When to this was added the Tractarian notion of 'Reserve' in the discussion and preaching of Christian doctrine,[3] it indeed seemed to many that the Tractarians were guilty not merely of flirting with 'popery' but of being downright dishonest into the bargain. Whether or not the charge was a fair one, by the early 1840s, it has been pointed out, the question of what it meant to be an honest Christian had ceased to be simply a matter of character and become, quite as much, a matter of intellect (Turner and Von Arx, 1982, p. 84).

By the mid-1850s, however, the focus of theological controversy in the Church of England was on the point of shifting away from the conflict between Tractarians and Evangelicals, to centre instead on the conflict between liberals and conservatives, Broad Churchmen and orthodox. *Essays and Reviews* provided the necessary trigger both for the emergence of the liberal-conservative clash as the new storm-centre of Anglican theological controversy and for a new phase of the debate about the ethics of belief.[4]

What is important in the present context is the fact that so much of the debate over *Essays and Reviews* centred on the honesty — or rather the alleged dishonesty — of the authors. They faced two such charges. The first was that, despite their prefatory statement to the contrary, they had written collaboratively and with the deliberate collaborative aim of co-ordinating a

---

[3] For the concept of 'Reserve' and its context in the emergence of Tractarianism, see briefly, *RVB*, I, 1.

[4] For the way in which, between 1830 and 1860, an essential consensus in Anglican theology was fragmented by the successive controversies over Tractarianism and Broad Church liberalism, see *RVB*, I, 1.

negative attack upon orthodox belief: the book was a conspiracy. The second charge was that — at least as far as the six contributors who were clergymen were concerned — their views were patently incompatible with the honest performance of their clerical duties and the honest retention of their clerical status.

It is instructive to note how the latter charge in particular was first hinted at, then made explicit, and then answered in the three famous and seminal reactions to *Essays and Reviews* from Frederic Harrison in the October 1860 edition of the *Westminster Review*, from Samuel Wilberforce in the January 1861 number of the *Quarterly Review*, and from A. P. Stanley in the April 1861 edition of the *Edinburgh Review*.

Harrison, once a High Churchman but by 1860 an ardent twenty nine year old convert to Positivism, praised the essayists for their courage and candour, and for their insistence upon the principle of free discussion, and he welcomed the fact that critical and scientific principles which radical and positivist thinkers had long urged were now preached from within the church itself. But Harrison also expressed regret that such principles were not yet frankly adopted and pushed to their legitimate conclusions by the essayists. If their views *were* thus pressed to their logical conclusions, the essayists would recognize that, far from being as they supposed defenders of a modern, critically conscious Christian faith, they were, in fact, now opponents of authentic Christianity.

> No fair mind can close this volume without feeling it to be at bottom in direct antagonism to the whole system of popular belief. They profess, indeed, to come forward as defenders of the creeds against attacks from without; but their hardest blows fall not on the assaulting, but on the resisting force. They throw themselves into the breach; but their principal care is to clear it from its oldest and stoutest defenders. In object, in spirit, and in method, in details no less than in general design — this book is incompatible with the religious belief of the mass of the Christian public, and the broad principles on which the Protestantism of Englishmen rests. The most elaborate reasoning to prove that they are in harmony can never be anything but futile, and ends in becoming insincere. All attempts to show that these opinions are not in accordance with Scripture, the Articles, the Liturgy, or the Church have little practical value, and do no small practical harm.
>
> (Harrison, 1860, pp. 294–5)

Thus Frederic Harrison challenged the essential honesty and sincerity of the essayists in the October 1860 issue of the *Westminster Review*. Three months later, in the January 1861 number of the *Quarterly Review*, Samuel

Wilberforce, rigidly orthodox High Churchman and Bishop of Oxford since 1844, not only announced his agreement with the Positivist Harrison as to the incompatibility of the opinions of the essayists and authentic Christianity, but also launched a scathing attack upon the essayists' lack of moral integrity. The alleged dishonesty, which Harrison had briefly suggested, became with Wilberforce a — perhaps the — fundamental issue. He had analysed their views at such length, Wilberforce said, and so far as possible used their own words,

> ... because, as honest men and as believers in Christianity, we must pronounce those views to be absolutely inconsistent with its creeds, and must therefore hold that the attempt of the Essayists to combine their advocacy of such doctrines with the retention of the status and emolument of Church of England clergymen is simple moral dishonesty ... They lay hold of the young and the ardent and the generous by their show of liberality, of reasonableness, of candour, of calmness, and by the specious glow of pietism with which they are invested ... It is impossible honestly to combine the maintenance of such a system and the ministry of the English Church.
>
> (Wilberforce, 1861, p. 274)

Wilberforce then proceeded to examine the way in which H. B. Wilson dealt with this very issue in his contribution to *Essays and Reviews*. Wilson, he pointed out, stated that he wished the freedom of opinion which belonged to the English citizen to be extended to the English churchman, and the freedom already practically enjoyed by the laity to be allowed to the clergy also. It was also, Wilson suggested, a 'strange ignoring of the constitution of the human mind to expect all ministers ... to be of one opinion at different periods of life' (quoted in Wilberforce, p. 274). Wilberforce then analysed Wilson's discussion of the latitude of interpretation which the wording of the Thirty Nine Articles might allow to a clergyman.[5] Wilson's position, Wilberforce asserted, finally amounted to that of a 'stammering, equivocating subscriber'.

Significantly, and in Wilson's case with painful tellingness, Wilberforce then referred his readers back to the controversy over Tract 90 some twenty

---

[5] Wilson had argued in his essay on 'The National Church' that, whereas it was commonly supposed that their subscription to the Thirty-Nine Articles imposed a great restraint on the clergy, in point of fact it was difficult to 'define what is the extent of the legal obligation of those who sign them; and *in this case the legal obligation is the measure of the moral one*' (italics added). He proceeded to demonstrate the degree to which the Articles were open to subtle interpretation and susceptible to the making of very precise distinctions of meaning. Subscription, he maintained, finally amounted only to 'an acceptance of the Articles of the Church as the formal law to which the subscriber is in some sense [sic] subject.'

years earlier. The Tract was, Wilberforce recalled, criticised in a public letter from four Oxford tutors for extending the bounds of the liberty of interpretation of the Thirty Nine Articles to a new and dangerous degree, and partly as a result of the tutors' letter the Hebdomadal Board of the University resolved that the modes of interpretation employed in the Tract 'evaded' rather than 'explained' the meaning of the Articles. Yet, Wilberforce triumphantly observed, one of the four tutors was none other than H. B. Wilson: well might Wilson, therefore, argue that it is strange to expect a person not to change opinions in the course of life. Then followed, yet again, a further reiteration of the fact that, whether right or wrong in themselves, the views held by the essayists were 'essentially and completely at variance with the doctrinal teaching of the Church of England, and cannot even under the shelter of any names be advisedly maintained by honest men who hold her ministry' (pp. 281–2).

The April 1861 edition of the *Edinburgh Review* contained an article which was both a response to Harrison and Wilberforce and a stout defence of the essayists' honesty, integrity and right to remain clergymen. Its author was A. P. Stanley, Professor of Ecclesiastical History at Oxford, close friend of Jowett, and consistent upholder of the breadth and variety allowable within the Church of England.[6] Stanley did not like the tone of *Essays and Reviews* at all. He found its manner and much of its content imprudent and also too negative in the general impression it created. But he presented a robust defence of the authors' moral position.

He first skillfully turned around the charge of conspiracy by listing other examples of opinions similar to those of the authors of *Essays and Reviews* which had been published in England in the last half-century:

> The style, the manner, the composition of this book may be offensive or peculiar. But facts and creeds are not revolutionised by manner and style. The principles, even the words, of the Essayists have been known for the last fifty years, through writings popular amongst all English students of the higher branches of theology. If there be a conspiracy, it is one far more formidable than that of the seven Essayists. For it is a conspiracy in which half the rising generation, one quarter of the Bench of Bishops, the most leading spirits of our clergy, have been, and are, and will be engaged, whatever the results of the present controversy.

(Stanley, 1861, p. 480)

---

[6] Stanley had, for example, also opposed the condemnation of the Tractarians, defended R. W. Hampden when he was attacked for his theological liberalism, and defended the Gorham Judgement on the grounds that the Church of England had always included and been meant to include opinions which were different to the point of contradiction.

Having thus indicated that the question of honest profession of beliefs, if raised in the case of the essayists, must also be raised in respect of very many others, including prominent clergy and bishops, Stanley then proceeded to discuss the question of honest subscription. Noting that the question of the actual truth or falsehood of the views under debate was being treated almost as a matter of indifference, Stanley made a series of points in defence of the essayists' position and their integrity as clergymen. First, he objected to the notion that clergy should have less liberty of thought and opinion than the laity. Second, he agreed that the present state of the question of subscription to the Church's formularies was unsatisfactory and in need of reform. He then asserted, however, that:

> ... still, as regards his own religious belief, the main question for a clergyman to consider is whether he can sincerely accept as a whole the constitution and the worship of the Church of which he is a minister. Those to whom, as a whole, it is repugnant will spontaneously drop off, in one direction or another, without any pressure from without. Those to whom, as a whole, it commends itself as the best mode of serving God and their brethren, will, in spite of any lesser differences, count it treason to the Church, and to its Divine Head, to depart either from its ministry or its communion.
>
> (p. 490)

If, Stanley continued, thirdly, there were any insuperable barriers in their terms of assent and subscription which would divide the clergy from the educated laity, then it would be the duty of both to tear down such barriers. In fact, however, this was not, in Stanley's view, the case: the Articles, in his opinion, were not sufficiently specific in the matters raised by the essayists to make outright conflict inevitable.[7] Fourth, Stanley conceded that *Essays and Reviews* did contain 'occasional contradictions ... to the language of some of the formularies', but promptly cited precedents for such statements from within the Anglican tradition, and then observed tellingly:

> Let him who agrees with every word and statement of the formularies cast the first stone at these variations. All clergymen, of whatever school, who have the slightest knowledge of their own opinions and of the letter of the Prayerbook and Articles, must go out one by one,

---

[7] Stanley actually cited the fact that no prosecution had been brought against the essayists as evidence of this point. The subsequent prosecution of Williams and Wilson weakened his argument — although the eventual verdict of the Judicial Committee of the Privy Council proved him correct, at least on the legal point.

beginning at the Archbishop of Canterbury in his palace at Lambeth, even down to the humblest curate … All laymen, too, who by virtue of their subscriptions in either University hold any office of trust or emolument therein, will remember that they also are bound by precisely the same obligations in this respect … What is open to the Professors of History and of Natural Science is open no less to the Professors of Divinity. What is closed to the Professors of Divinity is no less closed to the Professors of History and of Natural Science.

(p. 495)

In their attitudes to the question of the honesty or dishonesty of the authors of *Essays and Reviews*, Harrison, Wilberforce and Stanley thus provided a convenient summary of the essential division of opinion in mid-Victorian England concerning the ethics of belief and the moral demands upon clergymen who doubted or dissented from the traditional interpretations of the doctrinal formularies of their church. From the orthodox theological 'right' and from the radical Positivist 'left,' Wilberforce and Harrison challenged the honesty and integrity of the essayists' present position, and called upon them to become genuinely honest by acknowledging the clear incompatibility of their opinions on the one hand and the plain meaning of the formularies of their church and the popular understanding of Protestantism on the other. Stanley, meanwhile, on behalf of the Broad Churchmen, protested that honest participation in a church's life and ministry depended upon one's relationship to the worship and doctrine of that church *as a whole*, and that if *precise* and *uniform* acceptance of *every* word of the formularies was essential, then barely any subscriber to the Articles would pass such a test.

The controversy over *Essays and Reviews* culminated, of course, in the trial for heresy of Rowland Williams and H. B. Wilson and, in due course, in their acquittal in 1864 on appeal to the Judicial Committee of the Privy Council, after having first been found guilty in the ecclesiastical courts. The Privy Council, whilst not defining what the doctrine of the Church of England *should* be, (or even what it in fact *was*), ruled that the opinions of Williams and Wilson were not *legally* incompatible with the wording of the Thirty-Nine Articles.

Legally, it had thus been established, Broad Churchmen who held opinions such as those of Williams and Wilson were entitled to remain clergymen of the Church of England. But were they also *morally* entitled to do so? Were they *morally* entitled to remain Anglican clergymen on the basis of interpretations of the Articles which differed from the commonly held interpretations of them, and which clearly pre-supposed the need for their ongoing re-interpretation in the light of changing and developing modern knowledge and historical and scientific consciousness?

II THE CASE FOR 'PLAIN-SPEAKING'

The effect of the Privy Council judgement over *Essays and Reviews* was not limited to the establishment of the fact that the legal boundaries of the range of legitimate interpretations of the meaning of the Thirty-Nine Articles were considerably wider than the majority of Anglican clergy clearly wanted them to be. The judgement also had the effect of locating the responsibility for honest and conscientious subscription to the Thirty-Nine Articles and other doctrinal formularies of the church even more firmly within the realm of the individual conscience.

The Clerical Subscription Act of 1865 confirmed this state of affairs. In 1865, after the report of a Royal Commission which had considered the terms of subscription, Parliament passed, with surprising ease, an Act which modified those terms. Instead of the old formula which required the subscriber to say that he gave 'unfeigned assent and consent to all and everything' in the Book of Common Prayer, and that he 'willingly' and 'from his heart' subscribed to and acknowledged 'all and every' article to be 'proved by the most certain warrants of Scripture', the modified form required only a more general assent to the Thirty-Nine Articles and the Book of Common Prayer, and a correspondingly general statement of belief that the doctrine therein was agreeable to the Word of God. The change was important because of the way it deliberately made the terms of sub-scription more general and less precise.

Such expressions of the principle that *honest* subscription was not neces-sarily *precise* subscription, and was therefore in large part a matter for the individual conscience, did not end debate. On the contrary, it signalled, rather, the beginning of a decade and a half of intense debate, from the mid-1860s to the beginning of the 1880s, concerning the moral implications of 'lax' understandings of subscription and the moral duty of 'speaking plainly'.

As James Livingston has observed, representatives of widely different schools saw the decisions of 1864–5 as having potentially corrupting implications. Gladstone, for example, remarked that 'the general tendency and effect of the judgements has been and is likely to be hostile to definite teaching, and unfavourable also to the moral tone and truthfulness of men who may naturally enough be tempted to shelter themselves under judicial glosses in opposition to the plain meaning of the words' (quoted in Livingston, 1974a, p. 8).

Gladstone, however, was a churchman of orthodox theological views, even if also of generally liberal intellectual outlook: such a comment was what one might have expected from such a source. The reactions of repre-sentatives of two other groups to the degree of latitude in the interpretation of subscription which Broad Churchmen characteristically claimed were both more revealing about the nature of the Victorian debate over the ethics of belief, and also posed a more serious challenge to the position held by the Broad Churchmen themselves.

On the one hand there were the reactions of some leading Unitarians. The affinity between the Unitarians and the Anglican Broad Churchmen was noted in 1865 in the pages of the Unitarian journal *The Inquirer*. 'It cannot be denied,' observed an editorial in the issue of January 14th 1865, 'that there is much closer theological sympathy between ourselves and the Broad Church party in the National Church than there is between us and any section of orthodox Nonconformists'. That theological sympathy, as Dennis Wigmore-Beddoes demonstrated, included shared characteristic attitudes towards biblical criticism and biblical inspiration, miracles, hell, Atonement, the divinity of Christ, the use of similar liturgical styles and the actual concept of a 'Broad Church' (Wigmore-Beddoes, 1971). Such sympathies and affinities did not, however, prevent many Unitarians from finding the sophisticated nature of Broad Church subscription to and interpretation of the Articles, Prayer Book and Creeds less than entirely ingenuous. Thus *The Inquirer*, in 1860, found it, 'difficult to reconcile these conclusions [of the Broad Churchmen] with the ecclesiastical position of the Broad Church theologians and their retention of emoluments held on the condition of assenting to formularies which it is the whole tendency of their writings to disprove', whilst James Martineau — arguably the most outstanding Unitarian theologian of the nineteenth century — considered that until the formularies themselves had been altered, (which he hoped they would be), it was wrong and almost dishonest for many Broad Churchmen, including Stanley, to remain in the Church of England (Wigmore-Beddoes, 1971, p. 80).

Thus the Unitarians, in so many respects the natural allies of the Broad Churchmen, posed a challenge to their stance on subscription which was all the sharper because it came from such fellow liberal-minded believers. The second such challenge to Broad Church attitudes to subscription came from men like Henry Sidgwick and, perhaps pre-eminently, Leslie Stephen, who found in the legal decision concerning *Essays and Reviews* and the relaxation of the terms of subscription in the Clerical Subscription Act, not a relief of conscience but rather, as Livingston has put it, 'an added burden to ... sensitive minds who felt that the binding force of subscription was relaxed at the sacrifice of scrupulous veracity' (Livingston, 1974a, p. 2).

In 1869 Henry Sidgwick resigned his Fellowship at Trinity College, Cambridge. He did so because, although a layman, the terms of his Fellowship required him to assent to the doctrines of the Church of England and this he found himself no longer able conscientiously to do. Sidgwick had struggled with the question throughout the 1860s and found himself driven by the end of the decade to the conclusion that the demands of a rigorous intellectual sincerity and strict truthfulness of speech required that he resign his Fellowship rather than take refuge in the relaxed, (or in his opinion just plain lax), understanding of subscription and assent which had received legal sanction in the events of 1864–5.

If he was thus severe in the standards of intellectual morality which he set for himself, however, he was nonetheless also sensitive to the dilemmas facing clergymen of what he called 'progressive' opinions who felt both loyalty and commitment to their church and yet dissented from conventional interpretations of its doctrinal formularies. In 1870 he published a pamphlet entitled *The Ethics of Conformity and Subscription*, which reflected both his own acute sense of the moral necessity of strict honesty and plainspeaking, and his awareness of the dilemmas faced by theologically liberal clergy. Sidgwick was clear on the one hand that 'Reserve' was unacceptable, that the clear statement of a clergyman's true opinions was morally essential, that during a period of religious change and uncertainty it was absurd to demand that anyone in favour of change should cease to be a minister, that it was intolerable that a clergyman should be bound to perpetual agreement with the least progressive element in his congregation, and that, in present circumstances, the combination of an educated ministry *and* a uniformity of belief and worship were impossible. On the other hand, Sidgwick was also clear that it was impossible that 'a man can satisfactorily perform the functions of a pastor if his opinions are not more or less in harmony with those of his flock', and that the 'tacit understanding' whereby liberal clergy interpreted the formularies in a relaxed way was indeed 'tacit', not 'general', and therefore morally unacceptable. It was an understanding 'confined to the liberal clergy and a certain small number of educated laymen', but it was also an understanding, 'to which they dare not publicly appeal in favour of a dissent which they dare not openly avow'. The latter aspect of the situation was, for Sidgwick, intolerable, for it was clear to him that, 'the duty of making his position clear rests with the divergent; and if his position is not made clear, if the terms of membership are merely relaxed in the esoteric opinion of the enlightened few, if he gives other men fair reason for believing that he holds opinions which he does not hold, then his conduct can only be defended on grounds on which all other religious hypocrisy may be defended' (Sidgwick, 1870, especially pp. 19–37).

Sidgwick's pamphlet of 1870, clear though it was about the need for a strict, public and plain truthfulness in the matter of assent to and interpretation of doctrine, nevertheless retained a marked sense of the ambiguity of the position which Broad Churchmen found themselves in. Another essay, also published in 1870, on the theme of the Broad Church, plainness of speech, and the morality of assent in relaxed, general terms, presented a more definite and quite unambiguous answer both to the questions of intellectual integrity thus raised and to the matter of their practical solution.

Leslie Stephen was an Anglican clergyman and a Fellow of Trinity Hall, Cambridge. He had been ordained deacon in 1855 and priest in 1859 in order to accept a Fellowship which required that its holder, both as tutor and assistant chaplain at the college, should be in holy orders. By the early 1860s he had begun to question his faith. He disbelieved various specific matters, such as the story of the flood. More crucially, he revolted morally from participation in certain aspects of religious worship, (saying the creed, or reading a lesson, for example), which, if performed without any further explanation, might seem to imply to others that he believed things which he did not. And, at a more general level, he discovered not 'that my creed is false, but that I had never really believed it. I had unconsciously imbibed the current phraseology; but the formulae belonged to the superficial thought, instead of fundamental convictions' (quoted in Von Arx, 1985, p. 11; see also Livingston, 1974a, pp. 8–9). Accordingly, in 1862 he ceased to function as chaplain, and in 1864 he resigned his Fellowship altogether and embarked on the career of intellectual and academic journalism, historical writing, and the editing of the *Dictionary of National Biography*, for which he is chiefly remembered.

Stephen was the product of an Evangelical home and retained from his background all the moral earnestness of the Evangelical tradition. As Basil Willey once memorably put it, in Stephen the evangelical passion for salvation had been transmuted into an intellectual passion for truth and sincerity: 'what must I do to be saved' had become 'what must I think to be honest' (Willey, 1952, p. 121). Certainly, as Frank Turner and Jeffrey Von Arx have recently argued, the critique of both the Broad Churchmen and the Ritualists — in both cases for alleged lack of plain honesty and intellectual integrity — which Stephen presented in his writings, and especially in a cluster of essays dating from the late 1860s and the early 1870s, was prompted by more than merely the passionate moral earnestness of an agnostic conscience reared in an evangelical environment. As Turner and Von Arx demonstrate, the critique was clearly also prompted by Stephen's perception, at that time, of the existence of a crucial contemporary conflict between a Christianity (and in particular a Church of England) which displayed signs of institutional revival — and especially of *clerical* revival — and the efforts of a variety of agnostics and free-thinking intellectuals to construct a distinctly *post*-Christian intellectual and cultural synthesis as a basis for national life (Turner and Von Arx, 1982; Von Arx, 1985, pp. 20–30). At the heart of Stephen's perception of this fundamental cultural and intellectual conflict, however (as Basil Willey also acknowledged, albeit in rather different terms), there remained the question of honesty. Stephen did not approve of attempts to liberalise Christianity because he believed liberalism and Christianity to be opposites. Both liberalism which did not lead to agnosticism, and Christianity which attempted to be liberal, he considered to be essentially dishonest (Willey, 1952, p. 126).

In a series of articles published in the periodical press between 1868 and 1873, Stephen challenged the integrity of both the Ritualists and the Broad Churchmen.[8] Both the Ritualists' efforts to circumvent by evasion the consequences of legal judgements against them in order to continue their ritual practices, (as for example by mixing the wine and water in the chalice in the vestry not the church, or genuflecting without actually kneeling at points where kneeling was ruled illegal), and the Broad Churchmen's willingness to use traditional doctrinal language whilst investing it with quite new meanings, were in Stephen's view ultimately insincere and therefore dishonest.

In the present context it is Stephen's critique of the intellectual integrity of the Broad Churchmen which is of principal interest. His case against them was presented with disarming clarity in an article published in *Fraser's Magazine* in March 1870 and entitled simply 'The Broad Church'. Stephen acknowledged that Broad Churchmen were generally agreed to be honourable men who did not intend deliberate intellectual dishonesty, but, he asked,

> Is it desirable that men who believe that many of the popular views of Christianity are erroneous and immoral, but who believe nevertheless that Christianity in some sense will be the ultimate religion of the world, should hold on to the Established Church, should use the old formulae ... or that they should break with the old state of things and try a fresh start?
>
> (Stephen, 1870, p. 313)

To the extent that the Church of England still possessed the allegiance of thinking men (sic) at all, Stephen asserted, it was due to the presence within it of the Broad Church clergy, and he contrasted, (to their credit and to the discredit of the orthodox), the characteristic modes of apologetic of the Broad Churchmen and their opponents within the church. The latter, Stephen asserted, now characteristically avoided the question of whether or not orthodox doctrine was in fact true by attacking instead the competence of human reason to judge such matters, by insisting that criticism cannot *dis*prove the claims of orthodoxy, and by urging the suppression rather than

[8] See especially his essays, 'Ritualism', *Macmillan's Magazine* 1868; 'The Broad Church', *Fraser's Magazine*, 1870; 'Mr Matthew Arnold and the Church of England', *Fraser's Magazine*, 1870; 'Mr Voysey and Mr Purchas', *Fraser's Magazine*, 1871.

the discussion of critical questions. Such an attitude, Stephen declared, was 'essentially immoral', and he noted that

> The Broad Church, however, distinguish themselves by repudiating any such compromise in theory ... The great merit of Broad Church-men, in my eyes, is that they meet argument fairly, and admit in theory the importance of searching, fair and unfettered inquiry.

Unfortunately, however, Stephen continued, what they admitted in theory, the Broad Churchmen failed to carry through in their actual practice, not least because

> ... unluckily we have got into such habits of conscious or uncon-scious deception of ourselves and others that it is difficult to disinter a man's genuine faith from the masses of conventional language and insincere dogma under which it is habitually covered.
>
> (p. 316)

Thus, Stephen continued, the Broad Churchmen characteristically an-nounced their intention of simply setting out to ascertain the truth, yet their investigations always ended in opinions which they maintained were capable of expression in the words of antiquated theological formulae such as the Thirty Nine Articles — which were themselves, in turn, the result of theological compromises in the sixteenth century. Stephen again asserted his conviction that few, if any, of such Broad Churchmen were consciously dishonest, and acknowledged a degree of legitimacy in the claim that, since the Articles were not framed in a rigorously precise manner, it was accep-table that they should now be regarded as compatible with widely divergent sentiments. But he noted again the conflict between the Broad Church-men's own theological opinions and the language of the Articles.

In the hands of the Broad Churchmen, Stephen insisted, in a passage crucial to his whole argument, many traditional doctrines tended to melt away:

> The Atonement is spiritualised till it becomes difficult to attach any definite meaning to it whatever. The authority of the Bible becomes more difficult to define and to distinguish from the authority of any other good book. Everlasting punishment is put out of the way by the aid of judicious metaphysical distinctions. The sharp edges of old-fashioned doctrine are rounded off till the whole outline of the creed is materially altered.
>
> (p. 323)

At its worst, Stephen asserted, this process led to phrases which once appeared to have definite meaning being reduced to having no meaning at all, and to the gap between the ordinary interpretation and that now proposed by the Broad Churchmen becoming so wide as to seem diametrically opposite. In such circumstances Stephen proposed the use of a simple (sic) test:

> Let a man put out of his mind, as far as possible, all the old phrases with which he has become familiar, and simply express his thoughts in the clearest language he can ... If there is a palpable difficulty in reconciling them, the problem occurs whether he shall use the old in a new sense, or simply abandon language with so many misleading associations. The answer must be given by deciding which duty is just now the most important: to speak out with the utmost clearness, or to keep the Church of England together a little longer.
>
> (p. 323)

The paramount duty, Stephen insisted, was to seek to speak with perfect intellectual integrity. It was much pleasanter, he noted, to say that one believed in everlasting punishment, but to explain that it meant nothing which could shock a humane mind, than to simply denounce the doctrine as immoral and untrue. If only the Broad Churchmen would clearly adopt the latter course instead of the former one, then their influence on the mind of the country would be far greater. At present, their position in relation to the formularies of their church was one of systematic evasion. The more honourable course would be to call for the revision of such formularies, and, if this were not possible, to leave the church and 'speak the plain unsophisticated truth'. Since Stephen also acknowledged that the call to revise obsolete formularies might well be a hopeless course, his argument amounted to a call for Broad Churchmen to come out of the Church of England.

III   PLAIN-SPEAKING AND BELIEF: REALITY OR ILLUSION

The immediate strength of Stephen's position was its apparently disarming clarity. It asked that one should straightforwardly say what one meant, mean what one said, and not take refuge in special, private or esoteric understandings of the meaning of words. Measured against Stephen's call for such plain-speech, the attempts of Broad Churchmen to justify their right to remain clergymen whilst re-interpreting the Articles, Creeds and formularies of their church in a symbolic or spiritualized manner, often tended, (and could easily be made), to appear at best unclear and tentative, at worst evasive and insincere. But was the disarming clarity of Leslie Stephen's argument in fact as reasonable as it appeared? Was the matter of saying what you meant and meaning what you said in relation to creeds, formularies and confessions of belief susceptible of so straightforward a solution?

Obviously the Broad Churchmen themselves did not think so. James Livingston has suggested that for the majority of clergymen of theologically liberal or Broad Church opinions a response to Stephen's argument would have been based upon a combination of three principal arguments. First, that whilst some form of doctrinal standard or statement was necessary to express a church's belief, yet all particular statements are only approximate attempts to express truths and insights of a transcendant, spiritual kind. Second, that no single creed or standard would or could provide an adequate or satisfying statement of belief for every mind within the church at any given time. And third, that it was not possible for any creed to remain an adequate statement and expression of belief from one age to another (Livingston, 1974a, pp. 11–12).

For Broad Churchmen, then, both the nature of creeds and doctrinal formularies themselves, and the nature of the relationship between Christianity and modern liberal thought, were more complicated and ambiguous matters than critics of their position such as Leslie Stephen would allow. Stephen, like Harrison and Wilberforce in their famous responses to *Essays and Reviews*, wanted clarity above all else. He wished to establish that the relationship between Christianity and modern liberalism was a clear and decisive either/or: either Christianity traditionally conceived, or liberalism unreservedly embraced. If the *traditional* beliefs and the *traditional* expressions of those beliefs were now perceived to be untrue, Stephen maintained, then this should be acknowledged plainly.

The Broad Churchmen perceived the relationship of belief, modernity and honesty to be more complex and more subtle. For them, simply to jettison the traditional language of their church and its theological, liturgical and doctrinal inheritance would also have been, in a different way, a dishonest position, for that would have been to *wholly* reject and abandon something which they believed still contained within itself important insights, truths and resources. When the Broad Churchmen criticised traditional understandings and interpretations of their church's doctrinal formularies, they did so because they believed there was *more* to the doctrine than either the rigid interpretations of the orthodox or the allegedly 'plain meanings' of agnostic or positivist critics allowed. They sought to be honest by resisting the — to them — false clarities of both the orthodox 'right' and the unbelieving 'left'. As Jowett once put it, in 1873, 'Although we are in a false position in the church, we should be in a still more false position out of the church' (quoted in Chadwick, 1972, p. 143). Similarly Rowland Williams wrote, in 1868, that,

> There is hardly any doctrine of the Church of England, and here I include all such as the Trinity, and Baptismal Regeneration, which I do not systematically teach, and continue to teach: though it has seemed to me a sacred duty to avoid the exaggerations and misinterpretations with which these doctrines have been too often associated ... When I have been dead a century, somebody will discover that, upon the hypothesis of the Church of England being properly conservable, my method was the most logically conservative.

(Quoted in Crowther, 1976, p. 104)

Williams' statement neatly expresses the difference between his position (and that of the majority of Broad Churchmen) and that of Leslie Stephen. Williams believed deeply in what he understood to be the *underlying truth* of the doctrine of the Church of England, believed such underlying truth to be frequently obscured by *exaggerated* or *misinterpreted* versions of the doctrines, and considered the Church of England worth preserving. Stephen, on the other hand, considered the plain meaning of the church's doctrine to be just what Williams viewed as exaggeration and misrepresentation and did not regard it as desirable that the church itself should be preserved as an effective force and institution in national life.

There were, moreover, voices other than those of the Broad Churchmen themselves prepared to acknowledge that the matter of the meaning of creeds, the plainness of speech, and the demands upon the individual of the ethics of belief, was not altogether so simple. Rowland Williams' counsel at his trial for heresy was James Fitzjames Stephen, the brother of Leslie Stephen. Writing in *Fraser's Magazine* in 1864, in the aftermath of the acquittal of Williams and Wilson by the Judicial Committee of the Privy Council, James Stephen criticised the confidence, readiness, and ease with which orthodox clergy appealed to the 'known' or 'plain' sense of theological terms and doctrinal statements. It was the fundamental weakness of most theological writers, Stephen asserted, 'that they seem not to have any conception of the degree of precision of language which is required for the purpose of precluding discussion.' Theologians, he observed, were remarkably prone to impute treachery and dishonesty to those who differed from them rather than recognise that doctrinal formularies are to a large extent indefinite (quoted in Livingston, 1974a, p. 8).

The remarks are the more telling precisely because James Stephen was neither a churchman nor an admirer of Broad Church theology.[9] He

---

[9] Indeed, far from admiring Broad Church theology, he disliked it, even describing it in 1870,

retained, like his brother Leslie, a life-long interest in religion, but by the 1860s had already adopted the stance of an agnostic honest doubter.

The necessarily imprecise and indefinite nature of doctrinal formularies was, however, also taken up in the late 1860s by another legally trained commentator upon the subject of creeds and their interpretation, who was *also* a practising churchman, albeit not a member of the Church of England. The context and the theological tradition concerned — namely Scottish Presbyterianism and the legal status and position of its doctrinal standards — were quite different. But the discussion of the nature of creeds and confessions and of the meaning of assent to them, presented by the Scottish Free Churchman and Advocate, Alexander Taylor Innes, in his essay on 'The Theory of the Church and its Creed, with reference to the Law of Scotland', included observations as pertinent to the debate about the ethics of belief and subscription in the mid-Victorian Church of England as it was to the debates over subscription to the Westminster Confession which occurred in the Scottish Presbyterian churches from the mid 1860s onwards.

The essay first appeared in 1867 as an appendix to Innes' major work *The Law of Creeds in Scotland*. Having observed that a creed which was to function as a test of membership of a church must necessarily be of a limited kind, Innes listed a series of considerations which he described as 'truisms' concerning the nature of assent to creeds:

> ... taking it for granted that all the ministers of the Presbyterian Churches hold *ex animo* all the propositions which the Confession of Faith draws from Scripture, it is at least certain that each of these ministers (who has thought of these propositions at all) differs from

---

in a letter to his brother, as 'the most incoherent rubbish that ever entered the head of sane men'. In a legal and literary career of seemingly workaholic intensity, Stephen combined a successful career as a barrister with prolific writing — especially on religion and religious criticism — for the Victorian periodical press. In such religious writing, and in his participation in the meetings of the Metaphysical Society, he engaged in debate not only with the Broad Churchmen — whose writings he frequently criticized, not least for illogicality — but also with leading contemporary Roman Catholic writers such as Newman, Ward, Manning and Mivart, and with prominent freethinkers such as Frederic Harrison and Herbert Spencer. His dislike of their theology notwithstanding, Stephen acted as legal counsel for Broad Churchmen such as Rowland Williams and Charles Voysey and prepared a defence of Colenso, although in the event the Judicial Committee of the Privy Council ruled on Colenso without hearing Stephen's defence. He also acted for the Ritualist C. J. Ridsdale when he became the first clergyman to be prosecuted under the Public Worship Regulation Act. By the late 1860s, Stephen had become convinced that the theology of both liberals and orthodox involved degrees of sophistry which amounted to intellectual dishonesty. In the context of the present essay, however, it is also worth noting that, by the mid-1870s, although he had already given up belief in any traditional form of Christianity, he continued to attend church with his family. For details of these various aspects of Stephen's religious belief, attitudes and practice, see Livingston, 1974b, and Colaiaco, 1983, ch. 8.

every other in the precise meaning, emphasis, order, and relation in which he holds them; and further, that he differs from every one else in some of the ten thousand minor propositions which are outside the Confession. There is no honest and sane man who will pretend that any proposition in religious truth constructed by others exactly expresses his own view of that religious truth; and though it may be constructed with sufficient care and comprehensiveness to *include* the views of a great number of consentients, it is morally certain that every one of these consentients differ from every other, and from the objective proposition itself, in the exact sense in which he understands it. Confessions are limited, therefore, even when we look to what is attempted to be expressed in them. But this is clearer when we look to what is necessarily left out. The Westminster Confession is large enough; but for every one scriptural proposition there fixed, there are ten left unfixed — the larger the circle of truth ascertained, the larger is the circumference towards the unascertained outside. No Creed includes everything. For there are no two men who agree in the interpretation of every detail of Scripture, except those who decline to apply their minds to Scripture at all.

Innes thus showed himself to be acutely aware of the subtle differences which inevitably and necessarily existed between individual understandings of shared creeds and confessions. Once probed in detail, 'plain meanings' were inevitably apt to dissolve into a very wide variety of specific meanings, opinions and perceptions.[10]

The theme of the sheer variety of opinion which might co-exist within a single church, all of whose members officially accepted the same doctrinal formularies as their standard of belief, was one which Henry Sidgwick also took up. Sidgwick was no less passionate a believer in the moral virtue and ethical duty of veracity of speech and the open expression of opinion than was Leslie Stephen. But whereas Stephen concluded in his essay of 1870 on *The Broad Church* by seeking to argue the Broad Churchmen *as individuals* into the necessity of making a moral choice between sincerity of belief and profession on the one hand, and membership of the Church of England on

---

[10] When, some twenty-five years later in 1892, Innes republished his essay on the 'Theory of the Church and its Creed' (in a collection of his essays entitled *Studies in Scottish History, Chiefly Ecclesiastical*), he was able to append a further essay entitled 'A Quarter of a Century of the Development of that Theory', in which he noted and commented upon the extent to which the question of subscription and assent to the Westminster Confession had been debated, and the terms of assent to some extent modified or qualified in the Church of Scotland, the Free Church, and the United Presbyterian Church. For detail, see Innes, 1892, pp. 255–71. For a discussion of the wider context of such debates within Victorian Scottish Presbyterianism, see *RVB*, I, 3.

the other, Sidgwick concluded his pamphlet of 1870 on *The Ethics of Conformity and Subscription* by recognising the *institutional* dimension of the issue of the ethics of belief as well as its individual aspect.

Sidgwick concluded his pamphlet by relating the question of honest subscription on the part of the individual to the actual condition of theological diversity which already existed within the Church of England. The more familiar a man became, he said, with the present state of theology and the more he endeavoured to assimilate the results of recent research:

> ... the more he will find out that there is no sort of agreement among theologians in respect of principles, methods, or conclusions; that there is a complete scale of opinions, reaching from the extreme of mediaeval orthodoxy to the extreme of pure Theism, each separated from the other by a small interval, or shading imperceptibly into it; all held by men of undoubted learning, ability and character, and almost all by men of apparent fervour and piety, and declared attachment to the religion of Christ.
>
> (Sidgwick, 1870, p. 37)

As things stood, Sidgwick continued, the fact that clergy of liberal opinions did not generally and openly assert the burdensome nature of the subscription still required of them meant that the full extent and nature of this general *dis*-agreement over theology and belief was not commonly recognised and understood. What was desirable was that individuals should speak *openly* of their attitude to subscription and that the institution should *openly* relax its doctrinal requirement. Then, Sidgwick finally concluded,

> the actual state of opinion could be freely declared, and its consequences frankly faced; then we might fairly try what the spirit of compromise and conciliation, which, after all, is a virtue and not a vice of the Church of England, could do towards harmonising the inevitable conditions of a national ministry with the inexorable demands of theological thought.

IV POSTSCRIPT: AN UNRESOLVED ISSUE

This essay has sought to convey something of the nature, the variety, the intensity, and the ambiguity of the debate over the ethics of belief and the intellectual integrity of the Anglican clergy which occurred in mid-Victorian England, focusing especially on the decade which opened with the publication of *Essays and Reviews* in 1860.

As we noted earlier in the essay, this debate was not a creation of the 1860s but had emerged some two decades earlier in the controversies over the Oxford Movement. The events of the 1860s, however, and especially the publication of *Essays and Reviews*, the acquittal of Rowland Williams and H. B. Wilson by the Judicial Committee of the Privy Council, and the passing of the Clerical Subscription Act, raised the debate to a new pitch and, significantly, took it beyond the boundaries of the Church of England (where for the most part it had been carried on hitherto) and made it, instead, a part of that wider complex of conflicts between 'faith and doubt', 'conscience and theology', 'religion and freethought', which were characteristic of the mid-Victorian era.

The debate was one which, by its very nature, could not be pressed to a decisive conclusion. The acquittal of Williams and Wilson and the passing of the Clerical Subscription Act established the fact that, legally, Broad Churchmen were entitled to hold the views they did and remain Church of England clergymen. The debate was about whether it was also moral for them to do so. But that was an inevitably and intensely subjective question: it depended, among other things, upon one's temperament, one's perception of the nature of religious belief, and one's perception of the degree to which words and formularies were genuinely capable of being given precise and plain meanings.

The fundamental division which the debate revealed was not one between believers and unbelievers, but one between those who believed that the issue was essentially clear — an issue of either/or, either honest and conventional belief or honest disbelief — and those who believed that the issue was not a matter of black and white but of shades (and often very many shades) of grey. The Broad Churchmen and commentators such as James Stephen and Alexander Innes (and to some extent even so fastidious an intellectual ethicist as Henry Sidgwick) tended to see many shades of grey. The orthodox, such as Wilberforce, and those, such as Harrison and Leslie Stephen, who believed the future of society should be in the hands of a post-Christian intellectual elite, tended to see the issue in black and white.

During the 1870s the debate over the ethics of belief was continued in the pages of the leading Victorian periodicals and, especially, in the meetings and debates of the Metaphysical Society. The nature of the debate changed and broadened, however, and it became primarily concerned with the philosophical nature, implications and bases of various approaches to religious belief, rather than with the more immediate and practical question of the morality of clerical subscription and assent to doctrinal statements.[11]

Within the Church of England, the question of honest clerical subscription, the legitimate limits of honest clerical doubt, and the extent to which

[11] For surveys of the debates in the periodical press and in the meetings of the Metaphysical Society, see Livingston, 1974a, pp. 17–35 and 1974b.

a clergyman might modify traditional belief continued to cause concern. But the concern tended to surface spasmodically, in response to specific incidents and individuals. In 1880 the case of Stopford Brooke provided one such incident. By 1880 Brooke had come to the conclusion that he definitely did not believe in miracles. He therefore left the Church of England because certain elements of its doctrines and creeds were founded upon miracles. Brooke was respected for his integrity and most clergy thought it right that he should have left — although there were some Broad Churchmen who thought his action unnecessary and anachronistic (Chadwick, 1972, p. 136). Six years later the case for remaining a clergyman in such circumstances received forthright expression.

In 1886 there appeared a book entitled *The Kernel and the Husk: Letters on Spiritual Christianity*. It was written by Edwin Abbott, a liberal clergyman, biblical scholar and Headmaster of the City of London School. The book sought precisely to justify the position of a man who did not believe in miracles but remained a Church of England clergyman. Abbott's aim was openly pastoral: he wished to help to provide a 'religion which would wear' and would not end in causing complete *un*belief because it began by asking for *too much* belief. Abbott argued that the terms of general assent of the Clerical Subscription Act of 1865 would legally allow a clergyman to believe in a non-miraculous manner. But there then remained the moral problem of the public recitation of the Creeds in worship, the sensibilities of the congregation, and the degree to which, (in order to remain honest), the clergyman must speak out concerning his non-miraculous understanding of the Creeds. Abbott's solution was to argue that such a clergyman must admit his non-miraculous interpretation to his bishop, but should not preach it assertively from his pulpit. In preaching and in pastoral ministry Abbott advised such liberal clergy not to attack traditional *material* belief, but to preach their own *spiritual* belief: thus they would avoid aggressive disturbance of the faith of conventional believers in their congregation but would also preach truthfully 'without sacrificing your own convictions; and at the same time insensibly prepare the younger portion of your flock to detach the material part of their faith from the spiritual' (quoted in Livingston, 1974a, p. 41).

The Kernel and the Husk initiated a new chapter in the specifically Anglican debate over the ethics of belief and the nature and implications of clerical subscription. Abbott's position was attacked by Charles Gore in what proved to be the first shot of a more than thirty year long campaign on Gore's part against the acceptance of the legitimacy of non-natural (and hence non-miraculous) interpretations of the Creeds. If, Gore maintained, one could not accept the miracles of Christ's birth and resurrection, then one's mind was predisposed against the whole fabric of Christian super-naturalism, and this was inappropriate in a clergyman. Gore, of course, was also the editor of *Lux Mundi*, the collection of essays which, in 1889, signalled the break from the traditional Tractarian view of biblical inspiration on the part of a new generation of up and coming Anglo-Catholics. But Gore insisted that whilst biblical criticism had caused radical re-assessment of the historicity of much of the Old Testament, the historical trustworthiness of the New Testament was such that criticism would not undermine it — unless it were criticism predisposed to the impossibility of miracle, and therefore itself unreliable. The historical, natural, sense of the creeds in respect of the Virgin Birth and the resurrection must therefore be maintained as essential.

In 1895 Henry Sidgwick again entered the now re-opened debate and this time his contribution was less tentative than his earlier essay of 1870. He argued that, whilst for laymen the belief or disbelief in the historical items in the Creeds might be regarded as an open question, for clergymen it could not. If Creeds were to be spoken in public worship and not *openly agreed* to be understood non-naturally, then clergymen must either believe in the natural sense or leave the church. The expedient of private admission of one's precise opinion to one's bishop Sidgwick found quite inadequate.[12]

By the end of the century, however, such appeals to bishops were, in fact, becoming more common. The episcopal response would depend, as Chadwick has observed, not only upon the particular manner and merits of the clergyman or candidate for ordination concerned, but also upon the personal judgement, opinions and consciences of bishops. Different bishops adopted different polities (Chadwick, 1972, pp. 143–7). Moreover, as James Livingston has noted the position of the Church of England concerning subscription and the ethics of belief was, by 1900, an inherently unstable one. Some statements of some creeds (for example, the infamous 'damnatory clauses' of the Athanasian Creed) were commonly held to be open to non-natural interpretation by clergy as well as laity — a point on which even Gore agreed. Other statements, such as those concerning the Virgin Birth or the resurrection were not deemed open to non-natural interpretation, especially not by the clergy. But they were defended partly because their historicity was deemed to be demonstrated by the New Testament: yet the New Testament was itself now coming under historical-critical scrutiny at just such points.

The institutional response to this situation was to adopt conciliatory but manifestly ambiguous official statements. Thus, in 1905, a resolution was passed in the House of Bishops which, simultaneously, 'affirmed that the historical facts stated in the Creeds are an essential part of the Faith of the

---

[12] For a detailed account of both Gore's and Sidgwick's reaction to the case argued by Abbott, see Livingston, 1974a, pp. 42–5.

Church' and that denial of those facts went beyond the limits of legitimate interpretation and gravely imperilled sincerity of profession, whilst also recognizing the need for considerateness in dealing with the tentative and provisional thought and work of earnest and reverent scholars. But such provisional and tentative work included — and was well known to include — versions of belief in the Incarnation and Resurrection which did not accept the historicity of the events recorded in the birth and resurrection narratives in the Gospels. By the early twentieth century it was thus more clear than ever that Sidgwick's concluding remarks in his 1870 pamphlet on *The Ethics of Subscription and Conformity* were indeed apposite: the ethics of belief indeed possessed an institutional as well as an individual dimension.

By 1900, however, the debate over the ethics of belief and the honesty of clerical subscription was once more becoming (Sidgwick's contribution of 1896 notwithstanding) one predominantly conducted within the churches, and less a matter of general and cultural interest. Nor, indeed, is it surprising that this was so. Developments both within the Church of England itself and in respect of the Church's place in society conspired to render the issue of the ethics of belief on the one hand less clear, and on the other hand less pressing than had been the case in the 1860s and 1870s.

Within the Church of England the internal pluralism, already implicit in the 1860s in the alternating controversies between Anglo-Catholics and Evangelicals and between orthodox (both Evangelical and Anglo-Catholic) and liberals, had become steadily more obvious and more complex. It became increasingly clear that the Church of England was in practice a very Broad Church indeed — even if not quite in the way that the mid-century Broad Churchmen had wanted it to be. Defiantly combative and conscientiously disobedient Ritualist clergy had steadily extended the bounds of Catholic ritual and devotion within the Church of England. Theologically liberal clergy continued to take advantage of the judgements and legislation of the 1860s. In the publication of *Lux Mundi* a younger generation of Anglo-Catholics espoused critical theological views which, despite their conservatism on the historical clauses of the Creeds, were closer to those of the authors of *Essays and Reviews* than they were to traditional High Church or Anglo-Catholic orthodoxy. The ethics of clerical belief were still debated — but the debates were now inevitably even less clearly defined, the areas still resolutely and widely claimed as black and white inevitably much reduced, and the areas widely conceded to be grey much increased.

In respect of the Church's place in society, meanwhile, in the three decades after 1870 it became increasingly clear that the Church of England, although still established, had relinquished much of its effective power. The clerical and institutional revival within the church which agnostic and free-thinking intellectuals like Stephen had once feared might be an effective competitor for the intellectual and cultural leadership of society did not prove capable of any such thing. Society by 1900 was clearly more secular and more pluralist, and religion less central and more optional than it had been in the 1860s and 1870s. Because this was so, it became less pressing for secular and freethinking intellectuals to concern themselves with the intellectual honesty or otherwise of the clergy. The clergy were left, for the most part, to argue the matter among themselves, and the heirs of the earnest agnostic and freethinking debaters of the ethics of belief of the 1860s and 1870s inhabited a society and intellectual *milieu* in which religious issues and institutions simply did not prompt the interest and concern that they had a generation earlier. Whether either the church or the society of which it was a part, on balance, gained or lost by virtue of such intellectual and moral dis-engagement is a question worth reflection.

BIBLIOGRAPHY

*J. L. Altholz (1976) 'The warfare of conscience with theology' in J. L. Altholz (ed.) *The Mind and Art of Victorian England*, University of Minnesota Press.

O. Chadwick (1972) *The Victorian Church*, Part II, A. and C. Black.

J. A. Colaiaco (1983) *James Fitzjames Stephen and the Crisis of Victorian Thought*, New York, St Martin's Press.

M. A. Crowther (1970) *Church Embattled: Religious Controversy in Mid-Victorian England*, Newton Abbot, David and Charles.

G. Faber (1957) *Jowett: A Portrait With Background*, Faber and Faber.

F. Harrison (1860) 'Neo-Christianity', *Westminster Review*, No. 18, pp. 293–332.

W. Houghton (1957) *The Victorian Frame of Mind 1830–1870*, Yale University Press.

A. T. Innes (1867) *The Law of Creeds in Scotland*, Edinburgh, Blackwood.

A. T. Innes (1892) *Studies in Scottish History, Chiefly Ecclesiastical*, Hodder and Stoughton.

*J. C. Livingston (1974a) *The Ethics of Belief: An Essay on the Victorian Religious Conscience*, American Academy of Religion, Tallahassee, Florida.

J. C. Livingston (1974b) 'The religious creed and criticism of Sir James Fitzjames Stephen', *Victorian Studies*, Vol. xx, pp. 279–300.

H. Sidgwick (1870) *The Ethics of Conformity and Subscription*, Williams and Norgate.

A. P. Stanley (1861) 'Essays and Reviews', *Edinburgh Review*, Vol. 113, pp. 461–500.

L. Stephen (1870) 'The Broad Church', *Fraser's Magazine*, Vol. xx, pp. 311–25.

*F. M. Turner and J. Von Arx (1982) 'Victorian ethics of belief: a reconsideration' in W. W. Wagar (ed.) *The Secular Mind: Transformations of Faith in Modern Europe*, Holmes and Meier, pp. 83–101.

D. G. Wigmore-Beddoes (1971) *Yesterday's Radicals: A Study of the Affinity Between Unitarianism and Broad Church Anglicanism in the Nineteenth Century*, Edinburgh, James Clarke.

S. Wilberforce (1861) 'Essays and Reviews' *Quarterly Review*, Vol. 109. pp. 107–29.

*B. Willey (1952) 'Honest Doubt' in *Christianity Past and Present*, pp. 00–00, Cambridge, Cambridge University Press.

B. Willey (1956) *More Nineteenth Century Studies: A Group of Honest Doubters*, Cambridge, Cambridge University Press.

J. P. Von Arx (1985) *Progress and Pessimism: Religion, Politics and History in Late Nineteenth Century Britain*, Harvard University Press.

CHAPTER 10

RUDIMENTS OF SCEPTICISM AND ORTHODOXY.

The Free-Thinking Lucy. "Do you Know, May, sometimes, when I Hurt myself, the Place gets Well wivout *nobody NEVER* Kissin' it."
The Faithful May. "I don't Beyieve you, Yucy!"

THE CRISIS OF FAITH: REFORMATION VERSUS REVOLUTION

THE English ruling classes under Queen Victoria prided themselves upon the dubious distinction that their dominion over three kingdoms was impervious to the upheavals that swept the European mainland. They at least had had the foresight to tame their monarchy with an oligarchy of wealth. 'Your aristocracy and bourgeoisie', complained the French Positivist philosopher Auguste Comte to an Oxford disciple in the 1850s, '... consider England wholly protected in advance against the present crisis of the West by their dynastic Revolution of 1688' (quoted in Kent, 1978, p. 99). Subsequent events confirmed the safety of the ruling classes, although their sense of security was at least partly misplaced. Limited monarchies and reformed parliaments may fend off revolution, but not by virtue of their existence. Laws must be passed as deterrents, force must be used to stem unrest; and in the 'first industrial nation', where the manual working class was numerically dominant, the maintenance of public order also required a massive mobilization of consent. It did not take Elie Halévy in the twentieth century to point out that Methodism helped prevent a revolution in the 1790s, however much his famous thesis has had to be qualified. Victorians themselves, who peered piously through the mists at republican France, fancied their isles a bastion of Christian civilization. Endemic evangelicalism and natural theology were proof against atheistic materialism. The salvoes of 'false philosophy' passed harmlessly through the religious atmosphere, like bullets through a fog. Ideologically, as well as institutionally, Victorian England lay shrouded in reaction to the causes and the consequences of the French Revolution.

The reaction was not static. Revolution remained more or less of a threat until 1848, with commensurate institutional responses (Thomis and Holt, 1977). By 1870, however, one historical commentator announced that a 'revolution' had indeed occurred. In a remarkable series of lectures entitled 'The Revolution of the Last Quarter of a Century', J. Baldwin Brown, a prominent dissenting clergyman, offered urbane reflections on the period of his ministry to a prosperous congregation in suburban London. He ascribed the revolution through which together they had passed to inflammatory intellectual events, notably in science and philosophy; he also admonished his congregation that the social consequences of these events in the mid-nineteenth century required 'an entire revolution in our ideas'. Likening the times to the fall of the Roman Empire, Baldwin Brown traced the demise of feudalism from its 'death-wound' in the French Revolution to the *coup de grâce* administered in 1846 by the advent of Free Trade. The weakness of the feudal system was its resistance to the world's 'inevitable progress', but its strength was 'the definite order which it established in society'. Following its demise, 'the social sorrow of our times', he declared, 'is that men do not know their places.... All things are in constant flux' and men are filled with 'distress and apprehension'.

During these twenty-five years, the growth of a commercial civilization has widened the breaches and embittered the jealousies and
enmities of society. So far from a new order springing up under the
aegis of commerce, the world has seen, sadly enough, deepening
disorder; stern struggle and fierce hatred of classes; gigantic arma-
ments, tremendous wars, and universal distrust. The knowledge and
intercourse which have attended the progress of our commerce, by
means of cheap papers, cheap postage, railways, and telegraphs, have
stimulated rather than allayed the internal discords and miseries of
the great European nations.

England could escape the 'social revolution' thus portended, according to
Baldwin Brown, neither democratically, through universal suffrage, nor
through 'universal confiscation', the doctrine of the 'extreme Reds', but
only through 'the rearrangement of the thoughts, feelings, and principles of
individual human hearts'. English society required new divine sanctions for
a moral order suited to its needs, even as the Augustinian effort to 'justify
the ways of God to man', with its feudal doctrines, had answered to the
'remarkable crisis' of the Roman Empire in the fourth century. English men
of letters, the 'leaders of ... intellectual progress', would help provide this
bulwark against revolution. 'The world ... is full of dark, sad difficulties',
Baldwin Brown concluded his final lecture; 'theodicies under any conditions are hard'. But the task of reconciliation is 'the problem of the Church
of the future' (Brown, 1871, pp. 244, 250, 272ff., 283, 286–9, 345ff., 364).
    Baldwin Brown's quarter-century of 'revolution' was not the revolution
England had feared, for a *social* revolution was precisely what, he urged,
England could escape. Nor is his historical analysis beyond dispute. But as
a contemporary witness he calls attention instructively to a transitional
period in English religious history, a period when the ruling classes experienced a crisis as they sought a new ideological framework — a new
theodicy — for upholding industrial progress without revolution. The term
'crisis', like 'revolution', belongs primarily to the discourse of politics,
economics, and social history. Indeed, Baldwin Brown employed it precisely in that context. Conventionally, however, the only crisis to interest
intellectual historians of Victorian England has been a 'crisis of faith': a
spiritual condition of bourgeois thinkers beset by religious doubt in the
years round 1859. Only recently have historians begun to explore the wider
social perspective delineated by Baldwin Brown. This essay aims to contri-
bute to this re-evaluation of the conventional 'crisis of faith' by showing
how it may be viewed broadly as an ideological watershed in English
religious thought. For Victorian intellectuals, a religious 'reformation'
would quell unrest, forestalling revolution; a new creed would sanction
social relationships, no longer as providential dispensations to be redressed

in a future life, but as the by-products of an immanent progressive order that promised material salvation through moral achievement in history.

I   CREEDS IN CRISIS

Judging from the titles of literature dealing with the conventional 'crisis of faith', one would think that Victorian intellectuals lost their faith like the rest of us lose umbrellas. As if faith were some 'thing' that could be lost. As if there were some Victorians who ended up without beliefs. Susan Budd's important article on 'reasons for unbelief' among English secularists, entitled 'The Loss of Faith', is incorporated in her book *Varieties of Unbelief* (1977); Anthony Cockshut's graceful study of English agnostic thought is entitled *The Unbelievers* (1964); and two older essays, 'The Strands of Unbelief' by Noel Annan, and 'Unbelief and Science' by Jacob Bronowski, appear incongruously in a book entitled *Ideas and Beliefs of the Victorians* (1949). The partisan character of this emphasis on non-faith, or unbelief, should be evident from the fact that historically it has represented the viewpoint of the faithful — those who still believe. Vintage titles such as *The Battle of Unbelief* (1878) by Gavin Carlyle and *Unbelief in the Nineteenth Century: A Critical History* (1907) by Henry Sheldon were controversial in tone and apologetic in aim. Contemporary works by so-called 'unbelievers', on the other hand, advertized their authors' positive commitments. Consider just a single theme in titles by late Victorian intellectuals: *The Foundations of a Creed* (1875) by George Lewes; *The Creed of a Layman* (1907; first used 1881) by Frederic Harrison; and *The Creed of Science* (1881) by William Graham. There is of course a sense in which people like these authors gradually 'lost their faith' because certain Christian doctrines had ceased to shape their lives. But in the process, as one fair-minded commentator has observed, 'a faith was slowly forged by which men did shape their lives — the ideals of a humanist, secular, progressive, and scientific age ... It was in terms of this newer and confident faith ... that the truth of revelation was judged' (Brose, 1960, p. 228).

Let me pursue the theme of a 'creed' — that 'newer and confident faith' — a little farther.[1] Creeds, we must remember, were in dire straits during the middle decades of the nineteenth century. The basis of established religious ideology was being undermined at the same time (and for many of the same reasons) that the institutions in which that ideology had become a material force — an inertial force, I might add — were being pressed to reform. Thus members of the Universities of Oxford and Cambridge were officially obliged to subscribe the Thirty-nine Articles of the Church of

[1] See *RVB*, I, 8

England; in 1853 F. D. Maurice, a prominent theologian, lost his job teaching Anglican ordinands at King's College, London, because he had publicized his doubts about the morality of eternal punishment, doubts that had driven from the Church morally sensitive persons within his acquaintance, such as John Sterling and Francis Newman. The damnatory clauses of the Athanasian Creed, Maurice declared (1881, p. 410), 'could not be repeated by any honest or Christian man' unless, in effect, they did not mean what they had always been understood to say.

Here, as in many matters, Maurice was before his time. A decade later, not meaning what you said, or not saying what you meant, or just plain trimming, had achieved the sanction of law. The flap in 1984 over the consecration of Professor David Jenkins as Bishop of Durham in York Minster Cathedral, which later burned, was as nothing compared to the outcry in the early 1860s over the moderate unorthodoxies of the authors of *Essays and Reviews* (1860). Then as now, however, massive petitions and letters to *The Times* failed to stem the tide of events; and successive attempts to defend the establishment through litigation proved futile. In 1864 'hell was dismissed with costs' by the Judicial Committee of the Privy Council in the appeal of one of the essayists, who had denied the doctrine of eternal punishment, and a Royal Commission was appointed to look into the terms of clerical subscription. The Clerical Subscription Act of 1865 allowed for 'general', rather than 'unfeigned' particular assent to the Thirty-nine Articles. But if one still had scruples, a Clerical Disabilities Bill was in preparation which, on becoming law in 1870, made it possible for the first time for an Anglican clergyman to relieve himself of holy orders. In the same year the Royal Commission on Ritual issued its fourth report, stating that the damnatory clauses of the Athanasian Creed did not, in fact, mean what they said, or what most people had always thought they meant. This gave rise to a controversy that chuntered on in Convocation for several years, an arcane and unedifying dispute, it would seem, until we understand what was at stake.

For the threat of eternal incineration had been a credible deterrent in early Victorian England. Those who stood in the flickering shadow of hell-fire felt constrained to order and measure their lives in accordance with established moral norms. Hell was also an integral part of a creed or creeds that sanctioned the power and authority of the Establishment (Rowell, 1974, p.123). Those who found the deterrent *in*credible — that is, immoral — or who for other reasons could not subscribe the Thirty-nine Articles, were officially barred from taking Oxbridge degrees and thus, in effect, deprived of access to certain professions and to positions of social influence. The Universities Tests Act of 1871 relieved everyone in the English universities except ordinands and ordained appointees from the obligation to subscribe. But the problem of collective belief did not end there for dissident intellectuals. Whence public and private morality with the decline of hell? If the creeds could not be upheld by force of law — if, on the contrary, the law were seen to be weakening the basis of official ideology — then what hope for the Establishment? Clearly, the door was open to those who said what they meant and meant what they said, who thought freely and spoke plainly. Their new 'post-Christian intellectual synthesis' would have good claim to furnish the basis of public and private morality. It might become the new creed by which society, under their leadership, should be reformed (Turner and Von Arx, 1982, pp. 94–5).

Who, then, were the dissident intellectuals? How far is it justified to think of them not only as reformers, but as specifically religious reformers, constructing a new creed? To what extent may their emerging creed be identified as a new theodicy in the sense suggested by Baldwin Brown, an overarching framework of belief suitable for reconciling social expectations with social realities as an antidote to revolution?

II THE DISSIDENT INTELLECTUALS

The intellectuals who sought a new creed in mid-Victorian Britain were mainly the men — especially the young men — to whom Maurice felt a special mission after the untimely death of Sterling, his intimate friend, in 1844. Their increasingly unsuccessful 'struggle' to accept a 'system' of belief that had failed to underwrite real improvements in 'the condition of England' was, according to Maurice, 'more tremendous than any of us know'. Sterling had foreseen in 1840 a 'necessity for a great crisis in the belief in England' (Brose, 1960, p. 230; Maurice, 1881, p. 237). Twenty years later his words had come true. The fears and travails of the hungry forties, followed by the hopes and certainties of a decade set, as it were, in a Crystal Palace, spurred numerous conversions from the otherworldliness of Tractarians and Evangelicals. James Anthony Froude and Francis Newman, both scholarly refugees from Oxford with pious elder brothers, had searched High and Low for a viable creed. They marked their conversions with spiritual autobiographies published at mid-century. Froude's *Nemesis of Faith* (1849, p. 86) expounded the fundamental perception that society was unjust and the clergy were worse than irrelevant to its needs. Religious belief had to give real help to the poor and the suffering; true knowledge had to be 'linked on to humanity', to 'elucidate . . . some of our hard moral mysteries'. Newman, in his *Phases of Faith* (1850; 1865 edn., p. 135), stressed that the clergy were worse than irrelevant because of the immorality of their beliefs. Those who preached that 'the Lord is at hand' and stigmatized politics as a 'worldly' concern, thereby 'cut the sinews of all earthly progress'. They declared 'war against Intellect and Imagination, against Industrial and Social Advancement'.

While Froude and Newman (as well as the Unitarian industrialist William Rathbone Greg and other allies) remained professing theists, younger men who read Thomas Carlyle's seering indictments of industrial society passed through what Leslie Stephen later called an 'intellectual crisis', akin to a 'religious conversion', that left them without a recognizable belief in God (quoted in Harvie, 1976, p. 38). Inspired to boldness, however, by the heroic spirit of Carlyle's 'natural supernaturalism', convinced that the universe was on their side, they set out to remake society through plain speaking and righteous deeds. The careers of T. H. Huxley and John Tyndall, both scientists, were cases in point. Other young intellectuals underwent a similar though less dramatic conversion experience. Frederic Harrison drew inspiration not only from Carlyle, but from Maurice's and Newman's indictment of Christian creeds. 'As the supernatural died out of my view', he wrote of his years as an Oxford undergraduate in the early 1850s, 'the natural took its place and amply covered the same ground. The change was so gradual, and the growth of one phase of thought out of another was with me so perfectly regular, that I have never been able to fix any definite period of change, nor indeed have I ever been conscious of any real change of mind at all' (Harrison, 1906, p. 9). Harrison's organic metaphor of death and 'growth' was characteristic of the way the dissident intellectuals described their conversion to a fundamental belief in gradualism *per se*, the uniformity and continuity of nature. Stephen, again, whose personal crisis is well-known, put it like this (1907, p. 375): 'The old husk drops off because it has long been withered, and you discover that beneath is a sound and vigorous growth of genuine conviction'.

Years later the mathematician W. K. Clifford observed (1879, II, p. 250) that the movement of dissident intellectuals, of which he was by then a leading member, seemed to be 'not mainly an intellectual movement', spurred by destructive new ideas, but a movement that had 'grown out of the strong impulse given to the moral sense by political freedom'. Whatever truth there may be in this organically-inspired remark, it is beyond dispute that liberalism, first as an ideology and latterly also as a party political commitment, was the bulwark of the dissident intellectuals in their struggle with established religious authority. We can trace their skein of associations and alliances, influences and intrigues, from the early 1850s, when the wonders of the Great Exhibition lured them up to London to meet in the home of John Chapman at 142, The Strand. Chapman, a parvenu among publishers, had brought out their latest books: Froude's *Nemesis of Faith*, Newman's *Lectures on Political Economy* (1851), Greg's *The Creed of Christendom* (1850), and Herbert Spencer's *Social Statics* (1850). His catalogue was a sort of 'index to liberal studies in religion and philosophy'; it had been compiled by a young woman named Marian Evans, now better known as George Eliot.

With Eliot as his assistant editor, Chapman undertook to refurbish the old *Westminster Review*, which he had purchased, as a platform for his friends. The journal would advocate progressive 'organic change', wrote Eliot in the Prospectus. It would be 'an exponent of growing thought'. For the editors believed 'that the same fundamental truths are apprehended under a variety of forms, and that, therefore, opposing systems may in the end prove complements of each other'. 'Religion has its foundations in man's nature, and will only discard an old form to assume and vitalize one more expressive of its essence' (quoted in Haight, 1969, pp. 20, 32, 33, 42). The first number of the new *Westminster Review* appeared in 1852. Besides Chapman and Eliot, Froude, Newman, Greg, and Spencer, the contributors that year included George Lewes, George Combe, John Stuart Mill, and James and Harriet Martineau. In 1854 Huxley and Tyndall took charge of the scientific section of the journal. Here were the cream of the so-called 'honest doubters', free-thinking Anglicans and progressive Nonconformists, the preachers and the publicists of scientific naturalism in Victorian England. 'They are amongst the world's vanguard, though not all in the foremost line', Eliot declared. She also used a word, perhaps for the first time, in the sense we understand it today: in 1852 she called Chapman's circle of Westminster Reviewers an 'assemblage of intellectuals' (quoted in Heyck, 1982, p. 17).

The same names crop up repeatedly during the 1850s and 1860s in the controversies now associated most memorably with the conventional 'crisis of faith': liberal-minded men and women who supported Darwin, the authors of *Essays and Reviews*, Bishop Colenso, the second Reform Bill, disestablishment, and national education. New names also appear beside them in surviving lists of subscribers, petitioners, and members of institutions, lists that bear witness to the networks of power and influence among the Victorian intelligentsia. In 1860 it was a young man on the periphery of the Chapman circle, Harrison, who electrified the Establishment with his analysis of *Essays and Reviews* in the *Westminster Review* (Harrison, 1907, pp. 23, 28). Meanwhile an older member, Spencer, circulated the prospectus for his *System of Synthetic Philosophy*, the leading ideas of which had been canvassed in a series of essays in Chapman's journal. Among the subscribers to Spencer's *opus* were scientists such as W. B. Carpenter, J. D. Hooker, and Edward Frankland (Spencer, 1904, II, p. 484). Hooker and Frankland joined Huxley, Tyndall, Spencer, and the younger John Lubbock in 1864 to form the most powerful coterie in late Victorian science, known to its members as the 'X Club'. One of their first dinner guests was a bishop deposed for mocking Moses with mathematics, none other than Colenso. Earlier in the same year Colenso and Huxley had attached their names to an impressive petition in support of the bills to abolish religious tests in the universities. Other signatories were Maurice, James Martineau,

Dean Stanley of Westminster, and 'university liberals' such as Stephen, Harrison, Goldwin Smith, and Benjamin Jowett of *Essays and Reviews*. Stephen and Harrison, as well as Smith, who had subscribed to Spencer's *Synthetic Philosophy*, contributed to the famous liberal manifestos published in 1867, *Essays on Reform* and *Questions for a Reformed Parliament* (Harvie, 1976, App. 2, 7). Two years later they joined another of the contributors, R. H. Hutton, editor of the liberal *Spectator*, in a last-ditch attempt to patch up a consensus among the intelligentsia. Hutton described their organization as 'sort of Royal Society of Psychology and Metaphysics, — to contain men of all theologies and schools, — in the hope of leading to some fixed science at last' (quoted in Hutchinson, 1914, I, p. 101). The Metaphysical Society, as it became known, met monthly during the Parliamentary season, from 1869 to 1880. It enrolled nearly all the dissident intellectuals mentioned in this essay. Maurice, James Martineau, and Dean Stanley were among the earliest members. Rising lights of Liberalism such as Walter Bagehot and John Morley also joined in the polite but fruitless debates with bishops, archbishops, and other Establishment figures. Many of these individuals participated in more strictly political forums, the Century Club, founded in 1866, and its offspring in 1870, the Radical Club, which together eventually expanded into the National Liberal Club in 1882. Elsewhere in clubland the Athenaeum became a safe house for dissident intellectuals, the internal workings of which both exemplified and aided their political intrigues (Harvie, 1976, App. 5, 6).

III   A RELIGIOUS REFORMATION

If liberal reforms loomed large in the thoughts of those who had renounced the creed of established Christianity, what evidence is there that they sought to underwrite these reforms with a religious creed of their own? We have already seen that the dissident intellectuals frankly regarded themselves as religious individuals. Religion to them was the living kernel, theology the dying husk that it inevitably outgrew. Husk and kernel, accidents and essence — the root of religion, they believed, lay in the 'deeps of man's nature', in 'enduring instincts which will find expression in one form or another' (Huxley, quoted in Lightman, 1983, p. 158; Stephen, 1907, p. 81). The question, therefore, was not whether Victorian England would have a religion, but merely how it would be expressed. Religion, after all, was socially respectable; religious people held power that in other hands might be used for greater good. Religion had also been meat and drink to the dissident intellectuals. It had shaped their values, fired their ambitions, and inspired the supreme self-confidence with which they set out to change the world. Now, to use their own word, it would simply take a new 'form'. Most of those who called themselves 'agnostics' had an evangelical background. The X Club was a sort of Clapham Sect *redivivus*. Men such as

Harrison and Morley, who lived by Comte's *Catechism of Positive Religion* (1858), had come to intellectual maturity among Oxford Anglo-Catholics. Later such differences in denominational filiation among the dissident intellectuals would lead to open conflicts over the mode in which a new religion should be commended to the nation. But in the fifties and sixties, and into the seventies at least, everyone agreed with Francis Newman (1865, p. 175) that 'the age is ripe for ... a religion', a religion that would combine the best of Christian ethics with the intellectual rigour of 'the schools of modern science'.

The essential religiosity of the dissident intellectuals can scarcely be over stressed. Froude believed (1849, p. 42) that God had 'written the tables of His commandments' in natural laws, which clergymen should study 'in the cornfield, in the meadow, in the workshop, at the weaver's loom, in the market-places and the warehouses'. Spencer, whose *Synthetic Philosophy* began with a 'reconciliation' of religion and science, agreed with Froude to this extent (1889, pp. 306, 350), that 'the precepts of the current religion embody that which Biology ... dictates', and thus 'the inherited and theologically-enforced code ... has transcendent authority on its side'. Mill called attention (1875, p. 26) to the 'religious duty' of amending the material world, while Stephen urged that the motive for doing so must be shifted to the material world as well. His aim was to 'transform the whole theory' of Christianity 'consistently', to substitute a 'development of natural forces for a Second Advent'. Here Stephen revealed the centrality of evolution to the intellectuals' religious beliefs (Stephen, 1907, p. 123; *idem*, 1903, p. 82). 'Trust me', Tyndall in 1870 assured the British Association for the Advancement of Science (1899, II, p. 133), 'its existence as a hypothesis is quite compatible with the simultaneous existence of all those virtues to which the term "Christian" has been applied'. Indeed, as a basis of morals, according to Harrison (1907b, p. 147), it came to 'precisely the same thing, whether we say that human nature is adapted to a certain life, or that it was designed by a particular maker to follow that life'. But, unlike conventional theology, evolution held out a real hope for human nature, both individually and at large: adaptation will naturally and inevitably improve. 'The *baneful strife* which *lurketh inborn in us and goeth on the way with us to hurt us*', wrote Clifford (1879, II, p. 274), is a relic of savage life that must surely pass away. Meanwhile, 'by supplying us with a general conception of a good action, in a wider sense than the ethical one', evolution 'may be made to compensate us for the loss of the immutable and eternal verities'.

Thus ethics and eschatology were transferred to an organic, evolutionary basis, just as the notion of religious truth had been. The religion of science was to be founded on a science of religion. This 'naturalization' of religious beliefs, promising material salvation through moral achievement in history, formed the ideological resolution of the Victorian crisis and, as such, marked a profound transformation not only in intellectual culture, but throughout English society. 'Secularization' is the word now usually applied to this transformation, and the term is unexceptionable, provided that it is understood as the continuous displacement of one religious tradition, both ideologically and institutionally, with another. Indeed, this is precisely how the dissident intellectuals themselves understood the movement of their times. 'New doctrines' based on 'new revelations' were creating a 'new faith' that would proclaim a 'new gospel' for a new social order. To them the process was nothing less than a 'New Reformation' (Stephen, 1907, pp. 82, 388; Clifford, I, 1879, p. 37; Tyndall, 1899, II, p. 220; 1900, p. 45).

The slogan, a 'New Reformation', contained both a taunt and a truth. As controversialists, the dissident intellectuals took every opportunity to point up the ironies of the Church's position in relation to their own. Spencer argued (1889, p. 327) that the dependence of sociology on biology was evident from the First Book of Richard Hooker's *Laws of Ecclesiastical Polity*, the great Elizabethan apologia of the English Church. Hooker's view of individuals in society, he stated, 'needs but better definition and further development to make it truly scientific'. Huxley stressed on various occasions that his own objectionable views were consistent with, or at least theologically no more controversial than, the teachings of Augustine, Erasmus, Calvin, and Bishop Butler. Moreover, Huxley did not begrudge the fact that the Anglican Church as an institution was 'a great and powerful instrument for good or evil'. So engagingly, indeed, did he once describe 'an Established Church which should be a blessing to the community', one which 'no one would seek to disestablish', that an Anglican colleague was pleased to remark that the Church of Huxley did not differ greatly from 'the Church of Arnold and Maurice, Kingsley and Jowett' (L. Huxley, 1900, I, p. 221; T. H. Huxley, 1893–94, I, p. 284; Lubbock, 1894, p. 223). It was perhaps this ambivalence about the established Church — a coveting of its power and authority coupled with a loathing for its creed; an inclination to reform the institution tempered by an impulse to abolish it — that made the Protestant Reformation a potent metaphor for the dissident intellectuals. For the truth in their slogan, a New Reformation, was that they saw their new religion maintaining continuity with the old; the taunt was that they believed the new religion must be born by means of an intellectual and social transformation not unlike the one in which the Anglican Church had emerged from the Church of Rome (Cockshut, 1959, ch. 2).

The proximate source of the slogan may have been the phrenologist George Combe, who had written as early as 1847 of a 'Second Reformation' to be brought about in Britain through public education in the principles of naturalistic morality (Barton, 1983, p. 286, n. 122; Di Giustino, 1975, pp. 178–9). In 1853 Froude adumbrated the slogan in an article on the Book of Job. 'The whole question of life and its obligations', he said, 'must again be opened' as it was 'some three centuries' ago in the Protestant struggle with immorality and superstition. To Froude the Reformation was the hinge of modern history. The first four volumes of his *History of England*, completed by 1858, contained an impassioned plea for its principles in the context of an argument for English liberty and freedom of thought (Froude, 1853, p. 444; Paul, 1905, pp. 95–7, 103). In 1863 Francis Newman took up the argument in an article entitled 'The Reformation Arrested'. 'Bibliolatry' was 'the critical mistake of the first Reformers', the 'evil legacy' they had left the Church of England. 'A religious Reformation, in the very direction to which Colenso points, is demanded', Newman declared, 'by the most intelligent part of the nation'. Bishop Colenso, speaking for himself while under threat of deposition for his critical views on the Pentateuch, pointed out coolly that in the sixteenth century Cranmer, Ridley, and Latimer, although consecrated as bishops of the Roman Church, 'did not *resign* their sees as soon as they became *Protestant* bishops'. Anglicans, having based their church structure on one reformation, had no right to declare *a priori* that there should never be another (Newman, 1863, pp. 392, 393; Colenso, quoted in Cockshut, 1959, p. 100).

The risk attendant on justifying oneself by appeal to the example of three bishops who, in the event, were burned as heretics, was negligible by the 1860s. The 'Church of the Future', as Newman called it, had been born. A new faith was rising, phoenix-like, from the ashes of the old faith that had spent itself pursuing the likes of Colenso and the authors of *Essays and Reviews* (Newman, 1863, p. 393; Froude, 1853, p. 421). Within the Establishment, the Church of the Future and its new faith were weakly represented by clergymen such as Maurice and Stanley. In 1865 Maurice looked forward to 'a reformation more complete by far than that of the sixteenth century'; Stanley likewise had no doubt at the time that a 'new' or 'second Reformation' was being prepared by 'the various tendencies of the age' (Maurice, 1865, p. 171; Prothero, 1893, II, p. 239; Stanley, 1865, pp. 252–68). But it remained for one whose notion of a viable Establishment was said to resemble their own — it remained for that preacher of 'lay sermons' and self-consecrated 'bishop' of the 'Church scientific', T. H. Huxley, to press the cause of a New Reformation throughout a public career of more than thirty years. From his announcement of the theme in 1860 at the Royal Institution, to his extended analysis of Protestant principles in his 'Prologue' to *Essays on Some Controverted Questions* in 1892, Huxley maintained that 'a reformation ... is waiting to come', a 'wider and deeper change than that effected three centuries ago', or rather, he explained, 'a continuation of that movement'. If only people would live in accordance with 'that agnostic confession' which makes it immoral to profess knowledge of what cannot be known, this 'approximation to the millennium' would arrive (T. H. Huxley, 1898–1902, II, p. 393; *idem*, 1893–94, III, pp. 191–2 and V, p. 40; L. Huxley, 1900, I, p. 397; see Lightman, 1983).

Huxley's 'agnostic confession' never quite amounted to a creed after the manner of the Thirty-nine Articles. When Samuel Laing, the agnostic

railway entrepreneur, set down eight agnostic articles to oblige the Anglican prime minister, W. E. Gladstone, Huxley denied publicly that agnosticism was a creed. If a creed were to be compulsory, he preferred that of St.
Athanasius, the meaning of which, he said, 'I have on the whole a clearer
conception' (T. H. Huxley, 1893–4, V, p. 245; Laing, 1895, pp. 282–3,
286–7). Yet Froude, the devoted biographer of Carlyle, spoke repeatedly of
Carlyle's 'Creed' and its influence upon himself and other admirers, such as
Huxley. And little wonder. These young men and women, who by upbringing had been habituated to a creed as a vigorous summary of collective
belief, who had once recited a creed as an 'act of intellectual adoration',
could scarcely have used a better word for those 'other forms' of collective
belief arising, as Froude put it, from where the 'roots' of the old creed were
'cut away' (Tulloch, 1885, pp. 196–7; Hutton, 1899, p. 5; Froude, 1849,
p. 33; Kirkus, 1867, p. 541). To call one's new convictions a creed was to pay
them a compliment. A creed united its adherents; it represented their most
deeply-felt convictions. To some, *pace* Huxley, it was a moral necessity.
Besides, according to the dissident intellectuals, their old and new convictions were organically linked. To call the new convictions a creed signified
that the religious instinct underlying them remained unchanged. For just as
the 'old creed' was 'adapted ... to the wants of its believers', so, it was
said, a 'new creed' would be adapted to 'new social and individual requirements'. The old was 'decaying', the new 'growing' in its place. Society must
decide, wrote Stephen (recalling his own personal crisis), 'which creed ...
favours the faith which is the other side of energetic conduct', which gives
the 'clearest rules' by which to 'regulate our lives' (Stephen, 1907, pp. 124,
406; *idem*, 1903, pp. 10,51; Spencer, 1904, II, p. 468; see Badger, 1964). For
rigour and candour of reply, none excelled the high churchmen among the
dissident intellectuals, the followers of Auguste Comte. In the five dropsical
volumes of his *Problems of Life and Mind*, Lewes (1874–5, I, p. 2) laid the
'foundations of a creed' that would 'condense our knowledge, guide our
researches, and shape our lives', a creed based on the principles of scientific
method. Morley, in his famous essay *On Compromise* (1874, p. 124), foresaw
that 'a new creed by which men can live, ... an expansion, a development,
a re-adaptation, of all the moral and spiritual truth that lay hidden under
the worn-out forms', would one day be built by 'science'. 'Nothing but such
a basis', wrote Harrison (1907a, p. 151), 'can satisfy the mind of the inquirer
or give coherence to the social body'.

IV   A NEW THEODICY

English religiosity, a Reformed and reforming influence, could safely imbibe
its ideology from a critic of revolutionary France. Comte was 'the evange-
list of the expert'. His philosophy of Positivism culminated in a 'Religion

of Humanity' modelled on the structure and rites of the Roman Catholic Church. Stripped of its magisterium and its liturgy, its catechism and its saints, this religion furnished a creed resembling that of the dissident intellectuals at large. For them, a Low Church or Nonconformist formulary would impart 'coherence to the social body' just as well (Annan, 1984, p. 195; Kent, 1979, part 2). In Catholic France, Comte had proposed to 'recommence on a better intellectual and social basis the great effort of Catholicism, to bring Western Europe to a social system of peaceful activity and intellectual culture, in which Thought and Action should be subordinated to universal Love'. In Protestant England, the dissident intellectuals proposed to recommence on a better intellectual and social basis the great effort of the Protestant Reformation to bring about a social system of personal morality and intellectual freedom. In France the chief inspiration of Comte's proposal had been the revolution of 1848, which was thought to have ushered in history's 'positive' phase with the proclamation of a Republic. In England the dissident intellectuals were similarly inspired by the liberalizing tendencies evoked by Chartism and the Anti-Corn Law League, which took root in 1846 with the advent of Free Trade. On either hand, in France and in England, among Positivists and dissident intellectuals alike, the emphasis in their social prescriptions fell on continuity, moral authority, and progress. The best aspirations of an earlier religious tradition, they believed, would be better fulfilled by a new professional 'priesthood' — the term was used by Darwin's cousin Francis Galton as well as by Comte — who would place progress on a 'better intellectual and social basis' with the creed of scientific naturalism (Comte, 1880, pp. 268, 280; Galton, 1874, p. 260).

The Positivist motto, 'order and progress', summed up the theodicy inherent in the naturalistic creed better than the indigenous English slogan, a 'New Reformation'. Progress, according to the dissident intellectuals, was merely the natural order at work; the natural order throughout the living world maintained itself through uniform continuous growth. In reality, therefore, social relations were neither contractual nor conflictive, but vital and organic. 'The whole complex frame of society', Froude declared, 'is a meshwork of duty woven of living fibre, and the condition of it remaining sound is, that every thread of its own free energy shall do what it ought'. Spencer, who in 1860 spelled out the organic doctrine in minute detail, spent the rest of his life developing its ethical implications. This doctrine, which lay at the basis of Comte's sociology, also furnished the premise of the dissident intellectuals' commitment to liberal reform (Froude, 1853, p. 448; Spencer, 1860; see Greene, 1981, pp. 60–94). *Natura non facit saltum* — Nature makes no leaps: society must change gradually. *Natura nihil agit frustra* — Nature does nothing in vain: society grants to each their appointed task. Gradualism and functionalism in the new theodicy replaced the static teleology of the old: the rich man in his castle and the poor man at his gate might alter their relations, provided it was done slowly and harmoniously. And if the old theodicy had spared industrial England Tennyson's 'red fool-fury of the Seine', then in a day when the Paris sky again glowed red — in 1871 came the Commune — the theodicy of a New Reformation could promise nothing less. 'We have been to the brink of the volcano', wrote Stephen (1907, pp. 145, 147), of his forebears, 'and we did not like the glimpses we caught of the seething masses of inflammatory matter at the bottom. The effect was fairly to startle us back into any old creed which led to less disastrous results'. Just 'any old creed', however, did not suffice — Stephen referred no doubt to his own evangelical past — for in order 'that a creed may be permanent it must satisfy the intellect'. Among the dissident intellectuals, the creed of scientific naturalism filled the bill. W. R. Grove, whose doctrines of the correlation and the continuity of physical forces buttressed the naturalistic creed, spoke their mind when he reminded the British Association (1867, p.346) that revolutionary ideas and *a priori* reasoning 'are far more unsound and give us far less ground for improvement of the race than the study of the gradual progressive changes arising from changed circumstances, changed wants, changed habits. Our language, our social institutions, our laws, the constitution of which we are proud, are the growth of time, the product of slow adaptations, resulting from continuous struggles. Happily in this country practical experience has taught us to improve rather than to remodel; we follow the law of nature and avoid cataclysms'.

But in asserting that an anti-revolutionary creed must 'satisfy the intellect' if it is to be 'permanent', Stephen also acknowledged (1907, p. 147) that the first impulse towards its acceptance 'comes from the passions'. 'Therefore', he said, 'a revival of belief may be due much more to a change in social conditions than to any process of logical conviction'. Stephen wrote better than he knew. The 'revival of belief' in which he participated, whatever permanence it derived from the 'intellect' and 'logical conviction', owed its existence fundamentally to a 'change in social conditions' in Victorian England. Scientific naturalism was the creed of a movement that had 'grown out of the strong impulse given to the moral sense by political freedom' (Clifford, 1879, II, p. 250). The theodicy of the dissident intellectuals was related organically to the social crisis of their times.

BIBLIOGRAPHY

Portions of this essay have appeared in the author's 'Crisis without revolution: the ideological watershed in Victorian England', *Revue de synthèse*, 4th series (1986), pp. 53–78, which contains additional documentation.

N. Annan (1949) 'The strands of unbelief', in *Ideas and Beliefs of the Victorians*, pp. 105–6, Sylvan Press.

N. Annan (1984) *Leslie Stephen: The Godless Victorian*, Weidenfeld and Nicolson.

K. Badger (1964) 'Christianity and Victorian religious confessions', *Modern Language Quarterly*, Vol. 25, pp. 86–101.

R. Barton (1983) 'Evolution: the Whitworth Gun in Huxley's war for the liberation of science from theology', in D. Oldroyd and I. Langham (eds.) *The Wider Domain of Evolutionary Thought*, pp. 261–87, Dordrecht (Holland), D. Reidel.

R. Bithell (1883) *The Creed of a Modern Agnostic*, George Routledge & Sons.

J. Bronowski (1949) 'Unbelief and science', in *Ideas and Beliefs of the Victorians*, pp. 164–9, Sylvan Press.

O. Brose (1960) 'F. D. Maurice and the Victorian crisis of belief', *Victorian Studies*, Vol. 3, pp. 227–48.

J. B. Brown (1871) *First Principles of Ecclesiastical Truth: Essays on the Church and Society*, Hodder and Stoughton.

S. Budd (1967) 'The loss of faith: reasons for unbelief among members of the Secular Movement in England, 1850–1950', *Past and Present*, No. 36, pp. 106–25.

S. Budd (1977) *Varieties of Unbelief: Atheists and Agnostics in English Society, 1850–1960*, Heinemann.

G. Carlyle (1878) *The Battle of Unbelief*, Hodder and Stoughton.

W. K. Clifford (1879) *Lectures and Essays*, L. Stephen and F. Pollock (eds), 2 Vols., Macmillan.

A. Comte (1880) *A General View of Positivism*, trans. J. H. Bridges, 2nd edn., Reeves & Turner.

A. O. J. Cockshut (1959) *Anglican Attitudes: A Study of Victorian Religious Controversies*, Collins.

A. O. J. Cockshut (1964) *The Unbelievers: English Agnostic Thought, 1840–1890*, Collins.

D. De Giustino (1975) *Conquest of Mind: Phrenology and Victorian Social Thought*, Croom Helm.

J. A. Froude (1849) *The Nemesis of Faith*, John Chapman.

J. A. Froude (1853) 'The Book of Job', *Westminster Review*, new series, Vol. 4, pp. 417–50.

F. Galton (1874) *English Men of Science: Their Nature and Nurture*, Macmillan and Co.

W. Graham (1881) *The Creed of Science: Religious, Moral, and Social*, C. Kegan Paul.

J. C. Greene (1981) *Science, Ideology, and World View: Essays in the History of Evolutionary Ideas*, Berkeley, University of California Press.

W. R. Grove (1867) *The Correlation of Physical Forces*, 5th edn., Longmans, Green, and Co.

G. S. Haight (1969) *George Eliot and John Chapman, with Chapman's Diaries*, 2nd edn., Hamden (CT), Archon Books.

F. Harrison (1906) *Memories and Thoughts: Men — Books — Cities — Art*, Macmillan and Co.

F. Harrison (1907a) *The Creed of a Layman: Apologia pro Fide Mea*, Macmillan and Co.

F. Harrison (1907b) *The Philosophy of Common Sense*, Macmillan and Co.

C. Harvie (1976) *The Lights of Liberalism: University Liberals and the Challenge of Democracy, 1860–86*, Allen Lane.

T. W. Heyck (1982) *The Transformation of Intellectual Life in Victorian England*, Croom Helm.

H. G. Hutchinson (1914) *Life of Sir John Lubbock, Lord Avebury*, 2 Vols., Macmillan and Co.

R. H. Hutton (1899) *Aspects of Religious and Scientific Thought*, Macmillan and Co.

L. Huxley (1900) *Life and Letters of Thomas Henry Huxley*, 2 Vols., Macmillan and Co.

T. H. Huxley (1893–94) *Collected Essays*, 9 Vols., Macmillan and Co.

T. H. Huxley (1898–1902) *The Scientific Memoirs of Thomas Henry Huxley*, M. Foster and E. R. Lankester (eds.), 2 Vols., Macmillan and Co.

C. Kent (1979) *Brains and Numbers: Elitism, Comtism, and Democracy in Mid-Victorian England*, Toronto, University of Toronto Press.

W. Kirkus (1867) 'Morality and creeds', *Theological Review*, Vol. 4, pp. 534–52.

S. Laing (1895) *Modern Science and Modern Thought*, new edn., Chapman and Hall.

G. H. Lewes (1874–75) *The Foundations of a Creed*, 2 Vols., Trübner and Co.

B. Lightman (1983) 'Pope Huxley and the church agnostic', *Historical Papers*, pp. 150–63.

J. Lubbock (1894) *The Use of Life*, Macmillan and Co.

F. D. Maurice (1865) *The Conflict of Good and Evil in Our Day: Twelve Letters to a Missionary*, Smith, Elder and Co.

F. D. Maurice (1881) *Theological Essays*, 4th edn., Macmillan and Co.

J. S. Mill (1875) *Nature, The Utility of Religion, and Theism*, 4th edn., Longmans, Green, Reader and Dyer.

J. Morley (1877) *On Compromise*, 2nd edn., Chapman and Hall.

F. W. Newman (1862) 'The Reformation arrested', *Westminster Review*, new series, Vol. 23, pp. 376–96.

F. W. Newman (1865) *Phases of Faith; or, Passages from the History of My Creed*, new edn., Trübner & Co.

H. Paul (1905) *The Life of Froude*, Sir Isaac Pitman & Sons.

R. E. Prothero (1893) *The Life and Correspondence of Arthur Penrhyn Stanley*, 2 Vols., John Murray.

G. Rowell (1974) *Hell and the Victorians: A Study of Nineteenth-Century Theological Controversies concerning Eternal Punishment and the Future Life*, Oxford, Clarendon Press.

H. C. Sheldon (1907) *Unbelief in the Nineteenth Century: A Critical History*, New York, Eaton & Mains.

H. Spencer (1860) 'The social organism', *Westminster Review*, new series, Vol. 17, pp. 90–121.

H. Spencer (1889) *The Study of Sociology*, new edn., Kegan Paul, Trench & Co.

H. Spencer (1904) *An Autobiography*, 2 Vols., Williams and Norgate.

A. P. Stanley (1865) 'The theology of the nineteenth century', *Fraser's Magazine*, Vol. 71, pp. 252–68.

L. Stephen (1903) *An Agnostic's Apology, and Other Essays*, 2nd edn., Smith, Elder & Co.

L. Stephen (1907) *Essays in Freethinking and Plainspeaking*, new edn., Smith, Elder & Co.

M. I. Thomis and P. Holt (1977) *Threats of Revolution in Britain, 1789–1848*, Macmillan.

J. Tulloch (1885) *Movements of Religious Thought in Britain during the Nineteenth Century*, Longmans, Green & Co.

F. M. Turner and J. Von Arx (1982) 'Victorian ethics of belief: a reconsideration', in W. W. Wagar (ed.) *The Secular Mind: Transformations of Faith in Modern Europe*, pp. 83–101, New York, Holmes and Meier.

J. Tyndall (1899) *Fragments of Science: A Series of Detached Essays, Addresses, and Reviews*, 6th edn., 2 Vols., New York, D. Appleton and Co.

J. Tyndall (1900) *New Fragments*, 3rd edn., New York, D. Appleton and Co.

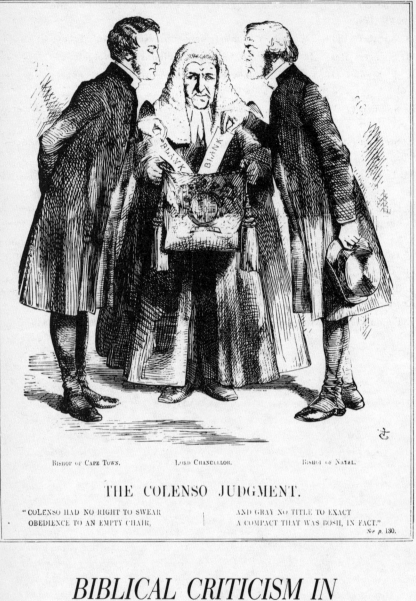

CHAPTER 11

BISHOP OF CAPE TOWN.   LORD CHANCELLOR.   BISHOP OF NATAL.

THE COLENSO JUDGMENT.

"COLENSO HAD NO RIGHT TO SWEAR   AND GRAY NO TITLE TO EXACT
OBEDIENCE TO AN EMPTY CHAIR,   A COMPACT THAT WAS BOSH, IN FACT."

See p. 130.

BIBLICAL CRITICISM IN VICTORIAN BRITAIN: FROM CONTROVERSY TO ACCEPTANCE?

G ENERAL surveys of the history of religion in Victorian Britain inevitably include accounts of the development of, and controversies over, biblical criticism. Along with 'genesis and geology', Darwin, and 'science versus religion', the rise of biblical criticism and the application of critical historical methods to the study of the Bible customarily feature as essential elements in the story of 'the Victorian crisis of faith'.

That this should be so is hardly surprising. In the 1830s and 1840s expressions of doubt about traditional views of the Bible were still rare from within the churches; most believers still held the Bible to be divinely inspired and took that to entail its also being inerrant and infallible in every detail. Biblical criticism, meanwhile, was commonly associated with dangerously lax and rationalistic German theology (for which the term 'neology' was coined), unorthodox groups such as Unitarians, or, worst of all, militant unbelievers whose infidelity extended to overt and polemical attacks upon Christianity as a whole.

By 1900 matters were quite different. If traditional views of the Bible remained widespread within the churches (which they most certainly did), they were nevertheless obliged to co-exist, willingly or otherwise, with a variety of 'critical' positions which ranged from the cautious to the radical. Biblical criticism was now practised — although still in the main by clergymen — in British universities with an academic professionalism akin to that which had already existed in Germany a century earlier. And, although militant secularists might still contrive to attack Christianity by criticism of the Bible, the automatic association of criticism and infidelity was now less common and less credible. Moreover, between 1830 and 1900 — and especially in the thirty years from the early 50s to the early 80s — the issue of biblical criticism had been the basis of a whole series of mid-Victorian *causes célèbres*, controversies, heresy trials, and court cases, as Nonconformist and Presbyterian ministers, Anglican priests, and even a bishop, found themselves both metaphorically and literally on trial for their application of critical methods to the study of the Bible.

The development of a broader range of commonly permissible and acceptable views of the Bible and its status, and the three decades of particularly intense controversy which accompanied that development, were indeed part of that wider ferment generally described as 'the Victorian crisis of faith'. Other essays in this collection challenge conventional interpretations of 'the crisis of faith' and seek to press beyond *both* the outdated model of 'the warfare of science with religion' *and* the more recent model of 'the warfare between theology and conscience' to offer instead an interpretation which, while retaining the recognition of the existence of conflicts between science and religion and between conscience, morality and (traditional) theology, also sets all this within a distinct and definite social and political context.[1]

The present essay will not attempt to offer a correspondingly extensive revision of the conventional account of the development of biblical criticism in Victorian Britain. It will, however, question certain aspects of that account — as conventionally presented — in particular the widespread assumption that the controversies of c. 1850–80 were essentially a clash between 'criticism' on the one hand and 'faith' on the other (intellectual doubt in conflict with traditional belief), and the frequent assertion that by the 1890s the churches had 'accepted' biblical criticism. It will also, briefly, seek to relate the predominantly clerical and academic orientation of the conventional account to a more 'popular' dimension of the history of changing attitudes to the Bible in Victorian Britain. First, however, we must review the basic elements of the conventional account.

I VICTORIAN BIBLICAL CRITICISM:
THE CONVENTIONAL ACCOUNT

As the introduction to this essay suggests, the conventional account of the development of biblical criticism in Victorian Britain encompasses three principal stages. In the first, running from the 1830s to the mid-1850s, traditional belief in the authority, inerrancy, and infallibility of the Bible is challenged by early Victorian science — especially developments in geology — and by increasing interest in and knowledge of the work of German biblical scholars. In the second stage of the conventional account, lasting roughly from the Davidson case of the mid-50s to the Robertson Smith case of 1876–81, traditional belief and biblical criticism confront each other *within* the churches and the classic confrontation of 'criticism versus faith' occurs. In the third stage, lasting from 1881 to the end of the century, as a result of the traumas of confrontation, *and crucially* as a result of the work of a later generation of more moderate critics, biblical criticism is 'accepted by the churches'.

In the light of the intensity of the Victorian controversies over biblical criticism and the Victorian fear of 'German rationalism and neology', the pre-Victorian history of biblical criticism in Britain is not without irony. Between roughly 1650 and 1750 it was in England that a critical approach to the Bible, or more accurately to the Old Testament, was pioneered. The English deist tradition of the seventeenth and eighteenth centuries included a critique of the Old Testament within its general attack on Christianity:

---

[1] See *RVB*, I, 8 and II, 12. See also *RVB*, IV, 8 and 9 for two important essays relevant to this theme by J. L. Altholz and F. M. Turner.

Germany at this stage did not lead but lagged behind (Rogerson, 1984, ch. 11). By the nineteenth century, however, the deist tradition in biblical criticism had suffered eclipse, along with deism in general. On the one hand, the theological tradition of Butler and Paley was commonly held to have answered the challenge of deism and rationalism, and to have provided a secure basis for traditional Christian orthodoxy, part and parcel of that traditional orthodoxy being a belief in the inspiration and authority of scripture. On the other hand, the powerfully conservative and biblical orientation of both Methodism in particular and the Evangelical Revival in general had fostered a renewed conviction of the centrality and inspiration of the Bible. It is true that, as John Rogerson has recently observed, even the renewed biblical conservatism of the Evangelical Revival allowed room for emendation of the biblical text in the light of linguistic and textual studies — not least because of the scope for new interpretation thereby created. But thus to relinquish *verbal* inspiration (the belief that every *word* is divinely inspired) was a strictly limited concession, and whilst belief in *plenary* inspiration (the belief that the Bible's statements on all subjects are inspired) remained intact — as for the most part it did in the 1830s and 40s — biblical criticism was bound to appear a threat (Rogerson, 1984, p. 250). With the decline of the deist tradition of biblical criticism and the rise of biblically conservative evangelicalism, British biblical scholarship declined and, after 1750, German biblical scholarship, in both Old and New Testament studies, decisively took the lead.

It was long customary to portray early nineteenth-century and early Victorian theologians as simply ignorant or unaware of contemporary German biblical criticism. Recent scholarship has suggested the need for a modification of this view. Certainly, knowledge of contemporary German scholarship was partial, largely secondhand, and predisposed to antipathy: there were relatively few British theologians fluent in German and thus able to read German scholars in the original; much of the reporting or translation which did occur appeared either in reviews designed to be hostile to 'critical' views or in series designed to present in English contemporary *conservative* German scholarship; and the periodic surveys of German 'neology' — such as H. J. Rose's *The State of the Protestant Religion in Germany* (1825) — were highly polemical in their rejection of 'rationalizing' and 'negative' criticism. Awareness of German biblical criticism in early Victorian Britain was, therefore, inadequate, polemical and subjective — but it was not, as sometimes implied, so rare as to be virtually non-existent (Rogerson, 1984, ch. 11; Crowther, 1970, ch. 2; Speller, 1979).

What was rare was *sympathy* for contemporary radical German biblical criticism or the attempt to develop similarly radical and critical approaches to the Bible in Britain. In England, prior to the 1850s, the only significant initiatives in biblical criticism from within Nonconformity were those of the in any case unorthodox Unitarians, and within the Church of England only early representatives of the Broad Church tradition showed sympathy for the approach. By the mid-1850s Unitarian scholars, both ministers and layman, had published studies which incorporated a range of critical views and arguments. In 1838 Charles Hennell published his *Inquiry Concerning the Origin of Christianity*; in 1847 came Francis Newman's *The Hebrew Monarchy*; in 1851 W. R. Greg's *The Creed of Christendom*; and in 1853 Edward Higginson's *The Spirit of the Bible*. Between them these books questioned the date and authorship of books in both the Old and New Testaments; recognized the piecemeal and composite nature of books in both Testaments; questioned traditional notions of inspiration and of the miraculous; and generally tended towards rational and naturalistic explanations. Those of Hennell and Newman, in particular, were commonly regarded as having contributed significantly to the 'unsettlement of faith' in the 40s and 50s (Wigmore-Beddoes, 1971, ch. 2).

Among early Broad Churchmen, the works of Coleridge, Richard Whately, H. H. Milman, Thomas Arnold, and Connop Thirlwall were notable for their awareness of a variety of critical approaches to the Bible. Thirlwall, as early as 1825, translated Schleiermacher's *Critical Essay on the Gospel of Luke* and defended its author's critical approach. Whately, in 1828, published *Essays on Some Difficulties in the Writings of St Paul*, and a year later Milman published his *History of the Jews* which, although not sophisticatedly critical, noted numerical and chronological difficulties in the biblical text, explained some biblical narratives as oriental poetry and allegory, and gave naturalistic explanations of some miracles. Thomas Arnold, in his *Essay on the Right Interpretation and Understanding of Scripture* (1831) and *Two Sermons on the Interpretation of Prophecy* (1839), argued that different passages of scripture must be read against their various historical settings and that distinction must be made between the inspiration of the Bible as a whole and the historical accuracy of specific books. Coleridge's *Confessions of an Inquiring Spirit*, meanwhile, published posthumously in 1840, gave early expression to the notion, later to be made (in)famous by Jowett, that if 'read like any other book' the Bible was capable of 'finding' the reader at greater depth than all other books, whereas the doctrine of verbal inspiration was a stumbling block, an invitation to hostile critics, and a deadening influence upon the spiritual potential of the text.

Such ventures in criticism could shock and outrage — the series in which Milman's *History* appeared was discontinued as a result of the anger caused by his espousal of a mildly critical position — but full-scale furore in the manner of the 1850s, 60s and 70s did not occur. The reputation of German criticism for being inherently destructive and rationalist, meanwhile, received apparent confirmation with the translation of Strauss' *Life of Jesus*, which first appeared in serialized and incomplete form in a radical secularist journal, and then in a complete and thorough edition by George Eliot in 1845. The image of German biblical criticism was not enhanced by a book which knew that miracles did not happen, held legend and history to be beyond disentanglement in the text of the New Testament, and anyway thought the myth more important than the history.

In Scotland, prior to the 1850s, there was sufficient awareness of German critical study (and among Moderate members of the Church of Scotland and leaders of the Secession church sufficient sympathy with a critical approach to the Bible) for conservatives to sound warnings and re-assert traditionalism. Thus, as early as 1828, the conservative Presbyterian Marcus Dods' *Remarks on the Bible* combatively and defensively warned against the tendency to 'reduce the Holy Scriptures to the level of other pious writings', and the ultra-conservative Congregationalist Robert Haldane published a precise and detailed defence of verbal inspiration. Most notably, however, in view of future developments in the 1870s, at the inauguration of New College, Edinburgh, in 1850, John Duncan, James Bannerman, Alexander Black and William Cunningham, the first professors of the newly created Free Church, united in a determined assertion of the vital importance of an infallible, plenary inspiration.

By the 1830s and 1840s, however, the biblical criticism of Germanically-minded theologians was by no means the only challenge to traditional belief in the inspiration and authority of the Bible. The discoveries of contemporary geologists were quite as challenging.

The clashes and controversies over 'genesis and geology' are not, strictly speaking, part of the story of biblical criticism in Victorian Britain, but rather part of that broader story of the changing relationships between the religious and scientific worldviews, the competing professionalisms of clergy and scientists, and the mid-century crisis of 'changing creeds'.[2] And yet it would be odd to attempt to account for the development of Victorian biblical criticism without some reference to the debates of the 1830s and 1840s over the significance for the understanding of the opening chapters of the Bible of the discoveries of geologists concerning the age of the earth and the species that had come — and gone — in that age. It would be odd to omit this episode for, in an era becoming increasingly aware of the challenge of critical *historical* methods to the traditional understanding of the biblical text, the conflict between 'genesis and geology' added another compelling example of the apparent conflict between 'modern knowledge' and 'the Bible,' and greatly sharpened the orthodox sense of the Bible being under threat. It did so, moreover, in a manner which was vivid to the *popular* imagination: geology was exciting, awe-inspiring, and exotic; and

[2] See *RVB*, I, 8 and II, 8 and 10.

the dinosaurs and other vanished species which it revealed were no less so — but dinosaurs were not mentioned in the Bible and clearly had not sailed with the Ark.[3]

The details of the interlocking and overlapping debates between moderate and sensible believing (often clerical) geologists such as Sedgewick, Buckland or Lyell, still seeking to hold together theology, geology and a sense of purpose and design in creation; less moderate geologists and natural historians such as Robert Chambers and his *Vestiges of the Natural History of Creation* (1844), urging rashly imprecise and critically vulnerable versions of evolutionary theory; passionately immoderate biblicists committed to the construction of Mosaic cosmogonies and geologies preserving six-day Creation and Flood; and equally passionately immoderate free-thinkers eager to beat Christianity with another critical stick — such details, although interesting and significant in their own right, are not important in the present context.[4] Nor, in the present context, is the real issue the *genuine* theological threat posed by 'genesis and geology' — which threat, as Tennyson's *In Memoriam* had recognized as early as 1850, was not to six-day Creation or Flood, but to the credibility of notions of purpose, design and moral order in an immense expanse of creation, uninhabited by human-kind, and littered with the fossil record of failed species. What is important in the context of the history of Victorian biblical criticism, however, is the fact that, for those committed to the plenary inspiration of the Bible, the challenge of 'genesis and geology' to six-day Creation and Flood and special creation of each species was *yet another* indication that the Bible was under threat — and therefore must be defended the more ferociously.

The ferocity took active shape in the three decades from the early 1850s to the early 1880s. In a succession of denominational investigations, official condemnations, heresy trials and court cases, English Nonconformists, Anglicans, and Scottish Presbyterians fought over the right of clergymen to espouse, publish and teach critical approaches to the Bible. Not every essay in criticism produced the same ferocious reaction: in England, for example, A. P. Stanley published a critical study of Paul's letters to the Corinthians (1855) and *Lectures on the History of the Jewish Church* (1865), both of which included the application of critical methods; and in Scotland not only liberal members of the Church of Scotland such as John Tulloch, but also A. B. Davidson in the Free Church, espoused moderately critical approa-

---

[3] To put the point in this way is not to trivialize it. The popular significance of the 'genesis and geology' issue lay in the conflict between the traditional assumption of the literal truth of the Bible and the intensely fascinating discoveries of early Victorian science.

[4] For accounts of these debates and conflicts, see briefly Chadwick, 1971, pp. 558–68, or in detail, Gillespie, 1959. For the historiography of the subject and the 'professional' dimension of the conflicts, see Moore, 1986.

ches and avoided prosecution (though Tulloch was, of course, by virtue of his membership of the more 'moderate' Church of Scotland, able to do so with an openness and boldness impossible for the Free Church Davidson).

In four notorious cases, however, traditionalists set out to suppress historical criticism and to establish its heretical nature and incompatibility with clerical status. The details of the Davidson, *Essays and Reviews*, Colenso and Robertson Smith controversies are well known.[5] In summary, in 1857 Samuel Davidson was obliged to resign from his post as professor at the Congregationalist Lancashire Independent College, having narrowly been judged guilty of denying the plenary inspiration of the Bible because, in published work, he accepted and practised a moderate biblical criticism, rejected Mosaic authorship of the entire Pentateuch, and asserted that belief in the general inspiration of the Bible did not require or imply commitment to its infallibility on all subjects. In 1860 came *Essays and Reviews*. Biblical criticism was not its only concern, but it was a central one. Benjamin Jowett's essay on 'The Interpretation of Scripture' enjoined the reading of scripture 'like any other book'. Rowland Williams and H. B. Wilson were tried for heresy, including the denial of the inspiration of scripture. They were acquitted on appeal, but the book as a whole was condemned, and the traditional conservative view of biblical inspiration was re-affirmed by over 11,000 Anglican clergymen in England and Wales. In 1862, the Bishop of Natal, J. W. Colenso, published the first part of his critical examination of the Pentateuch. Applying his mathematical training to the text, he demonstrated its historical inaccuracy by virtue of the inconsistencies and impossibilities of the figures stated. He too was tried for heresy but acquitted on appeal, albeit on a legal point, not a theological one. Finally, in 1881, after a five-year controversy, the Scottish Free Church scholar, William Robertson Smith, was deprived of his professorship at the Free Church's college in Aberdeen, because of his practice of biblical criticism and his publication of such critical scholarship in the *Encyclopaedia Britannica*. Importantly, however, through the efforts of Principal Robert Rainy, Smith was not deprived of ministerial status, and biblical criticism itself was not condemned by the General Assembly, only Smith's allegedly imprudent practice of it.

During the same period two other publications aroused marked controversy over the legitimacy and limits of a critical approach to the Bible. In the early 1860s two controversial 'Lives of Jesus' were published. In 1863 appeared Ernest Renan's *Life of Jesus*. Sentimental, romantic, vivid, realistic in style, and rationalist in assumptions, Renan's *Life* presented a purely human Jesus, a non-supernatural account of his life, and a naturalis-

---

[5] For the further accounts and discussions of aspects of these controversies, see *RVB*, I, 1, 2, and 3 and II, 4 and 9.

tic explanation of its various elements. It was a literary success because of its style, readability and 'feeling'. It was condemned by the religious as sceptical and impious. Two years later, in 1865, appeared *Ecce Homo*, published anonymously but in fact by John Seeley, Professor of Latin at London University. It was a critical historical work; it presented a compellingly human Jesus, concentrating on psychology and personality and not attempting a complete narrative. Seeley avoided the oriental romance of Renan. Half the book was an exposition of Christian moral principles. Most intriguingly, however, it was not a rationalistic or anti-theological book: it did not deny miracles or divinity, it simply avoided theological speculation. It was thus ambiguous and drew from the religious community a corresponding ambiguity of response. Across theological and denominational party lines, reviewers divided between those who condemned its lack of orthodox theology and those who found in its reverent ambiguity a potential stepping-stone to belief. It was also phenomenally successful and indicated a popular demand for such 'Lives of Jesus', which, clearly, would be supplied by the unorthodox if the orthodox could not do so themselves (Pals, 1982, pp. 32–50).

The ambiguity of the response to *Ecce Homo*, and the ecclesiastical politicking of Principal Rainy over the precise terms of the condemnation of Robertson Smith in the Free Church General Assembly of 1881, were both indicators of a changing, if not yet changed, situation in respect of the attitude(s) of the churches to biblical criticism. Jowett, looking back after Colenso's death in 1883, also noted such change: Colenso, he asserted, marked an epoch in criticism by his straightforwardness; the effect of his writings was permanent, even if they were no longer read. It has been customary to dismiss Colenso's *Pentateuch* as somewhat superficial, significant for its arithmetical clarity in the popular mind rather than its critical profundity (Chadwick, 1972, p. 91). Rogerson, however, has more recently suggested that, on the contrary, both Colenso and the more sophisticated of his opponents debated at a significant and profound level, and also that Colenso's very bluntness did indeed exhaust the scholarly credibility of the old orthodoxy. Colenso more than anyone else, Robertson argues, caused the old orthodoxy to disappear in *scholarly* circles from the 1880s (Rogerson, 1984, pp. 234–6). Certainly, Colenso's was the last English Victorian heresy trial specifically over the issue of biblical criticism,[6] just as Robertson Smith's was the last *successful* prosecution in Scotland.

The conventional account of the history of biblical criticism in Victorian Britain interprets the changing situation of the 1870s, 80s and 90s as 'the

[6] The successful prosecution for heresy of Charles Voysey in 1869–71 included the charge of heresy concerning the denial of biblical inspiration, but it also involved several other alleged doctrinal heresies. For the Voysey case, see Crowther, 1970, ch.6.

acceptance of biblical criticism' by the churches. There are, as we shall shortly note, good reasons for questioning the straightforwardness of that description, but at one level, certainly, there was, in the last three decades of the century, a steady acceptance of the possibility of the legitimacy of biblical criticism within the churches, and within the ordained ministries of the churches.

In the Church of England the leading players in the process of 'acceptance' were the so-called 'Cambridge Triumvirate' of B. F. Westcott, J. B. Lightfoot and F. J. A. Hort, and the group of Oxford High Churchmen, led by Charles Gore, who published *Lux Mundi*. In a series of commentaries, historical works, and an edition of the New Testament text, Westcott, Lightfoot and Hort, from the 1870s to the 1890s, between them refuted the more sceptical conclusions of contemporary German scholarship and demonstrated the possibility of using a moderate biblical criticism to reassure and to support a critical orthodoxy in doctrine and theology. In 1889, meanwhile, the publication of *Lux Mundi* signalled the acceptance by a younger generation of Anglo-Catholic scholars of a variety of biblical criticism unthinkable to their forebears. Their acceptance of a critical approach to the Old Testament, and Gore's willingness to allow that Jesus might have been ignorant concerning the authorship of the Psalms, drew protests from older Anglo-Catholics and Evangelicals alike. But there was no prosecution this time, and no *official* condemnation: on the contrary, the book came to be welcomed widely within the church. Alongside the almost proverbial contributions of the Cambridge Triumvirate and *Lux Mundi*, there also emerged a whole group of Anglican scholars committed to a critical, but conservatively critical, approach to the Bible. In Old Testament studies scholars such as J. B. Mozley, S. R. Driver, T. K. Cheyne and A. F. Kirkpatrick, and in New Testament studies William Sanday and F. C. Burkitt, gave ample evidence of the possibility of espousing a variety of critical views without suffering prosecution or condemnation.

Among Nonconformists widespread change did not occur until the late 1880s, but then took place remarkably quickly. The Congregationalists, the Davidson case notwithstanding, had been developing a more open position on the issue since the 60s: a succession of Presidents of the Congregational Union indicating their acceptance of biblical criticism.[7] By 1900 the Baptists, Methodists and Primitive Methodists had also accommodated a range of moderately critical opinions alongside their traditional views.[8]

In Scotland attempts to have Marcus Dods and A. B. Bruce condemned

[7] For which see, briefly, *RVB*, I, 2.

[8] For a detailed account of the way in which English Nonconformists accomplished this adjustment and broadening of their attitude to biblical criticism, see Glover, 1954.

for heresy in 1890, and George Adam Smith similarly condemned in 1902 (in each case for holding a variety of critical opinions concerning the Bible), all ended in failure. There was still conservatism enough in the Free Church to bring the issue before the General Assembly, but there was now also sufficient breadth of opinion to prevent condemnation.

Equally importantly, however, there developed, from the 1870s onwards, a tradition of 'orthodox' 'Lives of Jesus' in response to the earlier 'Lives' by Renan and Seeley. The most successful by far, and the basic model for a remarkable number of late Victorian imitations, was F. W. Farrar's *Life of Christ* of 1874. Daniel Pals has aptly characterized Farrar's *Life* as a combination of serious, critical, but conservative, biblical scholarship, orthodox theology and devotion; a bold intimacy of style in dealing with the biblical personalities; and a flavour of oriental romance. Above all, Farrar presented a Christ who was divine, and did so in a manner which was overtly devotional, in a *Life* which was manifestly the work of a believer. He reassured his readers. In so doing, Pals argues, he established a whole *genre* of late Victorian 'Lives of Jesus', in which *conservative* criticism combined with broadly orthodox theology to produce popular works that nevertheless included the basic *critical* notion that the Bible was not infallible, and biblical criticism not necessarily destructive (Pals, 1982, pp. 77–124).

II VICTORIAN BIBLICAL CRITICISM:
CONVENTION ASSESSED

The conventional account of the development of biblical criticism in Victorian Britain prompts at least three questions. Why did the period of intense controversy not begin until the mid-1850s? When it did occur, was it in fact essentially a conflict between criticism and faith, intellect and devotion? And in the 1880s what, more precisely, does it *mean* to say that the churches 'accepted' biblical criticism?

At first sight, the postponement of major public controversy over the issue of biblical criticism until the mid 1850s looks surprising. After all, as we have noted, German biblical criticism, if not well known, was also not unknown in the 1830s and 40s, and in so far as it was known, it was known chiefly as a dangerously rationalist phenomenon. Moreover, specific clergymen were known to hold views sympathetic to such criticism and antithetical to traditional understandings of the Bible, and in the background there rumbled the ongoing challenge of 'genesis and geology'. The absence of head-on conflict prior to the 1850s looks less puzzling, however, if the events of the 50s and after are placed in the context of the general mid-century crisis of 'creeds in competition and transition', and if the particular ecclesiastical status, roles and prominence of the controversial biblical critics of the 1850s, 60s, and 70s are borne in mind, together with the prominence given to biblical criticism itself within their overall work and theology.

By the mid-1850s there was increasingly widely *perceived to be* a profound crisis in Victorian religious life and thought. From the early 1830s to the early 1850s, scientists presented their findings in geology, astronomy and natural history; morally sensitive doubters announced their unorthodoxy or their departure from Christian faith owing to the moral dubiousness of traditional Christian doctrine; the 1851 census of religious worship confirmed what many had long known and more had long feared: disturbingly large numbers of the urban working classes were unattached to and largely untouched by the churches. But in the same twenty-odd years since the early 1830s, alongside the growth in scientific, moral and social doubts over Christianity and its teaching, there had also been a remarkable revival in religious feeling, intensity and activity: Nonconformists sensed the moment was at hand to challenge the established church; establishment felt itself threatened; the Oxford Movement revived theological life and debate within the Church of England and, crucially, posed the question of the limits of legitimate interpretation and the relative status of Creeds, Thirty-Nine Articles and Bible; in Scotland, confessional Calvinism had re-asserted itself in the General Assembly from 1830 onwards, and the Free Church had emerged from the Disruption as the standard bearer of Evangelicalism. In short, by the 1850s, the temperature was hotter, the pressure greater, the doubts and challenges more profound, the religiously conservative both more militant and also more embattled.

Into such a context came a series of works advocating biblical criticism from clergymen who occupied prominent teaching or pastoral positions in their churches. Davidson and Robertson Smith taught in church colleges training would-be ministers; the authors of *Essays and Reviews* taught in universities attended by Anglican ordinands; Colenso was a bishop. These, therefore, were challenges to Christian orthodoxy *from within*. Moreover, the orthodox protested, such challenges were, surely, dishonest, for they involved the rejection of doctrines which as priests and ministers of their various churches the authors had undertaken to uphold: yet now they published, not merely for fellow scholars, but for genuinely public consumption, opinions and criticisms of traditional belief which, it was held by the orthodox, would undermine or destroy faith. In a period of intellectual crisis and challenge to Christian faith, those charged with its defence were guilty of undermining faith by publishing their own intellectual and critical doubts.

That, at least, was how the orthodox perceived matters: a clash between faith on the one hand and intellectual criticism on the other. The advocates of a critical approach understood the issue somewhat differently. For them the conflict was not between criticism and faith, but between two types of faith. Davidson, the essayists, Colenso, and Robertson Smith were convinced that their critical approach was itself a genuinely faithful one: they were, to a man, *believing* critics. As R. A. Riesen has demonstrated in respect of the controversies over biblical criticism in the Scottish Free Church, the underlying issue was the meaning and nature of faith rather than criticism itself. 'What was at stake', Riesen observes, 'was the nature of the relationship between God and man'. The Bible was important, in the opinion of those who espoused a critical approach, not primarily for what it taught in doctrine, but for what it revealed (to the heart rather than the head — *pace* those for whom the critics were essentially intellectual and academic) of the relationship of God and humankind. 'It was for this reason . . . that criticism was justified: it made the Bible, in its essential historicalness and literariness — in its humanness — all the more real and accessible to those seeking, not abstract truths, not theology, but God himself' (Riesen, 1985, pp. 432–3; see also Rogerson, 1984, pp. 277–8). It was an orientation equally characteristic of the authors of *Essays* and *Reviews*. The theme which united the authors of *Essays and Reviews* was the abandonment of the traditional appeal to the *external* truths, evidences and proofs of Christianity (whether credal, scriptural or rational) and the grounding of Christian faith instead in the *internal* religious and moral sense and experience of humanity. Assent to doctrine and to logical, objective theology was replaced by the priority of subjective experience, relationship, and conscience — and whilst biblical criticism might threaten the former, it was a support to the latter (Ellis, 1971, pp. 397–8).

If the notion of a 'confrontation between biblical criticism and faith' thus merits re-interpretation in terms of a 'conflict between types of faith', what of the claim that, by the 1890s, the churches had 'accepted' biblical criticism? At one level, as we have seen, the claim is incontestably correct: from the 1880s onwards it became possible to hold, teach and publish critical approaches to the Bible and remain an accredited clergyman. Conservatives continued to protest — as in the *Lux Mundi* debates or the attempts to prosecute Dods, Bruce and Smith — but official censure was not forthcoming. But what, exactly, was accepted? The impression sometimes given by the conventional assertion that in the 1890s the churches 'accepted biblical criticism' is that, from being proscribed, or at least fiercely resisted, it became the norm, a common feature of church life, an assimilation of the views for which Davidson and Robertson Smith were removed from their posts, Jowett condemned, and Williams, Wilson and Colenso prosecuted. The latter impression is misleading. If 'being accepted' meant becoming a permissible opinion — and, even more specifically, a tolerable *scholarly* opinion — then biblical criticism was indeed accepted in the 1880s and 90s. How far it was genuinely assimilated into the life of the churches, however; or how far an increasing *de facto* division was being pragmatically accepted between the critical opinions permissible to the scholar in the study and the 'faith of the church' as proclaimed and presented by bishops and moderators, parish clergy and ministers; and what were the limits of the criticism genuinely acceptable in the latter; these are matters which are more ambiguous.

How far the principle of biblical criticism, even in a simplified form, was accepted into the life of the churches — into the pulpit, the Sunday school and 'popular' religious literature — is a question which merits much further scholarly investigation. Chadwick has observed that some of the sternest opponents of the growing 'acceptance' of criticism were the famous preachers: Liddon, Spurgeon or Parker, for example. He also cites the example of Bishop Moorhouse of Manchester, who supported the legitimacy of biblical criticism but urged his clergy to keep such matters out of sermons and confined to lectures (Chadwick, 1972, p. 107). It seems likely, indeed, that in matters of biblical criticism the majority will have kept to an imprecise and unspecific assumption of broadly traditional views. The number of clergy who will have openly sought to introduce critical insights is likely to have remained relatively small, and even then the critical insights introduced are likely to have been placed, in the manner of the orthodox 'Lives', firmly within a traditional doctrinal framework.

Such an approach from the pulpit would, moreover, simply have reflected the general manner in which the 'acceptance of biblical criticism' by the churches occurred. As recent studies have made clear, the crucial factor in the 'acceptance' of biblical criticism in the 1880s and 1890s was the development of a cautious, conservative criticism, a critical *orthodoxy*, a biblical criticism in which a moderate application of critical methods was wedded to a reassuringly orthodox doctrinal stance (Pals, 1982, chs. 3–5; Rogerson, 1984, pp. 234, 287–8).

Thus, the famous 'Cambridge Triumvirate' of Westcott, Lightfoot and Hort were acceptable not merely for their combination of moderate criticism with an essential theological orthodoxy, but also for the way in which they opposed and refuted the more radical proposals of German biblical criticism — especially German *New Testament* criticism. Old Testament criticism was more acceptable than New — especially if it was combined with a theory of progressive revelation whereby the critically evaluated sources of the Old Testament were held, nevertheless, to point clearly to God's providential guidance of Jewish history. Thus in *Lux Mundi*, the very symbol of the 'acceptance' of criticism by the churches, the acceptance of Old Testament criticism was founded on just such a notion of progressive revelation, which was itself, in turn, buttressed by the claim that this was indeed also what the early Fathers of the Church had taught. Significantly, what brought the conservatives — led by the older Tractarian and High Church warriors Liddon and Denison — to attack *Lux Mundi* was the fact that Gore and his associates claimed to write as defenders of orthodoxy, albeit in critical form, and the most sensitive spot of all was Gore's asser- tion that Jesus might have held a view of the status and authorship of Old Testament books which modern scholarship knew to be wrong. The closer criticism came to the New Testament, and therefore to doctrines about Christ, the more sensitive it still remained.

Equally significantly, the various 'Lives of Jesus' (pre-eminently that of Farrar, but also the many other imitations of the model) demonstrated precisely that a *cautious* criticism even of the New Testament *was* possible. But as Pals has demonstrated, what really distinguished these 'Lives' was their overwhelmingly re-assuring tone: moderate criticism was employed in the service of the nurturing of a devotionally and doctrinally orthodox faith: Jesus remained divine, miracles were not denied, the supernatural was not challenged, and the *essential* reliability of the gospels' record affirmed (Pals, 1982, chs. 3–5).

In assessing the extent of the 'acceptance' of biblical criticism by the churches, it is instructive to compare the nature and the tone of the criticism implied by, respectively, *Essays and Reviews* and *Lux Mundi*. Cer- tainly *Lux Mundi* was a tighter, generally more integrated volume: but then it was overtly collaborative in a way that *Essays and Reviews* was not, despite the orthodox charges of 'conspiracy' in 1860. Chadwick has observed that *Lux Mundi* was also more reverent. But 'reverent' is a loaded term, and its use in this instance is unfair to the authors of *Essays and Reviews*. What is unquestionably true, however, is that *Lux Mundi* was more reverent *of orthodoxy* and less radical, whereas *Essays and Reviews* was more radical in direction and happy to be *un*orthodox if *reverence for truth*, as the authors saw it, so demanded.[9]

That contrast, and the limits to acceptable biblical criticism thus im- plied even in *Lux Mundi*, extended beyond an Anglican context. The reas- suring criticism of the late Victorian 'Lives of Jesus' tradition had not opened the way for the acceptance of *radical* criticism or explicitly expressed critical views. The Scottish Free Church still faced attempts to convict scholars of heresy for their critical views, and in English Nonconformity the reactions to the Congregationalist R. F. Horton's *Inspiration and the Bible* (1888) by the Baptists (the Baptist Union cancelled an invitation to preach)

[9] Although Crowther has also noted the *relative conservatism* of which the authors of *Essays and Reviews* were capable (1970, pp. 77–81) and James Barr has drawn attention to a number of notably *conservative* aspects of Jowett's approach to scripture (1982 and 1983). But for a sense of the overall tendency of the thought of the authors of *Essays and Reviews*, and the Broad Church in general — especially in many of their later, often private and individual remarks — see Wigmore-Beddoes (1971). Barr also, it should be added, does not dispute the *essentially* liberal tendency of Jowett's position, but questions the extent to which Jowett's stance was genuinely *historically* critical.

and by some of his broadly liberal Nonconformist congregation (they left), demonstrated the potential strength of the residual resistance to criticism.

Moreover, as Pals has pointed out, after 1900 there occurred a new parting of the ways between criticism and devotion. The 'alliance' of cautious scholarly criticism and popular 'Lives' fell apart. Scholarly New Testament criticism became more radical, its conclusions less 'secure' and less orthodox; it also became more specialized and much more tentative. In place of confidence in the essential reliability of the gospels came increasing scholarly awareness of the gap between 'the Jesus of history' and 'the Christ of faith': a new contrast from which further and genuinely popular 'Lives' could not easily be made (Pals, ch. 5).

Moreover, the newer more radical New Testament criticism also carried with it disturbing doctrinal implications. In the decade and a half before 1914, theologians associated with the Anglican Modern Churchmen's Union (the heirs of the older Broad Churchism of the *Essays and Reviews* era) began to apply the historical principles of their biblical criticism to the criticism of doctrine and creeds. When the Virgin Birth and Resurrection were thus challenged, the orthodox — now led by Gore, the erstwhile 'liberal' of *Lux Mundi* — sought to secure the official re-affirmation by the church of the historical nature of such items in the Creeds. In 1905, and again in 1914, they succeeded in their efforts, although the bishops in Convocation also added to the re-affirmation a qualifying provision that there should be consideration for what was provisional and tentative in the work of honest and reverent students and scholars. After the First World War the issue was taken up again, and has been, periodically, ever since.[10]

By 1900 a new version of the old division between 'criticism and faith', 'intellect and devotion,' had taken shape between the rights of *scholars* to investigate and the *corporate* re-affirmation of the official orthodoxy (albeit now a critically revised orthodoxy) of the church as a whole. To be sure, the scholars were no longer to be tried for heresy or formally rebuked — however much some conservatives might seek it, the churches as institutions were now too essentially pluralist, and their leadership too pragmatically conscious of the Pandora's box such measures would open for them to be adopted. But the 'acceptance' of biblical (and now credal) criticism was a good deal less than wholehearted, and the gap between the churches' scholars and their laity — which the late Victorian 'Lives' had briefly seemed to begin to close — was widening once more.

---

[10] For the 1905 and 1913–14 episodes see Livingston, 1974, pp. 47–55 and Kreiger, 1984. Reisen similarly observes of the near-trial of G. A. Smith in the Scottish Free Church in 1902 that the *doctrinal* implications of Smith's biblical criticism were an essential element in the controversy (1985, p. 38).

III   THE POPULAR DIMENSION:
A 'CRITICAL' POSTSCRIPT?

The internal pluralism and licensed diversity which by 1900, was, in varying degrees, characteristic of all the Protestant Nonconformist and both the established churches of Victorian Britain was not only a matter of the institutional tolerance of a range of distinct, articulate theological positions, be they 'evangelical', 'catholic' or 'liberal'. There was also a popular dimension to the late Victorian diversification of belief within the churches.

Described pejoratively, it was a decay from within of theological precision and denominational identity, a drift into unspecific belief and lukewarm allegiance.[11] Described more positively, it was an assertion by the laity of the right to believe and worship in ways which 'made sense' to the laity concerned, even if the frequent inconsistencies and eclecticism of their faith did not correspond to the various 'official' versions of Christianity on offer from the denominations and their internal sub-groups.

How did the development of biblical criticism and the changing image of the Bible fit into this process? It is a question on which, as yet, we know too little and which — like most aspects of the history of the laity — deserves more study than it has received. We may, however, hazard certain preliminary suggestions.

As Pals has pointed out, the Victorian 'Lives of Jesus' were indeed a remarkable phenomenon. In 1906 a list of such 'Lives' ran to over 5000 items. By far the greater number sought to present a Jesus who was human, emotionally appealing, accessible and yet 'orthodox' in the sense that he conformed to traditional Christian belief. They also, even when employing a cautious version of biblical criticism, affirmed (or assumed) the essential historicity of the gospels. Not a little of their appeal and effectiveness, however, derived from their combination of vivid, imaginative and 'realistic' portrayals of the personality of Jesus with equally vivid topographical and geographical detail, descriptions of Palestinian life, and the discoveries of archaeology — like geology, a Victorian specialism with overt popular appeal and romance. Similarly, in the case of the Old Testament, from works such as Milman's *History of the Jews* onwards, and via later projects such as Stanley's *History of the Jewish Church*, there was a consistent enthusiasm for presentations of the biblical story that included the latest geographical, topographical and archaeological data.

But, as in the case of the 'Lives', the effect of such histories — even when intended to be impeccably orthodox — was to make the humanity of Jesus more real. The same was true of the Old Testament: even when God's providential intervention and progressive guidance was retained, to tell the

[11] For further discussion of this phenomenon, see *RVB*, I, 2, and 3 and II, 3.

story as history and to emphasize the people and personalities involved, was to humanize the affair. Implicitly if not explicitly, the biblical story was made relative and this-worldly. This was so even when history was used to oppose biblical criticism. By the end of the century there was a lively conservative attempt to use the 'facts of archaeology' to 'prove the Bible' and thereby disprove the critics (MacHaffie, 1981). But in so deploying archaeology as a weapon in their own cause, the conservatives in fact further historicized and humanized the Bible itself.

The churches also contributed to the process. As the doctrine of the Incarnation ousted the doctrine of the Atonement as the centre and focus of late Victorian orthodoxy, and as the churches found it easier to start from the historical Jesus and work towards the doctrine of his divinity (rather than the other way around as had been characteristic seventy years earlier), so an impression *of* Jesus became more practically important than a doctrine *about* him. Thus Ellis has observed of Farrar's *Life* that it presented a Pre-Raphaelite Christ, not a Chalcedonian one: coolly deliberate doctrine was replaced by warmly imprecise and ethereal emotion as the basis of would-be orthodox belief. R. Q. Gray has similarly noted the marked emphasis within late Victorian 'non-doctrinal Protestantism' upon the *personality* and *example* of Christ and other biblical figures (Ellis, 1986, p. 109; Gray, 1977, p. 149).

What seems to have emerged, by the closing years of the nineteenth century, was a *de facto* shift — aided and abetted by the critically orthodox themselves — towards a popular, semi-critical understanding of the Bible. The traditional orthodox opposition to biblical criticism — based upon specific doctrines of biblical inspiration — was less widely advocated. It had become, rather, the concern of specific and articulately conservative theological sub-groups within the churches. Similarly, the defence of a literal understanding of Genesis, or the resistance to all and any criticism of the historical accuracy of the Old Testament, was becoming the special preserve of the determinedly and committedly theologically conservative.

Outside the ranks of the self-consciously theologically conservative, Victorian Christians became willing to accept that much of the Old Testament might be mythical or historically inaccurate. But they remained much more conservative about the New Testament, and even in the case of the Old Testament a critical attack upon particular miracles might cause offence. For if the Bible had become more like a history book, it remained nevertheless a 'sacred' history book. The logic of much biblical criticism challenged that continuing status and thus remained suspect in the eyes of many of both the laity and the clergy. Thoroughgoing biblical criticism became, increasingly, an activity pursued in the universities and regarded with at best mixed feelings by the churches. In the ongoing life of the churches themselves the critical questions were avoided rather than addressed. The more extreme statements of the theological conservatives were widely rejected, but so were the implications of a thoroughly critical stance. It was an ambiguous and imprecise solution to the problem of the Bible in the life of the church in the age of biblical criticism: it has yet to find a successor.

BIBLIOGRAPHY

J. Barr (1982) 'Jowett and the "original meaning" of scripture', *Religious Studies*, Vol. 18, pp. 433–7.

J. Barr (1983) 'Jowett and the reading of the Bible "like any other book"' in *Horizons in Biblical Theology*, pp. 1–44, Pittsburgh, Pittsburgh Theological Seminary.

O. Chadwick (1971) *The Victorian Church* Part I, A. and C. Black.

O. Chadwick (1972) *The Victorian Church* Part II, A. and C. Black.

M. A. Crowther (1970) *Church Embattled: Religious Controversy in Mid-Victorian England*, Newton Abbot, David and Charles.

I. Ellis (1971) ' "Essays and Reviews" reconsidered', *Theology*, Vol. 74, pp. 396–404.

I. Ellis (1986) 'Dean Farrar and the quest for the historical Jesus', *Theology*, Vol. 89. pp. 108–15.

C. C. Gillespie (1959) *Genesis and Geology*, New York, Harper and Row.

W. B. Glover (1954) *Evangelical Nonconformity and Higher Criticism in the Nineteenth Century*, Independent Press.

R. Q. Gray (1977) 'Religion, culture and social class in late nineteenth and early twentieth century Edinburgh' in G. Crossick (ed.) *The Lower Middle Class in Britain*, pp. 134–58, Croom Helm.

F. G. Kreiger (1984) 'Sykes on liberalism and Liberalism on Sykes' in M. D. Bryant (ed.) *The Future of Anglican Theology*, pp. 87–101, Toronto, Edwin Mellen Press.

J. C. Livingston (1974) *The Ethics of Belief: An Essay on the Victorian Religious Conscience*, Talahassee, Florida, American Academy of Religion.

B. Z. MacHaffie (1981) ' "Monument facts and higher critical fancies": archaeology and the popularization of Old Testament criticism in nineteenth-century Britain', *Church History*, Vol. 50, pp. 316–28.

J. R. Moore (1986) 'Geologists and interpreters of Genesis in the 19th century' in D. C. Lindberg and R. L. Number (eds.) *God and Nature: Historical Essays on the Encounter between Christianity and Science*, Berkeley, University of California.

*D. L. Pals (1982) *The Victorian Lives of Jesus*, San Antonio (TX), Trinity University Press.

R. A. Riesen (1985) *Criticism and Faith in Late Victorian Scotland*, University Press of America.

*J. Rogerson (1984) *Old Testament Criticism in the Nineteenth Century: England and Germany*, S.P.C.K.

J. L. Speller (1979) 'Alexander Nicoll and the study of German biblical criticism in early nineteenth-century Oxford', *Journal of Ecclesiastical History*, Vol. 30, No. 4, pp. 451–9.

*D. G. Wigmore-Beddoes (1971) *Yesterday's Radicals: A Study of the Affinity between Unitarianism and Broad Church Anglicanism in the Nineteenth Century*, Cambridge and London, J. Clarke.

CHAPTER 12

CLERICAL ELOCUTION LESSON.

Bishop Punch. "NOW, SIR, LET ME HEAR YOU PUBLISH BANNS OF MARRIAGE."

Swell Candidate for Orders. "I—AW—PUBLISH BANNTH OF MAWIDGE 'TWEEN WEGINALD WOBERTH, CATCHLA, AND —"

Bishop. "STOP, SIR, STOP. THAT WILL NEVER DO FOR US. YOU HAD BETTER TAKE ORDERS—IN THE COMMERCIAL LINE."

THE MEN FROM THE MINISTRY

I N 1902 Charles Booth published his *Religious Influences* volumes as the third part of his voluminous study of *Life and Labour of the People in London*.[1] Although occasional historians have dipped into this religious material, it has been sadly neglected. For those who associate Booth's work with the charting of urban poverty, overcrowding and lack of 'respectability' it is important to note that Booth began this part of his work with the premiss that religion 'claims the chief part' of the 'other social influences which form part of the very structure of life' and that it grew out of a systematic research project. The basis of this project was a series of detailed interviews with Christian ministers of all denominations in the metropolis. These interviews were conducted by Booth and five assistants (Jesse Argyle, Ernest Aves, George Arkell, Arthur Baxter and George Duckworth). During the years 1897–1900 these men tramped from vicarage, to rectory, to manse, to priory, to mission to interview over 1,450 individuals. First of all they wrote to each minister or missionary and invited them to co-operate with Charles Booth's inquiry by granting an interview. With the letter was sent a printed schedule of questions: this was not to be filled in but was to act as a check list of the issues to be covered by the interview. When the interview was granted — and in the great majority of instances it was — it normally lasted up to two and a half hours and involved intensive questioning and frantic note-taking.

In this essay the issue which preoccupied Booth and his assistants — whether the churches, as institutions, were having a profound influence upon the poor of the capital — does not directly concern us. But the reports of the interviews, which contain many verbatim quotations accompanied by the shrewd comments of the interviewers, still exist and they provide the fullest surviving evidence of the work of the Christian ministry in late Victorian London. It is necessary to go back to the manuscript source as the printed volumes of *Life and Labour* are neither full enough nor accurate enough in their use of the interview material for our purposes. While exercising proper caution (necessary because the questions on the schedule inevitably shaped the nature of the responses and of the descriptions of pastoral and preaching work supplied) it is yet possible to deduce a good

---

[1]This essay uses the numerous interviews conducted by the social reformer and researcher Charles Booth and his assistants in the London of the last years of the nineteenth century to gain an insight into the life and work of 'The Men from the Ministry'. The pastoral ministries of seven men — drawn from the evangelical and ritualist wings of the Anglican Church; and from the Wesleyan Methodist, Baptist and Congregationalist denominations — are explored in order to throw further light upon the significance of that professional development (discussed in *RVB*, I, 5) for the 'church on the ground'. In particular the relevance of the development of educational institutions for the ministry to the actual problems which faced Victorian ministers is questioned. Additional material is drawn from the Booth Collection to support this detailed study.

deal from this rich archive which will shed light upon the extent to which ministers were prepared by their training for the reality of pastoral work and the extent to which their traditional roles were now under attack and felt by themselves to be under attack. Hitherto historians have drawn conclusions about the professionalization of the clergy, its causes and consequences, based almost exclusively upon the writings of a very few activists belonging to an élite within the church or denomination concerned and upon generalized and often abstract observations about the traditional roles of the ministers and the ways in which these were being eroded during the Victorian period and after (Russell, 1980, passim). Examining the ministries of even a few men — who could in no sense be described as extraordinary — can but provide a valuable corrective to this trend and may suggest some new questions which historians should be seeking to address in describing the ministry as a profession. It may be possible to suggest, for example, whether 'training' had a perceivably great influence upon the practice of a ministry. Or whether the training programme espoused by the various denominations was genuinely directed at the problems facing the Victorian churches. So, while it is important to remember that these ministers are individuals and that no claims are made for their 'typicality', equally, the individuals selected for special study are in no sense 'atypical' either.

II

First of all, the men concerned.

1 In mid-March 1900 Ernest Aves visited 'one of the best known parishes in South London', St John the Divine, Kennington, to interview Mr Brooke, 'one of the best-known figures among the South London clergy'. Brooke vigorously defended the Oxford Movement as the main spring of the church's work of the salvation of souls. Aves diligently wrote down his views and then gave his own opinions of the man: 'He is very rich and is unmarried'. Tall and bearded and fifty-five, 'he can smile you into a seventh heaven. If you don't see him smile, he remains unknown'; 'I felt all the time that he had a fluttering intellect. His body was always ready to bounce about and so was his mind ...' (B305, pp. 1 ff).

Charles Edward Brooke obtained a B.A. from University College, Oxford in 1869. He had come to St John the Divine as an assistant in 1869 before the parish was legally constituted in 1874. At this time he was still a layman: he was not ordained deacon until 1871. In 1872 he was ordained priest in the diocese of Winchester. Some time between 1869 and 1871 he had attended Cuddesdon Theological College. In 1881 he took over as Vicar of St John the Divine and by 1900 had two curates under him.

2   John Bishop Sharp, Vicar Designate of the Church of the Epiphany, Stockwell, who was interviewed by George Duckworth on 26 October, was at thirty-five altogether a younger man. He had come to Stockwell four years earlier from Forest Hill at the request of the bishop. Stockwell was clearly not the sort of middle-class parish that he had expected and that the bishop had described. Now the bishop wanted to move him to Gravesend to rectify the mistake (B305, pp. 75 ff.).

Sharp had been trained at King's College, London. In 1886 he became an AKC (1st Class) and was awarded the Jelf Prize. In that same year he was ordained deacon at Rochester and took up the assistant curacy of Kingsdown, Dartford. After four years he removed to become Curate of Christ Church, Forest Hill. He became Vicar Designate of the Church of the Epiphany, Stockwell, in 1896 and remained there until 1908 when he became Vicar of St Philip, Battersea.

3   'Gassy and insincere' and 'self-satisfied' was how Duckworth described William Douglas Springett, D.D. of St Matthew's, Brixton, on 30 October 1900. The portrait which Springett supplied him with was described as 'one of the most flattering portraits I have ever seen'. Springett was according to Duckworth about fifty-five years of age (he was, in fact, forty-nine) and he had been in Brixton for only two years (B305, pp. 127 ff.).

William Springett was himself the son of a clergyman from Brightwell, Berkshire. He had matriculated at Queen's College, Oxford in 1870 at the age of nineteen; had proceeded B.A. in 1873 (3rd Class, Theological Scholar); M.A. in 1877; B.D. in 1880 and D.D. in 1888. He was ordained deacon in 1873 and priest in 1874, both in the diocese of Lincoln. Prior to becoming Vicar of St Matthew, Brixton, he held a curacy in Nottingham from 1873–6 and in Hackington, Kent from 1876–83, the Vicarage of Herne Hill, Kent, from 1883–92 and the Rectory of West Tarring, Worthing, from 1892–98. He left St Matthew's in 1905 for further preferment as Rector of Pluckley, Ashford in Kent.

4   On November 8 1900 Ernest Aves interviewed the Vicar of St Paul's, West Brixton, J. Carnegie Brown, a Scot, 'genial and bluff, square and sturdy.' In 1900 he was about forty years of age and he had been at West Brixton for about six years. 'I suppose they would call me an Evangelical. At any rate I am old-fashioned enough to think that religion is something that one has to *be*.'

Carnegie Brown was described as next door to a teetotaller but one who 'smokes vigorously'. 'It's my own house' he said 'and I smoke everywhere, except my wife's bedroom. That is sacred' and then, as an afterthought, 'Unless I am laid up in it; then I smoke'. 'On the whole', thought Aves, 'a good, honest, muscular Christian' (B305, pp. 213 ff.).

Johnston Carnegie Brown was an M.A. of St John's College, Cambridge and had probably graduated B.A. in about 1885, for this was the year in which he was ordained deacon in the diocese of London, with the title of Curate of St Simon, Hammersmith. He was ordained priest in 1886. From 1887–1888 he served as associate secretary of the Church Pastoral Aid Society, North East District. In 1888 he became Vicar of St John, Hull, where he served until he was presented to the Vicarage of St Paul, Brixton, in 1894. His ministry at Brixton lasted for seven years. In 1901 he became incumbent of Christ Church, Jerusalem, as missionary in charge of the Jerusalem of the Jews Society.

5   On the previous day, 7 November 1900, George Duckworth had sat in the study of that 'scholar and unmethodical dreamer' J. Douglas, M.A., Pastor of the Kenyon Baptist Church on Solon road. This seventy-year old, white-haired widower, sat bent up in his arm chair, with his fingers to his white brows and his feet on the fender, as he described at some length how he spent 'hours daily on his knees in prayer & contemplation; wrestling with the Devil, in intercessory prayer, & on rare occasions, in seeing God & receiving his orders from Him directly' (B304, pp. 1 ff.).

Douglas was probably a graduate of one of the Scottish universities and his interview suggests that he was a man of considerable scholarship. He had been at the Kenyon Baptist Church for some sixteen years.

6   George Duckworth interviewed the Rev. Alfred Sargent, Minister of the Brixton Hill Wesleyan Church on November 13 1900. Sargent, who was head of a circuit, was between forty-five and fifty years of age and struck Duckworth as being 'just a little superior'. Duckworth went on to describe the church as 'practically the C of E without episcopacy', for 'in the morning there is a liturgical service, Church of England prayer book is used' and many church people attend. The liturgy is not used in the evening but 'The Congregation likes variety and sobriety' (B305, pp. 101 ff.).

Alfred Sargent spent one year of training at the Theological Institution in 1868. Then he moved from circuit to circuit — one year in Bradford; two years in Windsor; three years in Wallacestone, Runcorn, York (Wesley), Chester, Leeds (Headingley), Newcastle-upon-Tyne (Brunswick), Wolverhampton (Trinity), Kentish Town and Croydon, respectively, before becoming head of the circuit of Brixton Hill Wesleyan Church,

7   Meanwhile George Arkell was focussing his attentions on Camberwell. On 16 November he visited the Rev. Adam Averell Ramsey, of the Emmanuel Congregational Church, Barry Road, Dulwich. Ramsey was an elderly Scot who had been in the church for about twelve years. Arkell was struck by his person: 'In appearance he is the most clerical Congregationalist I have met, being dressed in regular clerical garb' (B306, pp. 1 ff.).

Ramsey seems to have been educated in Belfast. His ministry began in 1857. He came to Dulwich in 1888 to a church which had been founded in 1877. He was a member of the Congregational Board.

III

The Victorian period was marked by a movement for the professionalization of the various ministries.[2] This was characterized among other things by a conviction that ministers required formal academic instruction and training in order to properly profess their vocation. The degree to which one subscribed to the view that ministerial training of a specified type *qualified* a recruit varied from denomination to denomination.

Where the Protestant ministry is concerned there were considered to be other sources of 'knowledge' than an apprenticeship, a school, an institution, a theological college, or a university. A direct call from God gave the minister access to the most important *knowledge* of all — that of God's Will. It gave him ears to hear. It prepared him to receive and perceive the message of God's Word — the Scriptures. The balance between this knowledge and that imparted by human learning was delicately and variously struck in the different denominations.

With this in mind, it would clearly be inappropriate to make a direct, unqualified comparison between the preparation for the ministry of the seven men selected for special attention. They did not share a common preparation for the ministry. One Anglican was a graduate of Oxford and had received a doctorate in divinity. One had attended King's College, London. Another was a graduate and a product of Cuddesdon Theological College. Another was an M.A. of Cambridge, apparently with no specific training in theology. The Methodist had received his training at a Theological Institution. The Congregationalist probably attended an Institute in Belfast. The Baptist was a university graduate.

These differences are themselves instructive. How do the men concerned fit into what we know in general of patterns of recruitment and training among the relevant ministries?

In the early years of Victoria's reign the number of Anglican clergy expanded considerably. In 1834 there were approximately 13,000 Anglican clergy; by 1841 there were 14,613; by 1851, 17,463 (Haig, 1984, pp. 2–3). This meant that the clergy was transformed into a group of relatively young men and that recruitment and training became central issues. Throughout the century a substantial majority of the ordinands had graduated at one of the ancient universities or had been educated there. We must remember this as we move on to discuss the impact of the growth of the theological colleges — this was an interesting and crucial development but it was experience of a university education, not of theological college, which came closest to providing a common background and common intellectual baggage for most clergymen (Haig, 1984, p. 27). Over 80% of new ordinands

[2] For which see *RVB*, I, 5.

in the 1830s and 40s had attended Oxford or Cambridge. After this, the contribution of the universities declined but remained high. Moreover, the Anglicans continued to regard a graduate clergy as the norm and the ideal. In this context we should note that three of the four Anglican clergymen noted above had graduated from either Oxford or Cambridge. The fourth, John Bishop Sharp, A. K. C., (Associate of King's College) spent a good deal of his interview explaining to George Duckworth the differences between his preparation for the ministry and that offered by the ancient universities or the theological colleges. Clearly he felt somewhat set apart by the peculiarities of the King's College curriculum and approach.

Eighteenth-century Oxbridge had been too small to supply the church with a graduate ministry. By the early nineteenth century it looked as though it could do just that. This meant, in theory, that the bishops could tighten up standards of recruitment. It made it possible for C. J. Blomfield to turn away non-graduate candidates for orders at Chester, for example, early in the period (1824–28). In practice, the rapid population explosion put great pressure on the church to create new parishes and to multiply the number of its clergy. The number of clergy did not match population growth except in the 1840s and 1850s. These were pressures which led to some dilution of the graduate norm.

The universities continued to pour graduates into the Church of England throughout the Victorian period but these graduate ordinands formed a smaller proportion of the clergy than the hierarchy would have wished. Moreover, the church which had attracted graduates of high intellectual quality before 1850 signally failed to do so after that date. The calibre of graduate ordinands plunged particularly dramatically in the 1870s (Haig, 1984, pp. 48–9). Alternative careers seem to have attracted able students to the Church of England's detriment. In part the fall-off in able 'clerical' students may have been due to the increasing cost of attending the ancient universities and the difficulties facing poor but able students who sought outside financial support. The Elland Society, founded in 1774, did finance sons of poor clergy, clergy orphans and boys of unknown parentage to attend the universities and did require recipients of awards to repay their benefactors if they decided ultimately to enter any other profession than the church. On its own, however, it could do little to reverse the trend away from the production of an intellectually able graduate clergy.

It would be all too easy to exaggerate the immediate effects of this trend — three quarters of all ordinands in the late nineteenth century were graduates; a majority of vacant benefices were still filled with graduates. Nonetheless, the trend was established by this time and was greatly intensified in the next century.

The foundation of institutions to train non-graduate clergy was a nineteenth-century phenomenon. In part it grew out of the inability of the universities in the 1860s to produce sufficient graduates to supply the church. This was coupled with the demand for more clergy and better educated clergy in many quarters. The respectable lower-middle classes might not be able to afford an Oxbridge education for their sons (c. £300–400 per course) but they did covet and could afford a 'formal' education for them (at perhaps £100 per two-year course). Trinity College, Dublin; Durham; King's College, London, and Queen's College, Birmingham, were all beneficiaries of this development. The demand within the church for more clergy and an increasing conviction that ordinands should be in possession of a specific expertise before acceptance led also to the foundation of theological colleges. This was felt especially in the North and in the towns, which were less attractive to graduates. St Bees, for example, was set up in Chester Diocese, which suffered from a chronic shortage of graduate clergy.

St Bees admitted an average of forty young men per annum to its two-year course. It drew its entrants largely from the young, grammar school educated boys of the north west, with just a smattering of mature students drawn from other occupations. It was consistently the largest of the theological colleges: by 1870 almost three-quarters of all theological college students had been admitted to St Bees and even in 1890 it had admitted over half of the 5,300 students known to have attended Anglican theological colleges during the century.

There had been considerable debate within the Church of England about the role of the theological colleges. In the first half of the century they were essentially private commercial enterprises to which the bishops responded in various ways. There was no centralized theological college system. There were not even diocesan colleges. The idea found a kind of a acceptance — the education they offered was better than nothing but a graduate clergy was still the ideal and it was accepted that the universities would continue to produce the church's leaders (Haig, 1984, p. 138). The objections were voiced in terms of unease at the academic standards of the colleges as displayed by a few of their poorer products.

After 1869 the theological colleges were drawn more closely under the diocesan umbrella. In that year St Aidan's, which had closed its doors in 1868, re-opened with a diocesan, centralized organisation under a distinguished scholar. Highbury was the last theological college to be founded by someone other than a bishop. There was a proliferation of theological colleges and departments so that by 1870 there were diocesan colleges (partly or mainly for non-graduates) at Chichester, Gloucester, Lichfield, Lincoln, Salisbury and Truro and theological departments at King's College, London and Queen's College, Birmingham.

The content of the curriculum at the theological colleges was by no means dictated by the hierarchy during much of the century. It was felt that there should be an academic course with an examination. This would relieve the bishops of responsibility for the academic preparation of their clergy and free them to concentrate upon spiritual and pastoral aspects of their training. In 1874 the UPE (Universities' Preliminary Examination) was introduced. This was open to graduates and non-graduates alike. It proved especially attractive to graduates of universities other than Oxford and Cambridge and men from Durham, Queen's and King's. The theological colleges, however, opposed it: it was insufficiently practical in emphasis, thus discriminating against the non-academic candidate, and it had the effect of turning the colleges into crammers for an external examination.

At length, in 1881, the first of several conferences was held to discuss the training of candidates for Holy Orders and, specifically, the introduction of an entrance examination. In 1893 this CEE (Central Entrance Examination) was inaugurated. It tested proficiency in Greek and Latin translation, knowledge of the Bible, English History, and Euclid or Elementary Logic. In theory this would have the effect of excluding candidates without grammar school preparation. This seems to have precipitated the closure of several of the smaller colleges which were already suffering from falling rolls.

This attempt to raise academic levels at the theological colleges was indicative in part of the hierarchy's concern over the decreasing status of the clergy. The hierarchy had not resigned itself to accepting that new recruits to the church would probably be non-graduates. Theological colleges should properly offer detailed vocational preparation to graduates. In 1908 the Archbishop of Canterbury's Report again called for a wholly graduate clergy and for the association of training for the ministry with 'universities'. Under this plan, hostels at the new universities — for example, Mirfield at Leeds and St Chad's at Durham — would house and supervise the new recruits while they studied.

The Anglican clergy in our small group in some ways bear out this general picture. One would expect southern clergy to be of a high calibre and in a large majority of cases to be graduates of the ancient universities. Nonetheless, one is not surprised to see the role of additional vocational training appearing as important even for the traditional graduate nor the presence of a product of one of the newer theological departments. Neither is one surprised to see the interviewers settling upon the academic qualifications of the clergy concerned as worthy of notice (despite the fact that the schedule of questions that they worked with did not include such an inquiry) nor the AKC dwelling upon his superior training at King's! The status of the Anglican clergyman depended to a great extent upon association with centres of high social and academic prestige. This association was under threat even where the graduate of Oxbridge was concerned; how much more so did the AKC have to fight for status.

The professional ministry of the leading Nonconformist denominations was also large and expanding during the century. The following figures for mid and late century are instructive:

FULL-TIME NONCONFORMIST MINISTERS

Congregationalists	Wesleyans	Primitive Methodists	Baptists
1,400	1,125	518	1,577
(1847)	(1851)	(1851)	(1870)
3,000	2,202	955	1,963
(1900)	(1900)	(1900)	(1900)

(figures extracted from K. D. Brown, 'College Principals — a cause of Nonconformist Decay?' *Journal of Ecclesiastical History*, 1987, p. 236)

Inevitably, the nonconformist ministries were dominated by non-graduate recruits. The ancient universities had forbidden dissenters to matriculate and be admitted to degrees until 1856. Even then dissenters were excluded from the Faculty of Theology. The Scottish universities were the principal source of university education for dissenters. But in any event, the place of secular learning in the training of the minister was regarded very differently by Nonconformists. It was the direct call from God which made the minister; human intervention and human learning was traditionally discounted. However attitudes were changing during the nineteenth century in all the Protestant denominations. Gradually, it was accepted that while education did not 'qualify' a man *to be* a minister of God it could prepare him *to do* the work of the ministry to better effect. But it is important to realize that differing denominations reached this position at differing times.

For historical as well as immediate reasons, an alternative to education at the ancient universities was developed. The reform of Oxbridge was along secular lines. New institutions either appeared secular in emphasis (for example, the new university of London) or Anglican (for instance, Durham or King's College, London).

In some cases, the move to provide a specific training for ministers came early in the nineteenth century (as with the Wesleyan Methodists and the Congregationalists); in others it came late (witness the Primitive Methodists).

The movement towards formal preparation for the Baptist ministry was essentially a late Victorian phenomenon associated with the increasingly urban and middle class focus of the denomination (Munson, 1978, pp. 320–7). By 1870 there were ten Baptist colleges (England: six; Wales: three;

Scotland: one). Some of these were late eighteenth-century foundations. In 1870 half of the total of 1,577 involved in the active Baptist ministry in England had no formal education. By 1901 only 18% of Baptist ministers had no formal education. Only the Congregationalists had fewer uneducated ministers in their ranks (17% in 1901). The type of education received by Baptist ministers also changed considerably during these thirty years. In 1870 49% of Baptist ministers had received education in a Baptist college; in 1901 64% had done so. In 1870 only 1% had received any university training; by 1901 8% had done so. The 'scholar and dreamer' J. Douglas of the Kenyon Baptist Church was one of these. Of the twenty-five Baptists with degrees in 1870, only three had attended Oxbridge. In 1901 78% of the graduates had been to Oxbridge; although the majority still had degrees from London or Scottish universities. In most cases the London degrees were external — the men had not been in residence. The dependence upon the University of London was strengthened by the association of the Regent's Park College, the largest Baptist college, with the University.

As with the Anglicans, the Baptist colleges were not parts of a centralized system for the education of Baptist ministers. Whereas Regent's Park College (founded in 1810), affiliated with the University of London since 1841 and a constituent college after 1900, was academically respected, Spurgeon's College, founded in 1856, aimed to train 'a class of ministers who will not aim at lofty scholarship, but at the winning of souls — men of the people'. This 'non-academic' emphasis of Baptist ministerial training was long-lasting. There were proposals for a co-ordinated system, such as that suggested by Dr Green of Rawdon College in 1871. This contemplated a three-tier arrangement, whereby different colleges provided preparatory training, university education and theological education. In 1892 a special meeting of the Union proposed that all the colleges should drop their preparatory work and concentrate upon academically upgrading and broadening the course to include Hebrew and biblical Aramaic, New Testament Greek and Syriac, textual criticism, exegesis, systematic theology, apologetics, Christian history and literature, social economics, pastoral theology and homiletics. This proposal met with considerable opposition from those who felt that it would exclude from the Baptist ministry all recruits who had, because of expense, been deprived of an elementary education. The entire problem was shelved until the twentieth century.

Probably next to the Presbyterians, the Congregationalists were the denomination which placed highest regard upon ministerial education. Academies such as that of Hoxton (founded in 1778) had a long tradition. There were about seventy-five academies in existence after 1800 but many were tiny, one-man enterprises.

Highly the Congregationalists may have regarded education but in 1846 out of 1447 congregationalist ministers in England, 544 had had no formal education (that is, over a third). The remainder had attended fifty different institutions, all with unco-ordinated courses of study and no unified standards. Hoxton (which became Highbury in 1826) dominated the ranks of those who had a formal training — 29.6% of the trained men and 18.6% of the total active ministry. In view of the academic standards of Highbury, this is itself important. Highbury students were 'drilled' in the languages of the Old Testament, introduced to New Testament languages and coached in doctrine. Some formal education was assumed on entry. It is unsurprising, therefore, that many Highbury students were of reasonably well-to-do middle-class backgrounds with grammar-school or equivalent education. Academic standards seem to have improved over the century as a whole, commensurate with the increasing emphasis within the Nonconformist churches after 1830 on improving the ministry. This is not to say, however, that Highbury was highly academic. A contemporary who studied there claimed that most of his fellows 'had scarcely any other qualification than piety and a natural fitness for preaching'. Most entrants completed the course (Brown, 1983, passim).

Adam Averell Ramsey was one of the many Scots who entered the English Congregationalist ministry. His training had been in Belfast. He is representative of the large number of Congregationalist ministers with formal training.

During the nineteenth century Methodism had to accommodate itself to the fact that it was no longer a primarily evangelical force — there were settled Methodist congregations in need of pastoral care, even if Methodist ministers themselves remained unsettled. By 1851 there were well over a thousand Wesleyan Methodists involved in the full-time ministry. As the century progressed more and more Wesleyans received training in the centralized Theological Institution, which had branches in London (Richmond, 1843), Manchester (Didsbury, 1842), Leeds (Headingley, 1868), and Birmingham (Handsworth, 1881).

But the Methodist attitude to the education of ministers differed sharply from that of the Baptists or the Congregationalists. In general it was that the Institution would not make ministers but would fulfill a remedial function with those recommended by the Circuit and District Meetings for the evangelical ministry. For years only the worst educated were sent to the Institution. Although the course of study lasted two years, it was difficult to keep students for more than one. Sargent, who was perhaps one of the six new recruits in the first year at the Headingley Branch, spent only a year (1868) at the Theological Institution before his active ministry. You will recall that the Methodist Colleges were old-fashioned in their curriculum — preoccupied with the issues of the eighteenth century and seen by Methodists themselves as neglectful of modern theological scholarship, contemporary controversies and pastoral training. There was a fear in some quarters that improved education would be destructive of the ministers' spirituality. The Methodist Institution, then, unlike the Baptist and Congregationalist colleges, made no pretensions to academic excellence and did not seek association with the University of London, until the twentieth century. Its branches were also reluctant to introduce modern subjects into the curriculum.

IV

Now we can look at these statistics and these biographies and conclude that (a) the emphasis upon ministerial training was intensifying in the nineteenth century — particularly after 1830; (b) that this emphasis was being played out in the increasing number of ministers in all the denominations who had experienced formal education and (c) that this was part and parcel of the increasing 'professionalization' of the ministry — the tendency to separate ministers and people and to use formal education as one means of accentuating the difference. I would not dispute this. Nevertheless, we must also look at these statistics and say: all the denominations were feeling considerable pressure in the nineteenth century to try to win over souls in an increasingly hostile or indifferent environment. The new biblical criticism alone put great strains upon the ministry. To this were added the problems of population growth, urbanization, secular counter-attractions and the development of democracy. The institutions of formal education were seen as a means to a more laudable end than professionalization — to improving the 'efficiency' of the ministry as ambassadors of God's Word or ministers of the sacraments of the Church (depending upon one's denominational perspective). Seen in this light, the pertinent question is: did the training provided fit them for the task: was it appropriate?

Appropriate to what? The minister performed a variety of roles, which differed from denomination to denomination. He was the preacher, pastor, sometimes priest. He was teacher, tithe collector, comforter, youth leader, officiator at baptisms, marriages and funerals (Russell, 1980, passim).

Some of the clergy thought that their training had fitted them for the evangelical part of their ministry, and there can be little doubt that the training provided in the various colleges was directed towards this end. J. B. Sharp of Stockwell told Duckworth that 'King's College is different from either Oxford or Cambridge or the theological colleges in that there the students are specially trained to speak. They have to preach on Sundays. Their sermons must be shown up to the principal beforehand & corrected & commented on. There are special classes in elocution. For practice they are constantly called on to get up and "say a few words" to their fellow students. The result is that King's students start their church career very much better equipped in these respects than their university brethren.' Duckworth might dismiss him as having 'speech and manners [that] remind one rather of the drawing room entertainer' but Sharp was confident of his appeal. 'Well I am a good preacher, at least my congregation like to hear me & come in large numbers to do so.' He preached extempore, 'of course carefully prepared beforehand' and prided himself on his ability through sermons and lantern lectures to 'make the people see that religion had to do with everyday matters' (B305, pp. 75–9, 85).

Brooke of St John the Divine, Kennington, was also convinced that the success of his particular ministry was largely owing to the traditions of the Oxford Movement with which he had long been closely associated. 'People were being taught the good news of the Gospel message, and in ever-increasing numbers were seeking the forgiveness of their sins and the refreshment of their souls by means of the sacraments of the Church, and this together with the growth of personal holiness was the real secret of the strength of the movement.' 'It is hard now to realize the utter spiritual destitution of the people and the wilderness' which existed in 1866 when St John's was started on mission lines. Brooke has no doubt that his training within the tradition has enabled him to reach the people of Kennington (B305, pp. 5, 1).

The only other minister among the eight who mentioned his association with the training of ministers was the Baptist scholar, Douglas. He mentioned that he had for many years been appointed annually as a lecturer at Harley College because of his knowledge of Hebrew and Greek. We are left uncertain how far this scholarship affected his practical ministry, however. Duckworth described him as 'a man steeped in piety and otherworldliness'. To Douglas the 'only remedy' for general indifference to the Gospel was 'special intercessory prayer followed by a great mission which shall awaken the hearts'. Whatever personal store Douglas set upon biblical scholarship and the academic preparation of the ministers, the importance of his personal relationship with God was undiminished and the missionary strain of his ministry undiluted (B304, pp. 1, 11).

The education of a minister must match the demands of his constituency. The 'message' of each denomination appealed to particular sections of the community. By the late nineteenth century the Nonconformist ministers were resigned to the fact that their appeal was limited to specific groups, often on a 'class' basis. Sending an intellectual to appeal to the uneducated working classes was futile but the educated middle and upper classes needed a man with academic competence. In so far as the various denominations attracted congregations of different classes, they needed different types of men and of training. J. Reid Howatt, Presbyterian Minister of the Brunswick Square Church, Camberwell, explained that the Wesleyans drew the 'pious merchant', the Baptists the 'lower middle and working classes whose emotions [are] easily touched' but that the Presbyterians and to a lesser degree the Congregationalists 'attract the most intelligent section of the middle classes' and 'their ministers have the most thorough theological and philosophical training of all Ministers of Religion' (B306, p. 217).

This message was rapidly brought home to many of the ministers whom Booth's helpers visited. If there is one point that the interviews bring home it is that the individual's ministry was enacted within a 'congregation'. Membership of a profession, of a brotherhood of clergy or ministers is rarely mentioned, at a time when we are told by some historians that the ministry was very professionally conscious. The emphasis is upon the effort to achieve an effective rapport with a particular congregation. Many of the ministers concerned had learned to their cost that training was no substitute for experience and that, frequently, formal preparation ran counter to the lessons of experience.

It was people that the ministers had to associate with, not abstractions — people in all their variety. Carnegie Brown of St Paul's, West Brixton, '. . . finds the Londoner more difficult to deal with than the Yorkshireman. The former are too ready to agree with anything you may say, generally a sign of indifference. Also they fence better, and it is very difficult to tie them down to anything. They are apt to be full of excuses or full of acquiescence, but neither form of repletion helps very much. The Yorkshireman is much more likely to stand up to you, if he disagrees with you and then "you know where you are". Not so with the Londoner' (B305, p. 213ff.). Regional differences were not the only ones perceived. Douglas at Kenyon Baptist Church was well aware that his appeal to males was to city men, commercial travellers and clerks in offices, 'none of them men who would go to Theatres and Music Halls'. He saw his natural constituency as defined by wealth, class and the vagaries of human nature. 'In suburban London you may say that the rich either go to the Established Church or are Congregationalists'. This is because 'If you are a free churchman it is easier to become a Congregationalist than anything else: they are broader in their doctrinal requirements & interpretation of scripture than are the Baptists' (B304, p. 1ff.).

How did the ministers respond to the pressures of work in urban parishes? The spirit of competition is not terribly apparent in the Booth papers covering this part of South London. In some cases there was co-operation between the Free Churches; in many cases relations between the Free Churchmen and the Anglicans were cordial on the personal level but they never extended to active co-operation in religious matters. The Anglicans roused a degree of veiled hostility because of their 'exclusive stance' on ordination. But there was only a limited competition for souls. There seems to have been a general acceptance that particular social constituencies belonged to particular denominations. Tydeman, Minister of

Lordship Lane Baptist Church in East Dulwich explained that his ministry served 'better class working people' of the non-servant keeping classes and that 'Of the other churches, ... the Barry Road Wesleyan & Congregational Churches ... divide the better class people from Barry Rd etc. between them and are socially better off than his church, so much so that some Baptists belong to those churches rather than to their own denominations' (B306, p. 71). Ramsey, the Congregationalist, had a congregation which was 'mainly if not completely middle class ... drawn from all sects. Congregationalists, Wesleyans, Baptists and Episcopalians' (B306, p. 3). We are presented with a competition for the middle classes, in which the Nonconformists felt that they stood at a disadvantage to the Anglicans. '"... there is very little social intercourse between Church and dissent even in London" Still less in the country. The same applies to congregations as well as ministers' (B304, p. 117). But there were socially fashionable and unfashionable Anglican churches as well as nonconformist denominations. St Andrew's, Stockwell, had a congregation that was 'fairly comfortable working class. The well-to-do tend to go elsewhere' (B305, p. 51). The problem of retaining the middle class congregation varied in intensity from district to district. The ministers of Victorian London saw the prosperous middle classes fleeing to the suburbs, but this was not a problem which all ministers met. Nevertheless some districts did deteriorate markedly and for their ministers the lower middle classes and respectable working classes who remained when the more prosperous moved away seemed small recompense. No-one competed for the souls of the very poor.

The ministers accepted such people as presented themselves as 'congregation' (for reasons of class, alienation from their former church, convenience, style of worship) without necessarily actively seeking a wider constituency. Ramsey acknowledged that the Episcopalians in his congregation were 'as a rule driven from this Church by ritualism, quite lately Mr Ramsey named as a member a lady who was the daughter and the widow of a clergyman, but who was disgusted by the ritualism of her church'. Arkell thought that 'the attractions of the Church appear to be the music (the choir have been for some years first in some competition at the Crystal palace) and the preaching' (B306, p. 3). Occasionally one senses a more determined effort to win over some other church's congregation. In the morning Sargent's liturgical service — using the Book of Common Prayer — attracted many Anglicans; in the evening his evangelical service attracted a different type of congregation (B304, p. 107).

The Congregationalist Minister of Stockwell Green told Duckworth 'Our Church is not the Church of the poor, but among our own people our work is invaluable'. 'The Primitive Methodists are the only ones amongst us who touch the poor at all.' The big fear was that if the poor were touched they would turn away 'our own people' (B304, p. 83). Ramsey recognized, reported Arkell, 'the hopelessness of getting the poor in on any conditions: "the fine lady in silks" he said "will not mix with the lapsed masses" and while admitting that this attitude was unchristian seemed to think it was very natural. "Sometimes" he said "when I've been wedged into a third class carriage on the railway I've said to myself, 'If Hvn is worse than this I don't want to go there''' (B306, p. 5). Aylett, Superintendent of the Camberwell Green Congregational Church, observed the behaviour of the children in the Sunday School: 'Children sort themselves: poor sit next poor, well dressed next well dressed; the gutter children don't come ...' (B307, p. 25). The Vicar of St Andrew's, Stockwell, a church which 'for purely parochial success' according to Duckworth 'must about reach high-water mark for London', acknowledged that the poor inhabitants of the Bromsgrove Mission 'won't mix with the Church people nor the Church people with them'. In general the poor that the Church of England was able to attract seem to have been segregated in the missions. No doubt many justified this attitude as J. B. Sharp did; 'our people are courteous and kindly and glad to see you. I can't ask them to come to church because I know there is no room for them'. His mission church was filled with well-to-do outsiders (B305, p. 87). But when the poorest sections of the community were encouraged to attend church and participate in its life- there were other ways of achieving segregation. The evening service often attracted a less well-to-do congregation. Carnegie Brown described an evening congregation which included 'a few ordinary operative wage earners. They won't mix with those who come' (B305, pp. 35, 220). Brooke told Aves that the Guild of St John the Divine was 'for Communicants. Divided into "Wards", according to age, and also "practically according to social position. But we don't say so''' (B305, p. 17).

The ministers sought to retain their congregation. Visiting was seen as a means to this end: in general, visiting by the minister was confined to members of the congregation and, especially, the sick (B305, pp. 59, 91, 119; B304, p. 43; B307, p. 71). Springett confessed that this meant in his case spending 'every afternoon in paying calls "on the upper stratum of his people." Once a month too he has a social gathering at the Vicarage'. Tydeman, the Baptist Minister from East Dulwich, explained 'I am obliged [to spend four days a week visiting] in order to maintain the congregation' (B307, p. 67). At St Saviour's, Herne Hill Road, Camberwell, the Vicar visited the congregation and divided his team of visitors into three groups 'who represent roughly the 3 classes who make up the parish' (B305, p. 161). Sometimes ministers swooped like hawks upon possible backsliders. Mrs Milwood, wife of the part-time Baptist minister of Stockwell, told Aves that 'lapsing is rare, one explanation of this being that all are well looked after. Absence for a month, often for much less time would always mean that some one would go round and look the absentee up, find out the explanation, and see if help or influence was needed' (B304, p. 55).

There were other ways of attracting and keeping a congregation. Some Anglican churches created guilds of communicants which 'form a kind of inner circle of the whole body of communicants' (B305, p. 233). But there was scarcely a church or chapel without its cluster of societies, ranging from literary societies to Bible classes and mothers' meetings to sewing circles. With a very few exceptions (Sunday Schools were a partial exception) these were not missionary in their intent. They were intended to consolidate an existing congregation and, above all, to retain the children and youth of church members or communicants. Sargent's Literary Society — with its great discussions of the works of Marie Corelli, cricket and tennis clubs and Bible Classes — and Ramsey's mothers' meeting fit into this category, as do Sharp's 'Our girls' and 'Club for Girls' and Springett's Young Women's Christian Association, Guild of Willing Helpers, and Industrial Society. These agencies were certainly important; one clergyman contemplated a vanishing congregation should he close down the societies and rely only upon preaching the gospel to keep the people (B305, p. 59).

Some of the ministers acknowledged that their approach nonetheless excluded some of what they regarded as their natural constituency: menfolk. Tydeman said that he found it difficult to see the men 'and is now thinking of giving some meetings up so that he can visit them in the evening'. Brooke sensed that 'more were being done for the women than the men ... I rejoice more than I can say at the work which is now being done on Saturday nights and Sunday afternoons for the men of our parish ... Each Saturday the smaller room is crowded to excess with men bent on listening to some instructive lecture or discussing some topic of social and political interest, whilst on Sunday afternoons the large hall has had to be requisitioned in order to accommodate the men who come from all parts of the parish in order to take their part in the religious service ... they have the opportunity of listening to some of our greatest preachers, both clerical and lay ... Doubtless the excellent orchestra ... is no small attraction but I hope none will think that we have instituted anything like that modern abomination of a Pleasant Sunday Afternoon' (B305, Advent Letter, p. 10).

There is also a good deal of evidence that, no matter what their training and no matter what their personal preferences, many ministers of all denominations tailored their services and their approaches to suit the particular congregation. As Springett observed, many had no choice but to compromise to some extent; 'I never realised till I became the incumbent of a pew-rented Church what a difficult problem is set before a man who occupies such a position: namely, how to be "all things to all men" in the right way, and how to avoid being such in the wrong one' (B305, p. 1). For some this meant not forcing upon the existing congregation personal personal preferences in worship. So the Vicar of St Saviour's, Herne Hill Road, observed that there was 'Rather more music than I like personally but my predecessor started it & my people like it so I maintain it' (B305, p. 151). The Vicar of St Andrew's, Stockwell, explained confidentially, 'We are moderate High Churchmen here. My enemies say that I am too high or not high enough but the congregation is pretty content' (B305, p. 53). Sargent 'would willingly go [to the theatre], thinks the clergy ought to go, but for the misunderstanding it would cause with his own people' (B304, p. 111). True, this responsiveness to the congregations's wishes was not always supreme. Brooke was put into a predicament. His congregation had apparently favoured some external of worship which the bishop had ordered stopped: Brooke expressed his joy that the congregation had allowed him to submit to the bishop's command; otherwise he would have been compelled to resign as his conviction that he could not flout the authority of the ordinary far outweighed his own personal preferences or any belief in 'parochialism or congregationalism' (B305, Advent Letter, pp. 5–6).

If it was direct experience of a particular congregation which dictated to a large extent the 'style' of the church, then it was experience which also taught ministers how best to broach spiritual matters with their people. 'Asked as to how he dealt with people [Carnegie Brown] said that he had learnt by experience. Believing as he does in the personal nature of religion, (something of the nature of conversion), he used to go straight for a man and ask him if he was converted. But this plan does not answer, because having got your reply it leaves you rather stranded the next time a chance comes of speaking. It begins the subject at too late a stage and does not naturally lead on to anything else, if the man replies in the negative . . . In any case he may be said to have given up frontal attacks, and to resort to the old plan of winning men one by one and step by step. As to how he would try and deal with men, this would necessarily vary with the individual' (B305, p. 223). As one would expect, Nonconformist ministers were even more unprepared to venture into new avenues without the approval of their lay colleagues. Douglas believed that he had been chosen as God's instrument in a great missionary enterprise but announced it to the congregation only after consultation with the deacons (B304, p. 15).

It was not, however, a clear-cut situation in which the minister bowed to the wishes of the congregation. A. R. Wilson, a Congregationalist minister, confided 'As a preacher, after some experiments, [he] kept strictly to the Gospel in the pulpit. Once in Wolverhampton he had spoken politics. A deputation of working men was formed & begged that he would not do so again "not that we are not deeply interested, but we feel that it is not that that we come to hear from the pulpit"' (B304, p. 81). Yet Wilson was much impressed by the counsel offered by an old sailor who said 'don't shew them why they should be religious but give them your orders from the quarter deck & they'll obey you' and by the power of the Roman Church in Poplar, 'Lawless would go into a public house, lug out a man by the scruff & cane him in the street.' Wilson might bow to a congregation regarding the content of his sermons but he nonetheless saw himself in a position of authority over the congregation (B304, p. 81).

Those directly involved in such work knew that pursuing the calling of a minister of God in a late Victorian urban parish presented new and particular problems and pressures. The antiquated parish unit, so well suited to the village community, creaked on its hinges in London. It was too populous — the problem now was for a clergyman to know his people. Its population shifted. It was too poor. There were insufficient funds to endow livings properly or to support curates. Carnegie Brown observed that he had just had to sack two curates because of the poverty of the curates' fund: 'unless more money is forthcoming the parish of 10,000 will be left to himself a task which would be far beyond the powers of the most assiduous, able and energetic man that the Church could produce . . .' (B305, p. 227). It was essential to preserve pew rents and, therefore, to appeal to a prosperous congregation. This shortage of and poverty of ministers was common to all denominations. K. D. Brown has drawn our attention to the problems met by the Methodists in retaining their recruits (Brown, 1987, p. 241). Some of the Baptist and Methodist ministers interviewed in the survey were part-timers. They were forced to go out to work in other employment although they acknowledged the need for a full-time ministry (B304, pp. 51–5; pp. 67–71). The organization of other denominations was not necessarily more attuned to handling the problems peculiar to the city than was that of the Church of England. Ministers who remained with one congregation for a short time were likely to find the problems of 'getting to know the flock' even more acute than did the long resident clergymen. The circuit system of the Methodists was readily acknowledged to have this disadvantage. Sargent explained that, as head of a circuit and responsible for seven churches and missions, he had little or no time for visiting of individuals (B304, p. 115). It has been suggested that Congregationalist pastorates also tended to be short, because widely varying incomes and difficult relations with congregations encouraged ministerial mobility (Brown, 1983, pp. 13–15).

The education of ministers did not involve a practical pastoral component. The pastoral role was widely acknowledged but there was no teaching on how to be a pastor, especially in the new circumstances of Britain's big cities. In the Booth notebooks there is little evidence that the ministers encountered intellectual opposition to the faith that they preached but there is a good deal of evidence of the kinds of practical issues which ministerial training did nothing to address — how to win souls to Christ and retain their devotion despite the competing attractions of Victorian London. The

ministers concerned drew upon their personal qualities of human understanding, tolerance and compassion together with a certain pragmatism to
deal with these problems.

In conclusion I want to suggest that while it may be appropriate to
argue that the ministry was conscious of itself as a profession and that some
sections of the ministry were anxious to emphasize and develop the
'expertise' which the ministry possessed, we should not neglect other
aspects of the development of the ministry during the nineteenth and early
twentieth centuries. Even within the context of professionalization, this
would be dangerous. One feature of a profession is the professional/client
relationship. A profession is not simply a brotherhood of individuals with a
shared calling, expertise and code of ethics. It is a collection of individuals
sharing a particular relationship of authority and service with another
collection of individuals — the clients. Brian Heeney has shown that nineteenth-century Anglican clergy spent a good deal of their time in
'professional' gatherings discussing problems of pastoral care (Heeney,
1974, p. 216). By examining the ministries of individuals of all the leading
denominations we are able to come closer to an understanding of this
delicate professional/client relationship. For many of the clergy in Booth's
survey it was essentially a matter of give and take within a framework of the
pastor and his flock. One senses that for these men the service that they
offered (or felt that they were not offering particularly well) was far more
important than any appeal to the needs of professionalization as such.
While studies of the development of clerical education and training and of
the sense of cohesion felt by the ministers of the word are extremely important, therefore, it is time that we redressed the balance in favour of studying
the ministry on the ground. It was not until the twentieth century that
those in charge of the education of the clergy began to learn the lessons
taught by the experience of the pastoral ministry in the nineteenth century
— that ministers needed to be taught to be pastors as well as preachers of
sound doctrine and that some element of recruiting 'men of the people' as
well as men who could learn to speak to the people must play a part in any
successful programme for the preparation of Christian ministers.

BIBLIOGRAPHY

I have listed below works which are cited in the text. The reader will also find of use
items given in the bibliography to *RVB*, I, 5.

The following abbreviation has been used in the text:

B — refers to notebooks in the Charles Booth Collection, British Library of Political
and Economic Science, London School of Economics.

C. Booth (1902) *Life and Labour of the People in London*, 3rd Series, 7 Vols., Macmillan.

*K. D. Brown (1983) 'The Congregational ministry in the first half of the nineteenth century: a preliminary survey', *The Journal of the United Reformed Church History Society*, No. 1, pp. 2–15.

*K. D. Brown (1987) 'College principals — cause of nonconformist decay?' *Journal of Ecclesiastical History*, Vol. XX pp. 236–53.

*K. D. Brown (1987a) 'Ministerial recruitment and training: an aspect of the crisis of Victorian nonconformity', *Victorian Studies*, Vol. 30, pp. 365–83.

K. B. Garlick (1985) 'Ministerial training in Methodism and our colleges, 1834–1984', *Friends of Wesley's Chapel Annual Lecture*.

*A. Haig (1984) *The Victorian Clergy*, Croom Helm.

B. Heeney (1974) 'The theory of pastoral ministry in the mid-Victorian Church of England', *Historical Magazine of the Protestant Episcopal Church*, pp. 215–30.

D. A. Johnson (1982) 'The Methodist quest for an educated ministry', *Church History*, Vol. 51, No. 3. pp. 304–20.

G. E. Milburn (1981) 'A school for the prophets: the origins of ministerial education in the Primitive Methodist Church', Manchester, Hartley Victoria College.

*J. E. B. Munson (1978) 'The education of Baptist ministers, 1870–1900', *The Baptist Quarterly*, Vol. 26. pp. 320–7.

A. J. Russell (1980) *The Clerical Profession*, S.P.C.K.

CHAPTER 13

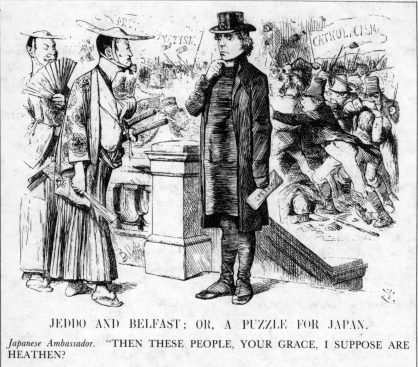

JEDDO AND BELFAST; OR, A PUZZLE FOR JAPAN.

Japanese Ambassador. "THEN THESE PEOPLE, YOUR GRACE, I SUPPOSE ARE HEATHEN?

Archbishop of Canterbury. "ON THE CONTRARY, YOUR EXCELLENCY: THOSE ARE AMONG OUR MOST *ENTHUSIASTIC RELIGIONISTS!*"

THE IMPACT OF OTHER RELIGIONS

A historian of our period has described it as 'The Age of Prestige and Expansion' (Thomson, 1950, ch. 8). The prestige he saw mainly in Europe, but the expansion covered considerable areas of the world and culminated in the British Empire. The same historian has noted of two of the high points of Victoria's reign, the Golden Jubilee of 1887 and the Diamond Jubilee of 1897, that in addition to the representatives of the new self-governing Dominions, the events were attended by 'Indian Rajahs and Burmese mandarins, Zulu chieftains and African headmen' (*ibid.*, p. 172). Prior to both events, Victoria had had conferred on her the title Empress of India. The expansion had much to do with straightforward migration and colonization, with the need of expanding trade with the colonies and other territories and with the development of imperial rivalry between the European powers. A historian of Christian missions referring to the same period said: 'The missionary enterprise of the Churches is always in a measure a reflection of their vigour, of their wealth, and of that power of conviction which finds expression in self-sacrifice and a willingness for adventurous service' (Neill, 1964, p. 323). The growth of British colonial power from about 1850 onwards matched an expansion of missionary activity unparalleled in the whole history of the Christian religion.

It is an exaggeration to say that the Christian religion advanced with the British flag. (There are plenty of exceptions to such an assertion. Even in India, where the religion did eventually enjoy imperial protection and patronage, the initial missionary endeavour took place in Danish territory because of the hostility towards missionaries shown by the East India Company.) These tentative missionary beginnings at the end of the eighteenth century became an increasingly confident expansion throughout the nineteenth century. By 1848 the Church Missionary Society claimed that it had accomplished the conversion of over 20,000 inhabitants of India. By this time a number of missionary societies were operating in many territories and their number grew astronomically by the end of Victoria's reign.

Neill suggests that there were five factors which contributed to this expansion. First, there was the supplanting of the East India Company by British government rule in India. Second, the door to China was opened by the treaties that ended the 'Opium' war with China in 1858. Third, there was the 'Second Evangelical Awakening', which began in the late 1850s in America, contributed to the intense revivalism which began in Ulster in 1859, and produced, among other things, new missionary societies, fresh support for the older ones and a surge of new recruits for all. Fourth, Japan was opened up by an agreement between the American government and that country. Fifth, there was a surge of Christian interest in Africa following the publication in 1857 of David Livingstone's *Missionary Travels and Researches in South Africa*, a direct result of which was the foundation of the Universities' Mission to Central Africa (Neill, *op. cit.*, pp. 323–5).

It is one of the ironies of the attempt to spread British political and mercantile influence and Christian religious and moral ideals that in order to govern, trade with and displace the religious beliefs of the new territories, government servants, merchants and missionaries had to study the religious faiths intended to be displaced by the Christian faith. What was intended to be a prelude to the destruction of alien, 'heathen' religions turned out to be a major force for the deeper study and popularization of those very religions in the west and their renaissance in their home territories. Even series of sermons in the City of London, for example, designed to 'be assisting to all companies, and encouraging them in any undertaking for propagating the Christian Religion to foreign parts', and essays designed to refute the claims of Hinduism and to 'establish the exclusive claims and authority of Christianity as an object of faith and rule of life to the whole of mankind', drew on the growing science of the study of religions and thus themselves added to and advanced the study of those religions.

In order to propagate the Christian faith among different linguistic groups the languages of these groups had to be learned and this process aided the publication of the scriptures of these religions in the original languages and in translation. *The Times*, reviewing books published by Trübner's of Glasgow in their 'Oriental Series' in the 1870s, compared the needs of the general reader of the classics of Latin and Greek with the current generation's need to study the Sanskrit classics. Trübner's, *The Times* went on, 'in a spirit of enterprise which does them infinite credit, have determined to supply the constantly-increasing want, and to give in a popular or, at least, a comprehensive form, all this mass of knowledge to the world.' Factors other than missionary expansion which led to the growth of interest in other religions included the intellectual interest of educated people in the new information on different cultures that was becoming available, the desire to apply the canons of scientific evolution to human cultures, especially the religious aspects of those cultures, and simple curiosity concerning the exotic. Taking all these developments into account we find that the period which saw the greatest expansion of the Christian religion in geographical terms also saw the greatest growth in the study of religions other than Christianity. The irony is that the religion which set out to supplant all other religions itself came under the impact of its rivals.

The impact was not evenly distributed and in some cases it is not easy to evaluate. Judaism is an interesting case. As the religion of the Christian Old Testament it presented a particular problem. To attack, let alone condemn, Judaism would in a real sense be to attack the very basis of the Christian religion itself. As David Englander has pointed out in an essay on Anglo-Jewry in Victorian Britain (*RVB*, I, 7), Christians had to find a way of rejecting Judaism without rejecting its historical base. To a very large extent, although adherents of Judaism were present in Britain in much larger numbers than any of the other major religions, the Christian attitude was to marginalize the Jewish religion in contrast to the detailed attention paid to some of the others. The volume of academic study and writing on the other religions far exceeded that on Judaism. The Christian Old Testament, the Hebrew Bible, of course was extensively studied, but the study of Judaism as a living religion hardly existed at all. In the sixty or so titles in Trübner's 'Oriental Series' Judaism figured no more prominently than Zoroastrianism in its Parsi (Indian) form, or the religion of ancient Egypt.

Islam was also a special case. There had been a history of conflict not only with Islam as a religion but also with those territories in which Islam predominated. From the time of the Crusades, Islam had perpetrated attacks against the Christian religion and since the fall of Constantinople in 1453 had posed a potential threat to Europe. As a result, there had been a history of deep animosity from Christianity towards Islam: this attitude of conflict persisted throughout our period, though there was considerable academic study of the religion under continental European influence. One of the more prominent exponents of this academic study was Thomas Carlyle who, under the influence of Goethe, defended Islam and Muhammad against their Christian detractors.

Not all religions that came within the orbit of British expansion were treated in the same way. The tribal religions of Africa and the Caribbean, for example, posed no intellectual, religious or political challenge. They were classified even by the most sympathetic anthropologist as 'primitive' and not in the same class as the 'high' religions, Islam, Hinduism and Buddhism, for example. The adherents of such 'primitive' religions were looked upon as much more pliable objects of proselytization and indeed were converted to Christianity in significant numbers in a way in which the adherents of the so-called 'high' religions never were, nor have been to this day. Of the 'high' religions, Hinduism and Buddhism had never been a threat to Christianity by their presence though they had been of intellectual and exotic interest for some time. Hinduism, being the religion of the territory regarded as the jewel in the imperial crown, came in for special treatment. More than any other of the 'high' religions, it became the object of intense missionary activity. Its impact was thus a complex one. It presented a religious and intellectual challenge to the West but it was also an example of the worst kind of 'idolatry' according to some minds. Buddhism was known largely for its intellectual challenge, was not known for gross 'idolatry', and was not a significant object of missions. The only other 'high' religious traditions which received attention in a significant way were those of Confucius and Lao Tze after the opening up of China, again mainly for philosophical reasons.

The way in which the impact was responded to on the Christian side was by no means uniform. Generally speaking the impact was met in three ways. First, there was the response of those who had a pastoral responsibility within the churches. Their response was essentially conservative, consisting partly of condemnation of other religions and partly of commendation of the Christian religion: a mixture of the pastoral and the polemical. Their response is found mainly in sermons and addresses, especially those addressed to members and supporters of missionary organizations. Second, there were those who also saw their task as pastoral, but who approached the task in a more liberal way, demonstrating the superiority of Christianity by a more rational, dialectical approach. Other religions were not condemned out of hand. Their religious claims were examined with a certain amount of academic dispassion. Ultimately they were all judged to fall short of what is true and perfect but they were allowed to retain some of their dignity and honesty. Third, there was a group of scholars, few at first but growing in numbers as our period progressed, who studied religion for its own sake. Some of these scholars eschewed any personal religious belief, although the work of those we shall be looking at was related directly to the Christian religion. They tried to engage in objective study — often referred to as 'scientific study' — of other religions, from their various disciplines, which included evolutionary anthropology, comparative religion, science of religion, history of religion and what is today called the phenomenology of religion. In this essay we shall be looking at some of the more prominent members of each of these three groups,[1] in order to gauge the impact of other religions on different sectors of Victorian Christianity.

I   PASTORAL AND POLEMICAL

The pressures of the Gospel command to 'make disciples of all nations' (Matthew, 28:19) made allies of churchmen of all kinds who viewed the other religions in almost identical light. It brought together High Church bishops such as Samuel Wilberforce and Christopher Wordsworth (nephew of the poet William), missionaries such as the Anglican Bishop Caldwell of Madras and the Congregationalist Joseph Mullens of Calcutta, evangelical Baptists such as Charles Spurgeon, and liberal Congregationalists such as R. W. Dale. All these, including Dale in this context, might be reckoned the conservative response to the impact of other religions. There is no attempt made to understand the other religions from their own perspective. Scrip-

---

[1] It should be recognized, however, that the division into groups does not mean rigid boundaries. The aims and motivations frequently overlap the divisions. The first and second groups, in particular, have much in common, their differences being to a large extent a matter of style and method. There is even, however, a partial overlap between the first two groups and one scholar in the third group.

ture read in a pre-critical way is viewed as rigorous in its demand for the condemnation of everything that is not Christian and the conversion of everyone who is not a Christian.

Spurgeon, in a sermon preached on Guy Fawkes' Day, 1854, takes the opportunity to attack 'Popery' but also any other religious or philosophical force which might challenge the Christian religion. Both Judaism and Islam are seen as threats to Christianity. Judaism is seen as something that had to be opposed by the early church but now has to be condemned, because its 'doctrines are now effete'. Islam, on the other hand, is the invention of Satan, 'in order to oppose the truth'. The church has condemned it also and now it is 'a bloated carcase, almost without life, not able to stand. The cross made the crescent wane' (Spurgeon, 1856, pp. 54-5).

Samuel Wilberforce, Bishop of Oxford (later a leading protagonist against the contributors to *Essays and Reviews*: see *RVB*, I, 1 and II, 9) in 1848 preached a sermon to members of the London Society for Promoting Christianity among the Jews. As might be expected, he argues strongly for a more successful mission to the Jews, but in effect blames the suffering and degradation endured by the Jews over the centuries on their refusal to accept Jesus as the Christ, and for submitting themselves to Talmudic and Rabbinic teaching 'in which the most fantastic legends of frivolous superstition are mixed with the dead generalities of the poorest deism'. Wilberforce claims that even in Britain, where 'the coarseness of more brutal times has passed away', Jews

> live dishonoured lives, by pandering to the worst vices of the most corrupt members of society. Their very aspect, that sad countenance, that downcast look, that hollow voice, bespeak the long inwrought results of ages of contempt and suffering. It seems to declare. . .that they who were the highest favoured of all nations, are now a people from whom God's face has long been turned away.
>
> (Wilberforce, 1854, p.224)

Wilberforce admits that much of the suffering inflicted on the Jews has been the work of Christians and that this should be a cause of shame, not for the offences themselves, but because of the hindrance it causes in converting Jews to the Christian religion.

The impact of Islam[2] on Europe was political as well as religious. In the summer of 1876 Turkish irregulars massacred between 12,000 and 30,000

[2] In the nineteenth century terms relating to other religions show a variety of spellings. Contemporary religious studies have regularized the terms and the following will be used in this essay except in quotations of the original text: Muhammad, Islam (Mahometanism, in various spellings, should never be used), Qur'an, Hinduism, Buddha.

Bulgarian Christians in reprisals for refusing to pay taxes to the Ottoman government. A few weeks later, Christopher Wordsworth, Bishop of Lincoln, preached a sermon on the topic 'The Mohammedan Woe and its Passing Away.' The sermon is an interpretation of a 'prophecy' in the Book of Revelations concerning some future woe which involves the ravaging of the land by scorpions and locusts and fearsome cavalry. The prophecy, Wordsworth maintains, is widely acknowledged as referring to the rise of Islam. He sustains the common view that the rise of Islam was largely due to the existence of heretical forms of Christianity at the time of Muhammad. Therefore, Islam 'was used by God as a scourge to sting like the scorpion, and as a plague to spread like locusts, and to chastise degenerate churches' (Wordsworth, 1876, p. 7). Wordsworth has very little positive to say of Islam but concentrates on its use by God as a judgement on heresy and on the command in the Qur'an to wage war on infidels: 'Has not this command been recently in the minds of Turkish pashas, and have they not thought that they had mission from God to execute it?' (*ibid.*, p. 18). The bishop sees some virtues in Islam, namely the strength with which belief in 'Divine omnipotence, omnipresence and omniscience' is held and the reverence which is shown to the Qur'an. He wishes that Christians would show the same depth of belief and reverence the Bible in the same way (*ibid.*, pp. 26-7). However, his last word is a prayer for the touching of the hearts of the Turks, that 'they should turn from the false prophet to the True, from the Koran to the Bible, from Mohammed to Christ'. Such a conversion 'would be an answer to the scepticism of the age, and a new proof of the Divine origin of the Gospel' (*ibid.*, pp. 27-8).

Bishop R. Caldwell, assistant Bishop of Madras, India, in the 1870s, was anxious to offset the intellectual attractions which philosophical Hinduism had for many Western thinkers. He attacked Friedrich Max Müller, whom we will look at in our third group, for questioning the religious claims made by the Christian religion and the way in which Christian missions were carried on. The bishop recognized in Hinduism three elements which were in a struggle for supremacy. There was the ordinary human element, the ordinary principles, sentiments and practices which, according to Caldwell's Christian standards, did not raise the Hindu very high. Then there was a higher element which could only be regarded as divine, for example 'the habit of seeing God in all things, and all things in God', but which could be traced largely to the influence of Christianity. Finally there was 'an element which can be scarcely described otherwise than as diabolical', for example the sensuous worship of Krishna. 'There is hardly a virtue that is not praised in some Indian book; but on the other hand, there is hardly a crime that is not encouraged by the example of some Indian divinity,' including the worship of devil or evil spirits (Caldwell, 1874, p. 7). The bishop admits that he does not know when the influence of Christianity on

Hinduism took place. The truth is that he is only speculating because he cannot conceive of Hinduism arriving at its 'higher elements', by which he means thoughts of faith and grace in the Hindu text, the *Bhagavad Gita*, without the influence of Christianity.[3]

The Rev. Joseph Mullens was a London Missionary Society missionary in Calcutta. He competed for prizes for essays refuting the claims of Hinduism and establishing the claims of Christianity. He was also involved in a controversy which followed the Indian Mutiny, or the First War of Indian Independence, in 1857. The controversy surrounded a Royal Proclamation issued by the Queen which dealt with many problems of government and law but also with religion. This part of the Proclamation read:

> Firmly relying ourselves on the truth of Christianity, and acknowledging with gratitude the solace of religion, we disclaim alike the right and the desire to impose our convictions on any of our subjects. We declare it to be our royal will and pleasure, that none be in anywise favoured, none molested or disquieted, by reason of their religious faith or observances; but that all shall alike enjoy the equal and impartial protection of the law. And we do strictly charge and enjoin all those who may be in authority under us, that they abstain from all interference with the religious belief, or worship, of any of our subjects on pain of our severest displeasure.
>
> (Mullens, 1859, p. 11)[4]

Mullens felt that this statement was ambiguous and open to more than one interpretation. While he welcomed the Queen's own avowal of Christianity, he would have preferred a clearer assertion of the status of Christianity as 'the only revelation from Heaven', and instead of some vague statement of solace derived from religious belief, a clear statement of the importance of 'the doctrines and promises of the Bible specially named'. He then proceeded to criticize the British government on their attitude to caste and for allowing Hindus to enjoy free time on their religious holidays. 'It must strike all thinking men, that to give holiday from public duties on days of heathen festivals, gives honour to the festivals, and associates with them notions of rest and enjoyment; their observance therefore tends to honour the idols celebrated as the days return'(*ibid.*, p. 21). Although Mullens was speaking of events in India, his words were published in

---

[3] In fact such influence never has been proved and modern scholars don't even consider it a possibility.

[4] See also Neill, 1964, pp. 323–4.

London and therefore helped to shape the British Christian response to Hinduism.

To label this group conservative and polemical is to identify them with the mainstream of the Christian religion in Britain in the nineteenth century. To take such an attitude towards other religions would have been considered by most Christians at that time to be 'orthodox', consonant with the demands of the Gospel and true to the vocation of imperial Britain. Members of this group were conservative and polemical in comparison with members of the two other groups that have been identified in this essay.

II PASTORAL AND LIBERAL

In this group are included F. D. Maurice, Rowland Williams and A. P. Stanley. Each of these persons engaged in some way with the impact of other religions and in contrast to the previous group may be appropriately described as 'liberal'. To call them liberal is, in one sense, merely to say that they were not conservative, and that they adopted a critical attitude towards Christian scripture, Christian doctrine, or both. This critical attitude goes some way towards explaining the way in which they dealt with the significance of other religions. These three clergymen, like their conservative co-religionists, were each engaged in an apologetic exercise on behalf of the Christian religion. Their language, however, is less condemnatory of other religions than those in the previous group, even if their final judgement is also based on the absolute demands of the Christian religion.

In one way or another these three, Maurice, Williams and Stanley, had a pastoral motivation in common with Wilberforce, Wordsworth and Spurgeon. In other words, they were straightforward Christian pastors or theologians with an apologetic vocation, i.e. they were paid to propagate and interpret the Christian faith. They were not professional historians of religion or paid to engage in comparative religion. Their task was to demonstrate the superiority of the Christian religion. To demonstrate anything else would have been an act of apostasy. Doing this by engaging in a comparative study of other religions was one aspect of their overall pastoral and theological task. Stanley was aware of the demands facing the church in response to the impact of other religions but did not engage in a detailed study himself. The other two only did so in a way that was tangential to their everyday task as theologians.

A. P. Stanley made his own attitude plain more than once in sermons on the mission of the Christian church. In a sermon in 1872 on 'Prospects of Christian Missions' he gave a number of grounds for greater confidence for the future of missions. We need look at only two. The first concerned the extinction of 'the once universal belief that all heathens were everlastingly lost', an advance which gave a better knowledge of 'the Divine nature'. The second concerned 'the increased acquaintance with the heathen religions themselves' (quoted in Max-Müller, 1873, p. 1). This second ground, the straightforward acquisition of knowledge, reflected what was happening in Stanley's day and what had been going on for some time as a result of imperial expansion. The first ground reflected the changes which had been occurring in certain forms of liberal theology going back to the influence of Friedrich Schleiermacher in Germany and Samuel Taylor Coleridge in Britain. Stanley commended both as a way forward in the missionary expansion of the church. He thought that the works of Maurice and Williams exemplified his own views and considered them as models of how to approach other religions.

It is not easy to define exactly F. D. Maurice's ideological stance. In the single work which he produced in this area of discourse he set out his programme on the basis that 'Faith is ...the most potent instrument for good to the world; has given to it nearly all which it can call precious.' He raises the question of whether there is

> ...not ground for supposing that all the different religious systems, and not one only, may be legitimate .products of that faith which is so essential a part of man's constitution? Are they not manifestly adapted to peculiar times and localities and races ?...Have we not reason to suppose that Christianity, instead of being, as we have been taught, a Revelation, has its roots in the heart and intellect of man, as much as any other system?
>
> (Maurice, 1852, p. 9)

It must be remembered, however, that, despite these questions about the cultural relativity of religions, Maurice's essential programme was set for him by the terms of the seventeenth century scientist Robert Boyle's will, under which the sermons given by Maurice were established. The preacher was to prove the Christian religion 'against notorious Infidels, to wit, Atheists, Theists, Pagans, Jews and Mahometans'. Maurice accordingly sets himself to examine Judaism, Islam, Hinduism and Buddhism, though Judaism does not receive as detailed a treatment as the others. He looks at all of them from the point of view of revelation and whether the Christian religion should give way to them.

Judaism and Islam are seen to have revelation in some sense. The Jews obviously were recipients of the same revelation that lies behind Christianity. Muhammad is defended by Maurice against the charge of plagiarism on the grounds that though what he believed was heavily reliant on the Judaeo-Christian revelation, nevertheless Muhammad made it his own to such an extent that it has the mark of revelation, by which he means that it is acknowledged that all 'is set forth as coming *from* [God]; He is, and He is doing...'. Maurice found this a particularly powerful part of the message of Muhammad. Furthermore Muhammad proclaims unequivocally the irrefutable Will of God. In Maurice's final analysis, however, Judaism is disqualified because it stopped short of the final stage of progress from an origin in a personal Being to a completion in a Person, i.e. Jesus as the Christ. Maurice's evaluation of Judaism differs very little from what we have seen in Wilberforce, even down to incipient anti-semitism. The Jews may think that they cling to the belief that God spoke to their fathers, but, 'Systems, rabbinical and philosophical, may choke that belief; money getting habits almost extinguish it' (Maurice, 1852, p. 152). Islam is disqualified on the grounds that the Divine Will is not seen to be a Loving Will 'fully manifested in the person of a man', and that the 'Divine and universal kingdom' inaugurated by this act of Loving Will is set at nought, is treated 'as mere imagination which outrages all simplicity'. Christianity is able to 'avenge the outrages and injuries of Islamism, preserving the precious fragments of truth which are lodged in it'.

Maurice sees in Hinduism the notion of Wisdom or Intelligence which is comparable to Jewish Wisdom. He also finds in the idea of the 'twice-born' a point of comparison with the Christian notion of 'being born again', except that only the higher castes enjoy twice-born status in Hinduism whereas it belongs to the whole body of the Church in Christianity. There are in Hinduism also notions of Incarnation and Sacrifice and it is in this last area that he sees that the 'controversy with Hindooism turns'. In Hinduism he sees only the terrifying aspects of the propitiation of Siva, which can errupt at any time in the 'form of terrifying wickedness in the likeness of some Man-God' (*ibid.*, 1852, p. 182).

This is contrasted with 'Christian Sacrifice, the sacrifice of the God-Man' (*ibid*). His conclusion is that the alternative for India and for England is quite simply 'whether we hold a system of opinions or a revelation from God' (*ibid.*, p. 184).

Buddhism fares little better at Maurice's hands. He sees in Buddhism's break with Hinduism an analogy for the Christian break with Judaism at Pentecost. The Spirit which came down at Pentecost figures very prominently in his treatment of Buddhism, since he finds in that religion 'a profound feeling of reverence for the human spirit'. This spirit, according to Buddhism, has great capacity, is not confined to one class or race, is in some sense divine. Buddhism shows 'the privilege of the divine man to contemplate the Divinity in His purity' by separating the mind from outward sensual things. This power of contemplation has been seen in the Buddhas. These and other beliefs that Maurice finds in Buddhism are matched and superseded by Christianity (*ibid.*, pp. 198-201). The big difference is that whereas the Buddhist sees these beliefs arising from a human ground, the matching beliefs in Christianity start from the divine ground. Spirit is the Spirit of Pentecost. The Buddhas are the saints, 'partakers of the ... Spirit'. The differences are summed up in the difference between 'the naked idea of a Spirit dwelling in man and identical with himself, and the idea of Him as given to men by the Eternal God through his Son'. There is, according to Maurice, a Buddhist side of Christianity as there are Islamic and Hindu sides, he can even speak of 'Christian Buddhism'. Original Buddhism, however, has been distorted by the *sangha* (the monastery community), by the fanatical exaltation of spiritual emotions and in the exercise of such human faculties as government and vision (*ibid.*, pp. 203-17).

Rowland Williams adopts an attitude which is reminiscent of the Apologists among the Early Church Fathers. His attitude is summed up in a passage in a sermon dealing with the person of Christ:

> He [Christ] concentrates and exhibits in his life, in his doctrine, in his death, and in the Holy Spirit whereby He ever lives, and wherewith He animates the whole body of His Church, the Divine perfection of those excellences, of which fragments, and shadows, and images, are scattered throughout the world elsewhere.
>
> (Williams, 1855, p. 395)

He further demonstrates his attitude in a passage from his notorious essay on Bunsen, the German diplomat and biblical critic, in *Essays and Reviews*.

> We cannot encourage a remorseless criticism of Gentile histories and escape its contagion when we approach Hebrew annals; nor acknowledge a Providence in Jewry without owning that it may have comprehended sanctities elsewhere. But the moment we examine fairly the religions of India and of Arabia ... we find they appealed to the better side of our nature and their essential strength lay in the elements of good which they contained, rather than in any satanic corruption.
>
> (*op. cit.*, p. 51)

Unlike Maurice, Williams did believe that other religions contained divine revelation, though the meaning he gave to revelation may be deemed less than orthodox according to the norms of his age. In his main work, a dialogue between a number of Christians and Hindus and a Buddhist (Williams, 1856), one of the characters in the dialogue is believed to express Williams' own view of revelation, which is a shift from the usual positive sense of revelation 'into a kind of spiritual growth, or something that more nearly resembles some Indian theories of a Divine spirit pervading and elevating humanity' (op. cit., p. 522).

Williams, like many of his contemporaries, treated Buddhism as a sect of Hinduism. Buddhism is seen as a reform movement in relation to Hinduism but not quite in the way seen by Maurice. In dialogue with the Buddhist monk, Blancome, the foremost of the Christian participants, attacks Buddhist doctrine, basing the attack on the usual Christian response that Buddhism is essentially a religion of 'total perishableness', such 'a dreary prospect'. If Sakya, the Buddha, preached such a doctrine then he could hardly be acknowledged as a deliverer. Even miracles claimed for the Buddha do not qualify him as 'a moral Governor of the world', for they can only be strange products of nature and 'convey no message'. 'The very contents of your doctrine then seem to negative the possibility of its being a Divine Revelation', whereas 'our sacred books which record this revelation of the Word of God made man, have all the characteristics which you thought might suit a Divine message' (ibid., pp. 528-31).

Blancome rejects the authority of the Hindu scriptures, partly because of the historical problems but also because they proclaim divinities like the sky, or storm, or fire, or some creature and create a bewildering mixture of 'conflicting deifications, an idol perhaps for the crowd, and a vague spiritualization for the few'. But even in this confusion it is not unlikely that the Spirit of God, which is, 'as Christ has taught us, like the *wind* which *bloweth where it listeth*', has given the Hindus a 'good hope for eternal life', and a hope of being delivered:

> Such a hope perchance you have; but it is Christ which brings us the deliverance, and gives us the gift. Might I not then say, your prophecies, or at least your desires, are fulfilled in Him.
>
> (ibid., p. 541)

In the dialogue there is a whole chapter in which the Buddhist monk is allowed to list eight objections to Christian belief so that while characters like Blancome are hard-hitting in their criticism of Buddhism and Hinduism the opposite view is allowed to be put. It may be worth noting that the objections to the Christian religion are objections to its Calvinistic expressions which are, of course, easily refuted as not characteristic of the proper Christian religion, i.e. Williams' own brand.

Towards the end of the dialogue, Blancome, 'after leaving to the Hindu religion only such power as the little elements of truth scattered through it may have to recommend themselves', goes on, in a series of propositions, to recommend Christianity as in origin divine, and points, for instance, to mission work which is why the 'Governor of the world gave into the hand of our Sovereign the sceptre of India'. Seeing the empire as a part of the

Christian missionary vocation was a common feature of the Christian religion in Britain throughout the nineteenth century.

In a final appeal Williams offers a number of convergent issues which might help the Hindu accept Christianity. There is, for example, the Hindu belief in *vach*, the Word proceeding forth from Brahma. This is not opposed to Christianity, indeed it might prepare Hindus to apprehend belief in the *logos* as expressed in St John's Gospel:

> With submission at least to wiser people, I do not think it a greater tampering with mixture of distinct systems, than the early Church doctors permitted themselves in setting forth the life of Christ after the phrase of Plato, if I say that your Vach appears a prophecy, or expression, of the everliving Word of God.
>
> (*ibid.*, p. 554)

What the Hindu says of incarnations, though they be 'poor expressions of the allholy and everblessed Spirit', might help them to understand the action that took place in Jesus. What is retained of the old 'superstitions' must either be able to stand in the light of 'clear reason' or must be reconciled with the faith of Christ, which rests on such clear 'Divine warrants'. Of course there are also numerous divergences. That Hinduism 'spares and even cherishes such things as idolatry is at best weakness; and weakness to such an extent in a religion is falsehood'. Williams cannot be expected, any more than Maurice, to give anything but primacy to the Christian religion, but his approach, which hardly received any attention after his fall from grace over *Essays and Reviews*, can now be seen as the embryo of much that followed in the twentieth century in the field of interreligious encounter and dialogue.

The persons dealt with in this second group represent a wider collection of clergy and theologians who were interested in the implications of the greater awareness of the presence of other religions in the world for the Christian religion. Such clergy were more active in the earlier part of the nineteenth century. While Maurice's work continued to be reprinted, Williams' work was soon forgotten. In the aftermath of the publication of *Essays and Reviews* the contributors planned a second volume in the same critical mould. For the second volume Friedrich Max Müller was recruited to write on other religions. That venture came to nothing and hardly any theologians after Maurice and Williams paid any attention to other religions. Indeed, neither Maurice nor Williams integrated their work on other religions into their own theology. As far as the churches were concerned, the other religions, being the religions of subject races, were not worth any attention. Along with Judaism they were marginalized in the latter part of the century. Christian theology continued to be written as if unchallenged by any other theology. Christian clergy were trained in complete ignorance of any other religion. Only in missionary circles was there any attention paid. Even after the Edinburgh Missionary Conference of 1910, when the challenge of other religions was forcefully put by those who considered themselves in the front line of the worldwide Christian endeavour, it took another fifty years and the migration of considerable numbers of Hindus, Muslims and Sikhs to Britain before the churches began seriously to take up where Maurice and Williams had left off a hundred years before. As far as the serious and detailed study of world religions in Britain was concerned, the subject became virtually the exclusive preserve of the don and the academic.

III THE ACADEMIC STUDY OF OTHER RELIGIONS

Scholars engaged in the academic study of religion, referred to as 'comparative religion' or the 'science of religion', included M. Monier-Williams, T. W. Rhys Davids and Friedrich Max Müller. These three and others like them were employed as academics in the study and teaching of other religions, although two of them, Max Müller and Monier-Williams, were also adherents of the Christian religion. Monier-Williams allowed his Christianity to obtrude into his studies and dilute his attempted neutrality, while Max Müller found himself in conflict with those who were primarily concerned with the problems of doctrine or belief resulting from the impact of other religions, and especially with those whose own stance in the matter was conservative. Rhys Davids was probably not an adherent of the Christian religion (his own religious views were obscure) but his approach to the study of religion nevertheless had important implications for Christianity.

One of the intriguing facts of our topic, which relates directly to two of the scholars in this group, is that knowledge of other religions was popularly made available to the British Christian public, more popularly than Trübner's series, by an organization founded, sustained and committed to the promotion of *Christian* knowledge, namely the S.P.C.K. Between 1877 and 1900 nine titles covering Buddhism, Islam, Hinduism, Confucianism and Taoism were published in the series *Non-Christian Religious Systems*. Monier-Williams' volume *Hinduism* was among the first of this series and went through thirteen impressions between 1877 and 1899. Another volume which became a classic of its kind, *Buddhism: Being a Sketch of the Life and Teachings of Gautama, the Buddha*, by T. W. Rhys Davids, was published in 1877 and had sold 22,000 copies by 1910. Thus, in spite of what was said about the response of the churches to the impact of other religions at the end of the previous section, in the last quarter of our period the potential for the impact of other religions on the indigenous religion of Britain was very considerable.

Max Müller and Monier-Williams were competitors for the Chair of Sanskrit in the University of Oxford in 1860, the latter securing the appointment. The two scholars remained in contention over their respective approaches to the study of other religions. Max Müller's emphasis on language as the key to understanding religion was soon discredited but his emphasis on the study of religious texts persisted. He is remembered not so much for his conceptual approach to the study of religions as for his leadership in the publication of a massive corpus of translations of oriental classics. His *Sacred Books of the East* gave an English-speaking readership access to a huge resource of material with which to study the religions of the East. His influence led to over-emphasis (both in the late Victorian period and in the twentieth century) on the importance of religious texts as a way of studying other religions and to the neglect of the study of religions as living communities. By comparison, Monier-Williams concentrated much more on the study of Hinduism as a living religion and provided the base for the scholarly understanding of Sanskrit-based religions with his massive *Sanskrit-English Dictionary*. In his work as a whole he is to be classified more as a phenomenologist of religion. In the preface to his dictionary he provides a glimpse of the tension between himself and Max Müller when in reply to the critics who wished he had devoted his time to translating Hindu texts he said that anyone who regarded such an enterprise as a guarantee of scholarship should go to India, something Max Müller never did, and 'associate with Indian pandits in their own country and ... find out that far severer proofs of knowledge and acquirements will be required of him there' (Monier-Williams, 1899, p. ix).

Max Müller and Monier-Williams also differed in their evaluation of the study of religions *vis-à-vis* the Christian religion. The former believed that Christianity should be studied in the same way as every other religion. Indeed, he went further than this and questioned the integrity of missionaries who tried to convert to the Christian religion those whom he considered to be living lives above reproach in their own religion (see *RVB*, III, 8.3.2). It was this kind of sentiment and his belief that all religions equally, including Christianity, sprang from 'the sacred soil of the human heart', that brought him condemnation from churchmen such as Bishop Caldwell. Caldwell, incidentally, condemned Monier-Williams for publishing a book entitled *Indian Wisdom* (1857), which, he claimed, showed only one side of Hinduism, 'for it would be easy to compile from the same sources not one volume of extracts merely, but many, which should be worthy of being entitled "Indian Folly"' (Caldwell, 1879, p. 10).

Monier-Williams, though he saw himself as an objective student of Hinduism, believed that the Hindus were 'a profoundly religious people', that their religion would 'stir the depths of the heart, and give room for the exercise of faith and love', resented Hindus being classed as 'heathen', nevertheless was committed to the primacy of the Christian religion in a way that Max Müller was not. It has been suggested that the Oxford chair was awarded to Monier-Williams rather than to Max-Müller because the former was considered more orthodox, though the contest was also complicated by the fact that Max Müller was a German and in league with the contributors to *Essays and Reviews* (Ellis, 1980, p. 157). Monier-Williams' inaugural lecture as Professor of Sanskrit was a detailed argument advocating the teaching of that language to every missionary bound for India so that they would be better able to persuade and dispute with the educated Hindu pandits. Another example of his advocacy of the Christian religion is seen in his excellent little book *Hinduism*, which is still worth reading as an introduction to the study of that religion. Having outlined the complexities of Hinduism, even down to a detailed list of major shrines and festivals, in the last two and a half pages he turns to a prediction that Hinduism is 'tottering and ready to fall', a condemnation of 'the degrading tendencies of idolatry', and a call to Christianity to step in quickly and win the souls of Indians before the 'Muhammadans' do it (*op.cit.*, pp. 184–6).

Thomas William Rhys Davids was like Monier-Williams in that he was completely devoted to his subject and had learned much of it 'in the field': he had gone to Sri Lanka to work as a colonial civil servant early in life, had learned Pali there and had studied the local form of Buddhism. But he was different in a very important respect: although he was the son of a Welsh Congregationalist minister he was not committed to the Christian religion. (Although he was a founder member and first President of the Buddhist Society of Great Britain and Ireland, it seems likely that he was not a Buddhist either.) He has been described as a freethinker, a not unusual description of a nineteenth century intellectual, nor unusual in an offspring of Welsh Congregationalism with its more than a dash of rationalistic Unitarianism.

Rhys Davids regarded himself as a historian of religious beliefs and he referred to the method he employed as 'the comparative study of religious beliefs'. While he espoused the comparative method he condemned certain ways of using comparison, in particular the way in which many scholars of a previous generation and of his own employed a subtle, and sometimes not too subtle, form of religious imperialism. They identified aspects of other religions which appeared to be similar to those of the Christian religion and deemed them to have been borrowed from the latter. He quoted the example of a Jesuit father who was struck by the similarity between Tibetan Buddhist and Roman Catholic ritual and deduced that the Tibetans had been deluded by the devil who led them to 'a blasphemous imitation of the religion of Christ' (Rhys Davids, 1891, p. 3). He was equally condemnatory of the use of comparison to suggest that there was a basis of 'universal and catholic beliefs' held by the majority of religious people. 'In matters of religious belief it is scarcely ever the majority of men, far less all men, who are usually right. On the contrary, the minorities have time on their side ...' (*ibid.*, p. 7).

Rhys Davids gave no priority or superiority to the Christian religion. If he referred to the Christian religion at all it was merely to use some familiar knowledge as an analogy for unfamiliar knowledge. Furthermore, he treated Christianity as he would any other religion in his general comments on the history of religions. He believed that all the major religious 'systems', 'Stoicism, Christianity, Comtism, Confucianism, Buddhism and all the rest' had failed, had completely disappointed the hopes of their founders and early adherents. While they had failure in common they had very little else. The striking thing about them was how much they differed in the particulars and the differences arose from, 'the one thing in which they are most essentially alike ... each is the natural outcome of an immeasurable past' (*ibid.*, p. 31). He admitted that such a view would only be accepted by those, like Max Müller, for instance, who believed that the history of Christianity should be treated like the history of any other religion. In other words such treatment was bound to be resisted by the Christian faithful. But given the increasing influence of the ethos of the European Enlightenment, with its questioning of moral or religious absolutes and the tendency to relativize cultural expression, Rhys Davids' approach to the study of religion was one that was bound to gain ground and even if it did not make a major impact on the dominant religion of Victorian Britain, the effect of his general approach to the study of religions has been considerable. In particular, his influence on the study of Buddhism persists to this day. What was seen in Rowland Williams as a liberal approach to other religions while retaining the primacy of the Christian religion, in Rhys Davids has become a full blown history of religions.

IV CONCLUSION

By 1900 attitudes towards other religions embraced a wide range of variations. In the main the impact of other religions was not really felt by the churches. Moreover, in some respects it is almost a coincidence that two of the main figures in this essay, Maurice and Williams, are treated at so much length. In each case their writing on other religions in fact arose from an external motivation, namely the requirements of the preaching of a series of sermons or the writing of a prize essay. The links between their work on other religions and their work on their own religion are at best tenuous, with Williams showing in his theology a more systematic basis for the treatment of other religions. In spite of the influence of Maurice and Williams, however, interest in other religions from pastors and theologians declined from what it had been in the early part of our period. In almost equal proportion, interest in the academic study of other religions grew and there was a growing general readership of books on comparative religion. The Victorian period could have provided Britain with the resources for meeting the influx of the adherents of some of the religions concerned in the second half of the twentieth century. Instead, the British population was almost entirely unprepared and uneducated in the face of a quiet, and in places not so quiet, social and religious revolution. Much of the racism experienced in Britain today is a survival of old imperial attitudes and a continuing intolerance towards the religions of the old empire which might have been better understood if some of the opportunities present in the nineteenth century had been taken up and not ignored.

BIBLIOGRAPHY

R. Caldwell (1874) *The Relation of Christianity to Hinduism*, R. Clay, Sons, and Taylor.

R. Caldwell (1879) *Christianity and Hinduism*, S.P.C.K.

I. Ellis (1980) *Seven Against Christ*, Brill, Leiden.

F. D. Maurice (1852) *On the Religions of the World*, Cambridge, Macmillan.

F. Max-Müller (1873) *On Missions* (with an introductory sermon 'The end and the means of Indian Missions' by A. P. Stanley), Longman, Green and Co.

M. Monier-Williams (1877) *Hinduism*, S.P.C.K.

M. Monier-Williams (1875) Indian Wisdom, Allen and Co.

M. Monier-Williams (1899) *A Sanskrit-English Dictionary*, Oxford, The Clarendon Press.

J. Mullens (1859) *The Queen's Government and the Religions of India*, Ward and Co.

S. Neill (1964) *A History of Christian Missions*, Penguin, Harmondsworth.

T. W. Rhys Davids (1877) *Buddhism*, S.P.C.K.

T. W. Rhys Davids (1891) *Lectures on the Origin and Growth of Religion*, Williams and Norgate.

C. H. Spurgeon (1856) *Sermons*, Vol. 1, James Paul (Alabaster and Passmore).

D. Thompson (1978) *England in the Nineteenth Century* (first published 1950), revised edn., Harmondsworth, Penguin.

S. Wilberforce (1854) *Sermons Preached and Published on Several Occasions*, London.

R. Williams (1855) *Rational Godliness after the Mind of Christ and the Written Voices of His Church*, London and Cambridge.

R. Williams (1856) *A Dialogue of the Knowledge of the Supreme Lord in Which are Compared the Claims of Christianity and Hinduism*, Cambridge, Deighton Bell and Co.

R. Williams (1861) 'Bunsen's biblical researches' in *Essays and Reviews*, fourth edn., Longman, Green, Longman and Roberts.

C. Wordsworth (1876) *The Mohammedan Woe and its Passing Away*, Rivingtons.

INDEX